# LUTHER COLLEGE GOES TO WAR: "SCUTTLEBUTT" AND THE WORLD WAR II LETTERS

## VOLUME I

**Also by Marvin G. Slind:**

*Norse to the Palouse: Sagas of the Selbu Norwegians*
(with Fred C. Bohm)

*Linka's Diary: A Norwegian Immigrant Story in Word and Sketches*
(Edited with Gracia Grindal)

# LUTHER COLLEGE GOES TO WAR: "SCUTTLEBUTT" AND THE WORLD WAR II LETTERS

## VOLUME I

Marvin G. Slind, Editor

iUniverse, Inc.
New York   Bloomington   Shanghai

Luther College Goes to War:
"Scuttlebutt" and the World War II Letters
Volume I

iUniverse books may be ordered through booksellers or by contacting:

iUniverse
1663 Liberty Drive
Bloomington, IN 47403
www.iuniverse.com
1-800-Authors (1-800-288-4677)

Because of the dynamic nature of the Internet, any Web addresses
or links contained in this book may have changed
since publication and may no longer be valid.

All photographs are reproduced courtesy of the Luther College Archives

ISBN: 978-0-595-52267-5 (pbk)
ISBN: 978-0-595-51027-6 (cloth)
ISBN: 978-0-595-62323-5 (ebk)

Printed in the United States of America

# CONTENTS

# REPORTS FROM OVERSEAS: THE ATLANTIC AND EUROPE

# THE PACIFIC THEATER AND ASIA

## RETURNING FROM OVERSEAS DUTY

# ACKNOWLEDGMENTS

This project has been possible because of the contributions of a number of people. As a faculty member in the History Department, I am very proud of the assistance which other members of that department have made to the creation and preservation of the letter collection. Most obviously, it would not exist without the efforts of the late Chellis N. Evanson. He not only made the commitment of his time and efforts to edit "Scuttlebutt," but he also recognized the historic value of the letters he received, and preserved them together with copies of the newsletter.

For many years, the letters remained in the drawer in which Evanson had filed them. When John R. Christensen became Chair of the History Department, he "inherited" the drawer with the letters. He also recognized their value, and facilitated their accession by the Luther College Archives. The next Department Chair, Richard Cole, worked together with Archivist Duane Fensterman to supervise a group of students who inventoried and filed the letters into a usable collection. Kara K. Burns ('91), Mark Andrew Lyon ('93), and John P. Bickel ('93) completed that project in 1992. Professor Cole also encouraged a number of other students to use the letters as the basis for seminar work and senior papers. When I joined the Luther College Faculty in 2000, he encouraged me to undertake this project of editing the letters. Similar support has come from the two Department Chairs who succeeded Professor Cole: Jacqueline Wilkie and Edward Tebbenhoff. Professor Wilkie authorized departmental support to cover duplication costs, as well as postage for my requests to Evanson's correspondents for permission to publish their letters, and Professor Tebbenhoff gave his enthusiastic support for my application for a sabbatical leave, during which I was able to finish the project. All four colleagues have continued to provide encouragement, as well as their personal insights about many of the individuals mentioned in the letters.

Kristell Benson transcribed the letters with remarkable accuracy. Even when struggling to decipher difficult handwriting or faded copies, her spirit seemed unflappable. Without her long hours of work, the project would have taken me many more years to complete. If Professor Evanson, an old Navy man, were to evaluate her work, I am sure he would have described her as having performed "yeoman's service."

As Administrative Assistant in my academic division, Chelle Meyer has helped this project in numerous ways. Even at a small college, it is sometimes difficult to find one's way through administrative procedures. With her assistance, those have always been easily completed. She also supervises student workers, including Ms. Benson (whom she recommended to me), and has provided technical and logistical assistance for my project since its inception. Without her efforts, my department, and several others, would have difficulty functioning effectively.

Rachel Vagts, Luther College Archivist, has given me invaluable support and encouragement from the moment I first asked her about the collection. She facilitated the photocopying of the letters, as well as scanning of the photographs in the collection. And I cannot count the number of times she has retrieved "just one more" file from the archives so that I could check a detail in the original letters. Without her cooperation and assistance, this project would not have been possible.

My wife, Mickey, has given me loving support and encouragement throughout this project. She has been a sounding board for my ideas as I struggled to develop an organizational structure, bringing a fresh perspective to the process. And her keen eye for detail has made her an invaluable editorial advisor.

Most significantly, I would like to acknowledge the role of Luther College in this project. Since at least 1943, it has lent its support. While Evanson's newsletter initially went to only a few men, the administration quickly decided that it should be sent to all former students serving in the military. Thus, even in a time of great financial difficulty, when the student body had been decimated as most of the men joined the military, the administration committed significant resources to prepare and distribute the newsletter. It distributed over 800 copies per month by first class mail. The College also devoted resources to the inventory project led by Richard Cole and Duane Fensterman, and as noted previously, the History Department allocated funds for photocopying and postage.

I am particularly grateful to the Office of the Dean, William Craft, for the award of Academic Administrative Assistantships. Those Assistantships funded Ms. Benson's transcription work in the 2001–02, 2002–03, and 2003–04 academic years. As noted above, without her work, this project would have taken me many more years to complete.

The Alumni and Development Offices at Luther College also provided support which helped to make alumni aware that this book was being published. I am particularly grateful for the encouragement I received from Keith Christensen, Tom Murray, and Sherry Alcock.

I am also grateful to the College for the award of a sabbatical leave during fall semester 2006. That period of concentrated work allowed me not only to organize the letters in a meaningful way, but to spend enough time working with them to develop a greater sense of the experiences these men and women had in the war, and their deep affection for their alma mater.

*Soli Deo Gloria.*

# INTRODUCTION

The Luther College Archives in Decorah, Iowa, contain a unique collection of letters written during World War II. Professor Chellis N. Evanson edited a newsletter, "Scuttlebutt," which was sent to former Luther students serving in the military around the world. He hoped that it would not only help them contact each other more easily by mail, but also facilitate the meeting of alumni in their various duty stations around the world. They, in turn, sent him letters, postcards, and "V-Mail" in which they often described their service life.

As a professor of history, Evanson recognized that the letters he received would someday be a valuable historical resource. When he received the letters, he often added important identifying information, such as the writer's last name. In some cases, the writers simply noted their nicknames, by which they were well known on campus. But today, many of those nicknames have been forgotten. (A list of the nicknames used in the letters is found in Appendix A, in Volume II.) Without his notations, many letters in the collection would be very difficult to attribute to their authors.

Evanson was clearly aware of the historical value of the letters. In the April 24, 1944 issue of Scuttlebutt, he noted,

> Today I looked through copies of what I had sent out, but discovered that I had failed to keep copies of all the letters I had sent out. From now on, I will keep a copy. Not that they are so valuable but, I think it will be interesting to look them over some day in the future. Of course, I have all the letters you men have sent me. and they are going to be preserved, that's for sure. What you have said in these letters is going to be pretty tame to what you will have to tell when you get back.[1]

Because they had all attended college, they were not typical of most soldiers serving in World War II. Some even commented on how that set them apart from their fellow G.I.'s, many of whom had not even attended high school. Their letters were not selected because their authors had more significant experiences than someone else. They are here because their authors wrote to Chellis Evanson, and he saved their letters. They offer a unique perspective on World War II.

A few of the writers receive more individual attention than most of the others. Following the flow of their letters provides a great deal of insight into the course of the war and their personal experiences. I have thus grouped their letters into individual sections for each writer. That is not because their experiences were more important, or because they made greater contributions to the war. It is simply because the collection contains more letters from them. For a variety of reasons, they wrote more letters to Evanson than others did. Many men and women could have written letters that might have been more characteristic of soldiers' experiences in the War, but a variety of factors may have prevented them from doing so. Furthermore, some soldiers and sailors had experiences they chose not to share. Most of the writers did not try to "blow their own horn" or embellish their experiences. On the contrary, most downplayed their actions. In a few cases, Evanson received word about awards for valor or injury from other sources, when the soldiers receiving the citations made little or no mention of them.

Evanson also solicited photographs, which he posted on his bulletin board. Many of those have been reproduced here to supplement the letters. In many cases, the pictures accompanied letters which contained nothing more than address changes, or notes of appreciation for "Scuttlebutt." Those letters have not been included here. Evanson also apparently received photos by other means, so there are pictures of individuals for whom there are no letters in the collection. Evanson also received many snapshots which are not of high enough quality to reproduce here. I have included as many

Paul Olson and Chellis Evanson
at the photo bulletin board

2

pictures as possible, even for those whose letters are not included. I hope that they contribute to a more complete understanding of the experiences of the Luther men and women who wrote to Evanson. Although it might be possible to obtain photographs of some of the writers for whom no picture is available, it seems more appropriate to include only those which are part of the archival collection. They are reproduced courtesy of the Luther College Archives. Identification of individuals in the photos is based on notes on the pictures themselves, or other information contained in the archival collection. I have attempted to be as accurate as possible using the materials available to me, but I am sure someone will be able to find an individual who is incorrectly identified. I apologize in advance for any such errors.

Many of Evanson's correspondents sent him sourvenirs from their travels, particularly samples of local currency. I have not reproduced images of such items.

In 1992, a group of Luther College history students, Kara K. Burns, Mark Andrew Lyon, and John P. Bickel, completed a "World War II Letter Project: Inventory of Topics Discussed in the Letters." Working under the supervision of Duane W. Fenstermann and Professor Richard Cole, who were then Archivist and Chair of the Department of History, respectively, they catalogued 762 letters and 50 postcards, as well as many other records, including news releases, photographs, and biographical information.

This published edition does not include every letter in the collection. Some are simply notices of address change, or a brief greeting, and perhaps a line saying, "Thanks for the swell newsletter." Because such expressions of appreciation are common among the letters that are part of this edition, it would be superfluous to include all such letters if they contain nothing more. Some are also repetitive, expressing the same sentiments as other writers. This work is already much longer than I had anticipated, so because of space considerations, I have not been able to include every letter. Instead, I have attempted to include those which seem to provide the best examples of different aspects of their war experiences.

For the same reason, I have deleted military addresses which the correspondents sent to Evanson. Such deletions are indicated by "[...]" Otherwise, however, the letters here are reproduced in their entirety. Although that risks including some passages that seem irrelevant, I do not want to risk altering the intent or feeling of the writers by interjecting my own twenty-first century attitudes or perspectives. A modern reader may perhaps wince at the frequent references to

"Krauts" and "Japs," but during World War II, those were the terms commonly used to refer to the German and Japanese enemies. American military forces were segregated until the Korean War. But while many of the writers may have held the common racial prejudices of the time, their letters do not reflect such views. The few references to "colored" troops are not pejorative, but rather reflect the general military classification of the period. Of the more than 800 letters and cards written by former Luther students serving in the military, only two, written from Latin America, contain critical racial (and anti-Catholic) views. Those letters did not provide a great deal of information of value to this collection; rather than cause possible embarrassment to the writer's family, who now live in an era where such comments are not generally considered appropriate or tolerable, I have not included them.

There is one case in which I have edited a writer's letters: a soldier made several humorous comments about a young woman who had been in some of his classes at Luther. Although the writer is deceased, I am sure that if he were alive, he would feel that his off-hand remarks to Evanson would embarrass the woman, and he probably would have refused permission for me to reproduce his correspondence. Although I have otherwise included the entire letters, I have removed the woman's name, and simply referred to her as "Miss X."

In the archival collection, the letters are catalogued in alphabetical order of the correspondents, and in chronological order for each individual writer. While that is a very logical and efficient system for a researcher, it does not give a reader any meaningful context or framework for understanding the letters. I have thus arranged them in what I hope are useful categories. Within each, the letters are usually arranged chronologically; in a few cases, however, letters by a single author are grouped together in order to follow a theme from one letter to another. In order to give them a clearer historical context, I have provided brief introductory comments for most letters, and in a few instances, I have provided some information about the military engagements in which the men participated. (My introductory or explanatory comments are printed in *italics*.) But I have not attempted to add any historical interpretation. Instead, I have tried to let the letters speak for themselves.

In transcribing the letters, I have followed the example of Andrew Carroll, who edited *War Letters: Extraordinary Correspondence from American Wars*. In his Introduction, Carroll writes,

Every effort has been made to transcribe the letters featured in this book exactly as they were written, mistakes and all. The intent is not to embarrass the correspondents but merely to capture their distinct personalities and nuanced writing styles. Certain errors also suggest the conditions under which these letters were written. Many correspondents wrote by moonlight in filthy trenches and flooded foxholes.... Punctuation and spelling errors abound because letters were written in haste, and certain words are indecipherable because rain or melted snow caused them to blur. Some of the servicemen, including George S. Patton, were dyslexic, and it is further evidence of how vital letters were to them that they would struggle for hours to write what would, in the end, amount to only a few pages. To clean up those letters or disrupt their natural pacing with one "[sic]" or bracketed notation after another, I believe, only diminishes what makes each letter so unique in the first place.[2]

Spelling errors are particularly common when referring to someone's name. Particularly with Norwegian names, letters might often be misplaced or omitted, and phonetic spellings were not unusual. Even the title of the newsletter, "Scuttlebutt," appears in several different spellings. As with other misspellings or typographical errors, these have not been corrected in the transcriptions. In a few cases, letters were typed using a typewriter that only had capital letters. My first inclination was to maintain such capitalization in the transcriptions. However, when set together with regularly formatted text, such capitalization gives an unwanted emphasis to the letters. I have thus transcribed such letters using normal capitalization format.

Some correspondents used "V-Mail," which was often hard to read. V-Mail was intended to reduce the bulk of mail being shipped to and from combatants. Letters were written on preprinted pages, which were then copied onto microfilm. Thousands of such negatives were sent on a single roll, and then flown overseas, or from overseas to the

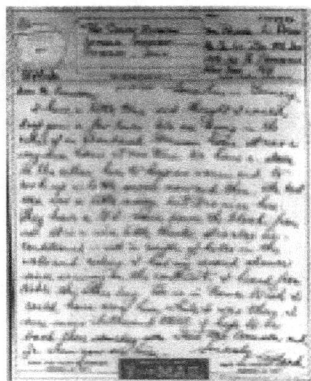

V-mail from Roland Dain

5

U.S., where they were processed at central stations. Copies were then forwarded to their intended recipients. This so-called "five-minute furlough" greatly reduced the bulk of mail, and helped boost the morale of service men and women, as well as their families back home; however, the 4 x 5 copies of the originals were often difficult to read.[3]

Fortunately, relatively few letters are illegible. Where words cannot be clearly transcribed, I have noted "[illegible]." The problem of legibility is more acute with the newsletter itself. "Scuttlebutt" was first printed on a ditto (spirit) duplicating machine (creating purple letters on newsprint), and eventually mimeograph stencils were cut, producing copies with black text of varying quality. In the transcriptions of "Scuttlebutt," illegible characters are indicated with "_" and words or phrases as "[illegible]." In a few cases, military censors blacked out words (or lines of text) in letters and V-Mail, and in one extreme case, most of a page of text was cut out; such instances are noted as "[censored]." Generally, however, the writers stayed clearly within the rules of censorship. In a few cases, the correspondents anticipated that something might be cut, and wrote "(censored)" themselves. Official censorship is indicated in brackets, while the writer's own notations are in parentheses.

As noted, many of the letters contain notations by Professor Evanson, indicating such things as the writer's last name, rank, or address. Such notations are identified in brackets. Similarly, when the writer used letterhead, such as from the base at which they were stationed, a hotel where they were temporarily quartered, or the unit of service in which they served, that has also been indicated within brackets. On the few occasions when I have added relevant information to the text of a letter, it is identified as "[Ed note: ...]"

"Scuttlebutt" was circulated from March 1943 to December 1945, with an additional "Plaque Fund Issue" appearing in December 1947, together with a similar flyer sent to World War I veterans. Unfortunately, the "Scuttlebutt" collection in the Luther College Archives does not include the first issue from March 1943; it begins with the April 21 edition. Transcriptions of the twenty-seven issues in the archival collection are reproduced in the last chapter of Volume II.

I have attempted to contact all of Evanson's correspondents who are still alive in order to obtain their permission to publish their letters. Some who did respond did not recall ever writing to Evanson, in some cases, even though they had written numerous letters. Yet, only one person I contacted requested that I not to include his letters—if he had written any. He did not recall ever writing to Evanson, and stated that he did not begin his studies at Luther until 1946. Through our correspondence, I discovered that he had accidentally been confused with another student with a slightly different name, who is now deceased.

One letter written in 1943, addressed jointly to Evanson and the College Registrar, ended with the request, "Please do not publish this letter. (Unnecessary to state, perhaps, but I prefer to let others do the advertising.)" Although the writer is now deceased, and the letter contained some interesting information about his service in the Pacific, I have honored that wartime request and not included his letter in this collection.

A note on citations: all of the letters reproduced in this collection are housed in the Luther College Archives. They are part of Record Group 15, Collection 130: "Papers of Chellis Evanson, World War II Letters." Within that Record Group, letters are sorted in folders, and each bears a unique identifying number indicating record group, folder, and document number. Those identifiers will be indicated in the citations in this collection. For example, the first letter quoted in this edition is document number 24, in folder number 19, cited as "130:19:24." Citations for "Scuttlebutt" quotations refer simply to the particular issue of the newsletter, copies of which are found in RG 15, Series II, Box 2.

# STATESIDE

—

# PRE-DEPLOYMENT

# CHAPTER 1

# The Origin of "Scuttlebutt" and the World War II Letters

Luther College, in Decorah, Iowa, was founded in 1861 by Norwegian immigrants. It is the oldest Norwegian-Lutheran college in the United States. Luther was originally founded to prepare young men to study for the ministry, but throughout its history, its students have entered a wide variety of careers. In 1932, the College dropped its classical curriculum and replaced it with a modern liberal arts structure. For its first 75 years, it was a men's college, but in 1936, it became co-educational.[4]

While it continues to maintain a strong sense of its Norwegian heritage, the men and women who attended the college were also strongly loyal Americans. When World War II broke out, they were no different from the thousands of other Americans across the country who quickly answered their country's call to arms, and joined one of the branches of the American military. In early 1943, Luther was home to one of the many "V-7" Naval Reserve Midshipmen's Schools in the United States. In March of that year, the first class of nineteen men finished that program at Luther, participated in an early graduation ceremony, and left for Midshipmen's school at Columbia University, part of the "V-12 Navy College Training Program."[5]

Luther College History Professor Chellis N. Evanson had served in the U.S. Navy in World War I. He recognized the morale value of soldiers maintaining contact with friends, so he started a newsletter to circulate news and addresses for the men from the V-7 program. As an old Navy man, he called the publication "Scuttlebutt," a nautical term for "rumor" or "gossip." Originally, "Scuttlebutt" was sent to the first contingent of V-7 men who went on to Columbia, so that they might keep track of one another after they finished the program there. But as word spread about the publication, others wanted to know where their friends in the military were stationed. The number of men receiving the newsletter gradually increased, until Evanson and the College administration decided that it should be sent to all former Luther College students serving in the military. Ultimately more than 800 men and women would receive the paper each month. The College also sent them copies of the student newspaper "Chips," and the alumni association's monthly "Alumnus." The College's administration, led by President Ove J.H. Preus, clearly made a strong commitment to maintain contact with Luther's former students serving in the war.

A 1918 graduate of Luther College, Evanson had been a member of the College faculty since 1919. In addition to teaching history, he had served as Dean of Men from 1925 to 1929, and he became Director of the News Bureau in 1928 (a position he held until 1950).[6] Thus he was well known to many students. In his history lectures, he talked about his experiences in World War I, and his preference for the Navy was apparently well known.

Former students serving in the military quickly began contacting Evanson, letting him know their whereabouts and, to the extent that military censorship would allow, often describing their activities. While his newsletter provided addresses, he also made brief comments that greatly personalized the publication, offering words of praise and encouragement, as well as occasional general advice, for the men and women who had written to him. The writers frequently commented on the value the newsletter had for them. And it is clear that in a number of cases, it facilitated the meeting of friends serving in the same theater of operations who might otherwise have never made contact.

It is obvious from some of the letters that he also wrote directly to some of his former students. Unfortunately, there are no copies of such correspondence, only what students wrote to him. Similarly, his son, Chellis Evanson, Jr., also wrote to many of the men. Because of asthma, he was not eligible to join the military. He moved to Denver for health reasons, and after finding a job there, he maintained correspondence with a number of his former classmates. When wounded soldiers were sent to an Army hospital near Denver, Chellis, Jr., also visited them. Although his correspondence does not survive, there are frequent references to it.

There is not always a direct correlation between the letters and "Scuttlebutt." In some cases, the newsletter included information that he received from other sources. At the same time, there are some letters whose writers (and their whereabouts) are not mentioned in "Scuttlebutt."

The letters in this collection offer a unique insight into World War II. They were written by men and women who shared a common experience: they had all attended Luther College, at least briefly. Some were graduates, while others had only attended the school for a semester or two. But even among those written by students who had only spent a short time at Luther, letters reveal a strong affection for the college. And it is clear that the "Scuttlebutt," which was their link to their common experience, also served to increase that affection. Similarly, many shared a common Norwegian-(or Scandinavian-) American heritage. References to traditional Norwegian delicacies, and the stereotypical Norwegian love of coffee, are common, even among those whose names do not necessarily suggest a Norwegian background.

A number of the soldiers and sailors had played in the Luther College Concert Band, under the direction of Carlo Sperati. The band made several tours to the Pacific Coast and other areas of the United States, and became an organization that generated great institutional pride. In 1936, the Band made a "European Diamond Jubilee Tour." Lasting three months, the trip included performances in England, Denmark, and Norway.[7] For the soldiers and sailors who had participated in that tour, it provided another common link, as did their fondness for Dr. Sperati, who died in 1945.

While a few of Evanson's correspondents were older, most were in their early 20's. Many had graduated from Luther College, but a large number had their college careers interrupted by the war. Under normal circumstances, they would have been living the lives of "typical" college students: studying for exams, preparing for a forthcoming ball game, hoping for an extra dish of ice cream at the "Boarding Club," or trying to build up enough courage to ask the woman in the next row in class out on a date. Instead, they were diving for cover from German artillery barrages, or attempting to shoot down Japanese kamikaze pilots before their own ship was destroyed. While most returned without physical injury, some were severely wounded, and others died while in service to their country. The letters in this collection provide at least a brief glimpse of what these men and women experienced in World War II.

# CHAPTER 2

# "Dear Chellis"—
# The First Letters

*The first issue of "Scuttlebutt" appeared in March 1943. But even before it was published, students had begun writing to Professor Evanson. While some used formal salutations, most took a more casual tone, which was encouraged by Evanson when he started publishing "Scuttlebutt." Students began sending him updates about their activities as early as December 1942. By February 1943, the letters came with more frequency, and with much more detail about the men's activities. Even before the newsletter had been created, it was clear that the former students were eager to hear news from home and from their alma mater.*

[Letterhead: Cuddihy Field, Corpus Christi, Texas]

2-19-'43

Dear Mr. Evanson,

When I was home over New Year's I promised I'd write you a letter. Although I'm a little slow in getting around to it I hope you will excuse the fact.

When I arrived here I had the sniffels and it developed into Cat Fever and thus I spent a month in the hospital.

Have been out 3½ weeks and that is the reason I've been so slow in writing.

I'm in basic training now and will check out of Squadron tomorrow.

Have completed all the flying in basic and am now in for a session with the 12 gage shot gun on the skeet range.

In basic you are given 2 instruction hops in the SNV, a ship of 450 horses and weighs about 3 tons, then you are given 3 solo periods to get the feel of the ships and a check ride.

Then you start formations. You fly formation until you swear you could do it blind folded. About 20 hours of formations. In the meantime you do night flying. At this base the last flight comes in at one oclock it makes a plenty long day of it when you consider that you get up at 615 in the morning. After you finish formations and night flying you check out in OS2V's.

OS2V is a service type ship much heavier than the SNV and with about 500 horses and is somewhat like flying a snack truck.

The SNV is the basic training ship the Army outlawed because it killed so many of their men but we've had only 2 accidents at this base in about 4 months and that's plenty good.

I think that is a pretty good showing of the Navy over the Army but think the Army was using them for purposes they weren't built for.

From now on flying becomes hard work. All that glamor stuff is for the magazines.

I had the most fun while I was at the E base in Kansas City.

In primary training there is some time to go off and do a little flat hatting but no time for it from here on out.

And flat hatting is really a lot of fun as almost any pilot will tell you.

From basic training a pilot goes to instruments and from there to advanced squadrons where a fella specializes in types of aeroplanes such as fighters, torpedo bomber, P boat on O S.

I hope to be able to fly "P" boats as I believe that multi engine stuff is the coming thing and will be of most value to me after the war. and the training is exceptionally fine. and I want the best training I can get.

I've come to one conclusion since I've left College and that is I really miss it and it makes a big difference. You can tell those fellas who are college men and those fellas who are not by just looking at them.

The college boy generally is more clean and mature. He's the fella who has gotten all the devilishness out of his system and really settles down and gets the job done. Also he's much more neater in his dress and appearance and in the navy both of those factors count a great deal.

I have one regret that I didn't finish College and get that sheep skin. I'm afraid when this war is over I wont be able to go back or will think I haven't the time. Never the less I still love and respect the Old School and will keep it as one of life's warmest memories and if I'm ever in a position to give her a boost That I will do. I must close now.

Please find time to drop me a few lines.
Respectfully, Your's
"Dill"          [A/C D. K. Donielson]
The best of all things good to you and your's.[8]

⊠          ⊠          ⊠          ⊠          ⊠          ⊠

*Because of its small size, Luther College's students and faculty knew each other well. Throughout the war, letters from former students referred to the closeness of the College community.*

Fri—PM—3/5/43

Dear Friend Chellis;-

Well how goes things in Decorah. It seems from Margaret's letter and the local papers that a lot more people are being moved around a bit. I have been here nearly two months now and we are kept very busy. I have been pleasantly surprised at the service that is given to the boys. Our equipment is very good and supplies are adequate. The officers almost to a man treat these kids as tho they were in their own offices. I really mean that. The Dentists in the last war didn't come out too well in the eyes of the service men. I'm sure treatment given this time is much better in both the navy and army.

I went over to see Hitly the other day. He is at the Destroyer base and you would hardly know him. He has gained about 20 lbs he said but look like 30 or 40 to me, He's had some trouble with his feet and been hospitalized a couple times. They wanted to survey him out but he requested Duty & got it. I'd like to have him talk to some of these young punks that squawk about being in at all. I believe Harry Sindeland's boy is out here but haven't found him yet.

Well Chellis I really started this to thank you and thru you all the fellows and girls that helped the family on moving day. It was a grand thing to do and I mean they appreciate it greatly as do I. When I got this letter telling about it I couldn't see very well for a few minutes. Means a lot to know such friends are at hand with the folks at home when one is so far away. Please thank them at the meeting and if you see them for me. It will be a grand reunion when we all get back.

16

Its getting close to chow time so must shove off. Am getting used to doing everything by the clock. Some difference for me but am beginning to like it. With the kindest regards to yourself & your family I am—

Sincerely yours—Chester [Lt. C.K. Peck][9]

✉      ✉      ✉      ✉      ✉      ✉

*A well-known member of the Luther College faculty was Herman E. Ellingsen. Well known by his nickname, "Tutor," he had taught physics and mathematics at the college since 1924. He was called into service during the war, and served in several capacities, primarily as an instructor. His first correspondence with Evanson is among the earliest in the collection:*

[Letterhead: United States Navy Yard, Boston]

March 21, 1943

Dear Chellis:

I have been about to write a few lines for some time and this being Sunday and no duty I shall see what I can do. I have been here almost a month but it seems like only a few days. I enjoy the work very much. We have a fine group of fellows here. Most of them are college or University teachers except the commanders who are Navy men. We have lectures, movies, records, material to read and spend about three hours per day giving instructions and running equipment for naval officers from ships. The last is perhaps the most interesting as we get new groups about every week.

Units like this will be set up at other places and we who are here now will be placed in charge of them. I am being detached from here on March 5 and will go to Key West for 5 weeks where we will try our attack procedures on friendly subs. They plan on having us return to Boston to await assignment. We will likely be stationed for the duration at that time.

The fuel oil shortage has been rather acute here. We have recently had the third coldest day in the Weather Bureau's history which was about 20 below. We ran out of oil at the place I stayed and just went to bed and piled on a bunch of quilts. I noticed the fuel oil man was around today so we may get some heat. We haven't had any so far today yet. The radiators are cold. Its been fairly nice lately and I would suppose the temperature rises to about 50 during the day. There is a raw wind almost all the time.

In about a week I won't worry about fuel oil. The fellows who have been down there say that it is already warm. I bought two suits of whites yesterday and from what I have heard you might as well leave blues in Boston as they never wear them. We work in kaki and they are very comfortable and rather inexpensive to keep clean. However one needs quite a few uniforms of each kind except possibly blues.

We have detailed reports of convoy trips that have been made. They are interesting to read. The radiator is making some noise and I may have a comfortable Sunday after all. I felt of the radiator but no go on that. Hope everything is o.k. at Luther. Bobby left rather suddenly but it seems to have been the thing to do. They have put a splint in the break and although its too early to know how it will turn out, it seems to be the thing to do. Greet every one around the place.

Tutor [Lt. H.E. Ellingsen][10]

✉    ✉    ✉    ✉    ✉    ✉

*Training provided many of the former students with more than physical training. Many had their first contact with weapons, not to mention the vagaries of Army bureaucracy. And the pressures of training could be increased if one encountered health problems.*

[Letterhead: The Armored Force, Fort Knox, Kentucky]

Monday afternoon [May 4—'43]

Dear Dr. Evanson,

Well, after six weeks of budgeting seconds in order to accommodate enough time to shine shoes, I find myself with almost 24 hours a day to myself. The only catch is that it took a case of the German measles to bring on this so-called furlough.

I imagine you've heard by this time that Noble, Dain, Borge, Larsen and I are in this outfit. All of us but Borge are in the same barracks and Paul isn't far away. Then, miraculously, all of us but Borge were chosen for clerical school which should start in a week or two. My only worry is that I'll stay in here so long that

18

I'll either be transferred or forced to start my basic training all over again. And that wouldn't be fun because the worst is over for us now.

I'll bet you wondered, as we all did, I'm sure, how Noble would stand up under army pressure. Well, I worried for all of us, reserving a large portion for myself, of course, when we were assigned to the armored force, supposedly one of the roughest, toughest, branches of the army.

Well, Noble has come through in great shape. He hasn't fallen out of any marches (we've had some rugged ones, too) and all in all, he's shown more guts than I gave him credit for. The first gun he ever fired was the .30 Cal. Springfield and, as you probably know, that's no gun for a beginner. Yet he picked off a good score.

We're all pretty well satisfied with Fort Knox. It's close to home for most of us, it's a big, clean camp and we're in one of the youngest, hardest-hitting branches of the services. This unfathomable Kentucky weather gets us down, though. Especially when we think how swell it must be around Decorah now.

Whom have you found for the news bureau now? I imagine it's a big job to find anyone for anything now.

I think the one thing that made us appreciate conditions at Luther more than anything else was the fact that Bob Hulsebus, last year a reserve outfielder, is now rated a starting pitcher. I'll bet trying to keep up with the schedule is really a problem now. It was bad enough before we left.

I think you'll find the while lot of us changed when we come back. Whether for better or for worse, I don't know. We'll certainly appreciate Luther, that's for sure. But I don't think we'll be so docile, either. No more of this putty-in-the-hand-of-the-professor stuff. That remains to be seen, though.

There's a kid in the bunk next to me who was with the British 8th Army in Libya for a year. He's had very few pleasant things to say about his experiences. He's the son of the McKibben who almost beat Kelly for mayor of Chicago in the last election.

[Pvt. Eugene Olson]          Sincerely, Gene Olson[11]

&#9993;    &#9993;    &#9993;    &#9993;    &#9993;    &#9993;

*The V-7 group that went to Midshipmen's School at Columbia University would undoubtedly have a very different experience there than they had at Luther College. In addition to the being in radically different physical surroundings, the men were also thrust into a new social group. In May 1943, Harold Heltne sent a progress report of his experiences in New York:*

[Letterhead: U.S. Naval Reserve Midshipmen's School New York, N.Y.]

Sunday, May 23,1943

Dear Folks;

I guess I haven't been very good to "write home" have I? I really have thought of writing to you many times but it's usually pretty hard to find time enough to write any letters around here.

I still haven't decided whether I like this school or not. Somedays when everything goes well you feel swell, but then the next something happens & you get awfully fed up with the place. At least I've found it that way. & I think most of the fellows around here have the same idea. The one thing I do like about the place tho' is the fellows around here. They really are a grand bunch of men. I've met some of the swellest fellows out here that I've ever known. However, you don't realize how nice it is to talk to a Luther fellow now & then. I don't know how I'd have gotten through the first three weeks if I couldn't have talked to them once in a while. It wasn't that I was homesick either, but everything was so new & different than civilian life that I was all fed up & ready to go back to the farm. They not only had us working half to death those first three weeks but they kept on giving us inoculations so most of us walked around here half sick for the first three weeks.

No fooling, never in my life have I ever spent such a terrible three weeks in all my life as I did those first three weeks. Every thing we had to do those first three weeks was entirely new to most of us and it was really a change. However, now that we have been here this long we've sort of gotten into the swing of things so it isn't so bad. We have five subjects that we are taking, and we have tests in them everyday. The subjects we take are, navigation, ordnance, damage control, seamanship, & communication. Not any of them are too tough, but we never have time to study them like we should. That's the big factor around here. We never seem to have enough time. Anyone could make this place if he had a little more time to study, but when you try & prepare three or four subjects in a couple of hours you really have to go through the material very fast. However, as they say, I guess we'll just have to keep our nose to the grindstone, & hope to get through the place. Our commissioning exercises are going to be July 28th, and believe me, there are about 1200 fellows around here that are just living for that day to come.

Now that all the graduation exercises are over for the past year I suppose you are getting ready to start summer school down there at Luther. How are the prospects of getting students next year? I suppose there won't be so very many men left. And how about this naval unit? Is Luther going to get one or aren't they?

I suppose you know that Betty is coming out here and work again this summer. I surely am happy about that. It's really going to be swell to see her again.

By the way, I surely don't think much of the city of New York. I much prefer the wide open spaces of Iowa. Never would I want to live in a place like this. Too many people, buildings, & dirt. I want to get back where you can breathe a little fresh air that isn't filled with dust & smoke.

Well folks, I think I better draw this letter to a close because I have some studying I want to get out of the way this morning so I can be free this afternoon. You'll have to give my greetings to anyone that might be interested & write me sometime if you have time. Letters are always appreciated you know, and I'll try to write to you folks again in the near future.

So long for now then—

As Ever, Just

Harold [Midshipman Heltne][12]

$\boxtimes \qquad \boxtimes \qquad \boxtimes \qquad \boxtimes \qquad \boxtimes \qquad \boxtimes$

*Like many former military men in World War II, Evanson was a smoker. That often gave students a subject from which to begin correspondence.13*

[Letterhead: El Encanto—Palm Springs—California

[July 16-'43]

Dear Chellis:

Saw by the paper that you fellows are collecting cigarette money for the boys over there.

Thought you might like to have one. Am sending you a package picked up at Christmas Island by a friend on his way back. He gave 'em to me.

American cigarettes, sent over thru normal channels, duty, etc., bring up to $2.50 U.S. money a pack from scalpers over there.

Have been here since July 4th. It's hot as hell here and by that I mean 142 today. Was 124 at 8 this morning.

Regards
[Lt.] Grant [H. Waldrum][14]

✉     ✉     ✉     ✉     ✉     ✉

*After graduating students from the V-7 program, Luther College applied to house a V-12 program, as many other schools had done. The application was not accepted. Word of the rejection spread quickly, especially among the men attending the V-12 program at Columbia.*

[Letterhead: U.S. Naval Reserve Midshipmen's School New York, N.Y.]
July 16, [1943]

Dear Dr. Evanson,

I should have written earlier, but the work keeps us pretty busy and I've had some pretty tough times, with Navigation, which kept me pretty worried and quite a bit busied. It was pretty hard to get down to real work, but no one can loaf and get through this place. In four months, we have to learn an awful lot.

It's too bad Luther didn't get a unit, but the loss of Old Main no doubt was too great. Maurice wrote and told me that he was in a school about the same style as Luther. He seemed to like it pretty well. He is rooming with Bob Hulsebus and Dick Anderson. They don't have quite the intensive training that we do, but they couldn't stand this for 16 months.

We have been counting the days for quite some time and now there aren't very many days left to count. We graduate July 28, but we finish our finals July 22. Naturally, the main topic of conversation is our assignments and whether or not we'll get any leave or not. We all made reservations, but some of them probably will have to be cancelled; everyone doesn't get a leave.

I hear all the latest down at Luther through Sara Marie, and it surely would be nice to get back. I understand "Chell Jr." is going to Colorado. That should be a good climate for his trouble.

We have an hour of marching and then on to Prarie State for a match. We get matches once a week without fail and we go down to Prarie State twice. The matches are much easier here.

Sincerely,
[Midshipman] Carroll Jenson[15]

$$\boxtimes \quad \boxtimes \quad \boxtimes \quad \boxtimes \quad \boxtimes \quad \boxtimes$$

*Some married men had to leave their families behind without seeing them for months or even years. But others were fortunate enough to be accompanied by their wives, who secured housing near their husbands' duty stations.*

3110 Shadowlawn Way

2 Aug 43

Dear Doc.,

I guess that it is about time that I drop you a short note and tell you what goes on at this place. First of all I am at Camp Elliott near San Diego, Calif. Isabelle and I live at San Diego at the address above. We like all the things but the high prices of food and rent. We are on to the ropes as to eating a bit now so we are getting along a bit cheaper than we did at first.

Since coming out here I have been in several different things. The first I was here I was in two different companies in as many weeks. Then because we were a bunch of extras who had come out during an off time in the setting up of companies they shoved some of us into a sort of a rounding out program. The first thing that we went into was a school in combat loading of ships and after that we went to a jungle warfare school. Then we were sent through a very rugged combat conditioning school and following that we laid by for a few days and then after a check of our activities before entering the Corps a few of us were picked to go into a Quartermaster's School in Administration. I have been in that now for the past eight weeks filling my mind with the gospel of the Marine Corps Manual. It is a very rugged school too on the academic side this time however. It makes the mind whirl quite often with all of the forms and the number of copies and who gets them after making them out. It will be good experience for me though even after I am out of the Marines. Oh yes, we have to learn to type the "touch system" too. I am up to about 35–40 words a minute now. We have only an hour a day for typing exercises. I'm a bit messy yet but it is improving.

I am on the list to ship out pretty soon and that means within a month or so. I will go out as an assistant regimental quartermaster. That means a lot of extra work. It is a good thing that everything is expendable after you leave this country.

Didn't finish this thing yesterday so will do so now in the next few minutes. I haven't much extra time from now on in either because I just got my orders this morning that I will be on the next replacement that ships out. They have been going out at two week intervals and the last batch went out last week.

Well, Doc, I guess that this will have to be all for awhile so take care of things down there and keep things moving. I'll drop you a line from across the water as soon as possible. One thing is for sure and that is that I will be in on the BIG PUSH on Japan when it comes. They keep us out at least eighteen months and something is going to happen for sure in that time. Greet everyone that I know there and I'll be seeing you some day in the future.

Sincerely,

[Lt. Helge]     Nasby '39

P.S. My wife sends greetings to you and your wife. Include mine to your wife too will you?[16]

✉   ✉   ✉   ✉   ✉   ✉

*Word of the newsletter spread by word of mouth, so that by September 1943, men were contacting Evanson, requesting to be put on the mailing list.*

Hq. 64th AAA Group, Camp Stewart, GA. Sept. 26, 1943

Dear Chellis,

A short time ago I was in Jacksonville to visit Ray Franck (Lt. J.G. USNR). At that time he was assigned to the Asst. Supervisor of Ships there but was expecting sea-duty shortly. We had a swell time rehashing our experiences at Luther. Ray said that you were putting out a sort of information sheet on the Luther Alumni in the services. I'd like to be put on your mailing list if it's possible.

I have been here at Stewart since July 1 this year. Got my commission as a Shave Tail from the AAA OCS in Camp Davis, N.C. on April 29 last. My present assignment is Asst. Intelligence Officer of the 64th Anti Aircraft Artillery Group.

Outside of Ray Franck, I have heard of only a few and seen no other Luther men in the services since I got in myself about a year ago.

Sure do miss Dr. Sperati and the band, I heard we have disbanded for the duration. That's too bad.

My brother, James.E. is also in the Air Corps and would also enjoy your publication. His address is: [...] He is an ex-46

If you have any charges please let me know. And thank you—!

Robert H. Hanson "the Babe".[17]

 

*While most of the recipients of "Scuttlebutt" were recent graduates or men and women whose studies had been interrupted by the war, older alumni were also serving in the war, and they appreciated the newsletter, too.*

[no date; probably late summer 1943]
Y.O.L. 26, Navy Pier 36th St. Brooklyn, N.Y.

Dear Dr. Evanson—

Thanks so much for your July "Scuttlebutt" received today. It has had a job to catch up with me as I have moved several times since it was sent from my home at Coon Valley. I really have gotten a big "wallop" out of it even tho there are mostly strange names—not so many of the fellows from the '20's are involved.

As you see, I'm now in Brooklyn assigned to a "Yard Oiler" refueling ships. Seems like a good deal. Went to Perth Amboy last Sunday to Services; "Christ" Preus was on his vacation but his brother "Nelson" really preached a swell sermon. Had dinner with him at a sister of "Billy" Hemker, I believe his name is, a student at Luther at the present time. Really had a swell time. Shall be going back to church there when "Christ" gets back from vacation.

Have enjoyed several big league ball games at the three stadiums here in New York. The caliber of play is pretty mediocre—the Luther teams of '24, '25, '26 could whip them! Also hope to get to see a few good football teams this fall if they still need my services in this man's navy in these parts.

I must secure as duty calls. Keep the "scuttlebutt" running! It quenches the thirst of the news-hungry service man!

Sincerely
R.G. Roalkvam '28[18]

   &#9993;      &#9993;      &#9993;      &#9993;      &#9993;      &#9993;

*The morale value of "Scuttlebutt" was recognized early, especially by those whose military responsibilities included similar duties.*

Leland W. Harris, Lt. A C
Stockton Field, Stockton, California

Friend Chellis,

Let us say this is a letter of appreciation for what you are doing for the Luther men in the service. A fine idea and will assure you that anyone would think so.

You see, this above reference is my business in the Army as well as many other subjects. How to keep the boys happy and contented? Boy that's a big order; not like beating Iowa or Northwestern and I use to think that was tough.

Dropped "Dusty" a line and also my camp paper as soon as I found his address in the Chips. I know a line won't hurt him and it may bring back memories as your letter, (getting worse every day) to the men in the service did to me. Talking of friends I ran into a cadet that was a junior in High School while I was there. Doesn't seem possible but I too am aging by the way. Grey Hair.

Wonder what has happened to Earl Berge from Bade, Jack Layton, Monk, Iverson, and that gang. Would you let me suggest that you refer the date of graduation, as to year, after names of men so we can think back and remember an old friend. Was proud of Steve to hear that he is now a chaplain. Many a problem will face him now, with the many new associations.

Will attempt to astound you with the duties of a Special Service Officer in the Air Forces: Theaters, Libraries, Orientation, Newspaper, Army Emergency Relief, Print Shop, Posters, Shows put on by enlisted personnel, Shows from Hollywood, (that's nice work thou,) Service clubs all entertainment, NCO clubs, and so it goes on into the night, a multitude of sins. Am the only Spec. Serv, officer in this wing who doesnt have an ass't.

Will send along a piece of the Christmas card my office is putting out to send to various stations. It is called rayon flocking and done by the silk screen process.

Better close now but good luck to Luther and especially to all Luther men in the service.

Lee

P.S. This is my 25 mo. in the service![19]

&#9993;  &#9993;  &#9993;  &#9993;  &#9993;  &#9993;

*By late 1943, word of the newsletter was spreading. Recognizing that the best way to distribute addresses was probably "Scuttlebutt," soldiers began sending others' addresses to Evanson, in addition to their own. They also occasionally passed on reports of what others were doing. Luther College had only become coeducational in 1936. But when most men were being drafted or enlisting in the military, the number of men enrolled at the College dropped dramatically. Most people recognized that this would have tremendous implications for the character of the student body.*

Hq. Co. CSCRTC Band No. 1, Camp Crowder, Missouri<br>December 12, 1943

Dear Chellis,

Helge Nasby has been telling me about the paper you are sending to Luther College servicemen. How about adding my name to your list?

I am playing the sousaphone in the Central Signal Corps Replacement Training Center Band here at Camp Crowder. Our band of twenty-eight pieces is a good musical organization, but it is far below Luther College Concert Band standards. Needless to say, I wish Dr. Sperati were on the podium.

Helge wrote to me recently. I gather from his letter that he is right in the thick of things. He says that he hangs his hammock in a nice quiet foxhole and goes to sleep. There are snipers around him, and a Jap plane crashed only a hundred yards away. He says that he can almost sleep through the dive bombing but the artillery still keeps him awake.

Selmer Norland sent me a Christmas card from England. We met here at Camp Crowder, and we struggled through basic training together. He went to OCS at Monmouth a year ago and then to England last spring. He said in his last letter that his English history comes in handy. Here is his address. [...]

Do you remember that skit the seniors always used about the changes coeducation would make in the boarding club by 1950? I guess the women took over sooner than most of us expected. I'm glad that they are carrying on until the men get back, but I'll bet they make pretty poor band material.

Say hello to Dr. Sperati for me when you see him. The best of luck to you and Luther College.

Sincerely,
Clarence I. Winden[20]

    ✉        ✉        ✉        ✉        ✉        ✉

*In some cases, the men called on Evanson for recommendations, particularly if they hoped to enter Officer Candidate School. The following letter is not dated, but it was probably written in late 1943 or early 1944. Ehrich was successful in his efforts; the October 1944 issue of "Scuttlebutt" refers to him as "Lt. Louis Ehrich."*

Pfc. Louis Ehrich, Drill Instructor 2nd. Br., Parris Island. S.C.

Dr. Chellis
Luther College, Decorah, Iowa

Dear Sir:

I'll get right down to the point and save you a lot of time. I hope this is O.K. with you.

I'd like you to write a letter of recommendation for officer training school. I've passed all other requirements and now have only to get my letter in.

Please address it to: The Officer Concerned, U.S. Marine Corps. It will help me greatly if you can do this soon, my C.O. tells me that time is an important factor in my case.

If you can see your way in writing said letter, well then send it to my address. You see I must give it to the Old man myself. Gen. E.P. Mores.

This is going to mean a lot to me. For one thing, I'll get off Parris Island. Dr. this is the only place in the world where a man can lay under a palm tree and freeze to death.

I'm looking for the day when this war will be over and I can come back to Luther and finish my education. Yes Sir, I really miss that place.

I hope that this finds both you and your family in good health.

Oh yes! Do you know any other College in the Country where a student could write a professor like this and get away with it? I don't.

Sincerely your

Louis Ehrich[21]

✉ ✉ ✉ ✉ ✉ ✉

*In addition to watching for former Luther students, Evanson's correspondents also looked for potential new students. Luther's enrollment, particularly male, dropped dramatically during the war, and the former students were looking forward to better days when hostilities ended.*

July 27, 1944

Dear Chellis,

Just a few lines to let you know I received your very welcome and interesting letter and will sure look forward to receiving the next one. It sure was nice reading of the old Luther boys, and what's happening to them. Quite a few of them are before my time but here and there I hit someone I know. Noticed that many of the fellows are attached to amphibious operations. When I spoke to Chellis, Jr. he gave me a lot of info on the fellows, how he saw Ted & Archie for a half hour and about Cal and Harold and Betty, Hap Jensen & a few others.

Got a couple Brooklyn recruits that will be heading Luther way as soon as this mess is all cleaned up.

Right now I'm on a pontoon crew and it's a working job and sure gives you a good appetite.

I'll secure now with Best Regards and telling you to take it easy Chellis

"Brooklyn" [John D Christiansen][22]

✉ ✉ ✉ ✉ ✉ ✉

*Some men's training or background fit them for high priority civilian jobs, which were deemed more important than contributions they might otherwise make in the military.*

West Branch, Ia
Oct 1, 1944

Dear Dr. Evanson:

I've been delaying this letter in the hope that I'd be able to write U.S.N.R. after my name. However, the Navy informs me that all Radar billets are filled at present, so I'm still working for the Office of Scientific Research. Also, I've been placed on the American Scientific Reserve List, which amounts to a freeze in my present job for duration or longer.

Skip and Art are in the same unit in the research lab. The work is interesting and ultra-secret, but sometimes becomes quite routine. The experience should be quite valuable after the war. It is concerned mostly with electronics and that will be a big field in the future.

Had a letter from Dyb. He's in New Guinea, and not to happy about it. His address is: Sgt. Vernon B. Dybdal [...]

We are living on a farm out near West Branch, birthplace of Herbert Hoover. It has pretty good pheasant and quail hunting. The Cedar River is just two miles away and affords some good duck hunting. Shot two teal this morning.

Your newsletter is really a welcome visitor in this household. I'm sure it's a real moral booster among the service men who get it.

Haven't heard a thing about homecoming yet. No "Chips" or "alumnus" have arrived as yet. However, I'm planning on getting up to Luther for a couple of days if possible.

Our daughter is growing like a weed. She has ideas about walking now and delights in tearing her play pen apart.

Gotta buzz off now. Best wishes for the most of the best of and greetings to Mrs. Evanson.

Arlo [Woolery][23]

✉   ✉   ✉   ✉   ✉   ✉

*Word of the newsletter spread among the larger Luther alumni community, and some former students who were not in the military also sent Evanson updates, and also requested to be put on the "Scuttlebutt" mailing list. Because of the prominent role Carlo Sperati played at Luther College, the Sperati family was well known to many of the students.*

826 Delafield Place NW, Washington 11, D. C.

21 November 1944

Dear "Chellis"—

May I be permitted to call you that, after having been away from Luther for a suitable length of time?

I've been intending to write to you for ever so long now, ever since I read the first copy of "Scuttlebutt" that I got my hands on. Even if I'm not in the service, do you think that I could be put on the circulation list? Stan and Helen Henderson have been letting me read their copy whenever they remember to bring it in—but I'd love to have a copy of my own, for addresses and such.

Another thing—would you also please send it to Bud Salisbury, ex '41? Although he only spent a short time at Luther, he is still a "Lutherite" at heart, and is always asking me about one or anther of his friends. The latest is Ld Hillman. Do you have his address, or know of his whereabouts?

Bud has been in the Army about four years now—was up in Kodiak, Alaska, at Fort Greeley, for about two and a half years. Shortly after returning to the States, he was sent out again, and is now "somewhere in France." He spent a little time in Paris, and is now in a small town, living in a chateau which was formerly owned by a champagne manufacturer. Lovely quarters—if it were only peacetime. His address is: Cpl Bud Salisbury [...]

Last weekend I just happened to run into Paul Strom in a bus station. Hadn't seen him for years. He's up in Ithica, New York, instructing.

Please greet Marilyn and the rest of your family from me.

Sincerely yours,

Beverly M. Sperati[24]

✉     ✉     ✉     ✉     ✉     ✉

*Most of Evanson's correspondents were young, either recent graduates or men and women whose studies had been interrupted. A few were older, however, and they often occupied significant positions in the military.*

[Letterhead: United States Coast Guard Academy New London, Connecticut]

11 January, 1945

Dear Chellis,

Out of old L.C. thirteen years, and I believe it's the first time I have addressed you "Chellis." These years do roll by. That I notice more than ever in Scuttlebutt where there are only scattered references to L.C. men of my day—and I'd not thought that so long ago. But I do appreciate the sheet, and I can imagine how much more it means to those of our boys who are in the "thick of it" and welcome the more news from friends and alma mater. Keep up the good work—and don't forget to give us the basketball scores, and our position in the conference.

I've been at the Academy since '38, when I left my position at Concordia. It's about a year and a half that I've been in uniform, and of course I am happy that I'm able to continue here as Academy librarian, and be with my family, too. Anthony Hubin, ex'33, is also stationed at the Academy. He's a Lieut.(j.g.) in the USCGR.

I've seen Valdemar Johnson, as well as "Porky" Hesla, that when they were at training at Harvard during the past summer. I envy Hesla his assignment. Also, there's a Johnson, class of '36, teaching music at Danbury, Conn., with whom I have visited recently. But unless I get to New York there aren't many Lutherites.

I like your idea of a Luther service plaque and would like to contribute $2 toward it. The remainder of my $13.25 check goes to the Century Club ($5) and the balance of my payment toward the Old Main building fund ($6.25). I'll appreciate the kindness if you'll allot it thusly.

Here's to an early reunion of service men on the L.C. Campus!

Sincerely,

[Lieut.] Ernest M. Espelie, '31[25]

---

[Letterhead: Office of the
Army-Navy Liquidation Commissioner
Washington, 25, D.C.]

Feb. 27. 45

Dear Chellis:

Please have my address changed on the various records there: [...]

After 2½ years overseas I am back here in the above organization as assistant to the Deputy Commissioner. Our job will be the disposal of surplus war materials et al in all foreign countries.

Had a very pleasant visit a few days ago with T.O. Kraabel (15) and Merriam Trytlen (16). Understand that Bryn Hovde and Gynt Storaasli are also here.

Your "Scuttlebutt" is interesting, but oldsters such as myself are out dated by it. I'd like to know—(if you have any such service) where members of the class of 1919 now live.

Sincerely B.A.Johnson
L-1919.

Please say hello to Pip—Ham Peterson—Tingle—and Pres. Preus—I don't know that I know any other faculty members.    B[26]

# CHAPTER 3

# "Getting a little restless"— From Training to Combat Duty: 1943

*Whether they were "ninety day wonders" completing Reserve Officer training programs, or enlisted men completing basic training, most men looked forward to the end of training and assignment to their "real" jobs in the military. For young men born and raised in the Upper Midwest, training assignments often took them to areas of the country they might not have otherwise visited. Earl Voelz, for example, described Parris Island, South Carolina, as "the section of the U.S. God forgot." 27 Despite the dangers they would face on the battlefield, many men wanted to "get into the action" and make a meaningful contribution to the war cause. Sometimes the wait seemed interminable, but at other times, men had a good idea that they might be seeing action soon.*

[Letterhead: U.S. Naval Section Base
Mayport-Jacksonville, Fla. Area, Sixth Naval District, Mayport, Florida]
June 25, 1943

Dear Chellis:

At the time I enlisted I promised to write but have not until now. I thought I'd drop you a line and let you know how things are shaping up.

After finishing Prairie State I went to a 4 month diesel school at Penn State College. After this I was assigned to a Coastal minesweep, and a few days ago I got my order to go to a fleet sweep that is building in Jacksonville. So at the present time I'm waiting for it to be completed.

I suppose you know I got married about 7 months ago to a girl from my home town. We went to high school together.

I'm getting ready to go home on a 15 day leave starting Monday. When they give you leaves like that out of a clear sky you can bet something is going to happen. So they'll probably send this fleet sweep overseas, I hope so might run into a little more excitement. I hope so, this minesweeping is awfully boring stuff. A lot of hard work, danger, and you never know what's going on until it's either too late or the mine has blown up.

Give my regards to the faculty and what members of the old gang I use to know.

Sincerely
[Ens] Ray Franck[28]

✉      ✉      ✉      ✉      ✉      ✉

*After receiving their commissions, the new Ensigns faced more specialized training, and finally an actual duty assignment.*

[Letterhead: Section Base, San Francisco, Twelfth Naval District Treasure Island, San Francisco, California]

Sept. 18 [—'43]

Dear Dr. Evanson,

Bill Aaker and myself have just been over having a good "bull session" with Ole Davidson. We ran across him one morning while we were having breakfast out here on the island and we've seen him quite often since that time. Needless to say, our conversation is almost always connected with Luther. It would be nice to drop by for a few days, but that will have to wait awhile, I'm afraid.

Perhaps you'd like to know what we are doing out here. Well, we were a bit disappointed to find that we were sent out here to an officer's pool, but we've gotten over that. We find that there's an awful lot to learn and that here is a good place to learn it. We go out to sea on the average of five days a week. We can't go very far out in one day; but we still get practice in navigation, ship handling, etc. The other day is usually spent on the gunnery range where we practice firing various guns. It is all very instructive, but both Bill and myself would just as soon be on our way.

We are supposed to spend six weeks here before we apply for a transfer and our six weeks is up next Wednesday. We don't know what we are going to apply for as yet, but we'll apply for something. Probably gunnery officer aboard a Navy cargo ship, mainly because orders seem to be coming through quickly for that particular branch of the service. It seems that those who stay here too long get in sort of a rut and we are trying our best to avoid that. It is easy to see how it can happen around here.

I was pleased to hear from little Chell just the other day. I had written him and he answered promptly. I'm glad to hear he likes it in Colorado. I also wrote to Heltne, but have received no answer as yet. That doesn't worry me. We know each other's writing habits pretty well by this time. Besides, it is very often hard to find time even to dash off a line. Ask Mr. Davidson, he knows. He seems to be very busy, but I believe he likes this work.

I'm sorry I couldn't drop by Decorah to say hello. I got to Spring Grove, but I had to go home the next day and I wanted to stay awhile in Spring Grove, so I had to forego the visit to Decorah. However, I hope to drop by on my next leave, whenever that will be. It's pretty early to start thinking of that.

It's about 0225 and I'm the Junior duty officer around here tonight. It's very dead and I'm trying my best to keep awake. However, I've been writing all evening so my arm is tired and with no better excuse than that, I'll close this letter.

sincerely yours

"Happy" Jenson [Ens. C.E. Jenson][29]

[...]

P.S. By the way, Bill and I room together. Pretty nice to have someone you know to room with.

✉    ✉    ✉    ✉    ✉    ✉

*While most of the men were training for the Navy or Army (including the Army Air Corps), there were also a few men who became Marines, such as Earl Voelz. Although he wrote several letters while he was in training, his correspondence with Evanson apparently ended when he was assigned to regular duty.*

9/19/43

Dear Chellis,

Another Sunday welcomed by everyone, for it signifies a day of rest and the passing of another tough week. With Sunday comes time for me to "get up" on my letter writing, for during the week time is limited.

36

Well, this makes it six weeks that we've been at Quantico. It's a much nicer and more interesting post than P.I. We do more of the really interesting things here, such as: working with and firing many weapons, and real tactical war problems of jungle warfare are actually practiced. Two weeks remain before graduation and commissions, then 12 more weeks of tactical work in Reserve Officer's Class. Time here is measured finely, for it is so scarce; however, the work is very interesting.

Thank you indeed for the letter containing news of Luther men in the service. Believe me, every bit of news from Luther is welcome, for this fall put a home sickness for the L.C. Campus deep in my heart. I'll be anxiously waiting for "Chips" later on. Homecoming is the time I will really miss, for the spirit and tradition is really unbeatable.

This detail is about ready to be called to a halt, so I'll sign off with—good luck, and God bless you in your work.

Sincerely yours,
Pfc Earl Voelz[30]

---

Quantico, Va.
11-22-43

Dear Chellis,

Thanksgiving at hand and Christmas just around the corner makes me think of home and Luther College. The <u>Messiah</u> is constantly running though my mind. It always added so much to the greatness in thought of Christmas.

Sunday was a wonderful day to me; for, as it was liberty weekend in Washington, D.C., I went to church on Sunday morning. Christ's Lutheran Church, a Missouri Synod Church, was the place of worship. I had been there before, but this proved to be extraordinary. Just as the pastor said that this church was the meeting place for Lutherans in D.C., so it proved. Beverly Sperati and Phyllis Knudson were there and older Luther grads also. You can easily imagine what was the topic when we congregated after the service. Luther College memories surely was the theme. It was indeed a splendid meeting.

Three more weeks remain in R.O.C. training—then an assignment. It's truly great. I like the Marines and feel proud to be a leatherneck. We don't have to brag for history and tradition speaks for us. I know the entire nation felt the same on

37

the celebration of the corps' 168th birthday on Nov. 10. I indeed like the work very much, and all has gone well in studies and work.

Greetings to your family and all L.C. friends.

I'm enclosing a photo you can use for anything you wish.

God bless you.

Respectfully, Earl F Voelz[31]

---

Quantico, Virginia
May 14, 1944

Dear Prof. Evanson,

I wish to thank you for the letter received from you just a short time ago. It's interesting for several reasons: to read what your former buddies and friends are doing, to know that your alma mater is interested, and to hear from a former teacher. These letters show (altogether) a lot of research and work on your part. This alone is a great enough compliment to you.

Well, time flies, and the world goes on its way which most of the time seems to be the wrong way. The war goes on, and I wouldn't even try to estimate its length of life. There may be a surprise ending, but most likely it will last for some time.

My work goes on and keeps me quite busy. Every twelve weeks we see our men—usually about 100—get commissions in the Corps. They are good men and are rugged. The training is wonderful and yet it is only part of the training they get on the whole. They study the weapons that will conquer our enemies, how they will be employed, and how to handle men—which is the most important of all.

Bertelli graduated just a short time ago and we get many so-called great athletes, and we find them to be quite serious and smart also. In my last platoon I had Werkkeiser (one of Mercer's Men) of Dubuque. He was good, rugged, and understanding in his work. All in all, it's wonderful to partake in making officers—through instruction and training—for the greatest corps of its kind in the world.

The course is constantly becoming more rugged as certain needs are seen and as more needs arise because of new weapons and organization. The rifle platoon of today has more fire power than the rifle company of the first world war. You'd be surprised at some of the new weapons and tactics. The bazooka, of course, is famous; but the 60 mm. shoulder mortar, the invention of a Marine Gunner, is quite wonderful. It is more accurate than the bazooka, and it is handy. Of course, it is more of an anti-personal than anti-tank weapon. That's just an idea of constant improvements being made to bring our enemy to his knees for peace.

Best wishes to you.

Respectfully,

Lt. Voelz[32]

*As an experienced teacher, and because of his age, "Tutor" Ellingsen was assigned to a training position. Evanson's letters to him do not survive, but it is clear that they had discussed the possibility of Ellingsen purchasing some items from the post exchange.*

[Letterhead: United States Naval Section Base, Little Creek, Virginia]

Oct 31, 1943

Dear Chellis:

Was glad to get your letter. We certainly have a number of Luther boys in the service. They have not gone unnoticed here at our base. Have been asked by several how big a college Luther is. They think it must be pretty large because of the number that come around. Ray Frank has been in lately for training. Had dinner on his ship yesterday and he has been up to our unit several times for training lately. I had his crew up for an hour and a half of instruction yesterday. Several of the boys are here. They leave for a few weeks and return. I usually don't know where they are going but always find out where they have been. Eric was out to sea for a day. He helmed the ship for about a half hour, put up signal flags, etc and had a good time. The Captain who is Lieut Comdr says he did very well and knew his flags.

I have looked at watches. They have Bulova at 18.75 which retail at about 33.00 and other makes less known but about the same quality and price. I wouldn't be able to buy any unless I get a chit. They only sell them to people who are assigned to ship but we can always arrange that thru friends and if you are interested in anything along that line I can arrange it. They have more expensive watches that run into (shock proof; water proof etc) They run up to 50.00 and these sell on the outside at about 100.00.

We are very busy. I give a procedure lecture about every other day and usually to about two crews at a time. We get a large number of ships from the south who are sent up to us for training. We operate evenings and take turns and get the next morning off which gives us time to go shopping and get around.

Last Sunday the family went to Yorktown and Williamsburg. Had a good time. We have a car which gets us around. We buy all our food at the commissary at cost. It will be hard to get used to civilian prices again. Also get our gas and oil at wholesale prices, the Navy is really well organized. They take care of everything for us such as gas rationing, fuel oil etc which makes it almost too easy. Well I shall have to close. Greet everyone at Luther. Hope that everything is prosperous and that the war will soon end. The colleges will have a real service to render after the war.

"Tutor"[33]

✉     ✉     ✉     ✉     ✉     ✉

*For the men in training, the wait for deployment could seem endless. And as many quickly discovered, their ambitions or personal interests were secondary to the decisions of the military bureaucracy. (They occasionally mimicked official news releases in their personal letters, to give them an air of seriousness.)*

Headquarters Station #11, Caribbean Wing ATC, Morrison Field
Immediate release ...
West Palm Beach, Fla., Nov. 27, 1943 (Special)....

Dear Chellis,

Got your very welcome Christmas greetings today. It's always great to hear news from and about Luther. Your communications, especially, cover just about everything that is to be covered. "Chips" and the alumni bulletin arrive here regularly, too.

It's about an hour before the Army-Navy game is scheduled to start and there is plenty of excitement around here. Most of the boys seem to favor the Navy, that is most of them with the exception of yours truly. I have my two-bits resting squarely on the boys from West Point. Was spotted six points to boot, too. [Ed note: Navy won, 13—0]

Got quite a surprise about a month ago when, opening Sunday Miami Herald sports section, I saw the score Cornell 27 (or was it 21?), Luther 0. "Chips" hadn't mentioned anything about a football team; it didn't even have a sports page. But "Chips" in a later edition and also your October communication explained the football situation. Pretty game of the few boys left to go out and keep the game going.

Speaking of football, I have seen one game so far this season. Watched Jacksonville Navy trounce Miami university 21 to 6 at Miami's Orange Bowl the first part of the month. I wouldn't be afraid to say that Luther's 1938 or 1941 teams could spot either of the two above mentioned teams 14 points and win with ease. Miami university, incidentally, is considered the top college eleven in the state.

Had a big reorganization on the field a bout six weeks ago. As a result our squadron, the 23rd Transport, along with all the other outfits, was broken up. Our Headquarters personnel was slated to form the nucleus of one of the three units, which were activated. However, on the day the jobs were passed out our CO was out fishing. Hence we found ourselves out of a job. Of course most everyone thinks his outfit is best, but I can say without reserve that we had the best outfit on the field.

Right now I am working in the Loading Section of Foreign Operations. This department computes the weight, moment, and index of all planes leaving the country. We do our work with an instrument called the "load adjuster", which is very similar to a slide rule used in mathematics. It is our job to figure out where to place the crew and cargo, how much fuel, mail, etc. should be taken, so as to assure the best possible balance of the plane while in flight. This department has four Lts., 2 Sgts., 2 Cpls, and 2 Pfc's. All do the same work, work about the same amount of time.

Have been on this field for fourteen months now and am getting a little restless. Was slated to go to Foreign Government school last summer, but my commanding officer couldn't see it that way and would not release me. Got a statement of availability from the new CO so am still on the school list, but the possibility of being called are plenty slim, as nobody has been sent to school from this field since last summer.

Our old 23rd was "alerted" twice, once last winter and again last spring, but nothing came of it. Rumor had it both times that we were all set to ship over, but nothing ever materialized.

By the way, I got a letter from Jim Holmlund last fall. He's a first Louie and is doing liaison work in North Africa. At the time he wrote he was laid up in the hospital with dysentery (bad stuff).

Heard from Loyal Radke some time ago, too. From what he said, he is most likely at Pearl Harbor, doing patrol duty. Said they were grooming him for a deck officer job. Haven't heard from Babe Moen since he was in California. Got his address from you last letter, wrote to him at Camp Gordon, but suppose the letter hasn't yet caught up with him if he is now in Tennessee. Babe has certainly come a long way in the enlisted ranks. I know a couple of fellows on this base that hold the position of Sergeant-Majors who have more power than some majors.

It's swell that Chellis Jr. can get home for Christmas. Bet he'll enjoy the pheasants Pete shot and his dad cleaned. I remember how I enjoyed the two canvas back ducks that were saved for me last Christmas. Chellis is in a good town; Denver is really great. Spent eight weeks there a year ago last summer and a person couldn't ask for a better place. By the way, you might ask Chellis Jr. if he remembers the time he tossed Big Babe Nordby out of my room.

The physical requirements for aviation cadet have recently been relaxed a bit (I previously couldn't make the grade because of a bad leg) and I am going to take another fling at it. Had an operation on my leg last fall, which kept me in the hospital nearly a month, but everything seems to be ship-shape now. I'll need three letters of recommendation when I go before the board next month. I know how busy you must be at this time of the year, but I would appreciate it if you would be so good as to bat off a recommendation and send it to me sometime before Dec. 15. Thanks, Chellis.

Had sort of hoped to get home for Christmas this year, but Foreign Operations is a little pressed for men and they just aren't releasing any men during the holidays. However, I am looking forward to a leave some time in January.

We have had a few celebrites through here lately including ex-cinamactor (now Captain) Jimmy Stewart, Generals Alexander and George. The boys really hustle when a brass hat is reported on the field. Hull was here several weeks ago but I didn't get very close to him.

They really gave us a feed here on Thanksgiving. There was plenty of turkey and all the trimmings, just like Charlie used to turn out at L.C. Boarding club. At ten-thirty in the morning there was a line two blocks long waiting for the Mess Hall to open at eleven. Don't ever let anyone tell you that the food in the army is bad, or even that it is only fair. It's plenty OK. Take it from me. And I have eaten in Mess Halls in the north, west, and south. Most fellows, at least on this side, are better clothed, housed, and feed than they have ever been.

You are certainly right in advising the boys to take out the maximum amount of insurance, Chellis. Anyone who doesn't have the full amount is foolish and anyone who doesn't convert a part of it and keep it up after the war is still more foolish.

If you don't hear from me before Christmas, here's wishing you and your family a very, merry, Christmas.

Here's the Army-Navy game and anyway I've gone on too long anyway, so will close.

Sincerely,

Dyb [Sgt Vernon B. Dybdal …]34

✉     ✉     ✉     ✉     ✉     ✉

*New assignments meant new responsibilities. But while many soldiers were obviously eager to describe their activities, they were also aware of censorship regulations.*

Dec 19, 1943

Dear Dr Evanson,

Just got your special Holiday issue of who's where. Thanks a million. Seems as if you get more subscribers with every issue.

My address changed about 5 or 6 weeks ago. It's now P.O. San Francisco. Guess somebody put a bug in the skippers ear that there was a war going on out here too.

Every time we hit port I hope to see some of the Luther boys but as yet no luck. Bob Thayer is now on a carrier. He may join us soon.

I'm still in the C&R dept. working on damage control etc. In another ten years I should know what its all about. Just like everything else I guess—you get to the point where you think you know the whole thing and then something else pops up.

Censorship regulations keep me from writing much of interest but someday I hope to have the chance to tell you all about the escapades of the mighty Cabot.

Best wishes to you, your family and Luther College.
Sincerely
[Ens] Harold (Butch) Bravick[35]

✉        ✉        ✉        ✉        ✉        ✉

*Similar experiences were found in the Navy, where "land-lubbers" from the Midwest had to adjust quickly to life aboard ship.*

USS LST 173

December 8, 1943

Dear Dr. Evanson,

I received your letter of November 23 and it was most welcome too. Needless to say I do enjoy hearing of our fellows in arms and our old school mates. Thanks a lot, we appreciate it.

Afraid to disappoint you but we're not on the loose yet. It is safe to tell you that we're still in "Da Chestapeake" as one of our deck hands, a Pennsylvania coal miner says. It's rather a drab, routine life but it gives us just that much more time to prepare for the big "putsch".

Haven't seen any of the L.C. boys for many a week now. I had the surprise of my life some time ago when I went to visit Heltne and found with him Sanford Sherry, already decked out with two service ribbons. He brought us word of Don Gjerdrum who went over the same time Sherry made his first crossing. Here's hoping we make ours soon. Never can tell the way things are shaping up.

My dad had been having a little trouble on the physical side, a nervous collapse, consequently his Naval service may soon end or be limited to special duty. He was just home on a sick leave.

I expect to get a "48" one of these weekends and take a trip to the big town (N.Y.) drop in on the middies and relax a bit. Haven't spent a night off this ship since I came aboard. Although we're always in sight of land we never get our foot on it.

The skipper finally let down and permitted me to do some ship handling. While cruising around with no particular goal in mind he gave me the conn and I played around a bit. It's pretty tricky but interesting. The "old man" is an ex-chief,

USN of 17 years experience. Typically tough but smart as they come. We learn a lot from him but get a lot of singed ears in the process.

Christmas cards and packages are pouring in and it seems most strange that the season should be upon us without the accompanying snow and cold of Decorah winters. Well, here's hoping that by a near Xmas we'll be back where we all want to be—home. Greeting to all of you.

Sincerely,<br>John Sorlien[36]

$\boxtimes$   $\boxtimes$   $\boxtimes$   $\boxtimes$   $\boxtimes$   $\boxtimes$

*Holiday greetings also provided the opportunity to report what the men were now doing.*

[Christmas card]

Dear Friends, Just to let you know I haven't forgotten you. I am getting along fine and am O.K. I am first aid attendant and drive ambulance at a port dispensary. I have been transferred here from a hospital where I was ward attendant for a while. We had a grand Turkey dinner for Thanksgiving and are promised an egg for breakfast on Christmas.

[P.F.C. George R. Dirksen, Dec. 6th 43][37]

$\boxtimes$   $\boxtimes$   $\boxtimes$   $\boxtimes$   $\boxtimes$   $\boxtimes$

*While most of the men assigned to the infantry probably wished they had different duty, a common sense of pride and camaraderie developed while they were in training.*

December 19, 1943

Dear Dr. Evanson, & family

Please excuse me for not writing before this but I received your letter the day before I went on maneuvers and this is about the first chance I have had to write. Also please accept my humble apology for not seeing you while I was home but some how we missed each other when I did get up on the campus.

I think your letter was a swell idea and I certainly enjoyed it. Seems like of the boys are seeing a lot of action and are really doing something great. I wish I could be doing something worth while instead of monkeying around here trying to teach some rookies something I am supposed to know. Seems like a waste of man power to me but I can't seem to get out of here.

It is nice to know what the fellows are doing and where they are but as far as writing is concerned it is nearly impossible. We are pretty busy around this place and it is pretty hard to find time to do any writing

As you probably know I am in the infantry. We all hate it but still we are proud of our organization because we know it is a tough outfit. We don't get any publicity and the men sent here aren't picked over but just the men put in the service and the Navy and Marines don't want them. Most of them don't want to fight when the get in here but when they leave they are ready to take them on single handed. We know the Navy gets us there, the Marines make the beach heads, the Air Corps softens them up, but the infantry takes the ground and holds it.

Don't think I am a one man publicity agent but someone has got it tell people something about the unknown infantry

Well I had better close and see if I can't get a little sleep before someone starts blowing that whistle.

My Christmas and New Year Greeting to you, your family, and everyone at good old Luther.

> Sincerely,
> [Cpl] Neal [Davis][38]

46

# CHAPTER 4

# "A guy keeps pretty busy"—
# From Training to Combat Duty: 1944

*Training activities continued through the winter of 1943–1944, and the recruits had to endure a wide variety of weather conditions. Those undoubtedly prepared them well for what they would later encounter in Europe.*

*Since the men had completed at least some college, they often hoped they might qualify for training that would make them eligible for specialized duty. One option some took was the Army Specialized Training Program (ASTP), but such plans did not always materialize.*

Fort Ord, California
January 25 1944

Dear Prof and Mrs. Evanson and Family,

California—here I am! The sky is a fair blue and the grass is green. It seems to be summer but the spanking breezes coming in from the bay quickly convince one otherwise. The first day I was here the weather consisted of alternate hours of California sunshine and California "dew." This fort is, however, a much better place than Fort McClellan—the barracks, food, weather, and everything in general is better. We will be here for a week at least but from there on, no one knows.

It was, indeed, a pleasure to have been your guest at dinner not so long ago I hope that you can sense my appreciation when I say, "Thanks a million."

When I was reclassified yesterday, it was explained to me that all the ASTP colleges have been filled and that no classes have graduated, as yet. Therefore no replacements are needed. Moreover, I did not make an army band; either there were no vacancies or I did not have sufficient ability. As a result, I am an infantryman—semi-skilled.

I was happy to read of Luther's victory over Upper Iowa about a week ago. More will undoubtedly follow if the army does not take too many men.

Sincerely,

Ole Storvick[39]

    ✉       ✉       ✉       ✉       ✉       ✉

*Officers' training was quickly followed by more specialized schools. For many, that also provided the opportunity to meet other Luther students.*

February 1st, 1944

Dear Chellis—

Just a line to thank you for your swell recommendation, and to let you know that I was appointed to the commission of Ensign in the Naval Reserve on December 7th in Chicago.

I reported here to Princeton University on December 15th for eight weeks "indoctrination" (which I need very badly, I might add). We leave here on Feb. 10th, & have until March 1st to report to our next training station—which is not yet definitely known. I am classified as "Deck Officer", and of course may go into several different branches, I am not sure yet which it will be—Armed Guard, Small Craft, or Communications.

My wife and daughter are still in Niles, Michigan—so you can continue to send my Luther Alumnus just as you have, & they will forward it to me.

Some news for you:

Kenneth Bergen is also here, studying Radar.

Met Carl Torgerson (String Bass on the European Tour) in New York recently. I believe he is at Ft. Schuyler in N.Y. City.

Almost got to Perth Amboy for the Luther College reunion a week or so ago—at Chris Preus' house. Missed Carlton Sperati, sorry to say.

Dick Reed is on a carrier in the South Pacific now—is a Lieut. (J.—g.) his address is: […]

Bob Melvold is a full Lt. and an instructor on sub classes in Florida.

Hello to all my friends around Luther—& thanks again for your very fine letter.

Sincerely—Ensign Lester C. DeNoyelles, USNR

611 Cuyler, Naval Training School, Princeton, N.J.[40]

✉  ✉  ✉  ✉  ✉  ✉

*In early 1944, more men were completing their training and preparing for duty overseas. But many quickly learned that "the Army way" did not necessarily follow what they considered standard logic; extensive training in one area might be followed by a completely different type of duty.*

[Letterhead: U.S. Army, Camp Callan, San Diego, California]

Hq & Hq Btry, AARTC

14 Feb 44

Dear Chellis

Thanks for the news and note. I hope you'll continue. I'm always eager for L.C. news.

I've just completed 17 weeks of basic, obstacle courses, bayonet, ocean jumping (in), hiking, bivouac, and general mayhem. We finished up with 2 weeks of desert maneuvers and when we returned to camp most of my buddies were sent to the infantry. This was a blow because we'd been trained on 90 mm anti aircraft guns.

I was one of the few lucky ones and have been assigned to the Classification office where I am learning the game of sitting much of the time behind a typewriter ... it's beginning to seem inevitable that I will spend most of my life behind a typewriter.

Callan is one of the best U.S. camps and only 4 miles down the beach from La Jolla, a beautiful little city. My wife lives in LJ and I see her every night and weekends, now that training is over. After six weeks on the post I can live off and so we consider ourselves very fortunate all the way around.

This might be of interest: About the only thing now available to draftees are Army school courses in radio, radio mechanics and radar operation. A prerequisite is algebra (1 year). Also any college course which has to do with radio would help. You might use this as a talking point for new students this summer session.

The climate here is fairly sunny but I miss the mid west and the spring, fall, and summer. I hope it won't be too long before I can spend some time again in Decorah.

Meanwhile, thanks again and very best wishes to Mrs. Evanson, Chellis Jr. and yourself.

John Hanson [Caroll (John) Hanson]

P.S. Will you record my new address on the mailing list. Thanks. .J.[41]

⊠      ⊠      ⊠      ⊠      ⊠      ⊠

*Even those who did qualify for their chosen areas of training faced setbacks when they experienced illness or injury.*

[Letterhead: Kingman Army Air Field, Kingman, Arizona]

2-17-44

Dear Sir,

I have surely enjoyed receiving your periodic letters. It's a darn fine way of keeping track of Luther friends wherever they are. I like your way of writing—its almost as if you were delivering a talk about it and we were the listeners.

Enjoyed the evening Chellis Jr. and myself spent together in Denver. I was sorry I hadn't known he was there before, as shortly after Christmas I shipped here to become an aerial gunner.

I had started out to become a pilot, but four months in a California hospital helped kill my prospects for this. Had a bit of virus pneumonia which left me not quite up to par physically. Am in fine shape now, however, and they finally decided to let me go along for the ride as a gunner anyway.

The work here is very interesting. What theory there is, we soon put into actual practice.

We do a lot of skeet shooting from moving trucks, which is really good sport. They teach us to regard the Caliber .50 machine gun as our best friend, and we do everything but sleep with it.

The B-17 is the plane we use to train in here. Hope to get assigned to one later on because it's a real piece of airplane.

If all goes well, this fellow will get a short furlough around the first of April, and if its at all possible, I'd like to have a visit with you.

Its very enjoyable to receive your letters, and I surely hope you keep them coming.

Thanks—

Best Regards,<br>Ronnie Larsen [Roald][42]

⊠      ⊠      ⊠      ⊠      ⊠      ⊠

*Some men found themselves in assignments that seemed "dead-end," and welcomed any opportunity they might have to improve their positions.*

Sec. "B", Buckley Field, Denver, Colo.[Undated]

Dear Chellis,

I have a favor to ask of you. Have had a letter from Lt. Colonel Williams in regard to a direct Commission as a Historical Officer for overseas duty. I would appreciate it very much if you would drop a note to him & give me a little boost. Just a few lines stating that you were associated with me & believe me capable of doing research along historical lines. Would surely appreciate it.

Have been instructing here since in Jan. '43 but school has closed now. Was on overseas shipment a wk ago but was pulled off until this other clears up. Has been rough here, no ratings at all. Have been a cpl. since Mch/43 & will always be unless I get into something better.

Must get this in mail. Say "hello" to "Larsens" if you see them. Have been wondering if the family is there or with the Doctor.

Here is address if you care to write. [...]

Very Truly yours

Lawrence Hof[43]

---

*For newly-minted officers, training did not end with Officer Candidate School. Specialized training was also required. For those lucky enough to be accompanied by their families, the dislocation was more tolerable than for single men.*

[Letterhead: Naval Training School, Harvard University]

7 March 1944

Dear Chellis;

Just a note to let you know i appreciate your last "lecture letter" (so named because it is confusing at first, being so highly concentrated and full of "bull", but on closer examination contains a great deal of valuable and interesting material).. no insults meant, naturally, as both Karl Torgerson and myself digested the entire two sheets several times.

After being detached from Princeton on Feb. 10 I had until March 1st to report to Harvard, so spent a swell two weeks with my wife and daughter in Niles,

Michigan. Spent one week-end in Chicago, and saw "Oklahoma" which I enjoyed very much.

We sub-let our house and furniture, and all three of us drove to Cambridge from Michigan. Had a good trip, and even stopped off at Niagara Falls for a "second honeymoon" ... of about an hours length. We went through several cities and towns that the European tour played in, including Angola, Indiana ... Cleveland, etc.

We were fortunate to be able to "share" an apartment with a young medical student and his wife. He just received his M.D. degree and is now an interne at the hospital and his wife works all day, so we have pretty much "free rein" of the place. It is a large 8 room affair, and very nicely furnished, only three miles from school.

This is a communications school that I am now attending, we will eventually go on boats, ranging from pt's, to battle-ships, as the officer in charge of all messages sent or received from that ship. Some will be on shore duty at advanced bases, but at the end of this 4 months course we will all (with very few exceptions) be outside the continental limits. Which is o.k. with me.

The work is very interesting, and I feel I am learning a lot. I most certainly do like it, and it appears that quite a few of us will get some pretty good billets on completing the course. All of our classes are two hours in length, with a ten minute break for smokes and cokes in between. We study such things as coding and ciphering, the morse code, signal flags, radio equipment, typing etc. (I qualified in typing over 45 words per minute with less than three errors which automatically excuses you from having to take the class ... hence the letter to you know) ... I mean now ... guess my success went to my head.

The food here is exceptionally good, almost unbelieveable. It so happens that my dorm doesn't compare too favorably with good old Larson Hall where Dick Reed and I roomed, but Jimmie Roosevelt and Franklin, Jr. both lived there at one time so I guess it is supposed to be a good dorm. What the hell ... after this thing is over you can post the names of the men who lived in Larson Hall, and have a damn good list of men. (pardon the "French", but sometimes I get almost too much of the pride Harvard takes in her illustrous alumnae.)

We are free from 5 to 8 every evening and also over the week-end until 8 o'clock Monday morning, so it gives us a good chance to spend some time with our families, if they are here.

As I mentioned, Karl Torgerson is also here, in line with my keeping everything posted on addresses. We are both interested in the item about Tutor Ellingson possibly coming to Boston. Incidentally my address is now: [...]

I sure will appreciate getting on that mailing list for your information sheet every month. Did I tell you Jack Layton (another Cresco boy from Luther) is now in the medical corp of the Navy ... a lt. J.g. guess I gave you Dick Reed's address ... care of Fleet Post Office San Francisco, etc and Kenny Bergen's at Princeton.

Glad to hear that the basketball, debate, and other activities are still going strong at Luther, give my regards to Pete for me. Tell him I will do my hurdling from island to island in the South Pacific this next season. Also am interested to know what Dr. Sperati is doing. Heard that they have a new man leading the concert band now.

Hope to see you all some day, thanks again for the letter

and so long.

Sincerely, Les de Noyelles[44]

⊠      ⊠      ⊠      ⊠      ⊠      ⊠

*While training was not something most would enjoy, some of the men were able to find humor in their situation.*

[Undated] Wednesday, Camp Crowder

Dear Chellis,

At last I'm getting around to writing you. It seems like every time I sit down to write somebody, some guy with a couple of stripes comes around looking for a yard bird named Linnevold that's wanted in the kitchen. I'm such a permanent fixture in the mess hall that they promoted me to admiral there. (You didn't know they had admirals in the army, did you? Yes, I'm admiral of all vessels; pots and pans to you. Ever since I first came in the army they've put me in the kitchen. In fact, at the reception center, a corporal came around looking for a college graduate who knew shorthand. Like a fool I stepped out of ranks and raised my hand. He said, "They're short in the kitchen. Get the h—over there."

I got another of your letters recently and enjoyed it very much. No fooling around, I suppose you've heard this a hundred times, but you can't imagine how much it means to us fellows to find out where our buddies are and what they're doing. In a way, besides the news you bring us, you sort of serve as a switchboard.

I'd lost all track of Ness, but got his address from your last letter and sent a letter to him today. Keep up the good work. In my opinion, you're doing more for Luther than the Alumnus, Chips, and News Bureau combined.

Say, did you know that Lorrie Ugland, (do you remember him) is over in the South Pacific. His address, unless it's changed, is S/Sgt. Lorrie H. Ugland—[...] I'm sure he'd appreciate your letters, too.

Right now I don't know just what's doing with me. I finished my course at Ohio State Dec. 4 and shipped back to here Jan. 21. I took 2 wks. basic training refresher course that was really rough. Then I was placed in clerk school, from whence this letter cometh. I heard we were released by the Signal Corps to the War Dept. the other day though (all ASTP graduates, I mean) so we'll probably be leaving here soon, I hope. Don't know where we'll go. It'll be nice to get out of the Ozarks to a place where people wear shoes again, though.

While I think of it, will you give my new address to the Chips and Alumnus, too, please. Also greet Fadness, Pete, Reque, and Karl Hanson from me, also, the Colonel.

I ran into Clarence Winden down here the other day. He's playing in the post band down here the other say, and he's still as fat and jolly as ever. It surely was nice to get together and talk over our experiences at Luther. You know, I've come to the conclusion long ago that, on the average you'll never find a better bunch of men than you'll find at Luther College. I know I spent my four happiest years there. I was far from a model student, but I believe I picked up a lot of worth-while information there too.

Before I get too maudlin I think I'd better close. Would you put Dave Preus's address in your next letter, please? I've lost track of him too.

Your friend,

Paul (Linnevold)

P.S. Excuse the paper, but it's the best clerk school furnishes. It's the best I can afford until next pay day. (A bit of advice—Never shoot craps on a blanket.)

P.P.S. Is Dr. Keiler still at Luther? Greet him if he's there, and if he's not why don't you enclose his address in one of your letters? I'd like to write him and I think some of the other fellows would too.

Also I still haven't written to Chellis, Jr. Tell him "hello" from me when you write.[45]

⊠        ⊠        ⊠        ⊠        ⊠        ⊠

*Some men continued to be reassigned to new training, even after they had served in active duty assignments. Moving around the country also offered opportunities to meet fellow Luther students.*

D.O.Q, Miramar Hotel, RM 4, S.C.T.C., Miami, Fla.

5 March, 1944

Dear Chellis,

I rather imagine that you will be surprised when this arrives, as it has been so long since I received your good letter. I've been planning to write dozens of times, but it seems I never did get at it and I'm truly sorry. I certainly enjoyed reading your lengthy letter and to thus locate some of my friends with whom I had lost contact since Luther days. They really are getting around and I hope they'll all return all right, too.

In my travels I haven't run into too many Luther people, but have seen a few. It is a real treat when you meet in far away places and it certainly is a good feeling. I've been in since Nov. '41 and Jan. of '42 found me in Sitka, Alaska as a Storekeeper 2/c. I spent a busy year up there and was then transferred to Seattle for duty, which I really appreciated, to say the least. While in Seattle I saw Martin Elstad when he went thru on his way to Alaska and I understand he's still up there. Sang in the choir out at H.A. Stub's church out there and had a lot of fun out of it. Met Nels Preus when he was there on his way to Alaska to fish that summer and also Carsten Smeby and a couple of others. From Seattle I went to Ft. Schuyler for Indoctrination and stayed on for two months of Advanced Training before being sent down here. Had lots of good weekends with Tony and Eloise Sperati out there and Ken Bergan was there, too, the last two months. Also saw Rolf and Paul Christopherson out there and all of us had some good get-togethers at the Speratis and at O.T.H. Preus' in Jersey City.

In between school periods I was fortunate enough to get about 3 short leaves and tried to include Decorah, but with the gas situation and short time, I couldn't quite do it. I certainly want to see Decorah and everyone again as soon as possible, but it looks as though it will be some time yet. During these leaves, I managed to get up courage enough to ask and get engaged to Agnes Engell. We're both very happy about the whole thing, but wedding plans are indefinite as yet. She is teaching music at Winona this year and she and Marge Helland, Don's sister, are living together as Marge is teaching there too.

Since finishing the basic course here, I requested and received the chance to specialize as an Ass't Gunnery Officer. I have one more week to go in that Course and am not sure yet what will happen after that. I'll either go directly to sea or else on to two more months of more study in that line. The school down here is the best one I've been to yet and has a wonderful reputation. They give you good dope and have the facilities to give lots of good practical experience at sea. I've been on several cruises and just got back Wednesday from a 3-day affair that was really good. Paul Preus and Solveig are down here, too, and Paul is just about through the basic course now. I also met Bob Jarnigan down here a few weeks ago. He was only at Luther the one year, 1934–35 and then went down to Iowa to finish. He went to Sound School from here and is now back in Miami awaiting his orders.

Had a letter from Joe and Jim Homstad a couple of weeks ago and both families are living together in Milwaukee and having a swell time. Joe is interning at one of the hospitals and is a Lt. (j.g.) in the Navy and expects to be called in in Sept. or so of this year. Jim was discharged from the army due to illness, but has now recovered and is working as a cost accountant in a Defense plant there.

Florida is a great place, especially during these winter months, but I don't think I'd ever care to live here permanently. It is nice to walk around in shirt sleeves all the time, to relax at the beach as often as possible etc., but prices are very high and the eternal dollar speaks a strong language to the people down here. We have nice quarters and eat good, so that helps to make life a little better. We do work hard and in a hurry, too, because time goes fast and there is so much to cover.

Thanks again, Chellis, for the letter and please give my regards to Sherm and all the others. You asked about the "Stephen." Its my first name, but I never used it until I began to draw salary from Uncle Sam. By the way, I don't think I'll be getting over to Norway, but Rolf Christopherson was hoping that he would be among the first to start operations over there, when and if. He's in the line of work which will be needed if Norway is retaken and speaks Norsk fluently. Mine is really pretty ragged.

Best regards, Chellis, and I hope you'll continue to keep me on your mailing list.

Sincerely, Tideman [Ens. Stephen T. Normann][46]

*In addition to the reports on "Scuttlebutt," Evanson carried on individual correspondence with many of the men. Unfortunately, that does not survive. In early 1944, he was apparently attempting to locate a set of old photographic negatives (perhaps of the 1936 band trip), to no avail. In his reply to Evanson's query, R.G. Hanson also took the opportunity to give a brief description of his current conditions.*

[Letterhead: United States Army, Camp Ritchie, Maryland
Co "C" 1st Bn. [Mar. 29—'44]

Dear Chellis,

About the films first, the last I recall of them was that I turned them over to Karl Hanson in the business office. This was I believe sometime in my junior year there which would make it '38–39. At any rate I'm sure that they were not turned over to the library at any rate not by me. At the time that I heard of the fire in Old Main, I wondered if the negatives went up with the rest. Helge Nasby requested that he be given all of his negatives back and that was done while I was at school and so far as I know he has his. The negatives of all the others were together as I recall. I hope that the negatives can be located.

Just a word about this place. I'm at a different camp in the mountains west of Baltimore. A wonderful place. The food is superb. I am attending a school here and wondering what will happen to me next. I have a sneaking idea.

Brother Jim is in Great Bend Kansas, a grand crew-man on the B-29 Super—Fortresses. Seems to like it a lot and is looking forward to a furlough.

Hope that the negatives can be turned up.

Yours Truly
"Babe",[Lt. R. H. Hanson.]⁴⁷

⊠　　⊠　　⊠　　⊠　　⊠　　⊠

*Since many of the men and women were originally from the Upper Midwest, a furlough or extended leave gave many of them the opportunity for a brief visit to their alma mater.*

June 15, 1944

Dear Chellis,

Just a few lines to let you know my change in address. Was home on furlough not so long ago, and was over to school but sorry I didn't get to see you. Saw Pip and Fadness, and some of the rest of the faculty. Meant to see Pete but he left just before I got to see him. Talked to his wife for a while and she had heard quite a bit of news from some of the boys. Also saw Ted, Curt & Archie while I was there. Sure good to see some of the old gang again. It will be a great day when the war is over so all the boys can come home.

I'm at Fort Ord waiting for an alert but haven't heard any thing as yet. Still in infantry heavy weapons but not assigned to an outfit as yet.

Well not much news except they can have California for my money.

As Ever
Dean Penney[48]

&#9993;    &#9993;    &#9993;    &#9993;    &#9993;    &#9993;

*Basic training brought many of the men to areas of the country they might not have otherwise visited. But the rigors of training were fairly standard across the country.*

U.S. Naval Training Station, Farragut, Idaho

Apr. 11—'44

Dear Dr. Evanson,

I guess I'm settled enough so that I can find time to write you some letters that should have been written before. They really keep a fellow on the jump around here. We don't have much time to ourselves.

I left Minneapolis on the 28th of March and we arrived out here on the 30th. We were fortunate in having Pullman accommodations on our trip. Upon our arrival, we were given our G.I. hair cuts and issued our uniforms. I timed the barber, and it took exactly 80 seconds to cut my hair. They really do some messy work.

Our first week was more or less routine work before going on a regular schedule. I didn't like it here the first few days but after you get used to it, you get to like it. It also helps when mail starts coming through.

Today I received an angel food cake from the folks and a box of cookies from one of the neighbor ladies so I'm living in style at the present.

I joined the Protestant Church Choir which I enjoy very much. I sang with them on Easter Sunday for the first time. It's really a good substitute for the Schola. There are some excellent singers in it and they really do a good job.

Today we had some mental examinations to find what branch of the Navy we are best suited for. Then we go before the classification officers who ask us our choice of service and then place us in some branch. I'm going to try for V-12. I sure hope the quota is not filled.

I will be here at Farragut for about five more weeks before graduation. I hope I can make a good enough record so I get some special training of some type after I leave here.

I guess I'd better bring this letter to a close and write some more of those letters I should have written before.

Sincerely,

Earl Narum

The folks sent me the last College Chips and I guess I've read it through two or three times. [49]

*Many men had hopes for placement in Officer Candidate School, which, despite its difficulty, offered a welcome change from the more mundane aspects of enlisted life.*

Wednesday, Apr. 11, 1944

Dear Chellis,

Here I be, wrapped up in the throes of another basic training. Physically it is not difficult enough to be healthy but the crap flows as in a mighty, indefatigable stream. Our company is pre-dominantly non-coms & all of us have been in the army for quite some time so they tell us how much they expect from us, claim not to get it, & thrust G.I. Parties & the like down our throat with reckless abandon. Being an intelligent group, however, we possess a fine sense of humor & even the most menial tasks can be funny. Hoots of derision & raucous laughter follow the calling off of the newest name for the G. I. Scourge—K.P. It is not to last long so nobody minds too much.

The Signal Corps has informed me that I am to return to college sometime during the summer to study more Japanese and in order to countermand that I am planning on making endeavors toward the one loophole, O.C.S. As I gaze at some of the boy scouts who are rampant here I feel that all hope is not lost. The quotas are, of course, fantastically low & I have no C.O. to buck for one but want to take a crack at it anyway. So, I should appreciate it if you would pause a few

59

moments & whip off a letter of recommendation for me. Also, I do not wish to have my parents know that I am applying as it may raise false hopes. Thanks a lot!

That much was done early this morning & I am now finishing up in a dirty furnace room—fireman 3rd class! Verily, if by no other means I certainly feel that I should be able to return to my Alma Mater some years hence as a rival of Teske. The only trouble is that I have not found my furnace keeping, floor scrubbing, window cleaning, wall washing, lawn manicuring, etc. etc., too much to my liking. That is, it would seem a bit of a chore to return to that sort of thing on a permanent basis.

Have spent quite a lot of time with Paul Linnevold even though he is on the exact opposite side of camp. Clarence Winden came over the other night & we had a gay old time over a few Px beers. He is a little more obese than ever I believe and hopelessly lost politically being a follower of Col McCormick. Personally, I think the Repb. Party lost me as a voter when Willkie bowed out—for President that is. Winden mentioned that Helge Nasby had been battling with dysentery down under someplace.

Hope to get in a little pole-climbing in order to get in shape. The chow here is excellent and my girth cannot stand much more. Sure would like to be in Decorah preparing to put in a king size garden.

Greetings to all,
Dave Preus[50]

   ✉      ✉      ✉      ✉      ✉      ✉

*Despite the dangers of the war, many men found themselves waiting for a "real" assignment.*

April 14, 1944

Dear Prof. Evanson,

"Too little and too late" might well be applied to this letter but, barring unforeseen circumstances with censorship rules and regulations, everything should be all right. As you can see I am not yet allowed to tell you where I am. I am still (after 6 wks) awaiting my assignment. It will presumably be in Infantry heavy weapons although it could conceivably be with an army band. Either would suit me fine—the infantry is O.K. and hvy wpns appeals to me very much. As to music—it is quite evident that I need much practice before I can follow Father's footsteps in the L.C. great Band.

We play "touch" football once or twice a week with 6–7 on a side. It really is a lot of fun. We also play volley ball and I generally take a short swim in the afternoon before retreat. During the day I work at Hq as a rule. This is just temporary, however, until I receive assignment.

I can't say that I have found many Luther men out here. About a month ago one Chaplain Shafland conducted Lutheran Communion services here. When he filled out a card for me in the National Lutheran Council—Service Commission he noticed my name. Following the service we had quite a talk. It developed that he was a Luther graduate—class of '29 I believe. He had played band music marked Storvick. He also was a classmate of Rev. Rognen at the seminary. Rev. Rognen was my pastor in Mason City.

Apparently all is well in Waterloo with David and Rosalie having successfully made the change from Mason City to Waterloo. Sonja, too, is busy in kindergarten. I can see that my brother and I will be at Luther at the same time. The girls, I fear, are too well set on going to St. Olaf.

From the U.S. Armed Forces Institute I am taking a course in Analytic Geometry. It isn't easy but I don't intend to be stopped. I don't seek any credit for I plan to retake my trig and analyt when I return. This course does, however, serve as a refresher in math and a link to school days.

I am singing second bass in the choir here and the choir is pretty good. On Easter Sunday we sang the "Hallelujah Chorus" from the Messiah and "Sanctus" by Charles Gounod. At the sunrise service the band played and the choir broadcast in the afternoon

The most important reason why I am writing is to thank you for your letters, the "Chips" and the "Alumnus." It is difficult to express in words what they mean to me. Of course I know very few personally but, having read the Chips since I was small, I remember many of the names.

Thank you again

Sincerely,
Olin Storvick[51]

*Those lucky enough to get into Army Specialized Training Programs faced difficult academic programs as well as the regular physical rigors of basic training.*

S.U.I, Iowa City,Iowa

[May 12, '44]

Dear Mr. Evanson:

Well, I'm in the army & already wish I weren't, but guess I can make the best of it.—

I was sworn in on the 2nd of May & was sent to Bozeman, Montana for training. I got there on the 6th & was immediately transferred to the Unit here at the University, so I'm just about where I started from.

My curriculum is physics, math, chemistry, hist., English, Military, & phy. Ed.—I'll only be here for 3 months & then I have to go to basic training. They really work you. Luther was a snap compared to this, & I already wish I was back there. Our lieutenant is a fairly nice guy, Lt. Smith is his name & he is very obviously a Southerner from his accent.

Well, I'll have to close. Really, nothing exciting happens that I can say. So, I'll sign off.—

Very Sincerely,

Pvt. David Tate[52]

✉    ✉    ✉    ✉    ✉    ✉

*While the men looked forward to their ultimate assignments, their training often was not as interesting or exciting as they hoped it would be. After qualification tests, many had to settle for something other than their first choice of duty.*

Randolph Field, Texas

June 14, 1944

Dear Mr. Evanson,

I have been wanting to write to you for some time but never seemed to get around to it.

I might as well come right out and tell you. I wish I was back at Luther. I left there at the end of the first semester Then I went to Radio School in Des Moines for 5 weeks then 5 days after I was 18 I was in the Army.

I took my basic at Sheppard Field, Texas & now I am here working on the line until they send me to pre-flight. There are about 8 or 900 of us pre-cadets here.

You see we will not be called Cadets until we get to pre-flight. Here we are known as aviation students. The work we do on the line is not very important. Most of the time we clean the planes. Only once in a while do they let us taxi. It is just training planes we work with so there is not much to taxing them.

I don't know where I will go after pre-flight. I did not qualify for pilot, only navigator and bombardier so I will most likely go to some school. That is if I dont wash out.

What is the enrollment at Luther this summer?

By the way when the "Pioneer" comes out will you see to it that mine is sent here. I guess I will be here for some time.

To whoever is responsible—Thanks for sending the "Chips" I find it very interesting.

Write if you find time please.

Your old student,
Donald Thompson[53]

---

*Later that year, Thompson reported a transfer to yet another radio school.*

Dec. 10, 1944
Sioux Falls. S.D.

Dear Dr. Evanson

I want to thank you for sending the Scuttlebutt but thought I better give you my new address so it won't have to go down to Texas all the time.

It's kind of good to be up in "Yankee land" again after being in Texas all summer but right now I could stand some of that Texas heat.

Radio school is O.K. but I'd give a lot to be back at Luther right now.

We had quite a tradgey here the other day. a plane crashed into one of the barracks. Seven in the plane were killed & 3 in the barracks.

There really is no news from this place. I just wanted to thank you for sending the Scuttlebutt.

Your former student [Pvt.] Donald Thompson[54]

*In addition to the tedious nature of some training, men were also irritated by the types of assignments they received. Unable to make what they considered a meaningful contribution to the war effort, they questioned the Army's logic in selecting them for particular training, and were frustrated when they could not apply for a different assignment.*

[July 8—'44] <u>Saturday</u>
[Ft. Custer Mich]

Dear Chellis,

Your most welcome monthly dope-sheet just received & thoroughly perused. Really, you embarrass me by invariably putting my address in each issue; Georgetown, Ft. Custer, Camp Crowder, sandwiched in amongst APO this & FPO that. However, all that will be changed quite shortly I suspect. Fact is, the lid blew off a week ago, POE orders in, but they were rescinded. But despite all admonitions to the contrary, coming voraciously from Sebastian, Jim Crain, Bob Knowlton, & about everyone else who has been that way, it seems that the South Pacific will beam on my sunny countenance soon. We are definitely hot, but you can't put much faith in this army, y'know.

As you so aptly put it, I am pretty burned up—I am not very proud of my contributions to its effectiveness. We are called a Prisoner of War Processing Co., yours truly supposedly serving as an interpreter. Now that is fine, it could be interesting, it could be important, but there are 25 Jap-Americans, mostly Hawaiians (and fine fellows) & ten of us whom the army has endeavored to teach Japanese. Needless to say, the Japanese I know is so insufficient that a prisoner could tell me the no of troops with him, the units, their positions, & what have you & I could not do much more than nod my head & look wise. Worse yet, I am an <u>essential technician</u> at Pfc.'s rating of course, and cannot even have the satisfaction of applying for something else. It's a great war & our boys are doing a fine job of fighting it.

Heard from Ness today—he too was in on the Big Show & could only say that he had had the honor of hauling in one of the (our) <u>Big Boys</u>. Those navy boys have a fine deal. Had swell weekend in Chicago with a fine Sioux Falls Norskie, (female). If there are any more guys at N.W. Mid'n School let me know please. I hit the Big Town almost weekly. Your sheet is really a fine thing Chell, keep 'em coming.

Dave [Preus][55]

64

⊠     ⊠     ⊠     ⊠     ⊠     ⊠

*The men's training assignments were often subject to the vagaries of military planning.*

0745—July 15, 1944

Hiya Mr. Evanson,

How's the old salt? Been thinking of writing to you for a long time but something always came up. So even if it does now, I'll get it done.

I'm still a dry land sailor yet—had about four days on a crash boat but that was all.

It's now 1100 and inspection is over. It seems wherever Acorn 29 is, something new is started. When we left our last place it was looking more like a concentration camp—high fences, turnstile and guards all over the place. When we first got there, there was no fence, no turnstile, and very few guards. Here at Heuneme when we first got here, there were no inspections, now all the units are having them.

Once I was a coxswain (for two days). Then I'm told the boatswain mate complement is full and so they take the rate away and say I will get it when we go over seas—when?

We're just on various training details now. I was chosen along with two other fellows to go to chemical warfare training in Denver Colo. The course was very enjoyable and beneficial. When out on liberty one night who do I meet—that's right Chell—Boy was I surprised. He took me out to one of the amusement parks and showed me around. It sure was nice seeing him. We talked over old times and about Luther fellows. That was alright. Denver is quite a liberty town too. We were the only sailors in the town and boy did we have fun!

Got weekend liberty now and am off to the races. Well take it easy Salty & be good

Brooklyn [John D Christiansen, S 1/c] [56]

⊠     ⊠     ⊠     ⊠     ⊠     ⊠

*In addition to the unpredictable nature of military orders, the men also had to deal with complications from medical problems.*

[Letterhead: United States Naval Training Center, Bainbridge, Maryland]

8/3/44

Dear Chellis:

Please pardon my extreme personalized greeting, but I trust that it will be accepted in the same tone as it is rendered.

I received the last 2 copies of your scuttlebutt via Karl Nordgaard for which I want to thank you greatly.

I have been here @ Bainbridge since the first week in May.

I was operated on for appendicitis on the 30 of June—during Captain's Inspection, so you can see how I rate!! ahem!! I've had great sport here, although my progress has been hindered by an abscess in the incision (which developed post operatively). I gave myself my own morphine hypos, and removed most of my sutures.

The med. officer on the ward (a full Comdr) invited my into the operating room and have witnessed several operations. It proves very enlightening. I hope to witness a delivery this afternoon.

Thanks for the news letter and I'll be waiting for the next issue.

Greetings to the Luther family—

Fred Giere[57]

&#9993; &#9993; &#9993; &#9993; &#9993; &#9993;

*Even though the specialized training was rigorous, the men tried to keep Evanson updated on their whereabouts and activities.*

10 August 1944

Dear Chell,

'Just dropping a few lines between jumps here, to say hello.

Bob McConnell and I reported here 30 July, and are rapidly being indoctrinated (or something). We have been lucky so far in that we live in the same room, are in the same company and platoon, and attend all classes together.

As for the training it's swell, except that it surely keep a guy going. We run between classes and to almost anything (including shore when we get leave). I like it a lot and feel that the training, although "pushed on you" is good. We have classes every day in Navigation, Recognition, Seamanship, Naval Regs,

Fundamentals and others, as well as drill, P.T. etc. Most classes are not difficult, except that the time allowed for study for each is limited.

The hotel itself is beautiful, the food is good, and the setup as a whole is excellent.

We will be here, <u>we</u> believe, about 8 weeks and then sent out to various duties. I've selected the three following in this order: 1.—Chemical Warfare; 2.—Destroyer Duty (Spec.); 3.—Amphibious Oper. (Spec.). I expect either #2 or #3.

How's everything back at Luther. I'd like very much to write several of the men back there, but just don't have time right now. I'd appreciate it very much if you'd greet them all for me.

I must close now and "hit" the books until 2215.

> Sincerely Marv [Ens Marvin Bachman]
> P.S. Say hello to your wife and Chell Jr. for me!![58]

⊠ ⊠ ⊠ ⊠ ⊠ ⊠

*The men frequently reported changes in their plans, as some programs were cancelled and new ones developed. The normal lot of a soldier often required considerable patience.*

> Fort Jackson, S.C.
> August 12, 1944

Dear Chellis,

I was very happy to receive your very interesting July issue of "Scuttlebutt" this morning. I had been losing contact with the grand old school, with the exception of the Alumnus, so it was great to hear about the fellows I knew and also about those older fellows who I had heard plenty about. To show my appreciation I decided to sit down and write. While I haven't seen action as yet, I've had a lot of interesting experience which I thought you might be interested in hearing.

Yes, I'm still pretty much of a rookie in this man's Army, although I have now been in the service 13 months. After reporting for active duty at Fort Snelling, I was sent to Fort Benning, Georgia, for basic training in an ASTP regiment. After four rugged months on the Georgia sands (and don't believe that fable about Georgia peaches), I was sent to Northeastern University in Boston to study basic engineering. I tried to get into Military Government, but no soap—not enough background. I was at Northeastern for one term—until the A.S.T.P. went on the rocks. It was a grand four months that I spent in the old Bean Town—for it is there (at Wellesley) that I met the girl I'm going to marry after the war. The whole thing was pretty much of a farce as far as learning anything was concerned because everything was repetition with the exception of chemistry.

On the 13th of March I joined the 26th Infantry Division which was on maneuvers in Tennessee. This outfit, more commonly known as the Yankee Division or YD, is rated as the best Infantry Division on this side, I am in Anti Tank company of the 101st regiment—an ammo bearer in a 57mm gun squad. It's a great outfit even if it is the Infantry. We hit Jackson on the 1st of April and have been sweating it out here ever since. There isn't too much I can tell you about our training, but I can tell you that we are definitely heading overseas. We are all packed up and will leave this camp inside of two weeks—heading for a staging area or possibly directly to a P.O.E. Of course, we don't know where we'll be going, but chances are we'll be getting in on the kill. There's a possibility that we may go to India, but I hope we don't.

On June 15, I was one of the first soldiers in this division to receive the Expert Infantryman's Badge. This is the highest award that can be given to any Infantryman short of actual combat. Besides wearing the attractive sterling silver badge, all recipients of the award receive $5 per month extra pay. We haven't received any back pay yet, but it is coming through this month.

It makes me feel something of a failure whenever I get news of my old college pals. Its seems that 75 percent of them are commissioned officers in the Army, Navy, Marines, or Air Corps. I guess my luck hasn't been with me—but then they say that our good Uncle knows best. I'm not complaining—I'm very content with my present association. However I did have a signal honor thrown my way which I don't imagine too many Luther Fellows have received. Believe it or not I was up for an appointment to the United States Military Academy at West Point, had passed the mental requirements, but then flunked the physical because of a slight deficiency in my right eye. But then I consider it honor enough to have come that close.

Despite the fact that I am far from Minnesota and Iowa, I often find my thoughts roving back to these glorious two years I spent at dear old Luther. No one who ever attended Luther could ever forget her. While at present it is almost impossible to plan for the future, I so hope to return to Luther someday and complete, or rather continue, my education, Truly, a person's education is never completed.

I would appreciate it very much if you would greet my former instructors for me. I don't know for sure just who is left but I'm sure that Dr. Preus, Dean Fadness, Professor Nelson, Coach Pete, Prof Reque, and Bob Juke are still around.

With best wishes for you and your family, and with hopes for another prosperous year at Luther, I remain,

An ex-pupil and fellow Norseman,
[Pfc] Roger Anderson[59]

$\boxtimes$      $\boxtimes$      $\boxtimes$      $\boxtimes$      $\boxtimes$      $\boxtimes$

*While many men hoped to become pilots, the Army Air Forces offered many other opportunities for those who did not qualify for pilot training.*

[Letterhead: U.S. Army Air Forces, Buckley Field, Buckley Field, Colorado]

August 20-44

Dear Prof. Evanson:

Well, I'm in Colorado now taking some training for air corps.

I've been classified as a remote control turret mech. Which is fancy for gunner on B-29's & I hope I make it. I start training for it in a couple of weeks, I hope. Probably at Lowery Field, Colo. which is 10 miles from here.

They are plenty tough here. Been here for about a month now & am about through. Go on Bivouac next week which is the finale for our training here. Work with 30 cal. carbines here & .45 cal. pistols & .45 Cal. Machine guns. Quite interesting, to say the least.

Ran into Paul Thompson about a week ago. He is here to in another section. Paul said that Wes Skadden is at Lowery & Earl Narum is at Boulder. I ran into a Cpl. Johnson—Luther '40 at Leavenworth. Seemed like a swell fellow. How is Luther.

I got your letter a couple of days ago. Are they turning Larson Hall into a girls dorm. Heaven forbid. It should never happen. Do you happen to know where Kenneth Olson is at present. I'd like to get his address if possible.

Food here is O.K., but I'll take the boarding club I think, & I didn't think much of it.

Well, keep plugging the history. Don't be too hard on the innocent frosh.— Your former & future pupil, I hope—Dave Tate[60]

✉        ✉        ✉        ✉        ✉        ✉

*In addition to information about themselves, Evanson's former students occasionally sent him cigarettes, which they could purchase at reduced prices in the post exchange (PX).*

[Postcard with Letterhead: <u>USO</u>]
From: Pfc. Dave Preus [...] Warrenton, Va
Thursday [Postmarked 4 PM Sep 21 1944]

Dear Chellis,

It took a long time for the army to let me accumulate enuf dough to get those cigarettes but trust that by now Barbara has sealed & sent them & you are basking in clouds of "M.F.T." smoke—or whatever it is. Had a fine time last weekend with Hale & wife & Barb. Were it not for a couple fighting brothers I should feel guilty here. But if the life is physically easy, I nonetheless have a satisfaction which has not been mine in other days. I still like it! How about those addresses?

<u>Dave</u>[61]

✉        ✉        ✉        ✉        ✉        ✉

*As they prepared for deployment, the men's conditions were often designed to prepare them for what they would be experiencing when they reached their combat assignments.*

Port Hueneme, Cal
1 Oct. 1944

Dear Folks,

I received your welcome letter this morning Dr. Evanson so I am going to drop you a few lines this afternoon. I am the J.O.O.D. this week-end & as there isn't much going on I do have a little time to get caught up on a little letter writing. It seems that a guy never does get caught up on that sort of thing.

Well, I am now getting settled into the routine out here too. They still don't quite what to do with me here as yet but they may figure out something yet. You see I am supposed to be the boat officer in the outfit, but as long as we are still in this country we don't get any boats so they really don't have any special job now. I am sort of a jack-of-all-trades at the present time. That is kind of interesting too for a while. It is a good way to get acquainted with the men anyway. I even built a football field for the boys the other day. You're probably wondering why the station doesn't take care of things like that, but you see we are out roughing it now. We are getting our final training with conditions as we will probably have them when we get to Island "X". We have taken over & are now operating an air field here. That is what we will be doing when we get over there. Except of course then we start from scratch & even build the air field and everything else unless the Japs have left anything that we might can use. We are living in tents etc. It is very interesting here for me tho' because I have never been around airplanes very much before. The planes don't seem to be in too good a shape, however, because they have had about four or five crash landings here in the past week. Fortunately there has been no one hurt at any time. Most of the trouble seems to be that they can't get the wheels down, & have to make belly landings. The officers that are in this outfit are really a swell bunch of guys & I am really glad to be with them. There is a lot of gold braid but they don't use it much.

I am surely glad to hear that you have so many students back at Luther again this year. I figure the enrollment is really pretty good with conditions as they are. Old Larson hall must be quite the place from the reports I hear. That is something that should have been done long time ago. Guess they had to get women in there first to get things done. ha! ha!

So Oct. 14 is homecoming again. I can surely remember some swell homecomings that we had while I was there. I am sure that I can say for myself & all the rest of the Luther fellows where ever they may be that we all wish we could be with you that day. It will be a great homecoming when we can all get back there for the first homecoming when this war is all over.

Both Betty & David are coming along just fine & dandy. She weighed him here the other day & he weighed a little over 17 pounds. So I guess he must be healthy & feeling O.K. He even has a tooth now. I figure that's pretty good but of course I don't know too much about it.

Well, folks I have an inspection to make about this time so I had better close for now. Greetings to all of you and I remain the same old—

Harold [Ens. Heltne][62]

$\boxtimes$      $\boxtimes$      $\boxtimes$      $\boxtimes$      $\boxtimes$      $\boxtimes$

*Although delays in receiving assignments were frustrating, they also provided personal opportunities that might not have been otherwise possible.*

[Letterhead: U.S. Army Air Forces, Buckley Field, Buckley Field, Colorado
Oct. 5—44

Dear Dr. Evanson:

Received your letter the other day & darn glad I was to get it.—As you can see, I'm still at Buckley. Been a "casual" (guy to be shipped) for over a month, but all tech schools seem to be full & they can't get rid of us.—Have hopes for this wk however.—

Ran into Keith King couple of weeks ago. He was here. He shipped somewhere.—Going into Radio, I guess.—

Congratulations to me this time—Larraine Hatfield, my girl from home, and I were married Sept. 30 at the Post Chapel here.—She came up for 4 days & that was all the time it took.—

Glad to hear the attendance at Luther is as well as it is this year. I sure miss the place. I'd give a lot to be back this year.—Am glad to hear they still have football. Hope the freshmen can beat the upper classmen as well as we did last year.

Well, regards to all especially to those whom I knew last year.—

As ever—

Pvt. David L. Tate[63]

$\boxtimes$      $\boxtimes$      $\boxtimes$      $\boxtimes$      $\boxtimes$      $\boxtimes$

*While some men were thrust into specialties for which they had no previous experience or training, others found positions in which they could "make themselves indispensable."*

9 Oct. 1944

Dear Chellis, Pete, Karl

Time for a Homecoming letter. This year I won't even come close to making it—no leave this year.

The pace on the Pacific Coast accelerates constantly. Ever since I had leave last October it's been a rat race around here. As far as I'm concerned I still have the best job in the Navy and wonder how I was so fortunate. All the other training officers on the Coast are either 3 or 4 strippers. The only reason they keep me in is that I was the first one on the West Coast. They had no idea then what I would turn into. Being an educator I soon had the place so full of graphs, charts, plans, curriculums, etc., that no one else could understand it. Then as the Bureau decided to put operational training on the No. 1 list and the men and officers started to pour in they made the mistake of having me do the planning for the whole Coast. That was all I needed. From that time on no one has been able to decipher anything and they are stuck with me.

My work consists of being responsible for the crews and officers of newly commissioned destroyers and cruisers on the West Coast together with all large ships—mostly transport and cargo—built in the Bay area. This includes the training for each rank and rate, the training of the instructors, getting of classrooms and buildings, requisitioning equipment—in short everything connected with training, its planning, and reporting. To help I have a schedule officer, two instructor training officers, a visual aids officer, and a planning officer. Also a staff of artists making training aids together with the necessary yeomen and storekeepers and about 350 instructors. So I couldn't have had a better assignment anywhere to tie into my civilian work.

Last week I was in San Pedro. They flew about a dozen psychologists out from the East Coast to meet with training officers as to their findings on the best way to train men. Next week I expect to go to Seattle.

After coming back from San Pedro I spoke at the Jr. College Fall Institute on Post War Veterans Education. Oct. 22 I represent the Navy at the State of Calif. Institute so I get a chance to keep my hand in Public School work, too.

Enough of such shop talk.

Happy Jensen and Bill Aaker come in quite often. Rudy Raftshol is here now. Edna Lee was here for a few days in August. Saw Rosholt '30 in San Pedro and found out he was stationed right here in San Fran. Art Bergee was here about 3 weeks ago.

With more and more transfers to the West Coast you might put my telephone no. in the Scuttlebutt—Exbrook 3931, ext. 376.

Trinity Lutheran Church have called Brown (Concordia) as pastor. If he doesn't accept they will call Ed Wilson '30.

A week ago I went to church in Los Angeles. Eggentrum (L.C.) was Pastor and announced his resignation that Sunday to take effect in Feb.

Keep the Schuttlebutt coming. It means a lot.

Again, I hope this is the last Homecoming I'll miss altho I have no hope of the war being over for at least two more Homecomings.

> Greet all
>
> Dave     [Lieut. A.O. Davidson, Treasure Island, Calif][64]

     ⊠       ⊠       ⊠       ⊠       ⊠       ⊠

*Many of the men who were in the Army Air Corps hoped to be admitted to flight training. Because of the limited openings in that area, they often had to wait, doing other related duties until an opportunity in flight training might present itself.*

[Letterhead: United States Army Air Forces]

Victorville, Calif

Oct. 23, 1944

Dear Chellis,

I've been thinking of writing to you for a long time but I just haven't gotten around to doing it. I'll tell you right now that this man's army doesn't stimulate one's ambition—at least I haven't found it so in my six months of service.

I am working on the flight line here at the present time. We are waiting to go to pre-flight but I don't know how soon that will be. I understand that Santa Ana has closed so I guess we're shut out in the cold. The Lord only knows what will happen to us.

I was very fortunate to be sent here because this is where my cousin, Capt. Dirks, is stationed. That gives me a "connection" that may help me a little. It's also very nice to go home with him for a good meal every now and then.

I've certainly enjoyed getting the "scuttlebutt". When a copy comes I drop my other letters and read every word before opening the other. I'm very anxious to know where some of my old L.C. buddies are.

Do you send out Chips to servicemen? If there is any change of getting it put me on the mailing list.

Willis and I were over to see Lt. Bob Lounsberry about a month ago. He shipped out for overseas about two weeks ago. He was flying a B24 at Muroc, about 60 miles from here.

I heard that the boys lost to Wartburg on homecoming day. I can understand why if some of them had never even seen a football game before. Maybe they can win the last three games.

I'd certainly like to be back in school again but I guess we've got to finish up first. I've been sweating out a furlough but I don't seem to be getting anywhere. Maybe next month—who knows?

Well Chell, 5:30 comes pretty early so I guess I'll hit the sack. Thanks a lot for everything.

Sincerely,
A/S Robert Dresselhaus[65]

⊠     ⊠     ⊠     ⊠     ⊠     ⊠

*As one might expect, even medical corps training attempted to simulate conditions the men would encounter in combat.*

[Letterhead: United States Navy, U.S. Naval Hospital, Farragut, Idaho]

Sunday Afternoon, Oct 29th—'44

Dear Mr. Evanson,

I want to thank you for the Scuttlebutt. It really is swell to get & read about the whereabouts etc. of all the other Norseman. I really appreciate it a lot. Thanx.

About the only Luther man I know out here is Karst Ulvilden. At the present time he's up in O.G.U. I've seen him several times & had some good old Larsen Hall bull sessions.

I have just five weeks left here in corps school. This is a 12 weeks course & just finished our 7th week Friday. At the present time we're getting Hygiene & Sanitation, Matern. Medic.. & Nursing. It's quite interesting. Have 6 hours of classes every day with 38 hrs liberty every other week which makes it pretty nice. On Sat. afternoons of the weekends we're not on liberty we get put in the woods & have transportation of casualties, which consists of the emergency first aid treatment on the field & transportation to a first aid station. All of our own splints, stretchers, dressings etc we have to improvise out of material available in the woods. It's lots of fun & good practice.

The other nite we had a little excitement around here when the wave quarters burned which was only about 3 barracks down from us. Our section having its fire station at the scene of any fires in the hosp. area to assist whoever needed at the fire, we got in on it all. Well I guess this will have to be all. Thanx again for Scuttlebutt & I'm looking forward to it each month & also Chips.

An Ole Norseman
"Bucket" [Milford Lunde S 2/c][66]

✉      ✉      ✉      ✉      ✉      ✉

*While most men found training a drudgery, some had unusual experiences which lightened their duty.*

McClellan Field, Calif.
November 1, 1944

Dear Chell,

Well, I have finally arrived in sunny California but we were greeted by one of the worst rain storms I've ever been in. Very typical of California this time of the year. It has been real nice today though but I'll still take the Midwest.

I will be on this field for approximately 3 or 5 weeks and then we will either go to Kerns, Utah; Greensboro, N.C.; or Seattle, Wash, depending on where we go overseas. McClellan is about 10 miles north of Sacramento, which is a very nice town.

I enjoyed getting back to Luther although I wished it could have been for a longer stay. I think of it often and am waiting for the day when we can all return.

Will you please put me on the mailing list for the Chips as well as your news letter so I can keep in touch with the school.

The one thing of this camp that strikes me is the fact that they wake us up in the morning with some hot Harry James records or otherwise. I think it is a very efficent way of waking us up because when we hear that swing music, we just get jumping and soon, we jump right out of bed.

Time for lights to go out so will close.

Sincerely,
Paul L. Thompson[67]

✉      ✉      ✉      ✉      ✉      ✉

*In many cases, new training assignments brought the opportunity to meet other "Lutherites," as well as take advantage of local recreational opportunities.*

[Bomb Disp School, Washington D.C.]

Sunday P.M.Nov. 6—'44]

Dear Chell,

'Just dropping a short line again to say hello to you and the gang up a Luther.

Since I wrote you last, I've begun a unique course here in Washington, at the Naval Bomb Disposal School. I like the setup very well, and, though the work is really "piled" on, the nature of the course is such that it's intensely interesting. I'll finish here about the 1st of January I believe.

We've had a couple of Luther reunions here since I came, both of which you've undoubtedly heard of. Chuck Arneson, Dave Preus, Selbo, Bev Sperati, Red Henderson and his wife, Cameron Hoff and several others had a party at Bev Sperati's. We ended a fine evening by singing "To Luther", and Norway's national song. (I can't spell it. Hi!) All in all, a very enjoyable time was had. We praised Luther to the sky. ('Course we're prejudiced!)

I've managed to see quite a lot of the important buildings here and also have seen some swell football games, both college and pro. We really pulled for Navy over Notre Dame, but they didn't actually need our help to take the Irish yesterday.

How're things back at Luther? I have Luther in my mind a lot, and am very proud to have been graduated there. I believe that goes for all of us, too.

Say hello to everyone there for me, if you will. I'd like to write many of them, but a guy keeps pretty busy most of the time.

'Must close now, and hit the sack.

As always, Your Friend, Marv [Ens M.C. Bachman][68]

⋈　　　⋈　　　⋈　　　⋈　　　⋈　　　⋈

*Evanson's correspondents often commented on remarks they read in "Scuttlebutt," and added their own opinions about changes taking place on the Luther campus.*

The I-N-D-E-P-E-N-D-E-N-T Territory of Texas
(Now overrun by Damyankees While Texans Wage & Win The War—!)
Nov. 9, '44

Dear Dr. Evanson:

Paragraphs or no paragraphs, SCUTTLEBUTT is a welcome periodical in this part of the country. Received Chips the other day—first time I ever saw an apology in Sawdust!!—and wish you'd correct the writer of the Servicemen's column. There is no "Kingham Field, Texas"—Cpl. Ronnie Larsen is stationed at "Kingman Field, Ariz."

I've heard a lot of good reports on the NEW LARSEN HALL. Larsen Hall-with-women is something I gotta see!! I'm making plans, and if the Army will concur with them, I should be able to see the premiere performance of "Ladies in Retirement."

But this, of course, will not happen until I return from 30-days "Special Services" course at Washington & Lee in Virginia. I leave for there Nov. 12th and know that the news will come as quite a shock to people who have had every right heretofore to assume that I am part of the topography down in Texas. The school will give me absolute mastery of the dubious arts of song-leading, skit-and-show-producing etc., so I should be well-qualified as an L.C. cheer-leader in that happy post-war time!

Best regards to you & faculty friends,
Marv. [Cpl. M.E. Lore, Sheppard Field, Tex.][69]

✉    ✉    ✉    ✉    ✉    ✉

*For officers wanting to get into "real" active duty, the wait for deployment sometimes seemed interminable.*

Port Hueneme, Cal
12 Nov. 1944

Dear Folks,

I have been on watch all week-end so I have been trying to get caught up on some of my letter writing, & according to records its seems that it has been quite some time since I have written to you people. So now I will try and scribble a few lines.

There really hasn't happened anything of interest since I last wrote to you. Everything is still going alone as usual. Same old routine stuff. I guess it is O.K. to get plenty of training before you ship out but I figure I've had just about enough training by now. I was pretty happy when I got my orders out here for additional duty outside the United States, but now again I am wondering if those orders meant anything. I suppose we will ship out eventually. But I am getting a little restless again. I feel quite sure that we won't be going out before the first of the year at least. The two other officers that I came out here with from Ft. Pierce have already shipped out with other ocean units.

Oh, yes, we are now getting some of that famous California "liquid sunshine." It's been raining pretty steady out here for the past week. I understand it keeps on for about three or four months too. By the end of that period I am afraid that I am going to be very tired of it all.

Say before I forget it. I wonder if you could send me Jack Preus address. You see there is an officer in our outfit that used to go to grammer school with him & I guess he hasn't heard from him or seen him for eight or nine years. The officer was wondering if I knew Jack because after he heard I went to Luther he remembered that Jack had gone there too. If you can send me his address it will be appreciated. Thank you.

I have been receiving the Chips fairly regularly & am very happy to get it. You can be sure that I read it from start to finish. It really is surprising, tho', how many of the names I can't recognize any more. And it really wasn't so long ago that I was there. They really are appreciated tho' and will be very happy to be kept on the mailing list. Your letters each month are more than welcome too Dr. Evanson. I sent the last one home to Betty & she said she got more news & enjoyed it more than the Chips.

Well, folks, it is just about time for me to make an inspection so I had better knock off. I hope this letter finds you all well and happy. As for myself I am well & so are the rest of the family. I hope I can see you all soon. I know I think of you all often enough. I also remember how swell you all were to me when I was fortunate enough to spend a few months at your home. I hope I can someday repay the kindness you gave to me then.

As Ever, Just
Harold. [Ens. J.H. Heltne][70]

*For others, new training gave them the opportunity to find more interesting work than they were originally assigned.*

[Letterhead: Section S, 33705th AAF Base Unit (TS), Lowry Field, Colorado]

Nov. 18—44

Dear Dr. Evanson:

I've been shifted again. This time to Lowry Field. I'm going to Photo school here. I got changed over from gunnery which was a break for me because I'll be here at least 17 more weeks if I don't wash out of school and I don't look that way yet. It's very interesting stuff, very best equipment etc. & darn good instructors. Quite a few WAC's stationed here going to school also. Lowry is just on the outskirts of Denver, takes about 30 minutes into the center of town. Denver is a real town for soldiers. Friendly etc. & really can't be beat.

Am glad to hear Luther is going to take ex service men under the GI Bill of Rights after a discharge for I am looking forward to finishing there if at all possible. Cannot make definite plans for anything at all any more. Had a letter from Oral Salbro in England the other day. Says he don't like it as well as the states. Tough break, his getting put in the infantry. Am going to try to look up Chel jr. as soon as I get time.

Well not much to say—

As always, my best to you and Luther-

Pvt. David Tate[71]

⊠     ⊠     ⊠     ⊠     ⊠     ⊠

*Although the men did not always get their choices for duty, they still remained hopeful of finding an assignment that fit their interests and backgrounds.*

[Letterhead: United States Navy]

Friday, 24, November [44]

Dear Mr. Evanson:

Just a few lines this evening to let you know that I am receiving your copies of the "Scuttlebutt." I always enjoy them, and read them with care because I'm always on the lookout for someone's name that is of particular interest to me.

I had the luck of "bumping" into Bud Eiden at Union Station, Chicago about 6 weeks ago. Sure was good to meet an old classmate. He is the only one I've seen since I left for the service 7 mths ago.

I got sidetracked at Great Lakes, they sent me to Electrician's Mate School, but hope to remedy that about the 1st of Dec. & get a transfer to the Hospital Corp. Be more along my interests at least.

They say "California for the winter", but believe me I'll have lots of snow for my winter weather, this rain just never stops coming down.

I had been hearing from "Gabby" regularly, but haven't had any word from him for some time now. From a picture I saw of him last summer I'd say he must weigh close to 225 pounds now. Really husky.

My brother Bob who is an Ensign now shipped out for Amphibious Operation in the Pacific last month. As luck would have it he left two days before I reached the coast.

Well I better knock off for now, and hit the sack. Thanks again for the Scuttlebutt, and if my brother isn't already receiving one, would you please send him one, I'm sure he'd appreciate it. With best wishes,

Sincerely Yours,<br>
Ernie [Ernest O. Overland F 2/c, Alameda, Calif.][72]

&#9745;    &#9745;    &#9745;    &#9745;    &#9745;    &#9745;

*New technology opened new areas of opportunity for the men and women serving in World War II.*

[Letterhead: Scott Field, Illinois]<br>
Nov. 25, '44, Friday Evening

Dear Scuttlebutt,

I've been receiving your letter now for some time and do I like it. Of course I do. It makes me feel just like I was back in Luther again. I wasn't there so long but long enough to get acquainted. I'm coming back too if it is at all possible.

I'm in the A.A.C.S. a comparatively new part of the Army. It is still considered as part of the Air Forces but has begun reaching out for itself in the last year or two. I'm supposed to come out as one of seven different possibilities. Radio

Operator is the one I want. I can sit over in Burma sending and receiving news from the whole world.

I'm now stationed at Scott Field Ill. My address is Pvt. Jim Geiselhart 37588970 Sec. H Brks. 778 Scott Field, Ill. There are at least two other Luther men here. Teddy Amundson and Keith King. We can get together every weekend.

I just got my home paper and I see Don Thompson is in Sioux Falls, S.D. I also got a letter from Paul L. Thompson today. He is stationed in Salt Lake, City, Utah. You may have his new address but just to make sure here it is. Pvt Paul L. Thompson [...]

I, as a whole have an exceptionally good deal here. Only six hours of school and a pass every weekend. I had better close now. Work to do in the Army you know.

> A Lutherite
> [Pvt.] Jimmy Geiselhart[73]

⊠          ⊠          ⊠          ⊠          ⊠          ⊠

*Navy duty often involved skills that the Midwestern "landlubbers" had never needed before, but which they had to develop quickly in order to complete their programs successfully. Those lucky enough to be accompanied by their spouses had the additional burden of finding suitable housing.*

29 Nov 44

Dear Chellis,

Thanks for the last two letters, they are the best means of keeping posted we have. I am now at ATB Solomons, Maryland—the same base Ted Jake [Jacobsen], Archie Ward & I guess Kenny Olson started here too. The word here now is that we are going to finish the training schedule here, but then they started to close this a long time ago. At any rate I am a stand by officer ready to take any crews (LCT), which might lose their officer by one means or another.

I had a letter from Ted & he was telling me what a good deal the LCT's were—just when I started training on one. It gave the morale quite a lift, cause I wasn't too happy when they ordered me here. We are probably shoving the same training ships around that those fellows used. I wonder how many dents Ted put in the bows of these ships. They run into each other so often the Base has put out

82

a Collision Form—To make up a report all you have to do is fill in the blanks. I guess we have to learn some way though.

Bob is still up at Harvard at Communications School. His wife is with him there & I guess they are having a quite happy time at the present. I have been in to Washington but haven't had time to look Marv B. up. I ran into Happy Jensen's younger brother the other day, but he was just shipping out and I was standing in ranks so our visit was short.

Lil is here with me, but it was quite a struggle to get a place to live. We moved six times the first week we were here. One night we got fouled up & I didn't know where she was, so I got another fellow's car and drove around the town till I saw my car. Lil was in the house beside the car & and there we stayed that night. So you see it is confusing some times.

Tomorrow we all are going out, I hope it will not be too rough because I am not too salty yet.

Thanks again and say hello to everyone back there.

Sincerely,
Bob McConnell [Ens. R. J. McConnell][74]

⊠        ⊠        ⊠        ⊠        ⊠        ⊠

*With the war effort progressing in the Pacific, men in critical positions expected to be involved in significant action soon.*

[Letterhead: U.S. Navy, Amphibious Training Base, Fort Pierce, Florida]
Dec. 13th '44

Editor,

Just a few words to tell you how thrilled and sincerely grateful to receive the "Scuttlebutt." I also want to inform you of my new address so the arrival of your swell idea will not be delayed.

At the present I am under going training preparatory to being assigned to a transport as an intelligence officer. I will be doing scouting just prior to the invasion so I believe I have something or other in store for me.

I want to thank you all again—I am really looking forward to your next issue.

Sincerely,
[Ensign] Leonard Nelson ex '46[75]

✉    ✉    ✉    ✉    ✉    ✉

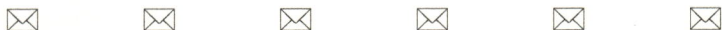

*Even Navy men sometimes found themselves assigned to posts far away from salt water.*

Boulder, Colorado
December 27, 1944

Dear Chellis,

Just a note of appreciation for the recent issue of "Scuttlebutt" which I received for the first time. I first saw it at Ernest Espelie's home in New London, Conn. and later at Moen's in Chicago. It is very interesting and I know that everyone feels you are doing a great service by editing it. I entered the navy on April 15th of this year and since that time have spent two months at indoctrination school in Tucson, Arizona and three months at communications school at Harvard University. I fully expected to go to sea from there but my orders were changed at the last minute to bring me here. Navy regulations forbid me to tell you what I am doing but it is very interesting and they don't leave us any too much spare time.

Best wishes for the new year and continued success to your publication and to Luther.

Sincerely.
[Lt.(j.g.)] Valdemar Johnson '33[76]

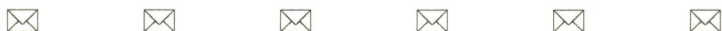

✉    ✉    ✉    ✉    ✉    ✉

*As 1944 drew to a close, some men were still just in the early stages of training. Coming from a small college like Luther, the vast, impersonal scale of "boot camp" was a drastic change for them.*

[Letterhead: United States Navy]

[Dec, 30, 44] Sat., The 30th.

Dear Mr. Evanson
(or Chellis)

You told me to write regardless how insignificant my business was, and that certainly is the case—I'm just as insignificant as sand in the Sahara—an apprentice seaman in an anything but small boot camp.

I imagine being in a mill such as Great Lakes is good for a person, but I prefer the smaller not cut-and-dried institution such as Luther.

Navy life suits me fine, but runs a poor second to the civilian life that I left.

One reason I wrote was to give you my address, as you directed. In case some should happen to the outside address, you'll find it below. [...] Great Lakes, Illinois

This'll be my address until Feb. 24th unless some changes are made or some accidents happen. This week one of our company became a scarlet fever victim which caused a lot of rumors about quarantine etc. Naturally I'll appreciate the "Scuttlebutt" and the "Chips".

I surely like the fellows in my barracks. I'm becoming very closely acquainted with those whose surname begins with L or M since we're arranged alphabetically.

My regards,
Donn [Gordon Luce H.A. 2/c][77]

# CHAPTER 5

# "Waiting around to be shipped out"— From Training to Combat Duty: 1945

*Sometimes the Army's changes in plans meant major transitions for the men.*

[Letterhead: United States Army]

1 January 1945—1630

Dear Sir:

I got the Scuttlebutt in the 27th Dec. You see I have transferred from the air base at Fort Dix. I could not quite figure out the set-up there. I was also told that it was a "jumping off" place. Well one day it happened (Dec. 6th) I was transferred into the infantry along with many other boys. We are down here at Camp Gordon in the I.A.R.T.C. (infantry advanced replacements training center). Three weeks of the six weeks training have gone by. It is a little rough but when one gets interested in the work it makes it easier to take.

Very truly yours,

Pvt Arthur L Martinek

LARTC, Co. B 21st Bn 6th Reg

Camp Gordon, Georgia[78]

✉      ✉      ✉      ✉      ✉      ✉

*The list of former students who received "Scuttlebutt" even included some men who had transferred to other colleges. Nonetheless, they had often developed strong feelings for Luther, appreciated the newsletter, and contributed to the Memorial fund.*

Lake City, Fla. Jan. 11, 1945

Dear Miss Hogenson,

I have been receiving the Luther College Chips for some time now and am happy to get it, in fact, I was surprised to be on your list in the Circulating Dept. You see, I attended Luther my Freshman year and then transferred to the University of Wisconsin, and hardly expected to receive the Chips. In every issue I'm able to trace the whereabouts of many of my class mates.

I am now at the Naval Air Station in Lake City taking operational training in the PV.a twin engine Navy land based bomber. Previous to my coming here, I was an instructor at the Naval Air Station, Corpus Christi, Texas.

Would you kindly send me the chips to my address at Lake City.

Inclosed is a check for $5.00, would you see that Prof. Chellis receives this for the Memorial Plaque I've read about.

Thanking you again for the Chips, I remain
Sincerely [Lt.(jg)] Edmund B Johnson[79]

✉       ✉       ✉       ✉       ✉       ✉

*Even though the war was entering its last phases in the spring of 1945, some men were just beginning their training*

April 11, '45

Dear Sirs:

First I had better apologize for not writing sooner. I haven't a very good excuse I'm afraid.

I have been receiving the Scuttlebutt regularly and enjoy it very much. In my last issue I read that Kenneth Kastner is now in the Philippines. I would appreciate it very much if you would send me his address. I chummed around with him quite a bit while attending Luther.

A couple of days after I arrived here I met Marlyn Vick. We have spent quite a few spare hours talking about the good old days back at Luther. (His address is the same as mine except he bunks in Everitt Hall).

I just finished my studies here and hope to be sent to Glenview Field at Chicago. I'll send you my new address as soon as possible, until then my present address will do.

That's about all there is to say so I'll close.
> Yours Very Truly
> Delbert Ingvalson [Chapel Hill, N.C.] [80]

⊠ ⊠ ⊠ ⊠ ⊠ ⊠

*Families also sent reports about Luther men, some of whom had rather unusual experiences with the military without seeing regular active duty. The information the families had about servicemen overseas was also often limited.*

> St. Olaf, Iowa
> January 16, 1945

Dear Chellis;

I want to express my appreciation for the splendid work you are doing in sending the "SCUTTLEBUTT" to the Luther men in the service. The last one sent to Nels was returned here. I am sending it on to him. However Nels is <u>not in active service</u>, due to his back injury, but I know he will be very happy to get the "SCUTTLEBUTT". He enlisted in the Army reserves while at Luther, but when he came to Chicago they would not accept him for active service. They did not give him a discharge, but kept him in the Army Reserves (no uniform, no pay) 2nd Lt. M.A.,A.Y.S. 0-1766537.

Nels Strandjord's address is: [...]

Again I want to thank you for your splendid work and with best wishes, I remain

> Faithfully yours,
> S.J. Strandjord

P.S. I understand that some sort of a service men's plaque is to be put up at Luther. I shall be glad to pay for Rolf when I come up to Luther.

Rolf's address is: [...] He landed in France, but I do not know where he is now. [81]

⊠ ⊠ ⊠ ⊠ ⊠ ⊠

*Since "Scuttlebutt" was a Navy term, some of the Army men tried to come up with a G.I. equivalent.*

[Letterhead: Section "A", 3706 AAF BASE UNIT (BTC),
SHEPPARD FIELD, TEXAS
Monday morning Jan. '29, 1945

Dear Chell:

Another great Scuttlebutt!!

I suppose the GI counterpart of this Navy idiom would be "Latrine Rumor."

But it's no rumor how much Lutherites in service appreciate this effort on you part—and I feel I can say, without fear of contradiction, that it is <u>effort</u>.

And despite the fact that I seem to be a permanent fixture here at Sheppard Field (who said there was no indispensable man?) and can make no news myself, I really look forward to each edition.

Best of it,

Marv. [Cpl. Marvin E. Lore][82]

In the February issue of "Scuttlebutt," Evanson commented, "Cpl. Marvin E. Lore, Pub. Relations Office,3706,AAF Base Unit, Sheppard Field, Texas, nothing 'new', just still in 'Taixas.' Don't know the Army word for Scuttlebutt, but the Navy for your term is 'Head', so try again, Marv."

---

*Within a few weeks of Lore's letter, Martin Elstad offered a similar suggestion.*

Training Aids Office, Sampson, New York
15 February 1945

Dear Chellis

Enclosed you'll find $1.00 for the PLAQUE FUND.

The latest issue of scuttlebutt came in today and the addresses are much appreciated.

The army word is "LATRINOGRAMS". which is of course almost pictorial in clarity.

How far have plans for a new main actually gone? Is there such a thing as a plan picture released as yet?

Best Greetings to you and all at L.C.

Lt.(jg) Martin K. Elstad.

I guess you've read about our 120 inches of rainfall.[83]

In the March 1945 issue of "Scuttlebutt," Evanson commented, "Elstad, your word for Scuttlebutt doesn't satisfy."

⊠        ⊠        ⊠        ⊠        ⊠        ⊠

*Although progress was clearly being made in the war in both the European and Pacific theaters, preparations had to be made in case surrender did not come quickly. Thus, even in the waning months of the war, men were still beginning training programs.*

Yuma Army Air Field
10 April 45

Dear Mr. Evanson,

I guess everyone must have made good use of their Easter vacation. I was up at Luther on Monday and I ran into two persons. One was the janitor and the other was Carl Hanson. I saw "Colonel" and several others downtown. They really have fixed up Larson Hall. I am looking forward to seeing the new building.

Decorah really came through with some beautiful Easter weather. I wore the same old hat I wore last year but I believe they are still in style.

We have had it very easy the last couple of months. Our program has been cut out so we have been laying around waiting to be sent to A-26 and overseas. We don't have to fly more than we want to. I have been flying quite regularly in order to keep up my proficiency in formation. Flying etc. in a B-26.

The weather here is very nice now. I have been swimming several times this year. It has been very nice golfing weather. Last Sunday afternoon I was out at the local course & with the aid of some unconscious approaching and putting, managed to shoot a 41 and a 40—par is 35. I sank a putt from the edge of the green on the last hole which was a 9 hole carryover so my game was very successful financially.

If we get the same deal as the rest of the fellows in our squadron got who have shipped out, we will go to Lincoln, Neb. to pick up a A-26 & a crew and then go to South Carolina for overseas training. I see by the chips that Arvid Olson is stationed here. I will have to look him up. I haven't seen a Luther man or a Decorah man in the army for over two years. The Chips and the Scuttlebutt really come in handy in locating people & in finding out what everybody is doing.

Sincerely,
Marvin Rohm[84]

**90**

---

[Letterhead: United States Navy]

3:15 P.M. Sun. Ap. 16,1945

Dear Chell,

Have finally gotten settled & found out my boot address. I left home Fri., the 6th., & didn't get here to boot camp until a week later, the 13th.

I don't imagine there's much I can tell you about Navy life that you don't already know. I don't suppose the Navy has changed too much since you were in.

We had a rather exciting night last night. We were just assigned to our cleaning details yesterday and didn't know too well what we were supposed to do, but we did our best and hit the sack (already using Navy slang) at 9:30 (2130 Navy time) At 2330 some officer, I don't know who, came in & got us all out & told us to be dressed & in front of the barracks in 5 minutes. We fell out & ran a mile for him (I suppose so that we could sleep a little better). When we got back we recleaned the barracks & good!—I stood a 4 hr. watch just the nite before too, so I'm just a little tired.

A bunch of the fella's went swimming today. I wanted to go too but figured I'd better write a few letters & wash a few clothes—Also, tomorrow we have tests all day & I don't want to be tired for them.

This is quite a company I'm in. About half the fella's are college graduates. Lots of them have had a yr or two of college, & the rest are just out of high school. The fellow bunking right next to me has had a yr. of pre. medic at Yale.—Then the other day an officer said that he's 'eat his shirt' if 15 of our entire company got thru radio school.—That sounds rough.—Hope he was just slinging a line.

Wayne is now back in the states. He was on Iwo for 10 days. He's now able to go almost anywhere, & thinks he might get transferred here to Chicago.—His address is: [...]

Don [Bravick, Great Lakes, Ill.][85]

⊠　　　⊠　　　⊠　　　⊠　　　⊠　　　⊠

*With the war in the Pacific Theater still an on-going concern, there remained a need for trained pilots.*

[Letterhead: Naval Air Station, Clearview, Tex.]
A/C Delbert Ingvalson, [...] N.A.S. Glenview Ill.

June 2$^{nd}$ [1945]

Dear Chellis:

Here's my new address I said I'd send so my letters will come direct again.

I met Beersdorf(sp) just before I left N.C. and two weeks after I arrived here he came too. We've had a couple Bull Sessions about the good old Luther days which is always a lot of fun.

I wrote Kenneth Kastner but haven't received an answer yet.

I'm through with one of the four stages of flying now which permits me to solo. So many solo's come in with Bashed in wing tips I'm beginning to wonder when my turn will come.

I'll close for this letter.

Yours, "Ing"

P.S. Please excuse all the mistakes, it's a wee bit crowded in here, the ready room.[86]

# CHAPTER 6

# "A grand session of intense study"— V-12 Programs

*Officer training was mentally as well as physically demanding. The former college men in V-12 programs had to adjust to a totally new course of study, with pressures and expectations placed on them that they had never encountered in college. After leaving Luther for the V-12 program at Columbia, some of the men found the course extremely challenging.*

[Letterhead: U.S. Naval Reserve, Midshipmen's School, New York, N.Y.]

June 25, 1943

Dear Folks,

Have a little time so I will drop you a few lines. You really have to use your spare time to write letters while you can or you won't have time to write any at all.

Quite a lot has happened since I last wrote to you folks. We have now had our semester exams, and that is really a relief. I don't believe I've ever worried so much about anything in all my life before. The tests were really tough too. All the tests but navigation were multiple choice. A person knew about 50% of the questions & the rest was just a guessing game. I guess I guessed pretty good though because I got through O.K. However, Happy & Iverson got put on probation. Happy messed up the navigation test pretty badly I guess; so that is the reason he got put on. However, I don't think he has anything to worry about because he'll get through O.K. I don't know much about Iverson, though. Time has really gone fast tho! We only have about three weeks of academic work left. Then I suppose we'll find out what this war is really like. We don't have any idea what assignment we will get. I guess we find out about 4 or 5 days before we graduate. I hope I get an assignment so that I can get a few days off before I have to report because I would like to get back to Iowa again. If I get any time off I hope to stop in at Decorah for a few hours anyway. If I do I surely will be up and see you folks.

How is summer school going? I have heard that there are a little over a hundred students. That's not so bad. How about the prospects for this fall. I suppose it's not too good. I don't see how there can be very many fellows left to go to school. How about Chellis Jr.? Is he still waiting for the army? He can consider himself lucky as long as he can stay a civilian. We do have a pretty good deal here but the civilian life is still the best. At least you're free then. Of course it might be better when we get our commissions.

This has been a pretty busy week for me. Last Monday I was on a cruise out in Long Island Sound. On these cruises you go out in Y.P ships & sort of run the thing on a small scale. We got to do some plotting of courses, act as helmsmen, etc. It's really quite interesting & fine experience. Then on Tuesday I stood watch all day & today I have been standing watch also. As a result I missed three days of school & messed up our weekly test in Navigation pretty much. This will most likely put me on a "tree" for the next week in navigation.[87] I've been pretty lucky tho! So far I've been on two trees, once in navigation & once in Ordnance. Oh yes, I was on conduct report once, too, because when the officer inspected our room he didn't think it was quite clean enough. I haven't been on any trees or conduct report this second six weeks yet tho!

We have been busy ordering uniforms the past week. It's really quite a job. One can certainly spend the money in a hurry, but then as long as we get $250 to pay for them it isn't so bad. It should be rather tough if we had to dig in our own pockets for the money tho!

Well, folks, I have some studying that is waiting to be done; so I guess I better get started on it. I realize that this is a pretty one sided letter because I have written mostly about myself, but there isn't much else to write about, I guess. Greet everyone that might be interested and I remain as ever—

Just

[Mdn.] Harold. [Heltne]

By the way, I almost forgot. Betty said I should greet you folks from her when I wrote to you; so "greetings" from Betty.

I rushed away so fast this spring, too, that I don't believe I ever thanked you folks for the swell hospitality you folks showed me the past year. I want you to know that I really appreciated it. Thanks very much. I hope someday I can do something for you folks too.[88]

⊠        ⊠        ⊠        ⊠        ⊠        ⊠

*Despite a difficult program of study, and some problems with subjects such as navigation, the V-12 students at Columbia finished their program in July 1943.*

[Letterhead: U.S. Naval Reserve, Midshipmen's School, New York, N.Y.]

July 7, 1943

Dear Dr. Evanson,

In the three months we have been here I have thought often of writing to you but as you probably heard the going is a bit rough and consequently not many opportunities for writing letters appear. However, tonight we've been granted an extra half hour of study so I'll make use of the time in writing a letter I should have written long ago.

Needless to say we think of Luther and talk of Luther almost daily and hardly a week goes by but what Heltne, Jensen, Gjerdrum and the rest of us get together and have a "bull" session. They all express a feeling of gratitude to you and the rest of the faculty for all the help and good advice you've given us. I know we all look forward to coming back to that grand old campus.

I'm afraid some of us showed up to be dry land sailors when we went on a cruise today. We were aboard a Y P (yacht patrol), 100 footer, out on the sound. It rained continually, there was a good wind and a heavy ground swell. We thought it great fun to feel roll and pitch but within the hour we were all out on deck and not a few of us hung over the leeward rail. At least we know now in small measure what to expect no doubt.

The plans are completed for our commissioning exercises which will be held the morning of July 28 in the largest cathedral of the world—St. John's the Divine. This move was made after it became apparent that the school's classes had become too large for the ceremony to be held in Riverside Church as was the custom. The Luther V-7's score in another conspicuous first! Rear Admiral Randall Jacobs, U.S.N., Chief of Naval Personnel will deliver the address. I am hoping that my father can come up for that date as he is only two hundred miles from here.

There are now nearly four thousand men in training in this vicinity; some 1000 midshipmen, 1300 apprentice seamen V-7, 1100 A-5, V-12 and others in surrounding schools. Recent figures show that about one out of five officers in the Navy now is a Reserve officer and some 8,000 of these have come from this school.

Lt. (J.G.) Kenneth Olson is visiting us now having arrived this afternoon. He has a recent promotion. Cal DeBuhr was over yesterday and we're planning an all Luther get together this Saturday. I wish you were here to complete the party.

I had a letter from Fure the other day. He is progressing in fine shape and in a few weeks should achieve his C.P.O.'s rating. His present address is [...]

It's nearly time for the buglers lullaby so I'll close for now and turn in.

Respectfully yours,<br>John Sorlien[89]

⊠    ⊠    ⊠    ⊠    ⊠    ⊠

*Even those who progressed quickly through Midshipman's School were frustrated as they waited for their future assignments, and often additional training.*

[Letterhead: United States Navy]

17 August 1944

Dear Chellis,

I know this letter should have been written long ago. I know I have received at least half a dozen letters from you since I got into the service but for some reason or another I have never gotten around to answer them. But in spite of it all I want you to know that I enjoy them and appreciate them very much.

Since I left Midshipmen school all I have been doing is travel from one place to another. I had hoped to see you while home on leave but time didn't permit. When a person is home on leave the time is always to short. But I guess I was lucky to get the time off I did.

Now I am beginning to get a little anxious to get started on something definite. The first time I was down here at Ft Pierce we were here about four days. During that time we did nothing but muster three times a day and go swimming in the ocean. At night we fought mosquitoes. I also got a chance to see Heltne. We talked over the good times we had back at Luther and wished we were back there. We are all looking forward to that first Homecoming when we can all be back.

It wasn't long before we got orders to report to Camp Shelton Va. They had what they called an Officers Pool up there and they took them as they needed them. They came there from all over. We had a regular schedule for classes there. They were refresher courses from Midshipmen school.

There were classes in Navigation, Seamanship, Gunnery, and Recognition. We went out on the firing range and fired the 20mm and 40mm. There we gained a lot of valuable experience and information. There were five of us from Luther up there. Mathy, Jenson, Ellingson, Ludvicka, and myself. I haven't been any place since I got in the navy without finding some Luther fellows there. Now we are back at Ft Pierce and Clifford Ellingson and Heltne are there.

Yesterday I saw the classification officer. He said that we should be starting our training within a week. I sure hope that he is right.

Ollie has been telling me about the baseball team they have had down there this summer. He really is interested in sports.

The living conditions are not quit as good down here as they were at Shelton but the Choir is much better. There are six of us in our hut. One of the fellows is from Princeton and he was quit an athlete back there. He was one of there football stars. I am also staying with one of the fellows I went to V-12 at Dubuque with. Speaking of Dubuque I got a letter from them inviting me to continue my schooling there after the war. But I can't quit see that. I'm sticking by good old Luther.

I'm scheduled to take my physical in a little while so I guess I'll have to close for now.

Sincerely
[Ens] Jim [Ulvilden][90]

   ✉   ✉   ✉   ✉   ✉   ✉

*Many colleges and universities around the country had V-7 or V-12 programs. Luther students receiving officers' training thus had an opportunity to experience a wide range of schools.*

Oct. 3, 1944

Dear Chellis,

Thanks very much for sending me the "Scuttlebutt." I enjoy it very much. The men of Luther are certainly very scattered around the globe, aren't they? I haven't had any sea duty yet, but I've seen a considerable part of the U. S.

I'm enclosing a copy of our school paper. This is a Catholic men's college on the order of Loras. I must say though that they treat us Protestants very fine.

My home town paper came today, and I noticed that Don Moore is overseas now—probably France.

Greet everyone.

Sincerely, Lt. (j.g.) Luther [Berven][91]

---

Monday morning, 10-30-44.

Dear Dr. Evanson,

Have enjoyed receiving copies of "Scuttlebutt;" hope they keep coming.

Am a student again; at Mt. Airy Seminary under the Navy V-12 program— only Lutheran Seminary in this program. I was in the Navy over two years when this opportunity came along so I applied for it and was transferred up here and reduced in rank to apprentice seaman. Expect to be here only two years under an accelerated program.

Saw Navy beat Penn last Saturday. Navy could have looked better but I expect them to beat No Dame and maybe Army. Navy does have a terrific line—Penn had a minus yardage through the line.

Receive the "Chips" so am quite up on Luther activities; together with Scuttlebutt I'm well informed.

Thank you very much.

[A.S.] Phil Fretheim[92]

✉    ✉    ✉    ✉    ✉    ✉

*In addition to training, the V-12 programs allowed the men to meet new people, including future wives.*

9 Oct. 1944

Dear Chellis,

I have been pretty busy as is everyone who comes here. Before for I go any further let me make apologies for this crude stationary. I just ran out and what with $5 every two weeks I'm not in any hurry to buy some more. I like it here real well and have seen several of the Luther fellows. Vernon Bly & Warren Berg are in the twentieth class and Eugene Olsen was in the 21st. class with me but he has been transferred to Great Lakes. We, the 21st. class, will be commissioned on 14 Dec. 1944. Right now I haven't any very definite post-war plans except that I will go back to college and I believe it will be Luther. I won't be coming back alone however as I am going to be married on 14 Dec. to Miss Arnolda Kornahrens of Summerville, S.C. and a senior at Newberry College. You can see that V-12 wasn't a bad deal at all. I enjoy getting your "Scuttlebutt" very much. I hear from Don Melaas & Cliff Ellingson quite often. Don is still at Newberry, but he will be leaving there soon. I have visited most of the larger churches here in New York City, and they were beyond all expectations. Riverside Church Cathedral of St. John the Divine, and St. Patricks are very beautiful churches. There isn't much to tell you about Columbia Univ. as all we do is go to class and study, study, study. I am in the Midn'.Band which is very good. I must close now and get busy on my studies. Looking forward to the next "Scuttlebutt"

Sincerely,

Art. [Mid AW Peterson[93]

---

2 August 1945

Dear Mr. Evanson:

It's about time I wrote and let my friends at Luther in on my good luck.

First of all, our ship received some lucky orders to take a top-secret cargo back to the states. We did and ended up in Seattle, Wash.

Found out we were going to be there for a while, and managed to "glean" a 7 day leave from the skipper. Flew home to good old Chicago in a B-25, and had 5 wonderful, glorious days and nights with my parents, sister, and girl.

Got myself engaged. She's the most wonderful girl in the world, and an Iowan, too. Hails from Dubuque, Ia. where I met her while in V-12.

We're kinda planning on going to Luther together after this war is over. Hope our plans materialize.

Saw "Cyc" Shroeder in the Officers' Club at Pearl, before we left for the states. He's bigger than ever. I'm mighty glad he's on our side.

We're on our way out again, From the looks of it, this is going to be much less a joy-ride than our last trip—already we're farther out.

Give my best to all of L.C. Enclosed is a snap and a couple of bucks for the Placque Fund. I'll do better next time. (Haven't been paid for a month and a half).

Yours, Warren "Meatball" Berg[94]

✉        ✉        ✉        ✉        ✉        ✉

*After midshipmen's school, more specialized training could bring a dramatic change of environment. Nonetheless, some men were able to maintain their sense of humor in most conditions.*

Fort Pierce, Fla.
Aug. 16, 1944

Dear Dr. Evanson,

I can't tell you how happy I was today when I received your scuttlebutt for the month of July. I'm taking time out right now to thank you.

I graduated from midshipmen's school at Columbia University on the 29th of June. I'll never forget that day as long as I live.

I was detached and sent to Fort Pierce, Florida but was there only four days. About a hundred of us, a number from Luther, were sent to Camp Shelton. We were there a month or so and then returned here yesterday morning.

Every one was sleeping when we arrived as it was 0400 in the morning. I heard someone say "this is it" but I didn't believe it until I felt a mosquito on my ear. Several of us ganged up on him, caught him by the leg and threw him overboard before he could do much damage.

We'll be getting under way with our work in a day or so. I've been out on a number of cruises in the Atlantic. Also have been swimming in the "salt water"

No matter where we go we'll always be thinking of good old Luther.

Sincerely,
[Ensign] C.T. Ellingson[95]

✉        ✉        ✉        ✉        ✉        ✉

*Besides the V-12 program at Columbia, Luther men attended similar programs at several other schools, including the University of Dubuque and Cornell University.*

14 October 1944

Dear Chellis,

After receiving another swell copy of "Scuttlebutt" I think high time I drop a line to the old friends at Luther. Don't think that I have forgotten all the swell friendship, but the Navy has a unique way of keeping a fellow busy every hour of the day. This is especially true since I got to Cornell midshipmen school.

I received your letters while at Dubuque and at that time managed to get back to visit the campus a few times. After shipping out to Asbury Park, N.J., I sort of lost my end of the contacts, but your letters kept coming. Thank you very much for keeping me on the mailing list.

The draft in which I was sent to Cornell brought me here 1 Sept. Since then it has been a grand session of intense study. I don't believe many Luther men have been stationed at Cornell previously. Right off hand the only one I can think of right now is Alvin Nickleson, who was my instructor in music in high school. He had shipped out of here long before I came though. Thanks to "Scuttlebutt" again for information about his address as well as the many others I have learned through your letters.

I'm very glad to hear that Luther is maintaining an even keel throughout the season. The athletics of course are at a low ebb, but never-the-less, I'll bet there is plenty of enthusiasm and spirit still there. After the shuffle has ended and all the gang gets back to Luther—it's going to be swell to watch the smoke made by Pete's teams again.

The addition notes by other members of the faculty in your last issue made one swell letter seem like letters from everyone back on the Campus.

While at Asbury Park I got into New York City and saw Warren Berg at Columbia along with several other buddies from the Unit at Dubuque. It seemed swell to see a Lutherite in the group.

I believe I'll have to bring this to a close now as I'm going on watch in a short time. Before I do I wonder if I could ask you to put my name on the "Chips" mailing list again. Thank you!

Also—I wanted to ask about Chell Jr. Where is he now? The last I heard from him he was in Denver and seemed to like it a lot.

My time is running short now so I had better close. Thank you for keeping the events at Luther close at hand through your letters. As all Norsemen, I too am waiting for the day when I can come back to the campus.

Sincerely,

[Mdsm] Glenn Larson

P.S.—This being homecoming week at Luther, really makes a fellow remember the good old days there.[96]

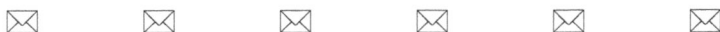

&#9993;    &#9993;    &#9993;    &#9993;    &#9993;    &#9993;

*The V-12 program was not always exciting, and the men's morale often received a boost when they got news about Luther.*

Nov. 18, '44

Dear Mr. Chell. Evanson,

I've been reading the October Scuttlebutt and I guess it's about time I gave you that letter I promised you in May. Thanks a lot for all those issues of Scuttlebutt.

I'm in the second term of V-12 here and the life is monotonous but I suppose its all right. There are no Luther men here but Warren Selbo's brother, Glenn, is here, but that is the closest I can get to Luther.

I read about the Luther Football team, although they lost all their games, we still have a football team. WMC lost all our games too (except the Homecoming game)

I guess I'd better sign off and tell you of my slight change in address, its […].

Sincerely
Kenneth Olson A.S.
[Western Mich. Coll., Kalamazoo, 45D, Mich.] [97]

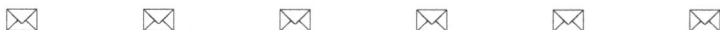

&#9993;    &#9993;    &#9993;    &#9993;    &#9993;    &#9993;

*There were obviously various gradations of physical qualifications. Some men might be eligible for military duty but not for officer's training. Others might qualify as officers, but have restrictions on the type of duty for which they qualified.*

19 November 1944

Dear Mr. Evanson,

I wish to thank you as editor of the monthly "scuttlebutt" column for all the news I have been able to get about my former classmates and friends at Luther. Without it I am afraid I would have lost contact with some of them, it is of course impossible for any of us by our own letters to keep up. Without your monthly column I'd have known very little of many of the friends I made at Luther.

I spent twelve months in the V-12 program at Dubuque and then for four months I was stationed at the Navy Yard in Philadelphia. At Philadelphia I was on duty under instruction in the Supply Department. While there I learned that my old roommate Dick Anderson and Bill Biersdorf were at Asbury Park, New Jersey which is only sixty miles from Philadelphia but I had rather poor weekend liberties there and was never able to get off long enough to run down and see them. I was rather disappointed, I would have liked to find out if Dick liked his V-12 duty as well as I did mine. If I'm not mistaken Bill had been transferred from the Navy Pre-flight school at Iowa City.

I reported here at the Navy Supply School, Harvard, on November 3rd. This is definitely the best duty I've had. I work rather hard, they throw these courses at us rather fast, but they aren't too hard to understand and are really quite interesting. I will receive my commission as a supply officer approximately four months from now.

Since I left Dubuque I haven't seen another Luther man. Warren Berg was in New York City until a short while ago, I haven't heard but I presume he has been commissioned by now. I thought perhaps "Meatball" and Glenn Larsen would have been given Supply School too but I guess the Navy took only specials for that. I'm slightly weak on color perception which is the reason I'm here. I'm not too sorry about that though, I really feel I'm learning a lot about the Navy here.

My brother, Percing, is still at Newport. I'll be able to see him quite often while I'm here. I suppose you've heard long before this that he was married. He seems to like his duty at Newport quite well, he's quite anxious to get back to the Midwest though, like all the rest of us.

My new address is: [...]

Sincerely Yours
Wilmer Fure[98]

⊠          ⊠          ⊠          ⊠          ⊠          ⊠

*As experienced men were rotated out of combat zones, new officers were needed. Training programs continued throughout the war, since there was no way of knowing how long the conflict would continue in the Pacific.*

[Letterhead: Navy Supply Corps School

6 July, 1945

Dear Chel,

Your June "Scuttlebutt" arrived today and I guess its high time I said "thanks" and all that for an O.K. little paper. I've sort of lost track of Luther but still like to see where all the old buddies are and what they are doing.

For the record—a little history. I got my commission in the 22$\underline{nd}$ class at Columbia on 8 March. Was sent up here to Boston to Supply school. We're better than half-way through the course and should be hitting the Pacific in September. Took the big step at the alter too, on May 12. Let me be <u>another</u> to repudiate the old adage about two living as cheaply as one!

I was down at Decorah on a Sunday around the end of March. Missed most of you scholarly professing gents, tho. The place looked nice!

I took notice of one of your hot tips and looked up Kermie Vanderbilt across the river in communications school. Other than Kerm, I've seen no L.C. men of late. Except Bob Larsen and Don Melaas down at N.Y. last March.

Since I missed the first issues of <u>Scuttlebutt</u> I don't know what this plaque fund is all about but it must be O.K. Hope $2 will help a <u>little</u>.

Miss the old boys from Larsen Hall and the five-hundred games we used to have. Wonder if the girls have taken up the game where we left off? They could probably find a table or two with decks on them up on the third deck east wing.

Best of luck to everyone at Luther and particularly to all those new teachers that are going out from the last class.

Don ("Doc") Strand

Ens. D.J. Strand [...], Boston 63, Mass. ('Til Sept. 5)[99]

# FIRST DUTY ASSIGNMENTS

# CHAPTER 7

# "State-side commandos"— Active Duty in the U.S.

*For many men, an assignment in the United States was simply a preliminary to overseas duty. Others, however, would remain stateside for the duration of the war.*

*"Tutor" Ellingsen's age and maturity gave him a different perspective than that of many younger men. As an instructor, his experiences were also unlike those of most of the Luther men. His correspondence with Evanson was also that of a colleague.*

[Letterhead: United States Naval Section Base Little Creek, Virginia]
Feb 6, 1944

Dear Chellis:

Sunday evening and a good time to write a few lines. Everything is about as usual. As a whole everything is going rather well. The weather has been wonderful since about Jan 1. We have onions in a garden behind the house, a few carrots and a few of these southern greens that I am not familiar with. They go strong for greens around here. Harold and Betty have been staying with us since the first part of Jan. He has rather long hours compared to mine and leaves very early in the morning.

I suppose you are wondering about the watch. I have seen some good buys in watches at Section Base but no Bulovas or Gruens. They had 65.00 Longines at 29.50 some time ago. Got 60 and sold them in a half day. They have clamped down on Ship service as they discovered sailors were buying lighters and selling them to Drug stores who in turn were selling them to the public. They require foreign assignments for many of the articles to be purchased. I get over to N.O.B. about once a week. Was there today but they had no watches. Amphibious had only about a half dozen last night and at times have hundreds of them. I shall however keep on a lookout. If your patience becomes exhausted I shall send back the check. Bobby bought a watch but only after looking over several hundred. They come at about half price. We bought an eversharp pen which retails at 9.75 for $4.85 last evening. Let me know what your desires are. Would you be interested in some other make if they are a good buy? We never seem to have Bulovas at Section Base. The housing situation is not too good. We were sub-leasing at Oakdale Farms but decided it safer to sublease at Norva Homes. Sub leasing is illegal at Oakdale Farms. Norva Homes are going to be sold so we won't be here too long. Bobby and Eric plan on leaving either for Decorah or west coast this spring or early summer. Its too hot around here and houses are too hard to find.

Schoeder has been transferred to Miami and no doubt you have seen him lately as he went on leave. I perhaps will go to Boston in the near future for a couple of weeks refresher and to become familiar with new developments. No doubt I shall return here unless the European situation changes. The interesting thing about the Navy is what one may be doing next. The boys are getting a real kick out of your letters Chellis. You at home don't realize how much it means to get these letters. You have a swell idea and the informality of the whole thing leaves a cozy feeling. The middle west is neglecting the boys who are in service. Many towns in the east sent all their boys bundles for Xmas which included almost everything one could think of. The boys enjoy Chips but your letters are tops with them. More should be done. It will be appreciated by the fellows and will pay dividends when this thing is over with. Some of the colleges are putting out special service magazines or whatever one may call them.

Eric has been going to the navy school at the operating base and likes it very much. The navy bus stops by the house and picks him up and returns him. He enjoys himself around here. Knows more about the navy than I do. He was given a war bond at a movie at Section Base. A commander won it and gave it to him. He naturally feels very kindly towards the navy.

We buy all our supplies for the house at Navy commissary. Prices are really very steep on the outside but we manage to stay clear of them. We buy our gas there also. They sell it for 6 cents per gal less than on the outside. They have a ships service garage on the base and manage to give real good service. We get a fair amount of gas. In fact I got more than I asked for. I am hoping to get a new tire for the car before Bobby leaves as she no doubt will drive thru. The trains are almost impossible around here. Betty and Harold are spending the afternoon in Portsmouth, they have a fine club there. Ping pong, pool, Bowling, dinners, drinks etc. We usually spend Sundays at Old Point Comfort or some place like that. It was raining today so we had our dinner at N.O.B. The Navy provides transportation to Old Point. They run a transportations service across the Black river and the bay for officers and their families. The Navy meals are always good and very reasonable. We had personal inspection yesterday at the base. Usually have them once a month. Will close for this time Chellis and hope everything is well with your family by now. The enrollment is encouraging.

[Lt.H.E.Ellingsen]                              —Tutor—[100]

$\bowtie$ $\bowtie$ $\bowtie$ $\bowtie$ $\bowtie$ $\bowtie$

*While stateside assignments might be safer than combat duty, soldiers often commented on the boredom, longing for more "action." They also often faced the reality that lingering injuries might hurt their chances for promotion, even if they did not disqualify them totally from military service.*

Feb. 9, 1944

Dear Chellis,

Thank you very much for the two interesting letters I have received from you. You will never know how much I appreciated them. They seemed to renew the atmosphere of the grand days I spent at Luther.

After reading about the excitement many of the other boys are having, my life out here in Oregon seems very dull. Of course, I have my wife with me which takes the place of much of the excitement created by combat experiences! Anyway, I'm still working with ammunition. However, I work only with the supply and do not handle the "real thing" very often. It is a nice easy office job but they get very tiresome at times.

You probably know that I was sent to Santa Anita, California for two months to attend a school on the supply of ammunition. Naturally, I enjoyed this very much. Harriet was with me there too. We visited Hollywood, saw some movie stars as well as the Rose Bowl and other points of interest. By the way, I met Blake Havell, the football coach of U.C.L.A. while I was there. Santa Anita was a very interesting place and the race track is very nice.

It was while I was there that my old back injury came upon me again and it appears that nothing can be done by the army doctors to cure me. It is disgusting to say the least and it naturally spoils my hopes of advancement. At least, I couldn't pass the physical for Officers' Candidate School.

We both think of Luther very often and enjoy speaking about the highlights of our years there. Thanks also for the Chips which comes regularly.

I hope Luther can continue to hold its own until the war is over. It will be fun to watch her grow.

I surely appreciate the history I learned from you and also the courses in Political Science dealing with the Italian, German, English and Russian governments. It helps to come to conclusions on matters that present themselves and affords a more correct opinion about the people concerned.

I am afraid morning will roll around too soon if I don't get some sleep. I wish you would include our greetings in your next letter. It certainly would be fun to drink a cup of that coffee you mention!

Sincerely,
Marvin [Norland][101]

---

*Norland provided an up-date of his whereabouts later in the year.*

October 1, 1944

Dear Chellis,

I have no satisfactory excuse for failing to write to you except that my evenings are usually completely taken up with my family, playing with Marcia and drying dishes! I seem to have good intentions all of the time but I seem to have trouble putting them into action.

Since I last wrote, I've moved to Kansas. I'm assigned to the U.S.D.B., Fort Leavenworth. My work is interviewing American prisoners who have violated some military law. I enjoy it very much because of the variety of the circumstances involved. My job is to cover their entire life in an attempt to reveal circumstances which might have had some influence on his offence and submit a detailed report to a medical board which consider if he is suitable for Restoration to the service, if he is suitable for a local Parole and for clemency.

We live in Leavenworth, Kansas which is an old town located about fifteen minutes from the post. The fort is not like an Army post because all the buildings are permanent brick affairs. The men live in a three story affair just outside the walls of the prisoner enclosure.

How are things at Luther? I have been receiving the College bulletins but I have missed your monthly news summaries. I realize the fault is my own for not informing you of my address. Larsen Hall must be an unusual sight this year.

Selmer is a first Lieutenant now. I saw several Luther men while I was in the seventieth division, including Kermit Hendrickson, Russ Garness and Stranjord. Kermit was a bugler for one of the regiments. We hear regularly from Norman Selness who is in France. Harriet's brother, Don, will soon be home from the South Pacific.

I must close now and dry some more dishes! Thanks for the letters you send. Greet Chellis Jr. when you write.

Sincerely, Marv. [Norland][102]

*Alvin Gisvold, a 1941 Luther graduate, was assigned to a training base where his athletic background apparently put him in good stead.*

Feb. 11. 1944
U.S.N.T.S., Farrogut, Idaho, Camp Bennin

Dear Chellis.

Received your very nice and thorough letter describing what was going on around old Luther and where some of the boys were located etc. One sort of wonders where all the old mates have branched out to and by the way the Luther men are doing right well by themselves. Leland Harris sure surprised me. His old line must have helped him considerable. Well I guess guts and a strong back go a long way these days:—

Well as for me I guess I am what you call a dry land sailor as I have been stationed here since I completed my indoctrination course at Norfolk but enjoy my work a great deal so feel well satisfied and I also have my wife and son with me and get home to them 4 out of 5 nights so things work out pretty good.

As you probably heard I am pushing Co's out here and have been doing the same since I came. I am now working with my 7th one and men are coming in faster than ever but our problems are mounting also at the same rate with them along the physical line. Some are really pretty well broke down and with a few days with the old Springfield we could put them to sleep for ever I believe if we bore down on them.

The main objective is to build men physically here it seems as in the training program physical fitness gets about twice as much attention as anything else so you see I am staying pretty well by my major.

Several Chiefs have been sent to foreign bases of late to handle Recruit and P Ed programs so my turn may be up soon also but so far we are short here on Company Commanders so we have to graduate a Co. in the morning and pick up the same day.

We are enjoying extremely mild weather this year with hardly any snow which is unusual for this part of the country. The past week there have been Soft Ball & Football games on the Grinder daily.

I heard Davidson who used to be Supt at Springfield and instructor at Luther has a good set up in Calif. We were good friends of the president of the school board in Springfield as was Davidson so we heard through them (Good people to know).

This letter has already dragged out so will cut it short and again I say well done Chellis as I am sure they all appreciate it as much as I did.

Will enclose a snap to give you an idea what an old Salt looks like if this thing don't end pretty soon I'll be wearing hash marks on my sleeve. I could put in for a commission but feel too satisfied with what I have.

Thanks again and greet Pete and the rest around and when you find time news is also appreciated although I am getting the Chips so have my line of sights squared away on quite a few mates now.

> Your Friend.
> Gizzie [Alvin G. Gisvold.][103]

⊠ ⊠ ⊠ ⊠ ⊠ ⊠

*As the war effort built up momentum, bases serving the transport of men and materiel became increasingly active.*

[Letterhead: Hamilton Field, California

6 October 1944

Dear Chellis,

Received the August issue of "Scuttlebut" in this afternoon's mail after it had been forwarded me from Camp Luna, New Mexico. Of course I had to take out time—even if it was G.I. time—to read it. Have been very busy recently to a new job I was assigned to Troops of the Air Transport Command on this base. This is THE aerial port of embarkation and what stories I could tell but neither time nor military security will permit. Everything that is flown in or out or to or from the Pacific regardless of direction, originates or terminates here.

Managed to get off an answer to Chellis, Jr. the first of the week that had been delayed about a week. Enclosed a typewritten copy of a letter I had recently received from Capt. Jim Holmlund over in Italy. Suggested to Chellis that he forward it on to you when through as it's a mighty good summary of all Jim has had action or taken part in since he went over.

Have some reports to get out so my note will have to be drawn short this time but want to list my current address as per your request in the Aug. issue of "Scuttlebut". It is: [...]  With best regards to you and L. C., I am

Respectfully yours,
Fred J. Rosenthal[104]

✉   ✉   ✉   ✉   ✉   ✉

*Although the end of the war was still months away, by late 1944 men were beginning to think about their postwar life.*

11-12-44

Dear Sir,

Rather a gloomy afternoon here in Arizona as we've been having one of our rare rainstorms. Everything is grounded and there's not much activity around the airfield.

As an aerial gunnery instructor, it means that I'll probably have tomorrow off also as there's not much sign of the weather clearing sufficiently enough for proper flying conditions. Nice prospect!

Well sir, it was very pleasant to have seen you a few weeks ago. It was certainly wonderful to get back to Luther for homecoming and find the friends and environment just as enjoyable as they had been remembered. Thank you also for the interesting letter I received—Scuttlebutt—as it is always appreciated.

Despite my affection for Luther, I have decided to immediately swing into a Law School upon my discharge. Don't know when that will be, and it looks like quite an uncertain stretch of time, but I want to have my post-war plans firmly fixed in my mind.

I have applied for post-war admittance to Northwestern University, and believe I'll be accepted. However, sir, I shall need two letters from former professors recommending my fitness for the study of law.

If you believe that I am so qualified, I would greatly appreciate your writing such a letter for me to the secretary of the Law school as soon as you find it convenient to do so.

Had a group of ten B-29's hit the field yesterday, and they certainly look huge compared to the B-17's we train in here.

Its rather dull being stationed here as an instructor, and certainly hope for something a little more exciting in the near future.

Keep the Scuttlebutt coming—it's a swell paper!

Well sir, best regards to you and yours, and I shall take the liberty of thanking you in advance for writing this letter for me.

Thank you,

        Sincerely,
        Roald A. Larson.

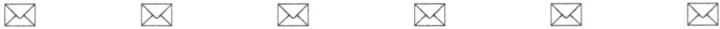

&#9993;  &#9993;  &#9993;  &#9993;  &#9993;  &#9993;

*Most of the men probably looked forward to their discharge from the moment they were inducted into the military. For some, especially older men, hope of that possibility seemed to appear well before the end of hostilities, but what might have seemed like a rational request to them did not necessarily fit the military's plans.*

[Letterhead: The Armored School, Fort Knox, Kentucky

        15 Nov 44

Dear Chellis:

I see at once that I'm making a bad beginning to carry out the main purpose of this letter—a change of address. This paper came with me when I left T.A.S. some 2 ½ months ago and happens to be the only stationary I have left. I've been intending to give you my new address but these GI change of address cards are such impersonal things. They also leave very little space for telling you that this present address has about reached its end also—I think—in the army one never knows.

The current address as of now: [...]

As you see this is a Provisional Company—in which men stay in varying periods of from 2 hours to 2 years. This one is rumored to come to a complete end by Dec 1. I happened to come here at the time the personnel office was being organized and became a personnel clerk from 12 noon, Sunday Sept 10 on. Since that time I seem to have become one of the indispensable men who works day + night 7 days per week in order that movements of men on special orders go forward as scheduled.

This outfit seems to have been set up to receive men from everywhere and to ship them out to almost the same places after their records have been corrected. Most of the men came here from basic training and go to either Fort Meade or Fort Ord for overseas replacements. I am still liable for such a shipment myself although men of my age (36 now) are mostly "quota fillers" who are shipped as a last resort because the orders call for a specified number of men. For any useful purpose 35 seems to be the maximum. After two months here almost anyone would become hardened enough toward the feelings of his fellow men to ship his anemic, crippled brother to China without a second thought.

I have recently applied for a discharge since I have become convinced that I can do more good to all concerned back at my old job. There have been either two or three men trying to take care of that job ever since I left it. Whether or not I'll be discharged I have no idea—my draft board is sorry if that means anything.

Outside of being utterly useless I haven't found Army life too bad. I got thru 8 weeks of basic without stepping on my tongue and qualified on every weapon with plenty to spare. The nine weeks at TAS were rather rugged too although I was third man in the class. I completed a 36 week course of Gregg shorthand in 7 weeks while there. The fact that I can remember very little of it now seems immaterial both to the Army and myself as I've never had occasion to use it.

I just heard a hot rumor that this place is moving lock, stock and barrel to Fort Knox next Monday—official too as the man had a towel over his shoulder. Maybe so & if so I may have another address for you before the next scuttlebutt reaches the mimeograph.

Your Scuttlebutt is, to me at least, a unique piece of literature. I'll have to admit it's not too interesting to me as it mentions very few of the men I know— which is neither here nor there. I'm not a navy man either—could have been a Lt JG, no less, but chose to be a private for reasons which I still think are good.

**115**

If I'm to write to my wife too tonight I'd better call off this personal history and get back to my favorite task as mentioned above.

I hope to see you next Homecoming.

[Pvt] Elmer [L Ulland][105]

---

*Nearly a year later, Ulland finally got his wish.*

Oct 10, 1945

Dear Chellis:

Just a note to tell you that I'm no longer cheating some poor 18 yr old out of $50 per month.

I was discharged at my own request (it <u>can</u> be done even honestly) Sept. 29 at Camp Attenbury, Ind. You will therefore strike me off your mailing list for GI's and consider me as just another civilian again.

My old job is begging me to come back but for the time being I have other more important things to do. Since last July my wife has been doing double duty as her father suffered a stroke and it has been necessary for to handle his affairs, nurse him and care for our 3 yr old boy—who has a lot more energy than his old man ever had. The wife has been unable to get help very much of the time and has had a pretty tough time of it. I figure the least I can do is help her out for as along as necessary. Then too her dad's home is 50 miles from Austin and in order to live with my family I'd have to be here—to any former soldier that becomes a pretty important thing.

I doubt that the Army did me any particular good or harm. My legs seem to have used up most of what was left in them, but that's probably nothing but advancing age. Conversely I don't believe I did the Army any good or harm either, but I seemed to round out the numbers needed—I also made a lot of payrolls, endorsed a lot of service records and quite a lot of the other Army chores.

I would like to be there for Homecoming this year, but won't be able to make it—next year perhaps. I haven't been there since Old Main burned and hope there will be a new Main by the time I get there again.

As ever

Elmer L Ulland, Bricelyn, Minn.[106]

⊠          ⊠          ⊠          ⊠          ⊠          ⊠

*When enlisting, the men and women could indicate their choices for training or future duty. But many, like Chester Porter, quickly learned that personal choice carried little weight in such assignments.*

Oct. 15, 1944

Dear Dr. Evanson,

I thought I just send a line or two to give you my address. I've stationed here at Great Lakes at a 16-week signal school. Our course consists of semaphore, blinker, flag hoist, spelling and procedure.

I don't much of it myself, but anyway it's what they shoved me into and in the Navy as you know you don't ask why so I'm here to stay for awhile.

Naturally our 32 hour liberty every other week end is our one consolation. I much rather prefer being back at good old Luther.

It certainly will be swell when this war is over so we can get back. Dick Ulvilden is stationed at Mare Island, California now.

Would you pass this address on to the Chips also because I'd like to get the Chips.

Sincerely,
Chester Porter[107]

---

[Letterhead: U.S. Naval Training Center, Great lakes, Ill.

Dec. 10, 1944

Dear Dr. Evanson

Just a note to give you a change of address. It is now: C.W. Porter S 2/C [...] I was in sick bay for about 10 days and I consequently missed about two weeks work so I will be in Great Lakes two weeks longer. This section is supposed to graduate about January 29th so I expect to be at sea sometime in February.

I like the work I'm in now much better than when I went in. It has proved to be very interesting.

Recently I saw Bob Larsen just before he was shipped out of Great Lakes. I also talked over the telephone to Neil Jordahl and Clayt Amundson.

It's really swell to get the Chips and Scuttlebutt and find out what's happening on the campus and to the rest of the Luther servicemen. Even though I wasn't at Luther very long, I certainly got to like the place and I look forward to Chips and Scuttlebutt.

My thanks for getting them.

It's interesting to read about Luther in the Chicago Tribune and Daily News on the sports page.

Sincerely,
Chester Porter [S 2/c][108]

March 3, 1945

Dear Dr. Evanson,

Well here I am once more with a change of address but I'll guarantee this one will be quite permanent for some time.

I finished signal school about the last week of January. Then we were in a transfer unit at Great Lakes for about one week. Then I was sent to the receiving station at Shoemaker, California on nine days delayed orders so I was able to get home before going out there. While at Shoemaker Milford ("Bucket") Lunde came over to see me from the hospital unit there where he is stationed.

Dick Ulvilden and I planned to get together one day in Oakland but I shipped out on the same day. I may get to see home yet if we stop in San Francisco before leaving the states for good.

| Personal for obvious reasons |
| --- |
| The ship I'm on is a patrol craft about 173 feet long and a complement of about 60 enlisted men and 5 or 6 officers. It is in port now for a general reconditioning. I'm getting a good taste of ship life though because we live aboard it in port. We get liberty every other night which is naturally very nice. |

My address for use of Chips also—[...]
Sincerely, Chester[109]

✉ ✉ ✉ ✉ ✉ ✉

*In 1936, the Luther College Concert Band had toured Northern Europe, making a number of stops in Norway. The men who had participated in that tour had fond memories, and a sense of camaraderie that stayed with them long after the trip. Martin Elstad sent Evanson this update on one of the more memorable people they had met on the tour.*

20 November 1944

Dear Chellis:

The Scuttlebutt items have been coming through. Thanks! The news of whereabouts of L.C. men is most interesting to read

Last week my phone rang and a very convincing voice said, "your orders are here. You are to proceed to U.S. Navy headquarters, in Oslo immediately after Norway's liberation. You will also visit Aalesund, Lillehammer, and Kristiansund. Then you will board the s/s MOSKEN."

I said "who's been on a Band Trip"? It was the Cornet man Geo Amundson. He's a PhM 1/c at the dispensary. L.C. Biology turned the trick for him.

"My"Anderson is here but haven't seen him as yet.

With so many of our boys overseas (in Europe) it might be well to print the following address in SCUTTLEBUTT with appropriate remark.

[Cap't. of "Mosken"—Tronheim to Oslo]

Capt Karl Jentoft

C/O J.Hay & Sons Ltd

45 Renfield Street

Glasgow—Scotland

Jentoft escaped with his ship & crew the day the Germans invaded Norway. He has had no word from any of his family since. He is the skipper of a bigger ship and has had some hair raising escapes in getting cargo delivered. I think he'd like to meet any of the band that might happen to be over there.

Enclosed is another $5.00 for the New Main. I hope to see her in commission soon after the war.

Since so many L.C. men are Navy I thought I'd send you a "Bond Sheet". The Navy is issuing a special NAVY SOUVENIER STAMP WAR BOND in this drive. In case you or others want a special NAVY ISSUE just fill out the blank or drop me a line.

Credit for the sale will be applied in the Decorah Quota if you wish.

Greetings to all.

Martin[110]

**119**

✉   ✉   ✉   ✉   ✉   ✉

*While most of the men entered the military in unskilled positions, others, especially older men, had highly valuable expertise that qualified them for much more significant assignments.*

[Letterhead: Administrative Command,
U.S. Naval Training Center, Great Lakes, Ill]

3 December 1944

Dr. Chellis Evanson
Luther College
Decorah, Iowa

Dear Chellis:

I see you often enough to be able to dispense with letter-writing, but since your December 1st issue of "Scuttlebutt" just arrived, I've got to to get this down in writing. I think this little paper is one of the most welcome things that could possibly come through the mails. I look forward to every issue. Next to Esther's daily scandal sheet and Bud's occasional scrawls, "Scuttlebutt" tops the list. More power to you!

As for Lt. Comdr. Jones's suggestion for a plaque, I'm in favor of that too, and am enclosing a little contribution to the fund.

I've just recently had a piece of good fortune, having been boosted from Laboratory Officer of the Epidemiology Unit here to Director of Laboratories for the entire USNTC, which puts me in charge of four labs. As we have the largest concentration of Naval personnel of any Naval station anywhere, the field for medical and clinical work is tremendous. This job has always been a Lt. Comdr's, but sorry to say, I got the work and keep my stripe and a half. I hope my orders, which are always lurking just around the corner permit me to hold on to this position for a while anyway. I know how lucky I am to have stayed here in the good old U.S.A. for 19 months already, and I'm afraid I'm stretching my luck. However, we in the Hospital Corps can console ourselves that we are doing a little bit by helping to get men out to the Fleet a bit sooner by keeping them healthy.

I ran into Lt. Carl (Bud) Wulfsberg at a football game here a few days ago. He is stationed in Chicago, and has been for nearly two years. Rasty W. is now a

Lt. Colonel, Einer W. is a Captain, and strange to say, all three of them are still in this country.

Well, Chellis, I'm going to be lucky again. I drew a five day leave at Christmas, so perhaps I'll be seeing you then. As for now, thanks again for "Scuttlebutt", and I really do think you're doing a swell job.

Sincerely,<br>
Harald E. Hoff[111]

$$\boxtimes \qquad \boxtimes \qquad \boxtimes \qquad \boxtimes \qquad \boxtimes \qquad \boxtimes$$

*Wives occasionally provided Evanson with updates on the men's activities, but they also had to be careful with censorship regulations.*

Dec. 5, 1944

Dear Chellis,

Here's another change of address for the "books": Ens. Kenneth N. Bergan, […] Ken's "school-days" were finished up the last of August. He is now a project engineer in the Radiation Lab at M.I.T. (Mass. Institute of Technology) in Cambridge. He enjoys his work very much, particularly the little flying he gets in once in a while. Of course his work is very "hush-hush", but I am permitted to mention that a B29 super-fortress was being exhibited, Sat. & Sun. at the airport where the MIT engineers spend some of their time. Would perhaps be best not to mention that in Scuttlebutt, however.[112]

We have been getting Scuttlebutt regularly and enjoy it tremendously. We pass it around to any Lutherites we run across.

Right now the only Lutherites in the city, that we know of are Norman Alstad, an engineer at Raytheon in Waltham—and Carl Sealander, who is attending the communications school at Harvard.

Lt. (j.g.) Valdemar Johnson was at Harvard until Sept. 30th. His present address is: Lt. (j.g.) Valdemar N. L. Johnson, USNR, c/o Professor of Naval Science and Tactics, University of Colorado, Boulder, Colorado.

We are attending Harvard Lutheran Church in Cambridge—Rev. Geo. Lillegard, L.C. 1908 is the pastor. They have eight children—wish we could talk them into sending some of them to Luther, but seems Bethany, at Mankato, is where they are going.

We have heard regularly from Josy who is in Africa. His address is: Capt. Herman T. Josendahl, [...]

We found out by devious ways that he is at Casablanca. His wife Ruth (1937) (and my sister) is teaching at Austin, Minn. this year.

Isabelle Collins Nasby is also teaching in Austin. Last we heard about Helge, he was "resting-up" at Guadalcanal after having been in on the Guam invasion. He has really been in the thick of most of the S. Pacific battle.

Haven't noticed in Scuttlebutt, Chips, Alumnus or even the Decorah papers about Lt. Willard G.S. Linnevold's marriage. We haven't his address, or even his wife's name so can't give you any details—but I'm sure Uncle Will would give you any and all of them. I'm sure that piece of news would be a surprise and very welcome to a number of fellows—Nasby particularly, since they were pretty good friends.

Seems I've about run out of news for this time.

Best of everything to all our Luther friends—and thank you so much for "Scuttlebutt".

Very sincerely yours,
Vivian Hamre Bergan
One more address:
Pfc. Melvin G. Aasen, [...][113]

With the increased importance of the air forces in World War II, meteorology gained added significance, and a number of men served at meteorological stations, sometimes being moved frequently.

[Letterhead: Gowen Field Officers Mess, Boise, Idaho]
11 December 1944

Dear Chellis,

I promised to write when I saw you in November, so here it is. This is my first letter back to Luther since I left in March of '43; it seems a long time ago, but Luther has been in my thoughts many times. I hope I'll be able to be back there one of these days when this "thing" is over.

I have met only one Luther Fellow since I left; Ens. Leland Sabbey was at Harvard while I attended Pre-metro classes at M.I.T.

I finished meteorological school at Chanute Field, Ill. on November 18 and was home on a delay enroute to Boise, Idaho when I saw you. I will be here for about a month or so and then where—I don't know.

I got my last Scuttlebutt forwarded to me here; I think it is a swell idea and I'd like to thank you and Luther for it and the other papers I receive.

Right now I'm forecasting in the Master station here at Gowen Field and enjoy it very much.

I'd like to say hello to Tutor Ellingson and the rest of the faculty.

Sincerely,
[Lt.] Roland Diddams[114]

---

[Letterhead: McChord Field, Washington]

27 January 1945

Dear Chellis,

Since I last wrote you, I have moved again farther west. I am at the Base weather station, McChord Field, Washington. The camp is about 8 miles southwest of Tacoma with Mt. Rainier sticking its peak through the haze to our east.

I am now only 35 miles from my brother at Renton, Washington. You probably remember him from the class of 1936; he is in public health work in Seattle and Washington.

I received a letter from Dick Helland of Spring Grove. He was at Luther at the same time that I was. His address is: Pvt. James R. Helland, 126th Gen. Hosp., A.P.O. 72 c/o PM San Francisco, Cal. He is in the medics in the Philippines and has seen lots of action there at and at New Guiana.

Well, I'm on duty at midnite so I'll have to get started for the station.

Sincerely,
Roland Diddams[115]

✉     ✉     ✉     ✉     ✉     ✉

*Diseases such as malaria compounded casualties from the Pacific Theater. Personnel working in hospital thus had a wide range of ailments to treat.*

[Letterhead: U.S. Naval Hospital, Shoemaker, California]

Monday Nite

12 Dec, 1944

Dear Dr. Evanson,

I just want to drop a short line & give you my new mailing for "Scuttlebutt." I came down here a week ago today & am now on ward duty here at the hosp. I'm on a malaria ward, about 90 patients on the ward but its good duty. Shoemaker is just about 25 miles out of Oakland. I'm hoping to meet Karst Ulvilden in there some weekend. He's up to Mare Is. which isn't far from Oakland. My new mailing address is:

Milford Lunde [...].

Merry Christmas & Happy New Year.[116]

✉        ✉        ✉        ✉        ✉        ✉

*Because they had at least some college experience, a number of men found themselves in teaching assignments.*

[Letterhead: United States Marines]

Lt. W. K. Selbo

OC Bn., Camp Lejeune, N.C.

Dec. 15, '44

Dear Chellis,

Guess I promised a line as soon as I got settled so I'll drop a few lines. Got my orders today and man! if "Tutor" could only see me now. I'm a math instructor in the officer candidate batallion here. The next few weeks will be more or less an indoctrination period and on January 3 I'll begin teaching, unless something unforeseen comes up by then.

Marge and I are somewhat settled about 10 miles from the base in a home with 2 old women but the place is pretty nice. I'll be home every night so it's really a good set-up.

I'm sure glad to hear of the basketball teams success so far. We may not be there to see the games, and we may not hear about the results for several weeks, but you can be sure our hearts are in every game just as though we were pouring in the baskets ourselves. My last year there will surely never be forgotten, not only because we had a fair ball club, but because of the way the whole student body acted. It's a sort of spirit that grows on one—a sort of spirit you don't find at any place but Luther. What a reunion that first homecoming will be! Maybe we'd better start making reservations now.

Well, enough for now. Greet "Tony" and any of the other gang still around and keep up with your "Scuttlebutt." It grows better every time.

Sincerely
Lt. Warren Selbo[117]

  ✉      ✉      ✉      ✉      ✉      ✉

*Depending on an individual's assignment, there were also opportunities for their wives to provide service on an informal basis. Hospital visits, particularly near the holidays, could contribute to soldiers' morale.*

[December 18, 1944]

Dear Ruth & Chellis:

If we could just put on the coffee pot and sit down and talk we would all have so much to talk about. A lot has happened since we last saw you in Iowa City.

Paul took his Internship at Methodist Hospital, Indianapolis. We enjoyed it very much. We left there the 20th Sept. to come back to Sioux Falls for a few days before Paul left for Medical Service School at Carlisle Barracks, Pa. on Oct 4th for 6 wks. training. He was then assigned to Drew Field [Tampa] and is in the Regional Hospital for the 3rd Eastern AAF. His first care was an OB which seemed a bit strange to deliver a baby his first day. He is assistant OB, Surgeon and Flight Surgeon so his work is varied. New orders come up the 1st Jan. Anything can happen and it probably will.

Judy is in S.F. It's hard to take youngsters out of school so felt it better she stay there. She is in the 4th grade & quite the little lady, she thinks.

Charlie & Harriet are in Olympia, Washington. He accepted his job in Public Health in Sept. Likes it very much. Their Public Health set-up is on Civil Service basis so felt it better for advancement in the field.

125

We enjoy your monthly news letter very much, believe me you deserve a lot of credit for what you are doing. It's a small world when one can keep up its contacts.

Without snow it just doesn't seem like the holidays are here. The roses and Poinsettias are in full blossom. It has been cold nites, but real warm during the days.

We will spend our Christmas at the officers Club & then over to the hospital after the dinner. Paul will be on duty part of the day & I shall visit with the boys. Its wonderful—those boys don't gripe and they have come back the hard way.

Paul is on duty tonite & I promised (him) I'd get our Christmas greetings so must get on to the next.

Hope this finds all of you well—(and) happy. Have a good Christmas—
Pete & Paul [Reagan][118]

✉    ✉    ✉    ✉    ✉    ✉

*Even those in critical training positions might find themselves reassigned to other duties.*

Jan 25, 1945

Dear Chellis,

I just received the January Scuttlebutt and the Chips. To be sure, both are more than welcome. There is something extremely gratifying about news of the whereabouts, etc. of one's fellow classmates. And surely, Scuttlebutt has proven itself; it is the interest and desire of the individual to maintain correspondence with as many 'associates' as possible—but this, for the most part—soon becomes sadly neglected. Consequently, your news letters, Chellis, save much time for me and the others and yet keeps us informed.

I have been more than busy, Chellis, since my furlough last November. For a time I was on a staff—as historian. Little did I realize that someday I was to become a writer. Guess I made a mistake in not taking any history courses from you—ha. Seriously tho', I did work nearly a month collecting and compiling data on the "History of Camp Sibert." This entailed much searching of old files of all kinds, old camp newspapers, and many interviews with several high ranking officers who have been at Sibert since the first tent was set up. The combined

126

works of four of us has been sent to Washington where it is to be rewritten by professional historians.

I am now working with a group of five other Radio Men. Indeed, we do have a tough row to hoe, for we are setting up a radio school here at Sibert—so that men will not have to be sent to Crowder, Mo.—for training. We had only a week to set up equipment—and draw up our training program, and without the aid of any books or manuals.

We are now teaching 4 Bns. of MPs & 1 company of smoke generator communication men. In the course we are teaching the use and procedure of six different radio sets—remote control units, telephone, telegraph—and allied subjects.

However, it looks now as if I'll be leaving Sibert in a week or so cause I've been on the alert list for the last two weeks, and it seems that the Lt. Col. in charge of radio school won't be able to keep me here.

Sherm Hosleth finally came through—didn't he ~? Another future Luther student.

Guess, it's about time to turn out the lights ~ so—"Hello to the faculty and students of Luther" and until again—

Sincerely
[Pvt.] Orland "Ole" Haugen[119]

⊠     ⊠     ⊠     ⊠     ⊠     ⊠

*Men serving in the Navy sometimes found themselves stationed far inland, and in conditions far removed from what they normally expected in the military.*

Jan 29, 1945

Dear Mr. Evans:

I've been going to write to you for a long time but for some reason or other it's been delayed.

I really enjoy getting the "Scuttlebutt" even though I was only a "Boot" at Luther I know quite a few of the fellows mentioned. It's really wonderful to know where they are and what they are doing.

I've been stationed here at Sun Valley for the past 16 months. I haven't seen much of the rest of the Navy but I don't believe there can be better duty anywhere.

This place is perfect. We enjoy all the recreational facilities that made this place famous in peace time and it doesn't cost us any thing either.

Right now the skiing is taking first place in recreation. The weather and snow are perfect. The ski lift is in operation so all we have to do is get in a chair, ride up and then ski down, some fun.

My duty consists of working in "Ships Service" and managing the Tailor Shops. I've spent some time working on the wards too but I enjoy my present job more.

I do hope it wont be to long before we can all meet on the Campus grounds again.

Enclosed you will find a small sum for the plaque, I hope it will be sufficient.

Sincerely:

James M Holey[120]

⊠      ⊠      ⊠      ⊠      ⊠      ⊠

*Some older men who had already served in the military now served in civilian positions supporting the war effort, such as the Red Cross Veterans' Administration.*

[Letterhead: American Red Cross, Office of the Field Director
Veterans' Administration, Dayton, Ohio]

January 26, 1945

Dear Chellis:

Have been receiving your Scuttlebutt right along and find it interesting to learn something about the whereabouts of the fellows. Of course there are a good many of them I do not know but I do recognize a large number of the names.

Danny is now at P O E in the East and presume he will be sailing pretty soon. Trust he will send you his address when the APO number changes as I know he appreciates getting the newsletter and Chips.

This is my first week on a new job. I am now with the Red Cross at the Veterans Administration here at Dayton instead of at Wright Field. This is quite an institution as they have the Veterans Hospital and provide Domiciliary Care here as well as house the Veterans Facility.

Will you please notify Chips of the change of address? Just make it Veterans Administration instead of Wright Field otherwise it is the same.

The Legion dues have been neglected and am ashamed to admit I do not recall the proper amount. It seems to be it was $ 4.00 and I shall inclose check for that amount. Should it be different kindly let me know. Here again use the Veterans Administration for my mailing address. Surprised to note that Dr. Hexom is leaving Decorah as did not think he would ever leave there. There are lots of Legion Fellows here as most of the men—especially the older ones employed by the Facility are Legion men. The Legion, V F W as well as the D A V have offices here and do the same kind of work as the Red Cross does.

Best regards
J. A. Lien[121]

✉  ✉  ✉  ✉  ✉  ✉

*While the men did not always have time to write detailed descriptions of their conditions, even brief notes were descriptive enough to give the reader a feel for their experiences.*

[Feb 25, 1945]

Dear Chellis

This is just a little note with a change of address. I have been receiving scuttlebutt and chips regularly and have enjoyed them very much. I am now a N.A.S. Melbourne, Fla. instructing flight pilots in their operational training. My address is Box 50 NAS Melbourne, Fla. I was married 10 months ago to a girl from Madison Wis. & we now have a little house here in Fla. Very nice—fishing—swimming, etc.

Sincerely
Lt. H.A.Bach USNR[122]

✉  ✉  ✉  ✉  ✉  ✉

*Some men found that entering a training program was no guarantee that they would be allowed to continue in that area of specialization. Sometimes programs closed, and men were reassigned to completely different kinds of duty.*

[No date—letter referred to in March 1945 issue of "Scuttlebutt"]

Greetings—

I can't put it off any longer, thanks most sincerely for the issues of your publication which I have received, and they have been coming through regularly lately. My only regret is that I didn't get my name on the mailing list sooner. Duane Sommerness put me wise to just what a great thing you folks were doing, and only then did I begin to fix myself up.

I have been at Fort Lewis, Washington for some six months now, and have been in the 1636th Engineer Construction Battalion since the twentieth of November, 1944 when it was activated. I noted in one of the issues that Omar Folven and Les Hjelle are out here too, but so far I haven't seen either of them. I believe that they are in the Medics, and if so, that is entirely another part of Fort Lewis. Nobody has as yet satisfactorily explained to anyone else just what the purpose of a battalion such as ours is, but I daresay we will find out before too long. Find out the hard way that is. But I have been most fortunate during my twenty eight months in the service and feel that I have had my share of the breaks. As a result, guess I can't complain too much no matter what happens. I have had a story much the same as what Dave Preus wrote of, was in A.S.T.P. at the University of Kentucky until the program folded up, and then off into the Engineers. We did spend a most enjoyable time going to school again though, even if it weren't at good old Luther. From the Air Corps to A.S.T.P. to the Combat Engineers in two quick hops might tell my story as well and as completely as anything else I could say. But this will have to be short, and with another thanks for everything, and a big hearty greeting to all my dear friends at and from Luther. My address for mailing purposes:

Ted. V. Jensen (Luther '41)[123]

⊠ ⊠ ⊠ ⊠ ⊠ ⊠

*A few Luther graduates had achieved high rank in the military. Because they were among the earlier graduates, they did not always appreciate Luther's change to a co-educational college.*

[Letterhead: Office of the Army-Navy Liquidation Commissioner, Washington, 25, D.C.]

19ᵗʰ March [45]

Dear Chellis:

I don't know how many years it has been since I have seen you, nor do I recall just when I last was at Luther. For the past 12 years, or so, since I went back into the service, my trips to the middle west have been few, and of short duration. Your letter is interesting, except that it makes me feel very old when you speak of having a son who is graduated already, and that Marie Shenekjem has a married daughter. I am a good deal older than Marie myself—so you can imagine! I used to go with one of her aunts at one time. Boy! That's a long while ago.

I appreciate the data on my classmates—and am more than sorry to hear about Sammy Daaler—there's another heart interest—Celia was a particular friend of mine, she played the piano well.

I have seen Trytten & T.O. Kraabel, and we all (the Luther men here) expect a get-together in about 2 weeks. I hope soon to see Bryn Hoode, Gynt Storaasli, and others.

Incidentally, overseas, I had in my unit a Harold Getty (since commissioned Infantry) and an Opdahl boy (both LC men), a bull fiddle player. One of my chaplains was a St. Olaf Lutheran, Rev. Gielstad, who had a charge in Wisconsin near my uncle Wilford. I had a colonel (dentist) by name of Gullicksen from Highland Prairie, where my uncle Nils holds forth, who knew Mike Larsen, Buck & their dad.

In rebuilding Luther, I do hope that the powers that be, build around that beautiful view of the river lowlands from the hill, Luther has been given by the Lord, and thru the foresight of our grandfathers, one of the most beautiful possible campuses in the U.S. I think that we can really have something, if we use our birthright correctly.

As I am soon leaving the country again, I have asked my wife to make a bond donation to Luther in memory of my dear Dad, and brothers, Paul & Harold— but I want absolutely no publicity on it and I must insist on that. As you probably know, we have no children and I hope someday to help Luther and the church in other ways. The Lord has prospered us, more than I (at least) deserve and I hope that I can make it up to Him in some way. I don't want to be bothered about it, Chellis—by having people come to see me—for I have decided on a definite program and I will carry it out in my own way. While I have never been in sympathy with coeducation at Luther, I have swallowed my sentiment on that.

This is a long letter for me. Best regards to all I know down there—I do hope that it won't be too long before we can all return to a normal way of life after which time I hope to get to Decorah & Spring Grove.

Sincerely

Bernard [B.A. Johnson. BrigGen. U.S.A.][124]

⊠     ⊠     ⊠     ⊠     ⊠     ⊠

*While they were away from Luther, the men tried to follow the results of the College's sports teams, which brought fond memories of their time on campus.*

29 April 1945

Dear Chellis,

I'm finally getting around to sending my contribution for the Plaque Fund. Sorry to be so slow, but hope that it will still be in time to help along.

I am receiving Scuttlebutt regularly and look for it each month. Certainly is a fine thing and I add my humble thanks and praises to the many which you deserve.

I don't write often, Chellis, because my duty is not very exciting nor fascinating and I know you must be plenty rushed with the mail from "out there." Key West is the same as ever and right now hotter than blazes due to the <u>sun</u>. I miss being able to see "Tutor" now and then and it seems not many Luther men get down this way.

I was certainly tickled about the recent basketball season at Luther and I hope that the baseball team will fare as well. It is good to know that you carry on so well and maybe before too long things will begin to get back to a somewhat normal state. It is good to think of a reunion gathering when this is all over and I know we all hope that soon, now, it will be possible.

I miss very much, the spring season, especially as it is in Decorah and I've no doubt that this year is no exception. It is a beautiful time of year and I'm very glad that I have the memories of it, at least.

Best regards, Chellis, to you and to the others.

Sincerely,

Ted Normann

"Tiedemann"[125]

⊠　　⊠　　⊠　　⊠　　⊠　　⊠

*Those who remained in the U.S. throughout the war often felt they could have been making a greater contribution to the war effort if they were stationed abroad.*

[Letterhead: United States Marine Corps,
Camp Lejeune, North Carolina

6 July 1945

Dear Chellis,

Just received a very welcome Scuttlebutt and made up my mind to send my contribution to the Plaque Fund which I have intended to do several times but never seemed to do. The Marine Corps still think I can teach mathematics so I'm still here and not exactly killing myself working. How much longer I'll be here no one knows. Marge is still here with me so we can't kick a bit. We were home over Memorial Day but only had 3 days at home so a trip to Luther had to be put off until the next leave.

Sure am glad to hear that Davey Preus got the gold bars—now I won't have to pay his way in case we meet in Washington again—maybe. Don't tell him I said so though. We managed about 4 week-ends together at the capitol last fall and they sure were 4 wonderful week-ends. Haven't seen many Luther boys for quite some time—Guess most of them like the Navy. Saw Lt. Louis Ehrich here several months ago and Fred Giere while home but that's all.

Your little word on Beiersdorf in the last news was the first I've heard of him for 2 years. I've often wondered just where he was.

Guess that's about all for now. We state-side commandos don't have much that's very interesting but before too many months are up I think I'll be on my way over. Thanks loads for your swell news sheet—keep them coming!

Best Wishes

Warren Selbo

Does our b.b. trophy still stand in the gym? Sure hope to get back and help keep it there.[126]

---

*In the July 1945 issue of "Scuttlebutt," Evanson replied,* "Yes, Selbo, that basketball trophy is still in the case in the gym, and we know there will be plenty of Norsemen ready to defend its permanent possession when things take up again."

    ✉        ✉        ✉        ✉        ✉        ✉

*While some men faced difficult conditions and were transferred from base to base throughout the war, others had more stable assignments. Some were even lucky enough to be stationed close to home.*

Iowa City, Iowa
August 31, 1945

Dear Dr. Evanson:

Please don't permit my remittance of the pledge I made long ago shock you too much, I've had lots of good intentions before this but just never seemed to get around to parting with the dough. Guess you may as well pay the pledge and apply a couple bucks to that fund referred to in "Scuttlebutt"

Perhaps you'd be interested in knowing how I've fared throughout the war. Frankly, I've been "damn lucky." Back in 1942 at Glenwood the draft board was practically <u>blowing</u> down my neck in hot pursuit. I applied for a commission in the navy & was elected March 17, 1943. May, 26, '43 I reported to Chapel Hill, N.C. for indoctrination for 5 weeks. July 15, '43, much to my surprise, I reported here at the Pre-Flight school & have been here ever since. It's only 40 miles from my wife's home so we were very pleased with the assignment. I've been in the military & athletic departments here the entire time. In addition to drilling & indoctrinating the cadets I've coached boxing, wrestling, track, soccer, baseball, football, gymnastics & hand-to-hand. It's really been very interesting and I've been treated more than nice. This last July I was alerted, that is I got my "flimsy," that orders had been initiated to the effect I would be placed on a carrier, we were packed and waiting for the word & two days after the Nips "threw in the towel" I was notified that my orders had been cancelled. At present it looks as if I and hundreds like me will be made into demobilization officers or replace men on carriers or island bases that are eligible for discharge under the current point system. I only have 39½ prints no I'm not apt to be out for sometime. But I've had it so very nice I'll be the last to complain about putting in time on some island or carrier. I'd hate to leave my wife and especially my little girl (2 yrs.) for any prolonged time but there are many that have done that in the past so presume I can to. Never can tell, I'll probably wind up as some aide to the ambassador or something if they start sending me out since I have a good foundation in International Relations—I sure used to enjoy our classes at Luther.

This is getting sort of rambling & incoherent I'm sure, besides sounding egotistical so will close. Give my regards to Pete & Pip, I've looked for someone from there around the U., here every time I go through town but to this day haven't met any one. Paul Preus was here when I first got here. Also an officer Amland class of '24, I believe. He got released to resume school work in St. Paul last winter. Sure a swell guy. By the way how is "Tobac"?

Best regards for a good year—
Lt. (jg) R. Satre USNR[127]

⊠     ⊠     ⊠     ⊠     ⊠     ⊠

*In some cases, "Scuttlebutt" provided families with more information than they received directly from their relatives stationed overseas.*

1st Lt. Ralph L. Estrem
16 Oct. 45

Dear Chellis,

Just a note to thank you for the fine work you have done in carrying on SCUTTLEBUTT and for including me in your mailing list. I have been sitting on the sidelines while I was completing my medical training at Ancker hospital after graduation from Minnesota, and so even though I have been in the Army since 1942, it has been on a reserve status until this summer. I am now working here at the army ground and service forces redistribution station. My address is shown above.

My brother Bob has twice been slated to come home from Europe but both times was suddenly transferred to another outfit from the one that went home. He is now in a field hospital in Czechoslovakia. his address: [...]

Incidentally last spring when things were hot for him over there in Europe and we weren't getting much mail from him, your note about him in scuttlebutt was our most recent news from him at the time so it was plenty welcome.

Thanks again for your fine work,

Ralph L. Estrem

Hope we can make it to homecoming next year.[128]

$$\boxtimes \qquad \boxtimes \qquad \boxtimes \qquad \boxtimes \qquad \boxtimes \qquad \boxtimes$$

*By November 1945, "Scuttlebutt" was no longer being printed regularly, and most men were eagerly re-entering civilian life. But because training had been an on-going process throughout the war, a few were just reaching new duty assignments.*

USS LST 461<br>% FP, San Francisco<br>Nov. 8, 1945

Dear Dr. Evanson,

I received an issue of Scuttlebutt not long ago so am dropping you a line so that I can be put on the Chips mailing list too. I really appreciate receiving them a lot.

I was just recently assigned to duty here, as I just graduated from Radio Tech. school in Chicago in Sept. Haven't run across any Luther men out here but am keeping my eyes open.

Am enclosing a five dollar contrib. to the Plaque fund which I hope comes through okay.

Very truly yours,<br>Luther Forde RT 2/c, ex 46[129]

# CHAPTER 8

# "I may become an old salt"—
# First Assignments: Navy and Marines

*Once the men received their actual duty assignments, particularly overseas, letters and news from home became even more important to them. Censorship regulations limited how much they could describe, however.*

[V-MAIL]

From: Lt. L. J. Sebastian [...] Feb. 1, 1944

Dear Chellis,

I received your letter mailed Nov. 23, and I really enjoyed it, its nice to hear from one's friends back at Luther. By the way would you step out of your back door and tell "Pete" that I have not received any mail from him since I've been over here.

I manage to keep quite busy most of the time; here are my duties—I am Bn. 2, P.X. Officer, ass't Bn. Motor Officer, ass't motor officer and I also go to school every afternoon learning artillery, which I find is very interesting.

Helge Nasby and myself came out on the same ship. We had a very enjoyable trip. I don't know how much longer we will remain on this island. We started in combat once but were ordered back.

This letter doesn't contain much interesting information but I want you to know that I appreciate the fact that you included me in your mailing list.

P.S. Write

Sincerely,
Gabby[130]

⊠        ⊠        ⊠        ⊠        ⊠        ⊠

*A major test for many men was the transoceanic trip to their Port of Embarkation. But some had relatively little difficulty getting their "sea legs."*

April 11, 1944

Dear Dr. Evanson,

There was a slight interlude while we crossed the great waters and betook ourselves to the sunny shore of North Africa. While time is still a bit free I'll avail myself of the opportunity of giving you the cold dope.

I see a faint ray of hope that I may become an old salt or a reasonable facsimilie thereof. We crossed the lake in something like three weeks and in all that time I used the rail as a stomach supporter only a few hours the first day. From then on in it was three a day and much more of an enjoyable trip. The weather was fine and we began catching the suntans we are sure to continue over here. We've had a minor bit of excitement, our "baptism" and have "la souvenirs de mc coy" to show for our first attack. One of these days I'll send you a fractional part of its wing.

It was one year almost to the day since I joined the Navy that we arrived here and I celebrated my 22nd birthday last Friday. Easter Sunday was conspicuously without the color and glitter so common to us at home but we did manage to maintain the true joy of the season by attending church on that morning.

Well, sir I hope to find one of your letters coming this way again soon. Mayhaps in the meanwhile I'll meet up with some of our buddies over here. Give my greetings to all.

Sincerely yours,
John C. Sorlien, Ensign, USNR[131]

    &#9993;    &#9993;    &#9993;    &#9993;    &#9993;    &#9993;

*While the younger men whose education was cut short by the war usually found themselves in the lower ranks, those who had already graduated from college were often officers, and quickly found themselves in positions of responsibility, especially training younger soldiers or sailors.*

8 November 1944

Kjaere Chellis,

The above is about the extent of my Norse at the present time and you don't know what fun Aggie and I had translating your very apt remarks re our marriage in your Scuttlebutt of a few months ago. Tusen tak!

No doubt you are wondering why I didn't hunt you up a few weeks ago when I was on the campus, but we just didn't have time. We picked a poor day, I guess, because Dr. Preus was the only one we saw. I hadn't been back since Oct '41 and I did want to take a look at the place I love so well even tho it had to be short. I had a hunting date with my brother-in-law in Spring Grove in the afternoon and as it was my only chance to get that in, too, the schedule was short and had to be met. It was grand to get back again and let's hope it won't be too long before we can all come back for good, tho no doubt many will miss it.

This leave I obtained this time was not for a happy purpose as you no doubt heard, but I am certainly thankful that I was near enough to be able to get home.

Things down here at Key West are going along as usual and I haven't been able to see Tutor since I returned. He is still here, tho, and I hope to be able to see him again soon. I'm out at sea all day and his work keeps him ashore and we're both usually ready for the sack pretty early in the evening. Aggie isn't with me, but is teaching again this year at Winona. She plans to come down for Christmas, tho, and stay thru Jan. at least.

Had a letter from Joe Homstad the other day and he mentioned writing to you, too. I guess you have gathered by now that the 1383, which I'm on, is a school ship attached to the Fleet Sound School here at Key West. Very routine duty and not at all exciting, but suppose somebody has to do that, too. I'm getting lots of valuable experience in ship handling and that will no doubt come in very handy. I missed the "big blow" down here as my leave came during that time, but the rest of the crew had had a jolly rough time of it. They came through without casualty, however, and that was good.

As far as I know, Tutor and I are the only Luther men here and I haven't seen any others since New York, while waiting for the ship. Then I saw Tony Sperati and wife, Paul Christopherson and Bill Sorenson, Lt,(jg) in the Chaplain Corps gave the prayer at our commissioning ceremony. My wife, Eleanor Dorrum, and the Speratis were my guests so the commissioning was really almost a Luther reunion. The Speratis now are the proud parents of a beaming son, Charles Robert, though you doubtless have heard before this.

I've been very lax in answering your very good Scuttlebutt letters, Chellis, and to tell you how much I appreciate them. You've certainly done a grand job and none of us will ever forget it. We always look for them!

The weather is fine down here now not too hot during the day and it cools off nicely at night. September was a killer and the heat really made one suffer. Should be nice now until late Spring.

Best regards to you and your wife, Chellis, and I hope all will continue to go smoothly. I'll be waiting for the next Scuttlebutt issue and hope it comes soon.

Sincerely,

Tiedemann [Lt.(jg) S.T. Normann, Jr., USNR[132]

⊠        ⊠        ⊠        ⊠        ⊠        ⊠

*In a few cases, soldiers' wives also sent Evanson updates. That was particularly the case when reassignment came unexpectedly.*

November 30, 1944

Dear Chellis:

When you mentioned your servicemen's photo gallery in the last Scuttlebutt it occurred to us that the snap of these four fellows might be an interesting contribution. At our homecoming party we discovered that we had present the Luther tennis captains for four successive years, so we took a picture of them. Hoff—'40, Henderson—'41, Preus—'42, and Selboe—'43: one a Navy Chaplain, one a Marine pilot, the next in the Army still a student, and the last a Marine who hasn't quite classified himself yet.

I'm sending along a picture of the group which isn't quite complete, but I think you can identify those present. Two of our Marine officers we found to be in hack on the big evening so they joined us just by telephone, and others (including Dr. Trytten) had already come and gone. In reference to the two boys in trouble I might say in order to ease your mind that neither offence was serious enough to warrant court martial proceedings.

Did you know that Beth Iverson Reynolds is in New York and now secretary to Bud Fischer, the creator of Mutt and Jeff? All descriptions of the job sound very interesting. Deacon is now in France.

Your Scuttlebutt is just as interesting to those wives who are fortunate enough to be with their husbands at present as it is to the fellows themselves. The fellows themselves think it's tops, and I've talked to plenty of them. Stan is still flying, shooting skeet, and he's assistant operations officer of the air station now so he battles that chain which keeps him at a desk half the time.

We consider ourselves lucky to be here where so many Luther people have seemed to congregate. Hardly a week-end goes by that at least a few of us don't get together, and it's really fun to be with "our kind of people" as we call it.

Sincerely,

Helen Henderson

[handwritten note following typed letter:]

P.S. Between the time of writing and mailing we have received a little surprise—the gist of which follows:[133]

———————

Quantico, Va.

December 1, 1944

Dear Friends, Relatives and suchlike:

War presents an excuse for almost anything it seems: even carbon copied letters. At 4:30 yesterday afternoon (Friday November 30) Stan received orders, and will be detached from this station on Monday. He proceeds directly to San Francisco and there boards a clipper for points west. He has no idea what type of duty he is getting—-it may be utility flying in multi-engines because he is now a first pilot for transports, or it may be dive-bombing again.

He is not getting any leave at all so there will be no opportunity to see any of you. We have been saving our leave for that purpose but so goes it. This whole thing caught us pretty flat-footed. We haven't decided where we will live while Stan is gone, but we are getting in the car Monday and driving West. We may go with him to the coast of we may stop off someplace along the way. All that will work itself out. In the meantime we are trying to get a family packed up and on the road besides getting checked out of here.

Howard says the thing he really hates about moving is having to start following a whole new set of funnies again. To say nothing of reading them in a good Republican paper.

But you'll hear from us again when I'll be able to give you addresses to reach us both. So happy landings!

Helen

(Mrs. Stan Henderson)[134]

✉ ✉ ✉ ✉ ✉ ✉

*Lester De Noyelles's wife had similar news for Evanson.*

Cresco, Iowa, July 14, 1944

Dear Mr. Evanson,

I would like to give you a change of address of my husband
Ensign Lester DeNoyelles, USNR [...]

He always enjoyed receiving the monthly "scuttlebutt" so much that I know
he doesn't want to miss a single one, especially since he's out of the country.

You may be interested in the address of another former Luther man.

Charles Salisburg—Ph.m 1/c [...]

Chuck has been in Londonderry, Ireland for the past two yrs. He is working
in the same base hospital since he's been there. He recently was made charge of
the technical part of the X-Ray Department.

Les was released at Howard May 26 and sent to San Francisco where he
expected further training but the Navy decided differently and after 2 wks there
sent him out. He is still in Communications.

Thank you for all they news in the past and I'm sure Les will enjoy all the
coming letters.

Yours truly,
Mrs. Lester De Noyelles[135]

✉ ✉ ✉ ✉ ✉ ✉

*Evanson was often asked to write letters of recommendation, particularly for men who
hoped to receive commissions in the Navy.*

Minneapolis, Minn
July 22, 1944

Dear Chellis,

I've had a guilty conscience for not writing sooner to thank you for your swell
cooperation in getting my transcript of credits and letter of recommendation.
Now I can report that your help was not in vain.

I received my "Greetings" before the application for commission had time to
work so went through "Boot" training at Farrogut. Wasn't too tough. As a matter
of fact, except for being separated from my wife and two little girls, I enjoyed it.

142

Had my 15 day "boot" leave on completing that training and when I returned to Farrogut was commissioned as a line officer, Lieutenant (j.g.). Might add to that that while in "boots" I was selected as "Honor Man" for our company.

I am now on delayed orders, reporting to Princeton University on July 25 for indoctrination school. That will last eight weeks, after which I will be sent to some sea port for sea going experience. When that is completed, I will be assigned to some vessel.

Thanks again, Chellis, for your help and best regards to you and my other friends at Luther.

Yours very truly

[Lt. (j.g.)] Robert M. Snouffer[136]

---

*In January 1945, Snouffer's wife sent this update:*

Bob has been gone since Dec. 22—and as yet I haven't heard from him so don't know just where he is—except on high seas. He went thru Boot Camp at Farragut—and took his indoctrination at Princeton Un. And final training at Camp Shelton, Norfolk Va. While there I know he met several Luther men. He has wanted to get back to Luther for a visit—but he has been home just once since entering the Navy last April—and then for 10 days.

Sincerely—

Mrs Robert Snouffer [1/23/45][137]

&#9993;  &#9993;  &#9993;  &#9993;  &#9993;  &#9993;

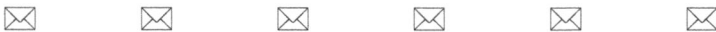

*Once they received their assignments, the men could not always be sure what their new duties would involve, or where their new posting would actually take them.*

[Letterhead: Alexander Hamilton Hotel and Apartments
O'Farrell Near Leavenworth, San Francisco]

Aug. 19, 1944

Dear Chellis—

One of the last letters to come to me before "shoving off" was the July "Scuttle-butt." It contained so much of interesting news that I want to thank you for it.

143

After 26 months at Great Lakes I find myself off to the Southwest Pacific to join the 7ᵗʰ Fleet. I have been looking forward to this for a long time and now I am very curious to know what my duties are going to be.

I notice that you are planning for a big year at Luther College.

In leaving I want to express my best wishes to the College and then will you greet friends for me.

Sincerely,<br>[Lt. Comd'r] Sig Steen[138]

    ✉      ✉      ✉      ✉      ✉      ✉

*When they received commissions, the new officers quickly found themselves in charge of entire units of men, with all of their accompanying problems to deal with. This was a dramatic change from their school days at Luther.*

[Letterhead: United States Navy]

Fort Pierce, Fla.<br>Aug.26, 1944

Dear Folks,

Hello, everyone. Yep, it is that old rooner of yours pounding out a few lines again. It has been quite some time since I last wrote to you folks, but when Betty was there I sort of figured that she would past on any news of any interest. Of course, being on this base there isn't any news of interest anyway. However, I will at least pound out a few lines and let you know how I am.

Well, we finally picked up our sailors here the other day. I now have 11 officers and 144 sailors to worry about. I have never seen such a dirty bunch of sailors in my life as those that I got in my group. I do have some good officers tho' and after we gave the sailors 24 hours to get their gear in shape we got them in pretty fair condition. Of course, you have to stay on their neck every minute or else they get back in the same old rut. I can really say that those sailors really do have the problems. I have never had so many questions and problems in my life. The prize one tho' is the other day a sailor come up to me and said that he got a little mixed up and now he has two wifes and he was wondering what he should do about it. He said that he didn't want to get in any trouble; so he thought he had better do something about it. That is the kind of stuff I get everyday except not that extreme. Everyone seems to have lost their gear and then they don't have any money. Some of these days we might get them in shape tho'. It does sort of get on your nerves now and then then. Now I can see how you must have felt with a few of us fellows in your History classes. I believe that I have even more problems than you did tho'.

Thanks a lot for that letter again for the last month. I really do wait for them. I know that if all the fellows that get those letters appreciate them as much as I do your time is well spent. By the way, Jim Ulvilden is back down here again. It is pretty nice to have a Luther fellow around again to shoot the breeze with.

Well, I am still trying to get out of here. I may be able to work it pretty soon out as yet I have nothing definite. I got my fingers crossed tho' because I have some logs on the fire at the present time, but I don't know just how it wall all pan out.

Well, folks, I haven't much more to write about and I have a couple other letters to pound out yet. So for now, so long and I will always be glad to hear from you if you have time to drop me a line.

As ever, Just
[Ens] Harold [Heltne][139]

⊠      ⊠      ⊠      ⊠      ⊠      ⊠

*One of the first stops for Navy men in the Pacific was Hawaii. For some, it was a brief stop for their ship en route to points farther West, while for others it represented a new duty station.*

Sept. 6, 1944

Dear Chellis,

Time for a letter again. Received your July issue of "scuttlebutt" and enjoyed it very much. I am sure everyone who received this "epistle" from you appreciates it as much as I do, and that is one hell of a lot. Have a little "news" of my own this time. I left 'frisco not knowing where I'd end up, or in what kind of duty. Note my new address if that will tell you anything, and you will see that I drew a darn swell job.

Our "working conditions" are almost to good to be true especially in view of what many of the boys have to go thru … we have an air conditioned room with fluorescent lighting and <u>very</u> interesting work, plus a swell bunch of fellows.

Our BOQ is just new, too, and we're blessed with clean sheets a wash bowl and mirror in the room, and even a couple of lounges. (however, we <u>don't</u> have anyone to draw our bath or shine our shoes, but that is about all).

Have been getting in a lot of swimming and surf boarding and also golf and tennis. Played on the course that Bob Hope played when he was here … you see they had to do the whole thing over again when he got thru. Haven't run any hurdles lately though. Have been putting on a little weight here and there … mostly "there" I admit … but really feel in the "pink." Just stocked up the room for midnight snacks, etc. with a half a dozen cans of pineapple juice (at 9¢ a can) a couple of <u>boxes</u> of gum, and all the cigarettes and whiskey a guy could want … personally I don't use much of the latter, but it sure goes a long ways towards making friends.

Ran into Dusty Hanson at the BOQ, he is stationed near here also. And ran into Al Mikelson at the officers club just the other day, he is on his way "out", and I hardly recognized him with his moustache. Ran into another "norsky" (from Boston, believe it or not) so enjoy a few "tak skal di har" and "ver so goo" (I never was very good at anything but Latin).

Enclosed is a snap of me, just so you can have somewhat of an idea to whom you are sending all these monthly letters. The jeep isn't mine "personally", but they sure do come in handy for "errands." Am glad to say I saw the President when he was here … there is enough "gold braid" around though that it took someone like him to even make a guy sit up and take notice. So far I've only used three expressions since I've been here.… "yes, sir," "no, sir" and "no excuse, sir" … and that seems to be all you need to know. Better "knock off" and hit the "sack". Thanks again for all the "news," and keep it coming. (my best to Pete and Pip and any more you see) … and the best to you too,

from [Ens.] Les De Noyelles[140]

✉     ✉     ✉     ✉     ✉     ✉

*Assignments to training ships or similar posts were often frustrating for men who wanted to make a more tangible contribution to the war effort.*

20 Sept. '44

Dear Dr Evanson,

I just got a letter off to Chellis Jr. and now I'll try one to the Sr. The ship is vibrating so much that my writing looks like I'm about 90 years old.

I was very glad to get your "Scuttlebutt" of July for I like to know what the fellows are doing & where they are. I hope you will put me on your mailing list

I'm glad you plugged the Navy the way you did at Luther for it has the Army beat—even though most of my former roommates are Army men.

I've been on this LST for 5 months but we got a bad assignment—a training ship. Our home base is Norfolk & we take out trainees from Camp Bradford for a two week cruise. We show them the ship and instruct them in all its operations—beaching etc. We've applied for transfer since the first but we are still here.

This cruise is O.K. for one of the officers training under me happens to be Bud Ludvigson, a Luther classmate. Boy, was I surprised when he came aboard. We've had quite a time shooting the bull about L.C.

I had a leave about a month ago & stopped in Decorah. The library really looks nice & Larsen Hall will too when it is finished. I was rather disappointed to see that the flag wasn't up. You know the Navy rules on that. How about seeing that someone takes care of it?

My brother Gerhard is still in England. He is a Navy man too, the Seebees. When I was in the cities we figured out that all our relatives are in the Navy—not a one in the Army.

Had hopped to see Jim Ulvilden, Mathre & Bulldog when they were in Norfolk but we were rammed one night so we had to go in for repairs so I missed them. That was a really hurricane that hit us last week. Sunk quite a few ships. Best wishes for Luther

E O Naeseth[141]

&#9747;  &#9747;  &#9747;  &#9747;  &#9747;  &#9747;

*While the men generally adjusted to the ships quickly, they nonetheless longed to be back at Luther.*

[Letterhead: United States Navy
Jan. 24, 1945

Dear Sirs,

I have been receiving the Scuttlebutt and the Chips for past two months and think the Scuttlebutt is very interesting as well as reading about fellow schoolmates and finding out were they are. Maybe I'll run across some of them someday. I did

147

run into a Luther graduate on the train back in 1943 while I was on leave but I can't remember his name so it doesn't help much. He graduated in '42 and is now a pilot in the army air force.

In case you can't decipher my address I will print it for you my writing is hard to decode. Arnold Sersland, PhM 2/c, U.S.S. LUMEN (AKA—30) [...]

I have been aboard ship for nearly a month now. And I like it pretty well. But good old Decorah is a better. We are still in the states but guess we will be shoving off before long.

I was in the hospital when I received the first Scuttlebutt. I had a little operation before I went to sea but I'm alright again now.

Inclosed you will find my contribution to the Jones Plaque. I think it a swell idea and I hope the former students of Luther respond as they always have. It seems quite awhile since I was in school at Luther but I guess it hasn't been so long after all.

Well I guess that will be all for now and I will be looking forward to the next issue of the Scuttlebutt.

Yours truly
Arnold Sersland.[142]

   ✉    ✉    ✉    ✉    ✉    ✉

*Navy men not only had the usual problems of traveling from training to a new duty station; if they were assigned to a ship that was at sea, it might take them weeks to finally reach their actual duty station.*

Bricelyn, Minnesota
2 March, 1945

Dear Dr. Evanson,

At last I have a chance to drop you a short line to add to the large amount of mail you receive from former Luther students. I have wanted to write you so many times, but up until now the time has been so filled that I've hardly had time even to write to the folks. At least I have enough time now to let you know how things are going.

On February 20 I finished the Naval ROTC course at the University of South Carolina and in a class of 63 finally received that long sought after commission. And let me tell you, it was a relief to know that we were all through. My orders are to report to San Francisco on March 7, so I just made a little detour and am now winding up 10 wonderful days at home. I have been assigned to the heavy cruiser, U.S.S Salt Lake City, so from Frisco I'll move on out into the Pacific and try to catch up with her. Two other fellows who finished with me have been assigned to the same ship, so that should make it pretty nice. Most of the fellows got amphib's and transports, so I was certainly happy to be assigned to a large ship—just exactly what I asked for. Amphib's are O.K., they say, but it means a little more, I think, to get on a large ship. About 25 of us report to the same place on the same day in Frisco, and about 20 report 2 days earlier, so we should have quite a reunion there. Certainly there will be plenty to talk over when we get there after just finishing a 15 day leave.

Have been receiving the Scuttlebutt regularly, Chellis, and have enjoyed every copy. You certainly are doing a swell job of keeping us posted on the old Luther Pals. I would imagine it takes a lot of time to read all the mail you receive & condense each letter to a few lines, but I'll bet you enjoy it anyway. As soon as I get a permanent address I'll drop you a line again so that the letter won't be sent to Columbia and then be forwarded from there. Maybe you'll inform Chips that I'm no longer at Columbia, too. Thanks a lot, again, and best wishes to you.

Ye' old salt,
Paul Narum[143]

⊠　　　⊠　　　⊠　　　⊠　　　⊠　　　⊠

*While most of the sailors were assigned in the more prominent Naval stations, such as San Diego, some were in less commonly used ports.*

19 March '45

Dear Chellis,

After a month of duty with the Commissioning Detail here in Portland I'm almost convinced there isn't a letter billet in the Navy. Living "on the beach" is really the nuty!

As the name of the Detail states we're in the commissioning business putting landing craft, auxiliary vessels, transports, and now carriers on the road to Tokyo. You might say we're the "middle man" twixt ship and shore; assisting in getting them outfitted, supplied and finally running up the pennant and ensign. I'm still in communications. The Lt. I was to replace has not received his orders yet which is fortunate for me. There are a lot of angles to pick up and questions to answer.

In the main the job seems to call for knowing who to see about what.

Portland seems to be a fine town. It strikes me as being just an over grown small town. Although crowded there aren't many service men. We are about the only "Navy" in town which makes it all the better. Both officers and E.M. in the Detail live on their own. We put in 8 hours a day, six days a week (one p.m. off per wk) and the rest of the time is ours. Just like having a civilian job. I'm at the YMCA right now in the heart of downtown and 7 blocks from the office. Hardly beat that. Usually manage to bum one meal a day off a ship—you know, just happen to drop around about lunch time.

Met a Luther man two weeks ago—Ens. Roland Hegg '39. He is communications and Stores Officer aboard the LCS (L)(3) 104. By this time he's about ready to jump off from Diego.

I have received couple issues of "Chips", the alumni Bulletin and all your back letters. Found lots of old mail waiting here for me. Really wasn't "old" though.

This has been a little sketchy but that's about enough gab for now. Thanks again for everything when I visited you.

Sincerely

[Lt.(jg)] John C. Sorlien[144]

# REPORTS FROM OVERSEAS: THE ATLANTIC AND EUROPE

# CHAPTER 9

# "Getting some practical sea experience"— Service in the Atlantic

*Men in the Navy expected extensive sea duty. Since most of the Luther men were from the Upper Midwest, however, few were accustomed to the sea. But many of them were able to adapt quickly.*

[Dec 9 1943]

Dear Chellis & family,

As you know by now, I finally got out of the States—perhaps foolish but one feels that he is doing a little bit more.—We had a very enjoyable trip across in that we stopped at several points of interest—However crossing in a 150' job has its bad features at times but I must say that I weathered it remarkably well. Truly an old Salt now but not battle scarred as yet. We have been here for a couple of weeks now and are enjoying the stay a lot. Feels good to set our feet on Tera-firma—go dancing, movies—stage shows etc—even an army nurse from Texas with a charming personality has accompanied me on several occasions—We have a good crew, the other 3 officers are very nice, about my age and we get along excellently.

Food is good—always a good bunk to crawl into—no rationing and very few strikes on the part of the exhausted men—Our mission won't be too dangerous so you see I'm faring very well—I don't have Chel's Denver address so perhaps you would send a greeting on to him and give him my address as a gentle reminder a trifle belated but still:

With Christmas Greetings and All Good Wishes for the New Year
From [Lt. (j.g.)] Kenny [I. Olson][145]

---

[V-MAIL]

From: Ens. C. M. Larson
U.S.S. Varian (DE7989) 18 August, 1944
Dear Prof & Friend,

Thought I would drop you a line to let you know that I'm finally getting some practical sea experience. Believe me Chel I'm getting very salty, but as soon as the war is over & the Armistice is signed that salt will rinse off and I'll bid so long to the Navy.

My duties aboard the U.S.S. Varian are as follows: 1) Ass't First Lt. 2)In charge of the men in the second division 3) Chief mail censor & 4) Sundays I give they boys a short sermon. We are now at sea in fact we've been out for about a week & we will be back about Oct 1st or maybe even Nov—I won't be able to mail this letter until we get to the—I can't tell—maybe I will beat it home. Now that you know my address, I would appreciate your letters once again.———

> I remain,
> Your ol' history student
> Curt Larson[146]

---

*Larson sent an update a few months later. While he had apparently adapted to sea life fairly well, there was nonetheless some monotony that he found difficult to adjust to. His thoughts about Luther remained strong, however.*

[Letterhead: USS Varian (DE 798)]

1 Nov. 1944

Dear Chellis,

Again I'm writing to you from the good ol' U.S.S. Varian—now somewhere in the Atlantic. This is my second trip across and somehow the time seems to just fly by. On second thought the last statement was slightly over exaggerated. The last crossing was fairly peaceful, but this trip—its been awful—Believe me Chell these DE's really pitch & roll. but as yet I haven't hit the rail—I'd better knock on wood.

After returning from our last trip I received a three & one half day leave—I flew home from New York to Chicago and it proved to be very interesting to me as it was my first trip by air. Oh, for the life of these bird men, but nevertheless a bunch of great fellows doing a bangup job—so here's to all our bird men with the funny hats. I'm very sorry that I didn't get to see you Chell, but I did see Pete—He was out with the football squad & believe me that sure brought back memories—those memories will become a reality again—Luther should have wonderful postwar athletic teams. A. Ward & I always talked about the football team Luther will have when the war is over & all the boys come marching home again. We will all be back again & more than likely we will be taking a few history courses, that is if you don't mind. Luther in my mind will always be something to hold on to—a person doesn't realize how precious a thing is until it is taken away from him. Yes. Chell it will be a great day when we are all back at LC and I'm sure every one else feels the same way.

I imagine I will get another shot there after this trip & honestly this time I'll make it a point to see you—Sorry about the last trip—

So until the middle of Dec. I remain—

As ever
Curt[147]

   ✉      ✉      ✉      ✉      ✉      ✉

*While the D-Day invasion involved thousands of ground troops, Navy ships were essential to its success.*

20 Aug. 1944

Dear Dr. Evanson

I was happily surprised yesterday when I received a copy of "Scuttlebutt" which, I take it, you have prepared as there is only one Chellis! It was very interesting although there were only a very few mentioned who I know. Naturally as time passes the older men loose contact with "Alma Mater" especially when you are in the service and far away.

I have been away from the U.S. since last January when we took a convoy over to England—a 47 day trip. Our crossing was uneventful but became rather monotonus and the last week our chow consisted of black-eyed peas, rice, coffee for dinner, rice, coffee, and peas for supper! But it was an experience for us moderns.

We had a part in the "D" day exercises; we took in the initial wave and then stayed a short distance off shore for 16 days. Our job—well I'll tell about that some other time. There was plenty of stuff coming our way; but—thank God!—neither men nor ship was even scratched. Exceedingly lucky I would say. We have since then had a few days of rest and relaxation in England; but have been along the coast of France on various duties, most of the time since then. We have had one liberty in a French port but I had the duty, so I'm still looking forward to setting my foot on French soil. I'm in charge of the engine room in one duty section so I must be fairly close to the job. The duty is pretty rugged—it's a rough ride when the old ocean gets to kicking up; but there are so many good features which compensate for it that I'm well satisfied. (Pardon the scribbling as it's trying to stay on even keel but can't)

I have not met any Luther men over here—I gather that there are many here but its just luck to run into them unless you had ship numbers or F.P.O numbers. What a grand homecoming we'll have when this show is over and we can get back to Civilian life. I'm not a 20 year man as the age is creeping slowly creeping up on me. It's over 16 years since I finished Luther; class of '28—old timers.

Well, it's soon time to relieve the watch. Give my regards to Hamlet and Mrs. Peterson; Sig Reque; Dr. Preus and any of the others who may still remember me. Greetings to all and especially to you.

Sincerely<br>R.G. Roalkvam[148]

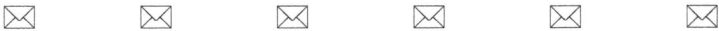

✉     ✉     ✉     ✉     ✉     ✉

*Even while aboard ship, the Navy men had occasional meetings with other Luther students. But their reports of their own activities aboard ship were limited by censorship restrictions.*

September 5, 1944

Dear Chellis,

I received your "Scuttlebutt" for July and to be sure, it was interesting—that was my first good complete newssheet from Luther since I took my leave from good old U.S. soil, and I had a good bit of enjoyment from it—thanks!

In my travels I have seen only two Luther men—Don Gjerdrum last winter back in Bizerte, and what a changed boy he was!! He spent the night with me and we had a good bull session on some of the days at Luther. The second Luther man was Carl Larson '38, whom I saw only a few days ago when his ship took us alongside for fuel, water, & supplies. I had him come aboard for a cup of coffee and in true Norse style we recalled days gone by—I even sensed a bit of Norse accent in the conversation! He seems well pleased in his position and assured me that the life wasn't too bad—guess there hasn't been too much work for them, must be running out of "game"! I had hopes of seeing Jim Holmslund, but the closest I came was to get a letter from him, and since that time we have moved to "greener pastures" so I doubt that I shall see him.

As for myself, things roll along pretty much uninterrupted and so far we have been able to stay clear of flying machines and all these so-called new fangled contraptions Jerry has pulled out of his dwindling bag of tricks. With the exception of getting to a point where I comb my hair with a damp rag—I'm none the worse for wear. I must admit, however—same as any human—I have been happy to have had clean drawers to change into on certain occasions!

Haven't heard from Dusty for almost 6 weeks but that is undoubtedly due to the fact that I haven't written—been a trifle busy you know. His last letter stated that he had been placed behind a desk to push a pencil around for awhile—my guess is that he certainly deserves it!

Well, Chellis—I'm always glad to hear from Luther and I hope soon to come back that way to see you all. Sorta like to see that youngster of mine, too. Greet the whole gang for me and if you have time, drop a line.

Best Regards
O.M. Walstad[149]

✉    ✉    ✉    ✉    ✉    ✉

*While some men stayed in Europe until the end of the war, others were soon reassigned back to the U.S., where they often found their assignments much less interesting than what they had experienced overseas.*

[Letterhead: Amphibious Training Base, Camp Bradford, N.O. B.
Norfolk 11, VA.]

30 January 1945

Dear Chellis:

It is one of those times when a guy gets to thinking that he has been neglecting his duty or some thing like that. I have been getting "Scuttlebutt" right along and enjoy every copy thoroughly and now I had better express my appreciation and contribute a bit of information.

The Columbia U. session was not really hard but just miserable and I guess even more so to a fellow like myself. Got the commission, as did 813 others, but still felt pretty good. Since them I have been very thankful I did make it. Feb. 24, 1944—guess I'll keep that date in mind. From then on, more liberty and more money. The next five months saw me in Raleigh, N.C., Diesel Engineering-good duty-good liberty—interesting—and something I could take to. I tore down some of those big babies the Navy uses on her ships and learned what made them tick and how to keep them ticking. I got to like the town and the people—and now several weekends find me right back there. It is quite warm there and it feels good to discard that top coat for a day or two. I had a couple weeks leave after I left Raleigh in July but didn't make it to Decorah. I had been there in Feb. and called on you but it must have been an odd hour. You weren't home and I didn't stay long. I flew across the brink in Aug. 19 hours New York to Ireland. Picked up LST-208 in England and went aboard as Chief engineer. In Falmouth I was in the process of enjoying a very slim Johnny Walker and soda and a voice boomed out, "You're Winter aren't you?!" I looked around and there was Lt. Ray Frank, and not a j.g. either. He was skipper of a YMS and was leaving the next day to sweep out the harbor of Brest! I made a few landing in Normandy and then our ship was ordered back home. 19 days it took to come back but we had no trouble and it was a good trip and I didn't get sea sick even though it was so rough we had to eat just sandwiches for a couple of days. Our ship was in need of repair so I stayed aboard her in Boston for a month supervising engine repair and then I got my 30 day leave. Was home from Dec. 4 to Jan. 1 which was pretty good, and believe me the time flew! I reported here on Jan 3, 1945 and her I still am doing nothing except watch an occasional training film and of course, make myself known a few times a day. It could be enjoyable, but the liberty is hardly worth making use of.

I forgot to mention that I flew from Boston to Raleigh in November and ran across Dillon Donielson, Lt. (j.g.). He was stationed near Providence, R.I, and is married. Had a good chat with him.

Red Mathre is here at Bradford, too, but as far as any other Lutherites go I don't know. I think he is working with gunnery.

I expect to be heading for the Pacific in a couple of months and won't mind it because here with nothing to do the time drags out too much. If I have nothing to do I would rather do it any other place than here.

I enjoyed being on the LST and had it very comfortable. I have a bunch of good pictures but I can't send them in the mail because I am not really supposed to have them. I'll guarantee you'll see them the next time I get to Decorah. Most of the officers aboard do get pictures even though they really aren't supposed to, but we are careful with them.

I read where Tutor was back at Luther and now your Jan. letter said he was called back again. I suppose he'll be in now until it's over.

I suppose it is not imperative that I give a discourse on the length of the war. I hope not because I very seldom say more than that it won't be over next week, but I haven't planned anything for couple of years yet anyway!

Again let me tell you how I appreciate your issues of "Scuttlebutt" and thanks!

Yours respectfully,
Bill [Ens. W. D. Winter][150]

# CHAPTER 10

# "Watching from the bench long enough"— Service in the Caribbean and South America

*While most of the men serving in the Atlantic Theater were sent to North Africa or Europe, some also served in the Caribbean and South America.*

Dec 17 '43

Dear Chellis—

Has been a long time since I've heard much about Luther College and I do owe you a letter and happened to have a lot of spare time which is very unusual in the Navy as you probably know being an old Navy man yourself. I'm located in S. America. below the Equator outside of that I cant tell you much more about the location as it is a Military Secret.

The climate here is very nice. Summer has come down here and it is hot in the day time but cools off at night so we have to sleep under blankets.

I don't think S. America is as great a land of opportunity as most people picture it. The natives here are very poor and dirty I don't believe they have ever heard of sanitation of any type as they don't practice it. The country abounds with Natural Resources but to work them would require a lot of Capital and then there are a lot of Hazards to be overcome. Both climate and governmental. The countries down here are anxious to have their resources developed but don't want any of the money to leave the country.

The U.S. Govt. Dept. of Agriculture is doing a lot of work for these countries to develop their soil etc. and to helping the Govt. clean up the towns which really need it.

The natives are mostly Catholic of the Church of old Spain and are very strong Catholics. I think they have church twice a day. Also there have been quite a few Political Refugees from Europe move in here and there are some Chinese.

The natives are a very short Race of People. about 5 ft tall and very dark and will work all day for about $.21 ¢ American money. The rate of exchange for American Dollars here is about 13 to one and we use all native money as the Japs put a lot of counterfeit American Money out here in S. America. So the natives won't accept it. Also the natives charge the Americans about 3 times as much as they do natives as they think we are all millionaires and would sell their birth right for a pack of American Cigarettes and all the beggars in town follow us around and you almost have to kill a couple of shoe shine boys before they are convinced that you don't want a shine. The larger cities have quite modern buildings in them and good streets and American Motor Cars. You see more 42 model fords down here than you do back in the states matter of fact almost all the cars and trucks down here are Fords or Packards. Have you ever ridden in a French Taxi where they blow the horn all the time The people down here drive the same way but a lot faster. and more reckless.

I have learned to speak Spanish a little because you should never pay the Price that is posted on an article as the proprietor feels hurt if you don't try and Jew him down and will usually come down at least half but its hard to put a fast one over on them. The backbone of the poorer classes diet consists of bananas and rice. They do raise potatoes up in the mountains and eat those in place of rice. Tropical fruits abound in the costal region as it is semi tropical and in the mountains they raise Cereals and some vegetables. Their diets must lack a lot of calcium as most of the people have bad teeth and the older ones no teeth at all. and in general they are verry illiterate and their vocabulary is rather limited to ordinary speech such as they would use everyday. I don't think its much over 400 words.

Guess this will have to be all for now so I'll toss out the hooks.

Sincerely
Yours
"Dill" [Ens. D.K. Donielson]

P.S. The <u>Best</u> of All Things <u>Good</u> To You and <u>yours</u>

Please write if you have time and let me know how all the Luther fellas are getting on.[151]

✉      ✉      ✉      ✉      ✉      ✉

*The Caribbean offered the men beautiful surroundings, but also a degree of poverty they had not seen before.*

30 May 1944

Dear Chellis,

I suppose the folks have told you where I am by now. I asked my father to give you my change of address, but he is so busy it may have slipped his mind. Right now I'm in Puerto Rico teaching the native soldiers how to speak English.

It surprised me not a little to find that so many of the teaching techniques and principles that I learned from you, Ole Davidson, and the rest, apply themselves so well in this situation. I guess teaching is a lot the same, no matter if the subject is high school history or the most elementary English. At any rate, I'm very grateful for what you all taught me.

This is a beautiful place. Many times I've wished I had a camera so I could bring back with me some of the things I've seen. I often go to San Juan on Sundays and swim in the ocean. The city itself is beautiful, but most of the people are underprivileged and live in poverty and filth that I didn't even imagine existed.

The island is at least 90% Catholic, but there are churches of all denominations here.

There seems to be no middle class here. The people are either quite wealthy or very poor. According to the little history and economics you and Dr. Keilor were able to pound into my thick skull this must be a very spineless country. Didn't we always learn the middle class was the backbone of a nation.

By the way, I lacked 1 hr. of teaching practice teaching to get my teacher's certificate. I wonder if the work I am doing now would apply on that. If you would find out and let my father know when you see him I surely would appreciate it.

Also, if you would put my new address in your next letter some Luther grad stationed near here might see it. I keep looking for someone I know here, but so far, no luck.

Have to get to my class now. Greet all the faculty and my friends from me, and keep up the good work with your letters. They're almost as nice to get as a "sugar report."

Your friend,
Paul. [Linnevold]


P.S. As I read this over, I see it's certainly a mixed-up affair. Excuse it, please. I just wrote as I thought of something.

In case my father did give you my address, it has changed a little, so please use the address on the envelope.[152]

———————

*Linnevold followed this letter a few months later with another one specifically related to his future teaching certification.*

[Puerto Rico]

23 August 1944
Camp

Dear Chellis

I'll only be able to write you a short letter because I'm enclosing 3 copies of a letter from the director of the program I'm in down here. You see, I'm trying to get credit for ½ hour of practice teaching I lacked and Prof. Qualley told my dad I should get a letter from the head of the program. Will you please see that they get to the right person? I didn't know who to send them to.

Got your copy of the "Scuttlebutt" recently and enjoyed it very much as usual. I'm having a fine time down here and learning a-plenty. I don't think we'll be here too much longer but am about ready to move on anyway. As you well know almost all my buddies are right in the middle of this war and I've been watching from the bench long enough.

Hope you can have a good enrollment this fall and that the college can enjoy a successful year. Please greet all the faculty and any of my other friends who might be around there.—Thank you very much for taking care of this letter for me. Sincerely,

Paul [Linnevold][153]

———————

*With the end of hostilities in Europe, troops started moving toward the Pacific Theater, which meant that men like Linnevold would be seeing more troops pass through their areas.*

13 May 1945
Hospital

Dear Chellis,

I got another Scuttlebutt just the other day—which gave me much enjoyment and also served to remind me I should write you. Since I'm just laying around here recovering from a siege of dysentery, I'm going to take care of it now.

Got a letter from Davie Preus. He's almost through O.C.S. Although my opinion of most officers is none too high, I hope he can swing it. He is one fellow I think would make a good officer.

I'm sending a picture of Kenny Nesset and I. He's a Decorah boy in the Navy down here—a chief carburetor specialist. The picture was taken in front of his quarters—which are really beautiful. They make my barracks look like the crudest kind of woodshed. Wish I could have made the Navy instead of the Army—but don't you dare to breathe that to any of the Navy boys.

There's getting to be a little activity down here now. I wouldn't be too surprised if a lot of the troops down here started following Greeley's advice—via the canal.

Dillon Donielson got in touch with me a few months ago as he was passing though. We had a long talk. He looks pretty good—quite a bit heavier. Guess war and married life aren't treating him too badly.

Did you know Lorrie Ugland and his wife have become three. It's a boy—Lorrie Hilton Ugland, Jr.

If you happen to have Morris Ness and Don Strom's latest addresses I'd surely appreciate seeing them in the next Scuttlebutt. I've lost contact with them.

I'm still at the same job down here—but it can't last much longer—I hope. After that, I don't know what gives.

My brother took himself a spouse last winter—a Florida girl he met while at Camp Murphy, and plenty nice, too. He's at New River, N.C. now but doesn't know for how long.

Have to close now. Would like to send a contribution to the plaque but left my money back in the company. Will send some in my next letter, or drop into your office with it on my furlough—which may come soon.

Your friend,
Paul [Sgt Paul D Linnevold]

P.S. I'm now in the 2^ND Bn. instead of the 3^RD. Message Center gets sore at me for not notifying people of my change of address so please take care of it. Thank you.[154]

⊠ ⊠ ⊠ ⊠ ⊠ ⊠

*Service in the medical corps involved a wide range of activities, including some that the men had not anticipated.*

South America
13 October, 1944

Dear Prof. Evanson,

After your reminder in one of the recent circular letters, which by the way I have enjoyed very much, I have decided that it is time that I wrote you a few lines.

Since I have been in this country I have had quite a number of duties, most of which have been rather interesting. At the present time I am back at the old medical technologist grind which gets rather monotonous once in a while. Allow me to elucidate a bit on this medical technologist terminology. While I was stationed at Quantico, Virginia I was chosen to attend the medical laboratory school. This is a six month course dealing for the most part in examinations of the blood, urine, sputa, and so on, chemically and microscopically. We also delve into bacteriology to some extent, but to a lesser degree than the aforementioned. To be sure the greater part of the work is in connection with Venereal disease which, as you know, is rampant in these climes. It seems that the Navy boys are no exception. Malaria is also a factor here and we have done much interesting work in this field. I think that Miss Betty Reque is engaged in a similar type of work somewhere in a civilian hospital. I was engaged for one month in a distasteful yet interesting work of Venereal Disease Control. This dealt to some extent in statistics, but the majority of my time was spent in contacting the girls in the very numerous brothels who were reported to have a venereal disease. You can easily understand that I was not a very popular man in the minds of these creatures. I had first to learn the language well enough to make myself understood, and second to use enough tact to keep the girls in a jovial enough mood not to use a knife on me. One month of that was quite enough for any person I can assure you. Even though I am the tallest member of the family, I am far from a Goliath-Ha. I was stationed aboard a PCE (Patrol Craft Escort) for one month on temporary independent duty which was more a vacation than anything. I was a relief for the man who went to the states on an emergency leave. This type of vessel is 180 feet long and has a beam of 35 feet. (PLENTY ROUGH) The remainder of my ten months here has been entirely in connection with the Laboratory with the exception of one month as night supervisor.

Life here is just about as soft as one could possibly expect in any branch of the service. Sometimes I feel like I'm not doing very much in the war effort, but the Navy seems to leave me here. However, after Germany folds I expect the Pacific, or the Marines.

About two weeks ago I was a member of a party which took a trip to the various churches in this area. One of these churches is approximately 500 years old and is a point of much historical interest here. The old paintings and murals still retain the luster which they had when completed. One of the other churches has a chapel which is covered with gold leaf over exquisitely carves rosewood. A very impressive sight, but when I see the apparent poverty of the lower classes I wonder if the Almighty might not rather have this wealth go to some better end.

Although I have not met any Luther men here, our Pharmacist is a man from North Dakota and knows some of the boys from his vicinity who went to Luther. When I found that his name was Iverson and that he was from N.D., I thought that he must surely have some acquaintances who went to good old Luther. We have been good friends ever since.

Had a letter from "Babe" quite some time ago, he sounded like he was doing all right. One of my main points to expedite when the war is over is to see him and hash over old times.

I am very glad to know that Luther is going ahead with the plans of expanding and reconstructing. I wrote to my sister tonight and asked her to send you some of that "stuff" that the school needs so badly, so you should hear from her soon after you get this.

Well Prof., I might get home sometime next year and if so I plan to have a look around the campus. SO, if you see a little guy in a Navy uniform bearing a red cross you'll know who it is.

Respectfully,

"Mac" W.C. McEnelly PhM1c[155]

# CHAPTER 11

# "This Italy is some country"— Reports from Italy

*Troops serving in Italy represented a number of military units. Some arrived there after serving in North Africa, and eventually moved up the peninsula and into France, and ultimately Germany. Others flew bombing missions over a wide variety of targets, ranging from German military targets to Romanian oil fields. (Additional letters from Italy are included among the "Individual Correspondents.")*

---

*As the American troops advanced into Europe, Evanson's former students often commented on what they observed. Sometimes they mentioned how it related to the course he taught. And as Evanson intended with the newsletter, "Scuttlebutt" facilitated meetings between men who were serving near one another, who might not have known their whereabouts otherwise.*

Italy
10 March 1944

Dear Dr. Evanson:

Just last night I received your second news letter. The first one (your Christmas letter) arrived well over a month ago. I want to thank you very kindly for them. They are very much appreciated over here. Chips is appreciated too but it takes your letters to give us the real low-down on all the Luther fellows in service and elsewhere. Would you be kind enough to thank Coach Peterson for me for the letter he sent at Christmas time?

It was in your Christmas letter that I noticed Bud Eiden's address. Immediately I got busy and found out that he isn't so very far from me. As it turned out, I had the pleasure of spending one afternoon and one night with him. Believe me, we had plenty to talk about! We discussed everything from the food we get to politics—and we included the many times we sat in your history classes a couple years back. But most of all, we discussed how much we would like to be back home. If things work out well Bud might be able to pay me a return visit soon. Surely hope so.

This Italy is some country. For the first three weeks here one could have bought enough wine for five dollars to fill a bath tub—but to get that much hot water it would have cost twenty-five dollars! But the old Engineers got on the ball so we now boast a real hot shower. This country has been steeped so long in Fascism that it will take many years for the people to learn to think for themselves again. That is, if they ever have. Things are run too much like the old feudal system to suit the Americans.

My job is still that of a Chaplain's Assistant. My boss is Chaplain John David Larsen, an Augustana man and a real good Chaplain. I am learning much from working for and with him. After the war the training should come in very handy at the seminary.

Thanks again, Dr. Evanson, for the letters. Keep 'em coming. Please greet the other faculty members that I know. And when you write Chellis, Jr. give him a very special "hello".

Please correct my address on your records.

Sincerely yours,
Cpl. Willard L. Conradson "Connie"[156]

⋈ ⋈ ⋈ ⋈ ⋈ ⋈

*For some men, "Sunny Italy" did not live up to its reputation.*

[V-MAIL]

From: Sgt. James A. Haugen [No Date]

Hello—

For the past three or four months I've been getting "Scuttlebutt," but it's been having a hard a hard time catching up with me through three or four army post offices. And so, to give the postal clerks a break, I'm sending the correct address.

I'm stationed in Italy, and my job is that of a tail gunner on a B-14. Our crew, which trained together in the States and is still reasonably intact, has been her quite awhile, but we've done no flying. We're getting acquainted with Italians, and incidentally, with Italian mud. You may have heard some tell fables about Italinan mud, but they're all true—in fact, they're probably masterpieces of understatement.

Thanks for the issue of "Scuttlebutt," and would you mind giving the address to the Chips office? Thanks.

Sincerely,
James Haugen.[157]

⊠      ⊠      ⊠      ⊠      ⊠      ⊠

*For many of the men who had participated in the invasion of Italy, news of the D-Day invasion of France reminded them of their own experiences.*

In Italia
27 July 1944

Dear Dr. Evanson

Let me thank you and your staff of helpers for the fine contributions of morale which have come through Uncle Sammy's Postal System. In good order have arrived the Scuttlebutt issues of April 24, May on July 3, and July 6 on July 22. It is a fine effort and certainly one that has my encouragement for continuance. Particularly compliment the girl that runs the mimeo machine for I recall how that thing used to balk when News Bureau was expanding.

Just the same how are things going with you back ther? I trust well, and that you are concluding another successful summer session. How are the summers back there in Decorah now? Just as hot as a summer can be?

You must excuse me for not writing previously. What with the broadcast business and the advance into and past Rome one can become disinterested in writing. I have fallen away behind and in fact I owe something like 50 people right now. Oh, well, I have always considered letter-writing as a sort of hobby with me.

Want to thank you for the comments regarding what I might have done. People will really think I have done something. I have a couple of clippings enclosed which might be of interest to you. They appeared in the Stars and Stripes. That paper is quite popular with the troops, and the same day it is printed in Rome it is with frontline companies.

You will probably notice that I have added a little extra tracking material, in the form of captain's bars, and this event took place July 7th. Had been a 1st Lt. for 20 months, and an officer for two years, total army time from Private to Captain three years. So what, I always say. Anyway I am much tickled, and Gen. Clark pinned on the bars. Enclosed you will find a picture.

Was wounded at Anzio March 16, and now I am able to tell it. Was a victim of German (kraut) fighter-bombers, when two 500 lb bombs were dropped on our quarter. Suffered concussion and still do occasionally, and leg and ankle wounds. Received the Purple Heart. Came ashore on D Day, and finally we were released by the boys who do the fighting so we rear echelon joe's could reap the gravy of Rome.

Yes, Rome was darn nice. The welcome was terrific, the city was fascinating, and the girls were lovely. I entered in a half track with our radiostations, and early.

Well, your papee has brought a reunion. Connie Conradsen, a T/5, was over soon after, and then I also received letters from Orlo Walstad and Deacon Reynolds. Hope to really get near them for a littlebit of session soon. Did I ever tell you that George Sundahl was in my oldtank outfit, and that he came through Cassino in good fashion. He was at one time a good bow gunner in our Shermans.

You bet, I'll give Luther College a plug hereafter. Ireally erred at the time, but I hope to do better hereafter.

Have now been overseas some and almost 19 months but bank on a good many more. I do want to see several things and that is the French Riviera, Paris, London and certainly Norway where I have many relatives. Wouldn't be surprised that they expect me to show up sometime.

As I recall it Les Anderson said at graduation in 1940 that the class of '40 would have if possible a reunion in 1944. Well, June 1944 is passed but tell Les and all that we ought to start thinking about one in June of 1946. At least most of us might be able to attend then.

I'm wondering where Norm Bredesson is by now. The last time I saw him was in Naples in December.

Confidentially, I'm told that this Miss Olive Sharpee is pretty sharp. Someday I hope to come around the greensward and meet some of these Luther lovlies. In the meantime I'll sweat out an answer to a letter from her, which she does owe. And here we fellows go overseas and some would disappoint us on letters.

Hope Charlie Whiting comes through the raps in Normandy. I'll wager it is no tougher than Anzio ever was. Someone referred to Anzio as the largest prisoner of war camp the Jerries had, and for a long time it was virtually so, with only one gate out.

How is family these days.? Do greet each and everyone. Thanks to Chellis, Jr., for listening, too.

Right now I feel I must close. Let's keep them coming, these fine, informative letters. In the meantime thumbs up, as we are certainly over here. Bye.

Sincerely,

[Cap't] Jim Holmlund[158]

---

*Holmlund sent a similar report to a friend in the U.S., which was forwarded to Evanson as well:.*

[Handwritten note at top of page, writer unidentified:] (Fred sent this letter to me & sugged I send it on to you. Perhaps Jim has written you all this before.)

Fred J. Rosenthal USN 16129733

Captain James O. Holmulund
31 August 1944
In Italy

Dear Fred,

Really am on a spree tonight, writing some five letters but I need to; I'm 51 behind. How are you Fred? Gol, I appreciated your interest in writing and thanks lots for the nice things you added to your letter. Now if I can only keep a straight face when I get home, and see if I can live up to all of that. Your V Mail of June 8 arrived June 22d, Are you still in Denver? And that reminds me is that the city sold on the particular sandwich? Rather corny, but I could go for one just the same. Next time you dash one off I would appreciate it if you could send some Luther chatter along. You know there's a place that I don't feel deserving of, for I really goofed off there in not applying myself and in my general conduct. I often hate to visit there for that very reason but always do feel good when I come away.

How is your assignment coming? Sorry about your tough luck on aviation cadet training. Flying has never appealed to me. I did like tanking. Mist the boys in the tanks aplenty. My old outfit is now in France. They were the last out of Cassino in Feb. when we had tradgedy, and then among the first into Rome. I crossed the Volturno with them and came ashore at Salerno on D plus nine. In Africa we trained and missed the Tunisia show, but made the Morocco landings, at least part of us. I've been over 20 months, by the time you will have received this. The in late Nov. I was evacuated from combat with jaundice. Went on the Anzio in Jan. and landed on D Day which was simple. It was what came afterwards that as rough. Was wounded there March 16 from a fighter bomber attack. Got the P. Heart. I can't recall the last time I saw you either, but think it was in Sept. 1940, just before taking a job on a paper. You were buzzing around Decorah on some new scheme, forget which. Do you still claim beer as your most potent drink? We are finally getting it over here now, we of the ground forces. I think the ration this week is 12 cans per man. I shall claim mine with rest. Now that I re-read yours and mine above (letters) I'm wondering. Did you say that you were training in flying in Denver as well? That was downright uncanny how you heard the program from Anzio. I appreciate the comments. We had some 88 broadcasts from there, and 66 of them were rated good or excellent by the commercial people. We had such meager equipment, too. I recall some of the conditions. One night I was on for test in April and Jerry laid about 15 shells in the neighborhood. I continued for no damn good reason, and then looked around. Athe assistants were gone. I soon followed. We shall begin again with this proposition soon. Of course, I was in Rome. Arrived early, and in a halftrack with a radio. The welcome was terrific, and the girls were terrific. I've been back since, once on leave for five days. Among the things I accomplished was to take pictures, attend opera Rigoletto Royal Opera House and have a Turkish bath. And, of cours, sleep between sheets. Recently have been personally introduced to King of England, and was in personal party with Winston Churchill when he was here. Also, Lily Pons and Andrew K. were here, and though I enjoyed it, they did not go over as well as they should have. How's the Elk's coming, and is Chellis and Elk-ite yet? Do tell him hello, and when you write your folks, as well. What you going to do after this war ol' man? For me—revive my mind, my love life, my play time and that includes some Heiliman's beer. Must close. See you, and sooner via letter. Bye,

Sincerely,
Jim.[159]

⊠ ⊠ ⊠ ⊠ ⊠ ⊠

*Holmlund's experiences included meeting some prominent Britons.*

[V-MAIL]
From: Captain James O. Holmlund Q-1010922; 16 Sept 44—In Italy
Dear Dr. Evanson,

Can't promise too much of a letter this evening. You see I'm entertaining a case of skin disease known as impytigl; not too serious but it sure make me keep my beard for a good while without shaving. How is the new school year shaping up? Seems to me it started two days ago. As you can read we are starting to roll again, and I hope we can finally clean this place out. Thank you again for the complimentary remarks made in your Aug 9th edition received the 20th. I had managed to stay out of Luther print for a few years and now I feel I've had sufficient for a good while. I'm not making any history anyway so as the censors do to copy over here will you do to my name there? Please, and don't be offended for I do like to read about the rest of the gang. Seems that most of Luther went to the South Pacific. Who knows but that I might wind up there as well. How does the News Bureau shape up for this year? Gol, I used to spend a lot of time in there, and enjoyed it, too. Don't know whether I'll carry on with my attempts at News work after this war or not. All of our lives will be one big adjustment after another. I'm thankful for one thing and that it that didn't marry before I took this rap. Gol, I started my 21st month the other day. Had a birthday, too; 26. Did I tell you that I had met and been presented personally to the King of England? Yeah, Gen. Clark did the presenting, and first I stopped, saluted and then we both grabbed on. (George and I). Then Churchill was here one day and wore us all out with his pace and his cigar fumes. Got into Rome for five day leave some time back, and managed an opera and a Turkish bath among other things of interest. Time to seal this up. Best of luck for the coming year. Greet Mrs. Evanson and Ch.. Jr. and all. We'll see you all before 1950.

(s)James O. Holmlund
Sincerely, Jim H.[160]

⊠ ⊠ ⊠ ⊠ ⊠ ⊠

*Picture postcards of famous landmarks provided the opportunity for some humorous comments.*

Dear Dr.

I think our engineers can straighten it.

John [Ensign John C. Sorlien] [161]

⊠    ⊠    ⊠    ⊠    ⊠    ⊠

*As the holidays approached, memories of Christmas festivities at Luther came to mind for many men.*

[V-MAIL]
From: Lt. M.E. Vrolstad 0719490 26 Nov '44
   Finally made it—in Italy. I'd like to get that Navy propaganda you issue & Chips. Assigned to a Fighter Group & will fly the P-51 with the 15th Air Force. Hope you've got some snow & the whole college enjoys its usual Christmas. Right now I miss that lefse supper.
                    —Merald[162]

⊠    ⊠    ⊠    ⊠    ⊠    ⊠

*The men recognized that while they were not all in direct combat duty, they each played a part in the overall war effort.*

July 26, 1945
Italy

Dear Dr. Evanson,
   Next month I will have two years overseas and have intended to drop you a line ever since I received the first "Scuttlebutt". I guess that is tops in neglecting

174

to drop a few lines of appreciation. I have enjoyed every issue of Scuttlebutt immensely and have always looked forward to each one.

I spent nearly a year in Africa and about the same here in Italy. All of my time has been spent with Allied Force Headquarters handling communications. I guess a lot of Luther men are doing a bigger part than I by defeating the enemy directly and being in the midst of it all. This is the job the army has given me and I am doing my best at it.

I haven't met any Luther men overseas but my thoughts have often returned to Luther and have made me very anxious to finish my education as soon as possible with renewed ambition. I feel it will give me great enjoyment to put everything I have into it.

I have enjoyed reading about the Luther men scattered all over the globe and am sorry I delayed so long the acknowledgement of appreciation for Scuttlebutt. Thank you very much. I am enclosing a money order for $5 which is my contribution to the Plaque Fund.

All the pictures I have taken here I have sent home so my family will be relaying one down there.

Thank you again for the interesting news in Scuttlebutt. I have also been receiving the college Chips and enjoying it.

Very sincerely yours,
John Meyer[163]

# CHAPTER 12

# "So Cheerio, all the best"— Reports from the United Kingdom

*In the spring of 1944, the number of American troops in Britain continued to grow as the Allies prepared for the D-Day invasion on June 6.*

[V-MAIL]
From: Lt. V.M. Larson, 0-873063 March 30, 1944
Dear Friends,

Just a few lines to let you know that I have arrived in England. As yet I haven't had a chance to do much sightseeing but what I saw of the country as we came to our present station seemed very nice. Things are beginning to turn green—I guess we came during the right part of the year. They say it gets pretty cold in the winter.

I don't know how many are left of the Class of '44, but if there are any around I'd like to say hello to them, as that was my old class. Maybe someday I'll get a chance to finish.

If anyone wants to write me, I'd certainly appreciate hearing from them.

Sincerely
Vernon M. Larson[164]

⊠        ⊠        ⊠        ⊠        ⊠        ⊠

*Men stationed in Britain had to adjust to a number of changes, not least of which was driving on the opposite of the street.*

9th APRIL 1944

Dear Friends Chellis & Family,& Luther College;

Another long lost but not forgotten soldier reporting to the line up of letter writers, to friends and comrades of Luther, Bly-me I have had the notion so many times to get a letter off to you and answer the many I have received from you and Pete and Dr. Preus and Mr Hanson I am ashamed of my self, to show up again here you should have received more letters from me than any one else in the service because I believe I was the first one to go of any with relations to Luther College. and I bet you Have received less from me than any one else in the service, I have been very angry with myself each time I received a letter that stated, letters were received from, so and so, with some interesting remarks following; My name was mentioned several times so I knew I was not forgotten But I haven't shown much appreciation of the fact I'm not a good hand at writing letters, I have an awful time keeping up with letters I receive from my own folks. Dwight and Gladys write me real often and if they get one letter to 3 they write they are very fortunate.

I RESOLVE now at the beginning of my fourth year of service with my dear old uncle sam to write more letters Its rather late but better late than ever, Yes the fourth year begins to morrow; Three years ago this morning I went and fixed the fires in Campus House and Sunnyside before breakfast, did a few other small jobs that were necessary went to the office and drew the portion of my wages I had coming to me thus far in the month and put a few t things together had a very good dinner, Chas. fried me a steak as only Chas. could fry, so I would have good substancal filling to stand the bus ride to Fort DesMoines this afternoon; Then at 1300 hours (1 O'Clock it was to me then) the college truck taxied me down town to the buss station shauffered by Adolph and I left for what I figures would be a 3 or 4 day leave just long enough to go to DesMoines to have it out that they couldn't use me or didn't need me in the army, but figures sure lies that time, 4 days later I was a soldier of the United States Army and in Jefferson Barracks Mo. and Have been getting further away every move I have made; Yes 3 years ago, and it seems like 3 centuries. 2 years,1 month 3 weeks and 1 day over seas to night. After a number of days on the North Atlantic and I'll say Rough with a capital R. Land came into sight, and I'll bet that Columbus wasn't half as pleased to see it as I was; I got sea sick the last 4 days of the voyage after having quick fried liver and onions for supper, fried nice and brown on the outside but very much alive on the inside, which tasted very good and I being hungry ate a good portion of it, and a few hours afterwards the fish got it second handed; I didn't get straightened out again till I got on land, I cant say dry land because it was raining when we disembarked in a city in North Ireland, where I enjoyed myself very much for 11 months living with the Irish. Than after an all night boat ride and a train ride the next day I was in England,[165] and have been in England and wales since. I was transferred into a medical unit while I was in North Ireland yet and have worked in that capacity ever since,(I put a new ribbon in this machine to get plainer letters, I got em). As soon as I got down here I started driving an ambulance,and that is the greater part of my duty for the past year; I have had British made ambulances to drive most of the time, the lend,lease,you know; We lend them ours and lease theirs and you drive on the wrong side of theroad with the steering wheel on the right side of the vehicle which of course is the wrong side from ours, shift with the left hand, pass another vehicle on the right side, and I do pass a lot of them. It took a long time to get use to all of that but it is quite natural after a year of it. I'll be needing an instructor to teach me how to drive on the other side of the road when and IF the time comes for me to drive on the roads back there. The other work in connection with medical work is very interesting thou not always pleasant, I have helped take patients from Hospital ships returned from Africa and other places as-Well its just not pleasant, enough said. and there is minor accidents etc. very often. I work in the dispensary when I'm not driving the ambulance on some trip; my trips take me to hospitals, other camps, ports, towns etc. its one way of getting around and seeing the country, and it would be much more interesting if the people or the engineers that constructed the roads in this country would have laid them more straight, you are constantly going around curves turning corners going up or down hill and quite often doing all at once, so I have to keep a close eye on the road, which dont give me much of a chance to look to the side of the road to get good views of the landscape through which I travel. it is very beautiful how ever, several times I have stoped on the side of the road on top of some hill just to get a good look around and it is worth it too. There are 3 dogs and 1 cat less in this country than before i started driving over here. outside of that I have not had an accident and dont intend to now.

In every camp I have been stationed in,I have got acquainted fast made many friends and also in the towns villages or cities which ever it happened to be, I have been to a good many private homes visiting and really enjoyed my self. due to the rationing over here which is a good deal less than over there the folks sort of feel discouraged, or ashamed,(would describe it better) that they cant serve a lunch of cake, pie iced cookies perhaps ice cream etc. that they are sure that we would have were we at our own homes, it takes a lot of explaining and describing to get them to understand that the war is having its effect on that country too maby not to the same extent as over here but they aren't having a lot of the things they had before too, and that is minor,it sure means a lot to us to be invited to some home and sit with folks and visit hear about the people and the country and get away from the rugged routine of the army camp for a few hours or days, as it may be. Some how or other I manage to make them feel very much at ease and they do set out a lunch very tasty and appreciative, they set out their rations and say help your self, and I know that if I take 2 spoonsful of sugar in my Tea, yes I say tea, that they will have to have a cup of tea some time or other without any sugar in, etc. I'm (personally speaking, because never drink coffee) very fortunate that I'm in a country where they drink tea to the extent they do and not coffee, or I'd sure be out of luck, so I have that to be thankful for.

I'm wondering if you have ever heard from any of the Nickoley boys, I dont remember that I have seen or read anything of any of them in your letters, and have looked for some word of them. I had a letter from Carl Nickoley at Christmas time and he told me about the boys but I havent heard or them since.

I have several letters from Earl Peters from North Ireland, hes a sgt. now. Thats what I should be, but I hope to be before long.

There is a dance being held here in camp to-night in our new recreation hall which has just been completed sort of an initiation or dedication, shall we call it. had a show in it a couple nights ago its 120 foot long and 70 foot wide, and a canteen where they serve tea and biscuits, plain cupcakes sandwiches and they aren't hamburgers or hotdogs either, they are jelly, lettuce, fish paste beet peanut butter, or else just plain Oleomargarine, of course they call it butter, If a fellow don't know the differents why hes just that much more satisfied. and draught beer on certain days,

Well I guess I have covered the highspots from the day I left Luther college It is hard to picture the campus with Old Main no more on it. and from descriptions of the changes that have been make in other buildings, How many changes have been in the staff? since I was there,that would be very interesting to know. Is Ole Korsrud still tending the boilers? and August,

179

Has Adolph got that truck wore out yet? and Martin Borgon still sweeping the gym, etc. Give my best regards to Mrs Molli, Mrs Harold Settje, that was a surprise, Is Mrs Olson still working in the B.C. That goes for her too and Mrs.??? (Bly-me I cant think of the lady's name that did the washing at the B.C. its plum slipped my mind) but that goes for her too, and now I must sign off thanking you verry much for the letters to us men in the service, I'm looking forward to meeting you all and gosh there will be a homecoming that the History of L.C. has never witnessed somewhere in the next couple of years I hope and prey that I will be one of them present, I shall write you another letter before long that will bear rather astonishing news of which I wont mention now. so Cheerio, all the best,

Cpl. George R. Dirksen[166]

    ✉       ✉       ✉       ✉       ✉       ✉

*Some men saw duty in several areas before D-Day, ranging from North Africa to Britain. The growing number of American troops stationed in the British Isles was a potential source of tension and problems in terms of relations with the local population.*

Somewhere in the British Isles
19 April, 1944

Dear Chellis,

Your letters have been such a pleasure and lift to me the last year that I feel the least I can do in appreciation is give you a little dope on what I've been doing and have seen as of late.

As you probably know, I didn't waste much time getting overseas. However, I had ten days in New York while attending school on Staten Island. While I was there I stayed with my uncle, Rev. Carl Lucky on L.I. That was too good to last, of course, so I was overseas and on my ship for the Salerno show which is an old story by now. That was really a hot affair, but I came through without a scratch. Since that, I've had a lot more respect for the British than I had before. While I was in that area, I had the opportunity of seeing such places as Tunis, Oran, Tripoli, Naples, and Palermo. I can sum my opinion of N. Africa up in two words. It stinks! Of course, the bizarre aspects of the country were interesting in spite of the fact that one has to hold his nose to enjoy them. The Arabs (Ay-rhabs), the mosques, palm trees, deserts and all, became reality rather than something

I'd read about in geography books. During a slack period I had an opportunity to drive to Tunis in a jeep and made an inspection of the ruins of Carthage with the assistance of an Arab kid, only two glad to show me around—for a price, of course. While I was there, I kept thinking how much John V. Halvorson would have enjoyed seeing the ruins.

The scenery in Italy and Sicily is beautiful, indeed. It's impossible to describe the rugged beauty of those countries. Their ruggedness doesn't seem to be doing us much good now, however, and from the condition of the people living there, I'd say it didn't do them much good either. Mt. Vesuvius and Isle de Capri gave me quite a thrill: I didn't have an opportunity to visit Pompeii which I regret very much, but there is a limit to the sight seeing a Navy man can do, too. The Italians were extremely friendly (once we got ashore) and even with the war front so close, they seemed to be more concerned over their opera than the war.

During the Christmas holidays I had a couple pleasant jolts when I accidentally bumped into Evans Knudsen and Orlow Walsted. Didn't have a chance to talk with Evans very long but I knocked around with Orlow for a couple of days. We had a wonderful time talking over Luther, the band, senior picnics, etc. You probably know he married a nice looking gal from Georgia and is exec on his Y.M.S. 28, […] Those are the only two Luther men I've seen so far. I knew "Crusty" was in that area but didn't locate him.

Although the Med. was interesting it was a break to get out of there. Yes, I know there is a nasty job coming up here soon, but I rather look forward to the event that's going to clean this mess up. It's not going to be very pleasant, but I hope I come through ok so I can get back to a lot of people I really miss. After all, that's what I'm fighting for. The Four Freedoms make a nice sounding phrase but it doesn't mean much to millions of boys who are playing a grim game that they didn't ask for. Well, guess I'd better not start talking to you about geopolitics and international relations.

Speaking of relations, the Anglo-American sailors are getting on quite well. The serious minded British frankly, although sometimes reluctantly, acknowledge the American invasion of England, a fact, their salvation. I've banged ears with enough British gold braid to know that they really are thankful for our presence here, in spite of any adverse publicity that may reach the states.

I spent a five day leave in London and really enjoyed myself seeing Westminster Abby, Parliament, No. 10 Downing, St. James Park, Trafalgar Square, the results of the blitz etc. London is still quite a town, actually (ek-tchually)!

Once again, thanks heaps for the "scuttlebutt." You're doing all of us fellows a wonderful service. Hope I get home this summer—if so I'll drop in and have a chat with you.

Respectfully yours,
Don [Gjerdrum][167]

---

*Gjerdrum's letter also contained the following description of his unit's mascot and motto:*

### "WE DELIVER"

One afternoon just after the fall of Palermo, Sicily; two junior officers were observed returning to the ship. In their wake a small Sicilian boy; laboring under the weight of what appeared to be a large stuffed bird. The gangway watch was heard to ask of the messenger, "What the hell is that?"

"It's a crane," said the messenger.

"No, it's a heron," said a bystander,

As the officers approached the ramp; the officer of the deck asked;

"Where did you get that sea gull?"

With dignity, the officer replied. "That, my dear sir, is a Sicilian stork, the bird that delivers."

This title was accepted and so it came to pass, the stork, named Palermo Pete, now stands, majestically, in a corner of the wardroom; and who is referred to as our mascot.

To look at Pete, standing in his corner, feathers ruffled, tail missing, and minus his starboard eye (the results of a terrific bombing) but still there he stands, looking satisfied and very proud. What does he have to be so proud of? We quickly recalled: He was the bird that delivers.

Having just participated in the successful invasion of Sicily; and having had the good fortune of being one of the first American LST's to enter Syracuse, (under attack by E-boats). There is no doubt: "Pete" and ourselves had much in common, because, we also had delivered.

"We Deliver" has become the proud motto of every man on board.

A short time ago Palermo Pete standing proudly as usual in his corner of the wardroom and, we all imagined, a determined expression radiated about him as he stared from his one and only eye while the Group Commander instructed officers of an assault group. There was going to be another invasion. As history will prove, Pete was correct.

The LST 357 carried out her part, gallantly and successfully, in the never to be forgotten assult on Italy, at Salerno. After the battle clouds had risen, those of us who remained joined with Pete to remind the world, with pride, that, "We Deliver".

When the end has come, the battle over, and we have won, the familiar antics shall prevail again the wardroom. Palermo Pete will stand—At ease. The. tension gone and the past a grim memory; a proud atmosphere prevails about the ship. We have accomplished a difficult task against the bitter opposition. With pride in ourselves, for the country we love————"WE DELIVER" [168]

⊠　　　⊠　　　⊠　　　⊠　　　⊠　　　⊠

*The men transferred to England generally found a warm welcome. Despite rationing at home, the men often had items that had long been hard to find in Britain.*

6-2-44

Dear Chellis,

Thanks very much for placing my name on the distribution list for your Christmas greetings. That general news letter certainly was a masterpiece. I don't see how you were able to accumulate and compile all the information therein contained. I also received Pete's greeting and the December issue of the Bulletin, both of which reached me after a roundabout journey reflecting glory on the accomplishments of the Army Postal Service. So much news from Luther College led an English officer friend of mine to comment on how well we are treated by friends back home and to observe that he could hardly picture an English institution or faculty doing anything comparable to it. Perhaps you are familiar with the monthly communique which Miss Cox at Iowa U. distributes to a fairly numerous and very scattered group of former students there.

Perhaps I ought to relieve your mind of any apprehensions which may have been occasioned by Harriet's sending over a few cosmetics. I was amazed at the reception such junk received from English women. If I could repack my footlocker now for a trip overseas I'd put in a supply of such stuff, for it's certainly popular. The same holds true for countless other articles. "American" candy, chewing gum, cigarettes, cigars, tobacco, clothing, dried fruits, canned goods, and dozens of other articles never go begging. At Christmas time I, a non-smoker myself, bought cigars at our PX for 4 d each and gave them to some of my English friends. They refused to believe that I could get what they claimed were very good quality cigars for such prices, while they often had to pay as many shillings for the very limited number available.

I've certainly enjoyed the months I've spent over here in England. I'm sure I have acquired a much more realistic picture of English life, government, character, and so on than I had before. I have discovered quite a number of things in which I think England and the English are very much inferior to us, but at the same time their strong points are very evident too. I've had an excellent opportunity to see England as it really is, since I have had private quarters ever since I arrived, first as a roomer in an English private home and later as a hotel "guest."

Thus far I haven't had an opportunity to see very many of the famous places I used to come across in English History. I have spent some time nosing about London and I once spent part of a day in Cambridge, but both places need a lot more attention and dozens of other sites are on the itineraries of whatever future journeys the exigencies of way may permit.

Thank you once again for the greetings and here's wishing you and Luther College the best of good fortune until we once again can do something more tangible than wish.

Sincerely, [Lt.] Selmer [Norland][169]

✉    ✉    ✉    ✉    ✉    ✉

*The D-Day Invasion of Normandy on June 6, 1944 was a major event, even for support troops who did not participate in the actual landing.*

[Letterhead: Officer's Club, European Theater of Operations]
12 August, 1944

Dear Chellis,

It's been too long since I last wrote to my old friends at Luther, so I'd better write now before I neglect it any longer.

Those news letters of yours are really swell—I certainly get a kick out of them, and pick up a few addresses that I've been wanting to know.

As yet, I haven't managed to run across any Luther men over here. I've been hoping to, but it just hasn't been my luck so far. You've mentioned lots of boys who are over here but I haven't made contact yet.

I've been keeping contact with a few fellows—Don Olikeid, Gene Olson, Gordon Benson to mention some of them. It will really be swell when we can all get back together again.

Larsen Hall really ought to look swell when they get through with it. I'll certainly look forward to a visit when this war is over—which I hope is soon. The reports sound pretty good from most places. It makes me sort of mad though to read about all the strikers back in the states. Some people get optimistic a little bit too soon.

So far, this stay in England hasn't been so bad. It's been quite nice lately—almost like summer in the states. Until recently, however it was usually quite cool.

"D" Day is over two months past now. I guess you folks back in the states "sweated it out" just about as we did over here. Our outfit took part, of course, but being a ground officer, I couldn't do much more than wait for the boys to get back. It certainly was a moment I'll never forget, and I doubt if anyone who had anything to do with it ever will. It was hard to realize just how momentous an occasion it really was.

Well, that seems to be about all I can think of just now. I'll be looking forward to your next news letter. I always hope you might give an address that might be close to me here. I don't recall any of the boys who got into Troop Carrier. I haven't heard of any yet who did. If you ever hear from a Lutherite who is in Troop Carrier, I wish you'd put his address in one of your letters.

So long for a while—

Vern Larson

P.S. I don't know whether you hear from any of my brothers or not so I might include a few words about them. Wendell is a Marine Lieutenant flying Corsairs and at present in San Diego. David is an Ensign instructing at the Midshipman's School at Northwestern. I believe he's teaching seamanship and damage control. My oldest brother Harold—I don't know if you have met him—is a Petty officer 3/c, I believe and should be in Chicago now too. He's in Navy radio and going to school yet.

I guess that's all now, so I'll sign off again
I almost forgot to mention——hat I was promoted to 1st Lt. in June
Vern Larson[170]

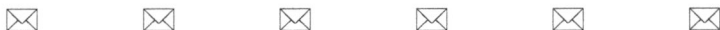

&#9993;  &#9993;  &#9993;  &#9993;  &#9993;  &#9993;

*On May 31, 1942, fire destroyed "Old Main," the central building on the Luther College campus. Memories of that event remained vivid for the students who saw it.*

Somewhere in England
August 23, 1944

Dear Chellis,

Thanks for the Shuttlebutt issue which I just received over here in blimey Britain. When I receive such items from the familiar campus I can look out over the landscapes of Europe and almost read into it the beauteous environs of the late Soli Deo Gloria tower we used to know at Luther. It's been only a little more than 2 years since I was dodging the firey and exploding embers of burning Old Main, but it seems like centuries.

Noble of you to include all the addresses of Luther Service-men in your Shuttlesheet—and I see a lot of names I know—but I shall utter terrible oaths if you don't include mine next time. I'm an old candidate for recognition in that sheet, this being not the first time I've written you.

The United States Army has involuntarily convinced me that what I'll have to shout about after the war will require a pulpit and considerable prestige, so let me speak my little piece for the Luther bandwagon by stating my intention to return to the campus there after the war. Please keep the functions of education from folding up until that time. Brigadier General Hershey has just stated that it would be cheaper to keep everyone in the army after the war than to feed them otherwise, but I assure you we shall assert our desire for freedom again one day.

Best regards to your history books and their victims,
[Sgt] Lloyd W. Ruid[171]

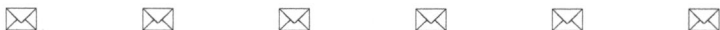

&#9993;  &#9993;  &#9993;  &#9993;  &#9993;  &#9993;

*Training did not stop when the men left the United States. Additional preparation overseas was common, and in some instance, it even involved entirely new activities.*

[Letterhead: United States Army]

Somewhere In England

Oct. 16, 1944

Dear Dr. Evanson,

Saturday I received your most interesting copy of the Scuttlebutt for August. Thank you very much.

I sure would like to see the inside of Larson Hall when they finish remodeling it. I bet it will really look nice.

I heard from Richard Ulvilden a few days ago. He also told me that Chet Potter, Karsten Ulvilden, & Jack Daley were all in the Navy. I also hear from Erling Jacobson quite often. I sure wish I was back there again now.

I have been in England about three weeks now. It has been raining a great deal here. It is also colder here than it was back in the States. Most of my old outfit has left me now. The only reason that I am still here is because I signed up for the paratroops. I tried it back in the States but I was to heavy then. I don't know as yet when our jump training will begin, I guess the first week of physical training is the toughest. The third day you have to double time fifty minutes without resting. We have been doing a little double timing & push up's by ourselves in the evenings in preparation for jump school.

So coach Peterson is playing a football team again this year. I sure wish I was there playing again—I feel as if I could do much better now that I weigh 185 pounds instead of the 210 lbs. I weighed last fall. Wish Coach Peterson & the boys all the luck in the world for me.

I wish you would greet Dr. Preus, Dr. Qualley, Dr. Nelson and the rest of the facility that I know.

I will be looking forward to your next issue of the Scuttlebutt.

A Luther member

Oral [Pvt. Oral A. Solbro][172]

⊠ ⊠ ⊠ ⊠ ⊠ ⊠

*A few of the Navy men served on British ships. With the invasion of Germany imminent, some expected to be transferred to the Pacific Theater soon.*

26 November 1944

Dear Chellis,

Just a word of heartfelt thanks for your splendid effort in extending to us the latest info on all our many friends in the service and at college. It is certainly appreciated and has enabled us to keep in contact with each other through change of address etc. By way of information my present address is Navy 416 and no longer #3952. Would appreciate it if you would make the change on your files. Might say that I have located Chas Whiting's camp and hope to see him shortly; thanks to your efforts. At present my assignment is quite interesting and secure but not too lasting as we all feel the call of the Pacific. Since coming off a Limy cruiser on which I served prior and after the invasion until August 13th, I have been Base Personnel officer at one of the bases in Southern England. It is pleasant but has its heartaches.

Thanks again, Lt. j.g. EN Larson[173]

$\boxtimes$      $\boxtimes$      $\boxtimes$      $\boxtimes$      $\boxtimes$      $\boxtimes$

*With the Allies advancing against German defenses, the men who were still serving in England recognized that their conditions were usually much better than those of their colleagues on the continent.*

[V-MAIL]

From: Lt. Selmer S. Norland 25-12-44

Dear Chellis, The arrival today of the September issue of Scuttlebutt not only served as a very effective stimulus to thoughts about home and friends on this Christmas day but reminded me that I should very probably receive these very welcome letters more punctually if you had the most recent version of my address, that given in the upper righthand corner of this letter. I'm glad that the College recognizes the interest displayed by Luther men and women everywhere in these letters and is cooperating with you in seeing that they continue. The job must have developed into a big one judging from the great number of people and incidents which are brought into each.

This is my second Christmas in England. Uncle Sam certainly did everything in his power to make it a happy one, particularly from the Christmas dinner point of view. I must admit that I have never eaten a more delicious meal. I'm afraid that a good many Americans on or near the front line have not been nearly so lucky. The Germans are proving themselves to be very resourceful and dangerous even when they apparently are on the run, but fortunately the end is inevitable.

It was fun to see the name Luther appear in the football score column in Stars and Stripes occasionally this fall, even if on the wrong side of the score. I hope it will not be long before Luther teams again become the team to beat in the Iowa Conference. Thanks again for keeping me on your circulation list and best wishes for a happy and successful New Year.

Greet Fadness for me.

Sincerely, Selmer Norland[174]

$\boxtimes$ $\boxtimes$ $\boxtimes$ $\boxtimes$ $\boxtimes$ $\boxtimes$

*In addition to planning to return to Luther to finish their own studies, the men also tried to recruit other students to join them there.*

[V—MAIL] [No Date]

TO: Mr. Carl K Norgaard
FROM: Sgt. Lyle Larson
Dear. Mr. Norgaard:

It has been a year and a half since I left Luther College. The school has kept me well informed in its happenings through Chips as well as the Alumni paper. I would be very glad if they would keep that up for me while I am across as well as when I am in the States. If it were possible for them to send me this year's edition of Pioneer, I would like it very much also.

I hope to return to Luther when this war is over and finish out my studies that I have for graduation. I have five other people who want to come to Luther when the war is over and start. I hope I will find more by the time I am ready to return.

I bet the school is changed a lot from what it was. Now there are more girls than boys, but still it cannot beat the ratio we have here in England—there are ten girls to every boy, which is really something. If one is walking down the street they will come up and ask you for a date.

If at all possible, may I have a list of men from Luther in England. Thanks

As ever,
Lyle Larson[175]

✉   ✉   ✉   ✉   ✉   ✉

*Evanson occasionally received press releases reporting the accomplishments of the former Luther students.*

Alumni Secretary, Luther College, Decorah, Iowa

An Eighth Air Force Bomber Station: England: Captain E.G. Mills of Fort Dodge, Iowa, has recently been awarded the Distinguished Flying Cross for extraordinary achievement in aerial combat.

Pilot on a B-17 Flying Fortress heavy Bomber, Capt. Mills has completed 30 daylight bombing assaults against Nazi Germany's war machine in Europe.

On a recent mission Capt. Mills was leading his group of bombers over Cologne, Germany, one of the Reich's most heavily defended cities, when a burst of enemy anti-aircraft fire knocked out one of his engines. It proved to be only the beginning of his troubles. Just before reaching the target, two more engines failed due to the malfunction of superchargers. The heavy Fortress bomber was dropping about 600 feet a minute as Capt. Mills fought desperately to make a successful bomb run. With his skilled flying ability and the combined efforts of the crew, the bombs plummeted earthward directly into the target area. The rest of Capt. Mills' formation of Fortresses were able to drop their bombs on his, and completed an excellent pattern of destruction on the target.

Unable to maintain the lead position in his squadron, Capt. Mills dropped out of formation and flew at a low altitude where superchargers are not necessary. The 23-year-old captain brought his crew back to England on three engines and landed safely at their home base.

Lady Luck flew with Capt. Mills again on a bombing attack over Brunswick, Germany. During this operation his formation was under constant enemy fighter attack for an hour. Though explosive bullets burst all around the aircraft, a highly successful bombing was done without loss of any aircraft or personnel.

Capt. Mills, son of Mr. & Mrs. O. H. Mills and husband of Mrs. E. G. Mills, 2002 6th Avenue N., Fort Dodge, Iowa, has also won the Air Medal and three Oak Leaf Clusters.

Before entering the AAF on December 9, 1940, he was a student at Luther College in Decorah, Iowa. Since his arrival in the European Theatre of Operations, Capt. Mills has been serving with the veteran 305th Bombardment Group.[176]

⊠        ⊠        ⊠        ⊠        ⊠        ⊠

*Almost all of the men and women writing to Evanson were serving in the United States armed forces. But at least one was in the Canadian army. His off-hand note at the end of the letter suggests the frequency with which such events occurred. .*

March 1, 1945

Editor of Scuttlebutt

Dear Friend:

In a way it seems like a long time since I attended Luther College. And, considering the many changes which may have taken place since then, it is a long distance back.

My address has changed from western Canada to—

E. O. Walker, H/Capt & Chaplain [...]

In Scuttlebutt I see many familiar names. And I am sure that the Luther men are well represented among the men of renown!

It will be a joy, someday, to see Luther again. And meet friends and old acquaintances.

We'll be remembering Luther with a "peace offering."

Greetings and best wishes, in His name,

Sincerely,

Emil O. Walker

Note: Sounds like a V2 just fell near, can be serious enough, indeed.[177]

# CHAPTER 13

# "The little guy with the rifle"—
# Reports from France and the Low Countries

*The D-Day Invasion at Normandy on June 6, 1944, dramatically transformed the war. A number of Luther men played active roles in that invasion.*

7 July 1944
France

Dear Chellis,

Received your last letter the other day & decided it was time to write a belated "Thanks" I really enjoy your newsy epistles & appreciate being on your mailing list.

I have a change of address, but don't know how definite this is so please keep sending to the '5+'. I've been here since the day the Big Show opened & have seen this place grow. Naturally I can't say much about it, but I guess you know it was quite a production—was glad to have had the opportunity to put my 2 cents.

I was a small boat (LCVP) officer aboard an LST & my future, as nearly as I can figure it out, is a big question mark. Sure would like to get a crack at the 'real' Navy.

My contacts with Luther fellows have been few, but I was fortunate enough to run into Eddie Larson a few times in Eng. We agreed that we're both looking forward to that 1st big reunion at old L.C.

About time to hit the sack so will sign off—please give my regards to Pete, Dean Fadness & the rest. Thanks again—[Ens. M.G.] Ness

P.S. Wish I could have put more time on my French—although my chances of using it are rather infrequent.[178]

---

*Ness' friend, Eddie Larson, wrote to Evanson at about the same time, just as he was about to leave England for the continent.*

Friday July 14th—'44

Dear Chellis,

Just a brief note to express my sincere appreciation for the newsy letters, which we are all so happy to receive. They have been the source of much enjoyment and have answered many questions concerning addresses of classmates, etc. Keep up the good work as there is nothing outside of spiritual means that brings more comfort to us than letters from friends. Thank you again.

I had the good fortune of having Ens. Morris Ness aboard for lunch yesterday. We had an interesting bull session re our experiences since our last meeting in England. He played a very significant role in the operation of D-Day and came out looking none the worse. I believe he is gaining weight and with his crew cut & split uniform he was hard to recognize. We may see quite a lot of each other. Ness' ability to handle men is indeed noteworthy.

While at an English base I was pleased to note the comments on another Luther man. I was engaged in lengthy conversation with Lt. Cmdr Dunn, who formerly was in charge of Welfare and Recreation at the Londonderry Base. He was succeeded by Butch Stolfa and had only the highest praise for Butch's ability and leadership.

As for myself there is little to say. I enlisted in USNR as a Yeoman after completing my junior year and as sent to Cleveland, Ohio, where I remained until March of 1943. The work there was quite interesting but very tiresome and hardly creditable as far as helping to win the war is concerned. It was with Naval intelligence and probably the biggest collection of "gold brickers" in the Navy. (This does not hold true for men & officers stationed outside the continental limits [with due respects to Lt. Haatvedt who I'm sure is doing a fine job]). The old man pushed through to BuPers my application for commission and I was sent to Northwestern where I received my commission on July 1st 1943. From there it was Little Creek, Va—Ft. Pierce, Fla, back to Little Creek, Lido Beach N.Y. England and now out. Don't know where it will be from here but trust it will be for the best.

Hope to see you again at Luther when this mess is over—made use of my pilots license obtained while at Luther, for a joy ride one Sunday in England.)

Sincerely,

E.N. Larson[179]

⊠        ⊠        ⊠        ⊠        ⊠        ⊠

The troops that had been gathering in England were now actively engaging the German army, which meant difficult fighting and the accompanying harsh living conditions of a combat zone.

France
July 26th [1944]

Dear Dr. Evanson,

I received your regular newsletter for the month of May yesterday and want you to know that I really enjoy them. I hope they keep coming. I'm in France now and have been for some time. When I get back to teaching I'll be able to say that I was a small part of the greatest invasion force ever assembled and so helped to make history. You'll probably be teaching about it soon too.

I can't say much about my actions since leaving England. I can say I've been pretty scared and have spent some hectic times over here. It still isn't much of a picnic, but is better than it was. I've seen some pretty unpleasant things and life in general has been pretty rough. I'm writing this from rather crude living quarters. I dug a large foxhole and then pitched my pup tent over it. When it rains my floor and blankets usually end up pretty damp, but I guess I can stand that part of it. Am wondering if any of the other former L.C. men are over here. I wasn't lucky enough to run into any of them while in England. Just today I got a letter from Lyle Larson, but he's in England so I'm afraid I won't see him.

The first piece of mail I got in France was an L.C. Alumnus which goes to show you that we get them quite soon no matter where we are. I noticed on my last letter from the college that they are still using my old address. Please note the one on the envelope as it is the correct one and I'll probably get my mail that much faster.

I'm glad to see L.C. carrying on its traditional functions even though numbers and material are quite small. I sure hope this mess will be over soon and we can all get back for a visit.

Must close for this time. Thanks again for sending those letters. Greet Pete and Sig Reque for me and tell Sig I could use him as an interpreter.

Sincerely,
[S/Sgt] Arleigh Kraupa[180]

---

*By September, Kraupa's unit had moved from France into Belgium.*

[V-MAIL]

From: S/Sgt. Arleigh L. Kraupa Sept. 17, 1944 Somewhere in Belgium

Dear Dr. Evanson,

Just a word to tell you I received the July issue of "Scuttlebutt" today. Seems good to hear from time to time what some of the gang are doing. As you will notice, I'm up in Belgium now. So far I cant see a great deal of difference between here & France. I got to visit Paris before leaving France and believe me it's a wonderful city. Very modern compared to most English towns & much cleaner & more well planned than London. I visited the Eiffel Tower, the Arch of Triumph, attended church services at the Cathedral of Notre Dame, saw Napoleon's tomb, the Louvre, Bank of France, Univ. of Paris and many other interesting places. Hope you have a fine first semester starting soon.

Sincerely,<br>Arleigh K.[181]

⊠     ⊠     ⊠     ⊠     ⊠     ⊠

*Although all the men missed their homes, those who left families behind particularly missed the U.S.*

[V-MAIL]

From: P 1/c J. S. Ree France—20 Sept. '44

Gentlemen

Just received the July issue of "Scuttlebutt" a couple of days ago. The length of time getting here is my own fault. Should have written you a long time ago, but you know how it is. It's really good to read about the old school-mates once in awhile. It appears that a great majority of them are somewhere in the service and doing good too.

Babe Moen is with the 3rd cavalry, but haven't seen him since we were in England and we've seen a lot of France since then. He had changed considerably since I knew him way back in 1939. How time flies.

Have been in the army a year now and have spent almost 3 months of it this side of the pond. That's not so long comparably speaking, but for an old married man with a family like me this last year has seemed rather drawn out, but one of these days this mess will end, maybe in the near future. A lot of us have our hearts set on being home by Christmas.

Now that you have my correct address maybe the "Alumnus" and "College Chips" will catch up to me again. I enjoyed them immensely back in the states. So long for now.

Yours truly,
Joel Ree[182]

✉  ✉  ✉  ✉  ✉  ✉

*When they were not in "hot" combat zones, the men occasionally had the opportunity to purchase picture postcards, which they used to document their travels.*

From: Ensign John C. Sorlien 29 Sept, '44
Dear Doctor
An object d'art de chamber de commerce no doubt and all for 2 Francs. A better port than others I've seen but the legend of the American dollar precedes us. Port looks good after having weathered a severe Mediterranean storm for several days. All's well and local scuttlebutt keeps us in consternation.

-John[183]

✉  ✉  ✉  ✉  ✉  ✉

*In some cases, the speed of their advance into Germany, combined with the press of their regular duties, meant that the men were not able to report on their experiences in France until they had already reached Germany.*

[V-MAIL]

From: Capt. Ray M. Lee 6 October 44 Germany

Dear Chellis:

Just time enough for a dehydrated letter to let you know that I think that sheet called "Scuttlebutt" is tops for Luther men and women in service. The style and contents are <u>great</u>. Keep up the good work!

By the way, I hope I'm the first Norseman to report in from the "holy rail of the German Reich."

I'm still with the old Second Division and still in communications work. Have a fine gang of old-timers to work with so I'm pretty happy about things.

After the Normandy campaign, the Division went over to Brest. Brest was a tough nut to crack but the job was our most interesting one to date. You can't possibly imagine what the siege of a well-defended naval fort can be like. The Navy, Air Corps, Armored Force, and plenty of artillery co-operated in the assault (which lasted more than a month) but the little guy with the rifle wrote the final chapter, as usual.

Oh, yes, I can't send you a check right now but consider this a pledge of $25.$^{00}$ to Luther College and I'll send it in a few days.

Best of luck,

Ray[184].

⊠    ⊠    ⊠    ⊠    ⊠    ⊠

*Some of the men had covered a lot of territory before reaching France. Since many of them were practicing Lutherans, they sometimes had to provide their own services if they wanted to have any kind of organized worship.*

France October 31, 1944

Hello Chellis,

Long time, no see, ever since I left old Luther. I have received the July and August issues of the Scuttlebutt. Sure glad to get it to find out what is happening to Luther men here and there.

I have covered a bit of ground and water since I left the Alma Mater. I went through N. Africa as a replacement and found my home (outfit) in Southern Italy and then to Anzio for a bit and now glorious France. Resurgum must be the

French motto too because it has again risen against the adversary and beaten him to a pulp—Viva La France.

I met Pluto at Anzio last Spring and I hear he was wounded since then. We had a grand visit that day. But I haven't seen any of the other boys since I left the States.

Since I hit France I have been holding protestant services for the boys of my outfit every Sunday. We haven't a chaplain of our own and it isn't always easy to get the services of one so I have taken that up for a sideline and like it a lot.

My present job is in the kitchen so I am faring well enough—in eats I mean. I haven't lost weight and seem to have put a little on.

I have been getting the "Luther Alumnus" regular. Thanks a lot for it.

My address is: Pvt. Robert H. Schlinkert [...]

Greeting to all of my Luther friends and profs. God bless you all.

As ever,
Bob[185]

✉  ✉  ✉  ✉  ✉  ✉

*While the men in Europe hoped for a quick end to the war against Germany, they also realized that they might also be called upon to serve in the Pacific against Japan.*

[V-MAIL]

From: Pfc. Roger W. Anderson 37572654
November 4, 1944 Somewhere in France
Dear Chellis,

I received your August issue of "Scuttlebutt" a few days ago and I assure you I was very happy to receive same. Its certainly great to read about the activities of my fellow Norsemen on the far flung battle fronts. Of course there are many that I do not know, but still I didn't skip a word of the letter.

You asked for change of address so the partial purpose of the letter is to comply with your request. My present address is as it is written on the outside address. I have now been in France about [2 words blocked out by censors] and have been on the front lines about [1 word blocked out by censor] of this time. I've been studying about them since I was a young boy, but I never dreamed that I would actually be on the so called historic battlefields of Europe. It still seems like a dream (or should I say a night-mare), but it's one dream that I hope will come to an end soon. Perhaps by the time spring rolls around, Germany will be about ready to capitulate, then those of us who will be fortunate enough to return can start to think about returning to our loved ones and resuming our lives which were so rudely interrupted by the fortunes of war. I, too, am among the multitudes of others who hope that we will not be called upon to finish the Pacific war too. Keep that old Luther Spirit alive! As Ever, Andy[186]

$$\boxtimes \qquad \boxtimes \qquad \boxtimes \qquad \boxtimes \qquad \boxtimes \qquad \boxtimes$$

*While many of the men served in the infantry or armored divisions, a few had more specialized jobs, including Counter Intelligence, which enabled them to cover a great deal of territory.*

France
1-11-44 [Nov. 5, '44]

Dear Chellis,

It's long past the time when I should have dropped you a thank-you for the "letter of the Lutherites" you sent last summer and which I received while in Wales. Much appreciated by all who received it, I'm sure. Unfortunately, I've moved about so much and changed addresses so often while overseas, that I've not kept up much of a pen-list, and have relied upon Dad and upon my wife for news of others.

Of what and where and when, there is little to tell, and why and how are—and will be for some time—trade secrets. However, this much you might pass on to the Alumni editor, if you care to do so. "Prior to the invasion, I was in Wales—and spent a hectic two weeks up to June 6. Several times, I went to bed at midnight and rose at two a.m. for CIC work. Here in France, the work has been very interesting and, I believe, very valuable. I have been able to work in Counter-Intelligence lines almost completely and have worked with the Frenchmen quite largely. Naturally, I have seen a lot of the countryside, for I jeep about a great deal. Around Valognes and St. Lo, it is too battle-scarred to be attractive, but the other parts of the country are exquisite—the cathedral at Chartres, the lovely chateaus, Paris, Tours. Among the headquarters in which I worked (or from which I worked) were a modern hotel with feather-beds, a café used by the Germans as an officers' canteen, and a Feldkommandatur (two of us had the latter—eight rooms with a bath) housed in a stone building facing a devastated area of incredible proportions.

Yes, it's very interesting, but I'm looking forward to a Luther Homecoming as much more interesting, by far."

Confidentially, at present things are fine. I just came into the headquarters last week-end, after five weeks during which two of us operated over an area including a number of towns, three small cities, and about a quarter of a million inhabitants. It's getting chilly, so it's a good thing to get into a nice heated hotel with feather beds, hot and cold running water, and a fine, intimate group of men. Which reminds me—

French cuisine is superb. The sauces our chef can concoct are innumerable and as variable from day to day as one could wish. We always have a dessert that reminds us of what "mother used to make"—apple turnovers tonight, chocolate ice cream last night, real custard the night before. Of course, we are fortunate in securing good quarters and food.

I have met no one from Luther or from any of my former "home towns" here in France; that is partly, of course, because I do not work with other army units and installations very often. I did meet Dirksen, the former L.C. janitor, at a dock in Wales just prior to the invasion—he was with a medical unit confined to the dock and I had some business with his C.O. one afternoon. We had a cup of coffee and talked for a short time. I hope to see some familiar face before long, now, as I shall be near a great number of them for some time now (subject to change without notice, of course).

While I am about it, I shall enclose a check for the Luther College Alumni Association. Will you please turn it over to the proper person?

My mail has been very irregular and out of any semblance of order, but I did get a letter of Dad's of October 21 yesterday. He stated that he enjoyed Homecoming much more than he expected to, although the enrollment is down and the vocal groups and band not what they were and will be (soon, I hope). I am glad that Luther is keeping up so well; the improvements Dad mentioned amazed me under the circumstances. With the Women's Dormitory and New Main, it will again be "the most beautiful campus in the Mid-West"—or any other place, to me.

Well, Chellis, must have a nip of wine (have had a goodly supply since landing, as the Germans left a lot behind in their hurry) and hie myself to bed. Please greet Pete, Pip, Tobak, the Speratis, and the other good Lutherites.

My best to you and Mrs.E.

[Mr.] Lyle [O. Estenson][187]

200

⊠        ⊠        ⊠        ⊠        ⊠        ⊠

*One of the many things the men missed while stationed overseas was their alma mater. The idea of returning for Homecoming became a common goal for many men.*

[V-MAIL]

From: Lt. V.M. Larson, 0-873063 France, 14 Nov., 1944

Dear friends,

I haven't written for some time so I figured it was about time I did so. The news letters have been coming regularly and they really are a treat to read. It's about the only way I have to keep tab on the Luther boys, as there are only a couple that I write regularly.

I won't be quite so close to Decorah when I get back, as my folks moved to Alcester, South Dakota, near Sioux Falls, in September. I'll still try to get over there if I can though.

I made homecoming a year ago, but it would have been pretty hard to do it this year. I thought about good old Luther though—it would be swell to be back there.

As yet I haven't run across any of my Luther friends over here. There are lots of them around though, so it could happen any time—

This letter might reach you early, but I want to take this opportunity to send you best wishes for a Merry Christmas and a Happy new year—

Good luck—

Vernon L.[188]

⊠        ⊠        ⊠        ⊠        ⊠        ⊠

*The advance across Europe was not always direct, as the routes of attack changed according to the success in a variety of battles.*

Nov. 28', 44

Dear Chellis,

By the card please don't think I am in Paris, at present we are in Belgium and have been in Germany and plan to return there really soon again.

I have enjoyed your paper Scuttlebutt very much, to find that Charlie Whitting was in France the same time I was, I believe at one time he was rather close to where I was stationed.

I am looking forward in returning with my wife back to Luther when we are finished here.

As Ever. Lyle Larson, Class of "45."[189]

    ✉    ✉    ✉    ✉    ✉    ✉

*The Army men were transported to Europe on Navy ships, and in the process, had a chance to compare the average sailor's conditions with their own.*

2 Dec 44
Eastern France

Dear Dr. Evanson,

Yeh, I know I haven't written much but you know how rapid this war can be. I just got two copies of <u>Chips</u> and I was suddenly reminded that Luther and all you swell people back there are still operating.

We're with the 7th Army over here and having a wonderful time. I haven't run into Butch Noble yet but our meeting is inevitable. We followed each other all over the states and then we both hit France. He's with the Third Army, I think. Even if he's up in Belgium, we'll still run into each other during the grand slam into Berlin.

I spent a lot of time around Marseille and agree with John Sorlien. The American dollar is precious all over the world. I was glad to discover that Marseille isn't France. I was pretty disgusted with conditions there.

I'm living with a French family. It's the first taste of billeting with them that we've had. I think they'll remember us more for the mud we drag into their homes than for the dishes we wiped for them.

I'd like you to know that I don't think much of the American Navy. Their enlisted men live like Kings; their officers live like potentates. It was my impression that they experienced very little of the filth, mud, and miserable conditions that are the GI's life. And next to absence from home, it is just those primitive conditions that make war so distasteful to us. I don't think you'll find any sailors who go for a week without washing. A shower is a thing of bliss to these guys. In comparison with the soldier's food, the sailor's meals were Ritz-Carlton stuff on the Transport coming over. Sure, lots of sailors are at sea for a long time, but they aren't sweating out the end of the war to get home as are most of the GI's here. For my money, the Navy is a racket and no sailor of this war or the last will be able to convince me that he went through more hell than did the average GI. Understand now, I'm not beating on my chest. The guys in a tank outfit have a sweet racket compared to the dogface in the foxhole. I'll tip my hat to the infantryman any day. I'm glad to see that his worth has been finally recognized by an increase in pay. I'll bet that if you talk Navy to some guy who sweat out the war in a foxhole, he'll never take another History course.

I'm taking a correspondence course from U. of Minn.—Political Science. Now all I need is the time and favorable conditions for study. I've got notions about Yale after the war. I've written to them and if I can cut the dough with the aid of the GI Bill of Rights, and Yale wants me, I'll probably be one of the absentees on Luther's campus come the end of the war. That's all very indefinite, though.

I think I discern another meal in the offing. Since feeding one's face is of paramount importance over here, I'll adjourn.

> Sincerely,
> Ole [Cpl Eugene B. Olson][190]

$\boxtimes$  $\boxtimes$  $\boxtimes$  $\boxtimes$  $\boxtimes$  $\boxtimes$

*The men who had participated in the 1936 Jubilee Band Tour sometimes returned to familiar territory as they advanced across Europe.*

France 1944

Dear Friends,

May God grant you a happy Christmas and a very satisfactory holiday vacation.

As we approach the scene of much interest (in 1936), my thoughts turn to our Jubilee tour and the wonderful time we had.

To a band reunion in the not-so-distant future,

> Yours sincerely,
> [Mr.] Lyle Estenson[191]

$\boxtimes$  $\boxtimes$  $\boxtimes$  $\boxtimes$  $\boxtimes$  $\boxtimes$

*Although the Allied advance across Europe would encounter some difficulties in the "Battle of the Bulge," early reports of their progress were very positive.*

[V-MAIL]

From: Pfc Glenn Vanderbilt

Dec 18, 1944

Dear Chellis

I just received the October Scuttlebutt and was very glad to learn how the other fellows are doing. As for me I've been very fortunate because I've been at this for quite a while. I missed seeing a few of the fellows on one move of our div. I have a hunch that Crusty and Mel Davis are near here but it's almost impossible to find any one at all when up in front. Really been moving lately and if it would be possible to keep it up we would hit Berlin by spring. Guess everything is going all right back there even with Hank as pres but it's the best school I've heard of yet so it can be expected. Well thanks a lot for sending the paper because I really appreciate it.

Sincerely Glenn[192]

☒        ☒        ☒        ☒        ☒        ☒

*Some men were able to write letters to a large number of recipients, including Evanson, but others had to resort to relaying information to him via family members.*

Rio Wis. Jan. 8, 1945

Dr. Evanson,—

Some time ago Harlan sent home a box of different articles he had picked up in France. Amongst them was a book which he asked me to forward to you.

Harlan is well and writes home often. Most of his letters come through in less then ten days while others take from four to six weeks. He went across in April '44. to England where he stayed till "D" day, where his division has been taking part in different battles. He has been through Reims, Metz, Nancy, Lunneville. He is in the 79th Div. field artillery. He works in the operational tent (he calls it) so is not in the <u>front</u>. He has very nice Officers to work for but all have to undergo a lot of hardship together. He does not complain but appreciates having a chance to sleep inside or in a bed, also getting a well cooked meal.

Harlan's address is [...]

with best wishes for the coming year for yourself and L.C.

Sincerely,

Mrs. Hans Kittleson, Rio, Wis.[193]

 

✉     ✉     ✉     ✉     ✉     ✉

 

*Even for men who had only been at Luther for a short time, the reports in "Scuttlebutt" sparked fond memories, and hopes of future reunions with friends.*

[V-MAIL]

From: S/Sgt. E. Omundson 37665753

3 Feb. 1945

Dear Scuttlebutt and L.C.

I was very much surprised to get a paper like Scuttlebutt and I really want to let you know I appreciate it a great deal. I wasn't at Luther very long but I did have a number of friends there and I do have a lot of pleasant memories of Luther. There are very few names mentioned in your paper that I don't know and I may be able to get in contact with some of them from the addresses I get from you.

You made an error in my address so I will give you my complete address at the end of the letter.

I am in the Combat engineers and at present I am in France going through much the same as a lot of other Luther fellows.

S/Sgt. E. Omundson [194]

 

✉     ✉     ✉     ✉     ✉     ✉

 

*For men who had been in Germany, assignment in Holland, even though temporary, provided a welcome respite. In addition to describing their conditions in Europe, the men also brought Evanson up to date with news about their personal lives.*

Holland

12 Feb. 1945

Dear Chellis & Pete,

Let me slip into my wooden shoes before I start this letter which should have been written months, or possibly years, earlier. At present we're "inactive," temporarily quartered in a Dutch home, & generally enjoying a few comforts which we don't normally expect.

These are fine people. My travels have taken me through Belgium, Luxemburg, France, Scotland, part of Germany, & of course England, but I still say with a little extra emphasis, "<u>These</u> are fine people." They're industrious, sanitary, & deeply religious, & all of those characteristics haven't been common to some of the folks which we've met.

Let me tell you how much I enjoy the editions of the Scuttlebutt, & also Pete's messages. Although I don't write too often, I still keep a sharp eye on what happens at Luther, & your letters have served perfectly to keep me well informed. It is quite impossible for you, I'm sure, to understand how much we appreciate hearing about other Alumni in the various services. I'm in favor of recommending the Bronze Medal to ye Editor of the Scuttlebutt for meritorious services.

I guess it's about time that I should come through with the details of my marriage. Doris & I had known each other for twenty years, had been more than casual acquaintances for about twelve years, and, while we didn't want to rush into this thing, we decided it would be well to be married while I was still in the States, rather than to wait until I arrived overseas & then have it done by proxy. So we were married, and a couple of days later I was shipped across. Some oldtimers have told me that some guys have all the luck, but I don't quite see eye to eye with them on that statement. Doris is principal in the high school in my home town this year, & again, the oldtimers tell me it's good to let the wife work if she feels so inclined. It wouldn't be courteous to disagree with everything they say. That home town, by the way, is LANSING, over in Allamakee County, & there are lots of good Republicans in that neighborhood.

I think it's remarkable that Pete can produce such a good basketball team with manpower as scarce as it is. He's carrying on in a style which makes us all proud of our Luther ancestry. Now, concerning the football season——! Don't worry, we're proud of those boys too.

My conscience has troubled me no end because I've received two statements reminding me that I've failed to pay my Century Club dues. In order to clear the record, I'm enclosing a check for the 1944 & 1945 dues, & in addition checks for the servicemen's plaques & the building fund. It's a little hard to take care of these things promptly overseas, but we definitely want to be reminded of our obligations at frequent intervals.

My chest is as barren of medals as my head is of hair, but I've "enjoyed" a couple of good campaigns. In Nov. & Dec. I was over here with another armored outfit & we had a couple of good engagements. Recently, we had another little party. All of these have been on German soil.

At least I can say that I have been indoctrinated, but I'm not exactly suffering from battle fatigue.

Over here we're very well fed, usually well housed, and quite warmly dressed. Cigarettes seem to be plentiful for those who want them, & other PX rations are issued automatically to the men each week. We definitely get what we need.

Les writes from his lonely outpost occasionally, but of course I never hear any complaints from him. I'm amused to read in his letters such expressions as "hit the sack," & other phrases which have endeared themselves to every man in the service. Six-syllable medical terms have always been his usual language.

To all friends at Luther I send my sincerest greetings. I hope that many of us will be able to spend next homecoming on the Luther campus. No harm in being optimistic.

Very Sincerely,<br>Ira Larson

Data for Chips & the Archives:
Married: Sept. 30, 1944 at Shreveport, Louisiana: Ira E Larson, '36 to Doris E. Veit (ISTC), both of Lansing, Iowa.[195]

⊠     ⊠     ⊠     ⊠     ⊠     ⊠

*Despite some frustrations the soldiers experienced when they tried to connect with fellow Luther men, notes in "Scuttlebutt" did facilitate some meetings as the troops advanced across Europe. Even when the men had not known each other previously, their ties with Luther were a common bond.*

Friday Noon, February 23, 1945<br>Somewhere in France

Dear Chellis,
I guess it is high time I wrote you all back in Decorah as I have been receiving the "Chips" and your "Scuttlebutt" for some time now and have made no effort to thank anyone for it. Received the January issue of Scuttlebutt recently and noticed the address of Glen Vanderbilt as one of the companies in the same

regiment as my company. I made a note of it and as it happened a few days later I was out on detached service with his company and had a chance to meet him personally. I am transportation Corporal at the present time and had three trucks working with his company and we were parked behind a house where his platoon happened to be quartered. We had a long talk together and as near as we could remember he was in a class I had in practice teaching in Decorah high school back in 1938. He seemed to be a nice sort of a kid who has seen his share of this war and who wants to return to Luther when this is all aver. He had a Lutheran Herald with him, which contained a picture of Rev. Ingvoldstad and three of my cousins (Johnny was missing) so I mailed that home to mother in a recent letter.

While I think of it Chellis—my mail from Luther still goes to an old address I had in the states. It would speed up delivery some if I gave you my present address and thank you very much. This Vanderbilt boy is the only Luther man I have come into contact with since leaving civilian life, which incidentally seems like years ago.

Received Pete's letter at Christmas and was glad to hear he has a strong basket ball club again. He mentioned the fact that Dick Elliot was coming to the front this season. I remember him well when he was in high school because he always caused us a lot of trouble every time we played Harmony. "Dusty" very likely remembers him too for the same reason.

I could give you some information on this country of France but I imagine from all the fellows who write you most of it gets to be repetitive. I know these people have been through years of war and occupation, nevertheless I've decided it is no place for me. I believe a majority of us over here would agree with that.

We have a baby boy now in the family born Nov. 25th—getting to be quite a lad now and weighs twelve pounds. Hariette has a baby girl born December 3rd—her husband is a medical captain with the 9th army. So Mom & Dad became grand parents twice over in a short time this winter. Jane has been with her folks at Le Sueur, Minnesota since last August. Beth's husband—a lt. in air corp—is still in the States and she is living in their apartment at Stillwater, Minn. and that about accounts for our family.

Certainly appreciate hearing from the school, Chellis, and your efforts are most worthwhile. I'm sure all the alumni feel the same way about it. Seems like ages since I've been in Decorah, but will make it a point to get there when we all get home again. My greetings to you again and your family.

Sincerely,

[Cpl] Don Moore [196]

✉    ✉    ✉    ✉    ✉    ✉

*Even with the pressures of flying missions over Europe, "Scuttlebutt" helped keep Luther and one's fellow students in mind.*

France
March 2, 1945

Dear Friends,

I've started receiving the Scuttlebutt rather regularly and I want to express my appreciation. That seems to be about my only contact with everyone from Luther. I have met no Luther men since entering the service and it really is swell to hear what they are doing.

I'll try to send a little contribution to the various things you have when we get set up. I don't think this French money would be much good for that, then the limit on the amount put on by censorships is quite low.

Ran into Rolf Norstag down in Barksdale at Shreveport, Louisianna. He is a radio instructor there preparing the radio operators for combat.

As for myself I'm flying a B-26 Marauder and really like the plane. I have a good crew. Half are Southern and half northern. Nearly have my copilot talked into going to Luther after the war. He hails from Alabama and is quite interested in our climate of the north.

This will be all. Thanks again for the scuttlebutt. Lets hope this war is over very soon.

Joe [Lt. Robert M. Josephson][197]

✉    ✉    ✉    ✉    ✉    ✉

*While the men most frequently commented on things related to Luther, they still managed to include brief observations about what they found in Europe.*

Somewhere in France
6 March [1945]

Dear Chellis,

Just received the January Scuttlebut before embarking and the February issue her at my new address last night. Surely didn't take long for you people to make us of that change of address card. Thanks a lot.

Naturally, both issues were very interesting. Am watching closely now for addresses of fellow-classmates in this area.

Met both "Jumbo" Strom and Paul Borge on our trip across, and am sure they are now in this same vicinity, also.

As yet we haven't seen much of this country, but am sure it won't be very long before we do some more traveling. What French cities we have been able to visit have been very interesting, years behind the times compared to our cities, tho.

Had a short visit with Jack in the cities a few weeks before we left, and also spent a few days with the folks in Dayton. So I fared very well on that score, although I didn't have enough time to take in Decorah. So now I guess I'll just have to wait till its all over, and then come back and go right back to Luther.

The plaque fund sounds like a very good idea, and will enclose my "fare" as soon as I am able to change a few francs back.

So long for now,
Danny [Pfc Daniel W. Lien]

P.S.—have been unable to find any American currency around, so I have instructed my father to send the money to you. D. W. L.[198]

✉    ✉    ✉    ✉    ✉    ✉

*There had been a tremendous buildup of manpower in Europe prior to the D-Day invasion in June 1944, but new troops were still being assigned to the European Theater until after hostilities ended on "V-E Day," May 8, 1945*

March 27

Dear Chell,

I guess I have been owing you a letter for quite some time. I guess I felt pretty cheap for being in the states for so long, when all the guys were over here. I have been here a little over a month now. Really had quite a boat ride over. Paul Borge was on the same boat together with Danny Lien. Paul right now is a couple of miles from me. I have seen him a couple of times. Was really surprised we would be so close together. Have been receiving the Scuttlebutt regularly. Enjoy it very much. Sorry I didn't get to see you when I was there on my last furlough. Don't know what my next move will be but I imagine they didn't take me over here just for the boat ride. The news seems pretty good right and if it keeps up as such we may be home before very long.

Glad to hear you had a pretty good season in basketball. Did pretty well to keep on during the war. That's more than a lot of the bigger colleges did. Well that's all I have for now say hello to everyone for me.

As ever

Neal [Strom][199]

⊠     ⊠     ⊠     ⊠     ⊠     ⊠

*As the push into Germany intensified, the men did not always have time to write both to family and to Evanson, so reports to families were forwarded on to him.*

[Letterhead: American Red Cross, Office Of The Field Director Veterans' Administration, Dayton, Ohio]

April 3, 1945

Dear Chellis:

Danny sent instructions some time ago that I should send you a check for $ 2.00 for the Plaque Fund for him as it was so difficult for him to get a money order where he is. Same is being enclosed.

We have been hearing from him regularly but have had no word the past ten days or so and we assumed that to mean he was invited to go along on the push into Germany. The last word we had from him was "still in France but not for long".

Jack was here for Easter vacation and we enjoyed his visit. He really thought he had come south as he was quite thrilled to see trees and flowers in bloom as it is a little early for that in Minneapolis yet.

Best regards,

J. A. Lien[200]

⊠     ⊠     ⊠     ⊠     ⊠     ⊠

*After their wide range of experiences in Europe, the men often expected future duty in the Pacific Theater.*

France, 28 April 1945.

Dear Chellis,

I have been getting the Scuttlebutt regularly, as far as the mail service will permit, but I am as lazy as ever and have just been procrastinating on the writing. Needless to say, I enjoy and appreciate your monthly epistle. Scuttlebutt is hardly the term used by the Army, but the material is essentially the same.

So far I have run into only one Luther man and that was Chet Hoven, whom I met in England last May. We met in Cambridge and had a real old "session". My brother, Lawren is over here but I have been unable to see him yet. He is in a medical unit attached to a Field Artillery unit and Air Force units, such as ours, rarely occupy the same localities. I am hoping that we can get together soon. I did see a cousin if mine who has been in Africa, Corsica, Italy and now France and maybe Germany by this time.

My wife and son are living in Wall Lake, where I was coaching. The boy will be two in June and I haven't seen him since he was two months. I hope he will make a good man for Pete in about 1961. That is the worst part of being overseas, not being able to see your family.

I have been fortunate enough to see quite a few places of note. I visited London quite often while we were in England, fighting a "Gentleman's War" and I have been to Paris on numerous occasions. The two cities are almost exact opposites and both very interesting. My history major made both places especially interesting to me and you can be sure I visited most of the places of historical interest.

Right now we are "sweating out" the end of hostilities here and then whether or not we will go to the CBI.[201] Personally, I am sure of coming home via San Francisco in about 1947. I am hoping against it, but the brass will do the deciding.

I wish I could write to you regarding our operations, location, and other more interesting things but you know what censorship is. I hope I can come to another Homecoming and soon. Give my regards to your family and thank you for Scuttlebutt.

Yours,
Paul [Nesset][202]

⊠      ⊠      ⊠      ⊠      ⊠      ⊠

*The fighting ended in Europe in May, but men serving in the Counter Intelligence Corps (CIC) were still busy throughout the summer of 1945.*

LeHavre, France
1 October 1945

Dear Chellis,

Finally got a few pictures developed, so I'm sending them through for the board; the one in civilian clothes was taken in front of the wall surrounding our little home, the one in civilian uniform was taken inside the walls and in front of the house, none of which, unfortunately, shows up very well. The date they were taken (5 September) is indicated on the reverse.

I just returned last week from a ten days' leave in England, mainly spent in a civilian home in a suburb of London, with a week-end at Hastings thrown in. Ran into my first LC man over here while staying in the Jules Officer's Club right off Piccadilly Circus the night before my return to LeHavre—Dr. Kenneth (?) Green, a dentist and Captain stationed near London. We looked each other over with eyebrow up for a few minutes but finally popped Luther into a sentence and recognized each other. As I remember, he finished in 1939 and came to Luther from North Dakota. My first LC graduate since I was "swallowed up in the war effort," not to coin a phrase. with Dirksen, the ex-janitor, the only other man I've met who had a direct connection with Luther—and that the week before the invasion of Normandy.

Have been sweating out an essential billing, but the danger seems to be passed, and the addition of another battle-star this month (awarded this month, that is) has put me in to the "eligible-in-October" class. However, I don't expect to leave until the last of the month or the first part of November. There is a good reason to hope for a return to civilian life by Thanksgiving, with Christmas at the outside. And that's something, with the uncertainty of one-to-two years' work in Germany out of the way.

As you perhaps know, my brother Don is now in Austria, his Field Artillery Battalion assigned to MP duty near Salzburg. He is hoping to get back to Luther, but will probably have to sweat it out until next fall. With the addition of "summer points," he now has 37 points, which isn't many, but includes 28 months (27 of which count) of service, almost six of them overseas. I hope he gets a chance to play basketball this winter.

Must drop off my contribution to Old Main and Century Club dues when I get near the APO later this week. Hope things work out so that the building program can be well-started by next summer.

Regards to your family, Pete, Pip, and the rest of the "old guard."

Sincerely,

[Mr.] Lyle [Estenson][203]

&#x2709;    &#x2709;    &#x2709;    &#x2709;    &#x2709;    &#x2709;

*While most of the troops remaining in Europe after V-E Day were in Germany, there were still a number of units in other areas, especially ports where troops departed for the U.S.*

Marseilles, France
30 November, 1945

Dear Chellis,

I'm afraid that I have been a bit delinquent in the matter of letter-writing, but rather than go into a rambling discussion of how busy I have been suffice it to say—"my head is bowed"—.

After having been pulled off a boat heading for the South Pacific on V-J Day, I now find myself in Marseilles. I am Aide-de-Camp to Gen. Ratay, commanding General of Delta Base Section. This Base Section controls the Port of Marseilles, Riviera Recreational Area, Biarritz University, and an area equivalent to 35% of France. It's really a big business and a very interesting one.

My job here in addition to the usual duties of an aide entails much contact with the French (my French parlez[ing] is picking up every day) and also taking care of the numerous VIP's (Very Important People) that come through Marseilles and to the Riviera. In the past few weeks we've had Winston Churchill, the Duke and Duchess of Windsor, the Aga Khan, and numerous generals.

Although this spot has held up my promotion a couple of weeks longer, I've more than compensated for it in the experience gained.

I've enjoyed your little news sheet very much Chellis. You've done a very good job with it. Every now and then I catch a Luther football score in the Stars & Stripes, and judging from the score, the season doesn't seem to have been too bad. I'm currently "sweating-out" the Army's tiff with Navy tomorrow. Not on the outcome, you understand, but just the score. Navy's got the material to give us a pretty hard run.

How's the younger member of the firm doing these days? I've been more or less out of touch with the news from Decorah the past few months. The last I knew of Chell was that he was still in Denver. I wish you'd greet him from me.

Mother tells me you have really risen in Legion Circles. Congratulations!

Well, I must hurry off as I have to fly in the General's C-45 to pick the "old man" up. Please greet your wife, Dr. Preus, and Prof. Nelson from me.

Sincerely,
Lt. LeVerne Blount[204]

# CHAPTER 14

# "A good look at part of the Reich"— Reports from Germany and Central Europe

*One of the benefits of "Scuttlebutt" was that it helped the men keep in contact with their Alma Mater. For many of them, celebrating Homecoming on the Luther campus became one of the things they wanted to enjoy as soon as the war was over. Until peace was achieved, the event was frequently on their minds.*

Dear Chellis—

Just a note to accompany the money which I pledged to the college a few days ago.

Tomorrow will be Homecoming at Luther. Needless to say I think of the event with no small feeling of nostalgia. Since I was "knee high to a grasshopper," Homecoming was one of the big events of the year for me. The illumination of Old Main, the pep meeting, the big game (and how I loved it when we smeared St. Olaf!), the reunion band concert—they all added up to a thrilling event for me.

Sorry I have to miss it this year but maybe next year—

Sincerely,

Ray [Cap't Ray M. Lee]

Germany—13 Oct 44[205]

✉     ✉     ✉     ✉     ✉     ✉

*With the pressures of Army life, especially in combat zones, the men did not always have time to write to as many people as they would have liked. This was particularly the case if they wanted to write detailed letters describing the conditions they were observing as they moved across Europe. In some cases, Evanson received copies of letters*

216

*that were sent to several readers. While they were not necessarily "personal," some of them nonetheless contained valuable insights regarding the conditions they observed.*

[Mimeographed letter sent by Ens. Roland Hegg, October 20, 1944]

To you I am a total stranger. To the people of Riceville I hope I still remain in their memory even though I have been gone for some time. I can best introduce myself to you as the roommate and classmate of Ensign Evans I. Knutson, formerly of Adams, Minnesota, and therefore you can verify my high estimation of this young Ensign through your relationships with him. It was my very great pleasure and opportunity to room with him all four years that we both attended Luther College. He at present is serving with the United States Navy somewhere in Italy; I am performing duty with the 750th Tank Battalion somewhere in Germany. Thus our experiences are of a very different nature, and it is going to be extremely interesting to compare experiences after this war is brought to an end.

I have been informed that the letter which I wrote to my parents describing my trip across the Atlantic Ocean was published not long ago in your paper. From letters I have received since then from Riceville, it seems that they are interested in hearing of the various experiences we in the service encounter in our traveling to the various fronts of World War II. At present we are located "somewhere in Germany", and therefore I feel that I am observing and witnessing many sites that would be extremely interesting to you in Riceville. To me it is very revealing to watch the reaction of the German people, and also to see how the war is affecting the country from which this war originated. Since several have requested that I wrote a letter on Germany, I have attempted to put into writing incidents and reactions I have witnessed since coming into Germany. Bear in mind when you read this that it is written by only one of many soldiers in the Reich for the people of a small community.

Germany is suffering tremendously in this war. It is hardly feasible for them to continue from what we are witnessing here in Germany, but yet we also must stop and realize that we have just penetrated Germany proper. I am assigned to the First American Army, and we are the farthest into Germany of any Army fighting on the Western Front. I shall never forget the day I entered Germany. I crossed the Holland-Germany border, going through a town which was divided by the borderline. The section of town that was located in Holland was hardly touched. The other section of town which was located in Germany was in ruins, and every mile thereafter has been partially or completely damaged or destroyed. This town sums up the entire story in the most perfect manner I can possibly show you. As the American soldier advanced and fought his way through France, Belgium, and a small sector of Holland, he was fighting and giving his life as a liberator, having in the back of his mind always one objective—GERMANY! He was moved by the reception he received in some of the conquered countries, puzzled by the reaction in others. He was glad to participate in the liberation of countries such as Belgium, but his greatest desire was to get home again. The way of acquiring that greatest desire was to reach Germany, to invade Germany, to conquer Germany, to bring her to her knees in such a manner that she would not be able or even desire to start another war for some time to come. The American soldier is now in Germany, and if I were asked for my opinion as to whether the American soldier is fulfilling his vow, my answer would be most emphatically "Yes."

Why do I say "Yes?" To fully answer why I believe the American soldier is fulfilling his vow, I will have to describe the manner in which the war is affecting the German civilian. The United States has set up Military Government in some of Germany's occupied cities. They deal fairly with the German civilian, but harshly, for they intend to have their orders carried out. Orders given by a MP are to be obeyed. Germans are not allowed in certain restricted areas. If violations of these orders are reported to the Military Government, imprisonment may be imposed as the sentence ranges from three to nine months in some cases. If violations of these orders still continue more drastic action is taken. I am subject at all times to a fine of $65.00 if I am caught fraternizing with a German civilian.

The larger German cities are near chaos, and I am perfectly right in saying that 80% of the German homes are now rendered unhabitable. In these homes a soldier can find the necessary protection against the weather and other forces of nature which would make his life unpleasant here in Germany, but they are beyond repair as far as being a permanent home for German civilians is concerned. It is without question a huge problem for the German to confront to find a liveable place in which he can be reasonably comfortable through the coming winter. We are fighting hard, very hard, for every inch of ground we are now taking. That CAN'T be accomplished without a great deal of destruction and a huge amount of shelling to "root" the German out of his positions. That is the main reason for the tremendous amount of destruction we witness whereever we go in the "Deutschland."

What about rations and clothing? The German Army took with them all accessible food that was left when they retreated. Their German population

218

had orders to evacuate before the advancing Army. Why they didn't is hard to determine. Perhaps they were afraid of more bombings. Day after day I can look out my window from where I an now located and see waves of bombers and fighter planes going over. On this side of the front, the German does not have to run for the cellar each time. On the other side he would have to. He would only keep retreating on the other side. Here it will be over with sooner. What about fuel? I have reason to believe it is not too plentiful. The American Army does not intend to feed and clothe the German as it did former civilians in France and Belgium, for it can't be done as our transportation facilities are crowded to the maximum as it is.

How does the average German take the coming of the American soldier into their homeland? This is a very hard question to answer as yet. We are not allowed to fraternize with them, and my contacts with them have not been too great. However, the American soldier definitely does not trust the German civilian. He can't afford to take the chance, for as we say "he has too much at stake." The German civilian returning to his home looks very bewildered and dejected. Many are living in the cellars of the cities, for the German army completely tunneled the cities for fighting purposes. I went down into one cellar in a fairly large town. I could have walked for blocks underground, for huge iron doors connect many of them. This brought havoc and destruction for our infantry in taking the town. I was in front of my Company Headquarters one day, the Company having been among the first to move in after the Germans had been driven out of the town. Two German ladies walked down the street toward our Orderly Room. Just before they reached it, they started to run and kept running until they were well past. The same procedure was repeated when they returned. I do not know what the German is thinking in his mind and heart, but I have seen decided dislike in the eyes of some German civilians. The Americans—they love souveniers. That, however, it strictly forbidden by the Army.

The Americans have an entirely different feeling toward the German population in contrast to the feeling held toward the Belgian or French people. Here in Germany no G-I lives in pup tents, but either lives in a German home or in public buildings. It is not uncommon for soldiers to be living in one-half of a German house with the German civilian living in the other half. I am at present working with higher Headquarters and not with the Company. We have occupied German barracks which would be a definite credit to any Government. Their feelings and attitudes toward the American soldier and his policies will come more prominently into the picture as we move further into Germany proper.

This is Germany as I see it today, the Germany that is facing her first winter with war being fought in her midst. Is this Germany learning enough about war and all its destruction to think twice before she decides to prepare for another one? The American soldier can't be blamed for feeling as he does toward the German civilian, for here he is among the "core" of the war. He is now fighting in Germany, and this time he intends to finish it, making the German sorry for the woe and destruction they have caused other people.[206]

⊠     ⊠     ⊠     ⊠     ⊠     ⊠

*As the U.S. Army advanced into Germany, units hoped to claim the honor of being the first to enter Hitler's "Third Reich."*

[V-MAIL]

From: T/S A. Buckneberg 6 Nov. '44 Germany
Dear Chellis,

By making the primary purpose of this V Mail the notification of changed address I can perhaps evade the business of apologizing for neglecting this particular bit of writing. Anyway, I enjoy "Scuttlebutt" and even though it has taken the August issue until today to catch up with me, the dope there in was very interesting.

Saw Sgt. Ruid in France a while back. Had opportunity to spend off duty leaves for several days with him while our show was attached to his division.

Have had a good look at part of the Reich and I might say (off hand and unofficially, with no intention of stirring up an argument) this tour unit was the first G.I. stage show over the line. Sorry I have no local newspaper clippings to bear out the statement.

Contemplated expansion & stabilization of "Scuttlebutt" fine (no doubt) but don't let it divorce the homey gossip and pregnant paragraphs from the original.

"Buck" A. Buckneberg '34[207]

⊠     ⊠     ⊠     ⊠     ⊠     ⊠

*The men hoped to connect with friends while abroad, but the reality of combat usually made that difficult, particularly as the Army was speeding toward Berlin.*

[V-MAIL]

From: Pfc Glenn Vanderbilt Dec 18, 1944

Dear Chellis

    I just received the October Scuttlebutt and was very glad to learn how the other fellows are doing. As for me I've been very fortunate because I've been at this for quite a while. I missed seeing a few of the fellows on one move of our div. I have a hunch that Crusty and Mel Davis are near here but it's almost impossible to find any one at all when up in front. Really been moving lately and if it would be possible to keep it up we would hit Berlin by spring. Guess everything is going all right back there even with Hank as pres but it's the best school I've heard of yet so it can be expected. Well thanks a lot for sending the paper because I really appreciate it.

Sincerely Glenn[208]

    ⊠      ⊠      ⊠      ⊠      ⊠      ⊠

*Although "Scuttlebutt" did not carry any notices of deaths in the war, such notices did appear in the* Luther Alumnus, *which the men also received. During the winter of 1944–45, the men advancing into Germany experienced weather that sometimes reminded them of home.*

Saturday Jan, 45.

Somewhere in Germany.

Hi Chellis:

    Just as I was sitting here and just waiting for some kind sole to bring news of my mail, I was handed a Luther Alumnus so have finished reading it. Was surprised to hear of the death of two of my classes mates in Maurice Mace and Junior Bickle, they were sure two great fellows on the campus and will be missed by us all when we return back to school which I hope will be soon, very soon, I hope.

    I have a fellow here as our mess seargent who is from Mason City, who has been interested in Luther fore quite some time and when I get mail from you all back their, I pass it on to him, he has played ball with Denerur, Cary, Olson, and knows most of the fellows his name is Dean Gilbert, he as well as I want to return to Luther as soon as possible. It will be sure swell to go back and be on the campus once again.

We are having weather here as we had in Iowa snow and plenty of it plus a lot of wind, but when you live in a fox hole, with wood and dirt over your head you may be considered a very fortunate person for when on the front lines it is rather hard to get lumber for your holes.

In one of your last papers you had written about a plaque for those men who have died in the battlefields of this war, I have on the way to you through my wife a contribution for that plaque which I believe is a great idea, so in one of your letters will be a check enclosed.

I am rather anxious to see what our basketball team has been doing, one of the things I as well as several others are missing is the games and support we could give them.

I would like to know if it would be all right and be put on credits of mine if I were to take a course in American government here for a credit in Education I have to have?

Well Chellis I guess it is time for chow now so will close for now.

[SGT.] Lyle Larson.[209]

$$\boxtimes \qquad \boxtimes \qquad \boxtimes \qquad \boxtimes \qquad \boxtimes \qquad \boxtimes$$

*As the Army advanced into Germany, the men quickly encountered the massive bulwarks constructed to protect the "Fatherland." Even months before the German surrender, many of the men were thinking of the future, both for themselves, and their alma mater.*

Germany
12 Jan 45

Dear Chellis and Pete:

Now I hope, after that salutation, you both won't denounce me as a brassy young whipper-snapper but somehow it just didn't seem right when I thought of calling you Dr. Evanson and Coach Peterson. After all, you probably know that you've always been Chellis and Pete to all of us—privately, if not publicly—so why not do it now?

I've intended for a long time to sit down and acknowledge those delightful letters you both send out to us. Seriously, those letters mean a whole lot to a whole lot of Norsemen these days when we're scattered to the four winds. We need and want something like that to keep us in touch with Alma Mater and our old friends. We know that there's a lot of work involved in getting them out but you may be very sure that it is not in vain. So, thanks a lot for the kindness.

This pecking on a typewriter reminds me of the days when I used to peck one for Chellis in the News Bureau office. I thought that was pretty hot stuff. There was Ulland, Sealander, Jim Hanson; and I brought up the rear. After games we'd roar down to Western Union and dash off the reports.

Well, tonight I'm pecking a machine under slightly different circumstances. "Home" tonight is in one of the massive bunkers of the Siegfried Line. Wish you could see it. When the krauts built this place they didn't figure on any depreciation. This one is typical of others in the neighborhood but each has slightly different features dictated by consideration of terrain and tactical mission. In the states this thing would cost a fortune to build but in Germany with the cheap labor of the Todt organization it didn't cost so much.

The roof is of re-inforced concrete at least ten feet thick and the concrete is covered with six or eight feet of dirt, so that even heavy shells with impact fuse don't even touch the concrete. The walls, except for the two firing embrasures, are six feet thick. And the embrasures, which are only about a foot square, can be closed by shutters of four inch armor plate.

Entrance to the bunker is by a long flight of steps leading down into a dark hall which is covered by a machine gun embrasure at one end so that even if troops do gain entrance by blowing a steel door they still have to fight inside. One room, about twenty by twelve, contains ten steel bunks for the garrison of super-men. Gun rooms, ammo rooms, and sleeping rooms are all separated by heavy steel doors. Each room contains a big manually operated air-filter and all doors have gas-proof seals, so that the occupants can sweat out a gas attack indefinitely. Even the heating stove is gas-proof.

These bunkers are formidable obstacles but they can be—and are being—reduced by plain ordinary Yank infantry. This one wasn't destroyed by even the Jerries because they headed for Mecca when one of our companies approached it.

I've wasted a lot of space describing a simple pill-box and I hadn't intended to do that.

By the way, I noticed in Stars and Stripes last night that Col. Gynther Storaasli has been appointed supervisor of all the chaplains in the Army Air Force. There's a tip for the Chips editor to follow up. Luther can well be proud of that man—

he's one of the top chaplains in the Corps and I'll bet that he will be Chief of Chaplains before he retires.

It's strange but I never run into any Luther men. Everybody else (according to Scuttlebutt) runs into everybody else whether it be in Guam, San Francisco, or Belgium. But I never do. It seems that I've explained the "L'35" on my class ring to everybody in the United States Army and I'm still waiting for somebody to rush up announcing himself as a fellow Norseman. If you ever hear of another Luther man winding up in the Second Infantry Division, please give me a buzz so that I can look him up.

Got a big kick out of Pete's Christmas letter, especially when you talked about some of those big boys coming back for a little workout with the current crop of cagers. Somewhere between '35 and '45 they must have slipped in a few big hunks of meat. We had some big boys back in those days but the only one I can remember who tipped the scales at 270 pounds was Guy Larson and he didn't play anything except the clarinet. You casually mentioned a few who weighed 222, 211, 231, and 270. Well, as long as they keep turning out Norskes like that Luther's line should be strong.

Now for a little personal news. Had a couple of letters from Mother day before yesterday telling about Dad's illness. I knew he wasn't well before I went overseas so I've been hoping he would improve. Now he has been operated on at Lutheran Hospital in La Crosse and I'm anxiously waiting for word that he is getting along all right. I'm awfully sorry I can't be with Mother at this time because I know that she needs me.

My little daughter, Linda Louise, was three years old on January 30th and from all reports she's getting to be quite a little gal. My wife is a University of Minnesota grad so we've been feuding for three years on the question "Will it be Luther or Minnesota?" Oh, well, we still have about fifteen years in which to continue the argument and I hope to be home in time to get in on the rebuttal at least. Don't get me wrong—it's not a very serious argument. It's something like the pseudo-riot that breaks out when I tease my wife by telling her that the only way I can remember her birthday is by remembering that it comes the day before Luther Homecoming. Perhaps she wouldn't be too happy having me tell tales like this for I might give the impression that we scrap. That isn't the case at all for Clara is beyond a doubt the grandest girl in the earth—and she's 100% for Luther College. We've been married five years and she has attended three homecomings in that time.

I've been wondering what plans have been made at the College for the post-war years. It would seem that the so-called "G. I. Bill of Rights" will be a great thing for the colleges. Every effort, in my opinion, should be exerted at this time toward contacting Norsemen in service with a view to continuing or completing their education at the college after discharge from the armed forces. Perhaps it would be wise to plan refresher courses—courses designed to re-orient discharged service men. No doubt the Faculty has already discussed the problem at length.

Another angle which might be considered is that of military training offered as an option. Compulsory military training at Luther is a thought which would be revolting to all Norsemen. But, if compulsory universal military training is introduced by the Government after the war, it would seem that the colleges which offered courses in military science and tactics to prospective draftees would enjoy a distinct "selling advantage" over those which did not. Mr. Talle, who is close to all the discussions in Congress, should be an excellent advisor in this matter

Well, this has been a screwy letter but at least my intentions have been good. Before I close I'll add a word about myself. At present, I'm a battalion Executive Officer and with the same battalion in which I served as a company commander when I was back in San Antonio.

That sounds rather insignificant but it really means a lot to me, for I'm back with many of the same old magnificent Regular Army non-coms that I loved so dearly in those days. Lots of them are gone now but many remain—just as loyal, just as tough, and just as efficient as before the war. These old non-coms are the backbone of this outfit. Together with the new young men they make a grand team. Those old-timers were good before D-day but between the beach at St. Laurent-sur-Mer and————————Germany, they have learned a lot and are absolutely superb.

It's not considered good taste to apologize for one's writing but this job really smells. The last time I touched a typewriter was in Ireland and that was a long time ago.

Again, thanks for Scuttlebutt and the other letters which you send out to us. Let's hope we can thank you in person in the not too distant future.

Please convey my greetings to all my good friends on the faculty.

Sincerely,

Ray [M. Lee][210]

⊠     ⊠     ⊠     ⊠     ⊠     ⊠

*Conditions near the front lines were potentially dangerous for physicians, as well as for the men they helped in surgery.*

8 April 45
Capt. R.D.Estrem

Dear Chellis et al,

"Scuttlebutt" has been following me through several APO changes so it's about time I let you know where I am. I've been with the 86th Cavalry Recon. Squadron Mecz., troubleshooters for the 6th Armored Division, since Dec. '44. Joined them on the way to Bastogne and have travelled with them since then. Before the call came for more medics on the front, I was enjoying myself doing general surgery with the 90th Gen. Hosp in France.

To date, I haven't had the good fortune of meeting up with any Luther men, but have greatly appreciated getting the news via your compact monthly edition.

I enjoyed reading in the Alumnus about my old roommate Sax's experience in Iceland. His address wasn't given, but if you have it I would appreciate very much getting it.

Right now I am sitting deep in the heart of "nowhere" with only the clothes on my back and my sleeping bag, hoping that my driver, jeep and all my personal possessions have not been requisitioned by the Krauts. He (my driver) started back up from ordnance two days ago, ran into some action on our rear and hasn't been heard from since then. And so it goes.

Best wishes to all down Decorah way.

Bob Estrem[211]

⊠     ⊠     ⊠     ⊠     ⊠     ⊠

*As the end of the war approached and troops advanced through Germany, the men were able to observe the effects of Allied bombings. They also had thoughts about Germany's future after Hitler.*

226

Germany
May 2, 1945

Dear Chellis:

This is a German typewriter so you may see some unfamiliar symbols such as these: [four lightning bolts] ß ä ö . However, the main difference is that the y and z are interchanged.

Enclosed find Money Orders for the Old Main, Century Club, and Plaque Funds. I obtained them sometime ago but have not gotten around to mailing them to you until now. More later.

Since sometime last fall, your "Scuttle Butt" has been arriving regularly. I look forward to each issue. Having never been fortunate in meeting anyone from Luther in the service, I hated to see the address feature discontinued.

The countries we missed on the Tour in '36 are included in the quite different GI itinerary this time.

All of the various phases of war (not in the book) that you described to us in your classes have come true. I also recall your dismissing a class to listen to a Hitler speech, another time when Phylis Johnson looked a bit weak after a vivid bayonet story.

Hitler is said to be dead and the latest radio report is that the German army in Italy has surrendered unconditionally. I hope that Hitler does not become a legend to the German people who have taken a terrific beating. This is to be seen everywhere one goes in Germany. The Air Corps did a swell job on the Ruhr. On the Ruhr, as far as living standards in homes and clothes are concerned, the standards were very high for Germans and filthy for the imported slave labor. Also the diet of coffee and bread in the morning, soup at noon, and soup at night was of the worst.

Over here it is not hard to realize the size of the jobs yet to be done in Europe and the Pacific.

Almost time for a hash mark. "Where to next?" and "How many more Hershey Bars?" are the questions. I've found my work in S-2 and S-3 at Div Arty Hq most interesting. Have been well all of the time and lucky most of the time in being on the sending end rather than the receiving end of artillery fire.

Also Enclosed is a short Div History. Perhaps you are receiving copies from the other boys and will have enough to make a file.

Best wishes to all of you at Luther. Greet Dr. Sperati for me when you see him.

Hope to see you again at Homecoming not to far in the future.
Sincerely,
Harlan

Sgt Harlan G. Kittleson[212]

✉    ✉    ✉    ✉    ✉    ✉

*Throughout Germany, occupation forces saw the destruction firsthand.*

[V-MAIL]
From: Pfc. Robert H. Schlinkert July 6, 1945
Dear Dr. Evanson,

Just a few lines to you this time to give a change of address. It is now Co. C 15 Engr. C. Bn, APO 9, NY, N.Y. I was transferred out of my old unit into the 9th division for the occupational army . Please give this address to the Chips & Alumnis Offices. Also, send my copy of the "Scuttlebut" to this address.

I have enjoyed the Scuttlebut a lot. It has been a swell effort on the part of Luther College to send it to the servicemen from the College.

I am still in Germany between Nuremberg & Munich. It is a swell country but the weather is no good. It is cold all the time and there is plenty of rain. Never saw so much rain during the summer in all my life.

I was camped in Munich for 49 days. Moved in there May 1st. It snowed there that day. Munich is pretty well beat up. Most of the damage was done by Arial bombs. Nuremberg is nearly flat. I camped just across from the stadium there. Got a few snapshots of both places. Also I saw the hitler hidout at Berchtesgaden. That is the prettiest country I have seen., right in the big middle of the Alps.

This is all for now,
As ever,
Bob[213]

✉    ✉    ✉    ✉    ✉    ✉

*A number of men remained in Europe as part of the German Occupation. Although they might have preferred discharge and a return home, this was a marked improvement over combat conditions.*

July 30 1945
Gross Gerau Germany

Dear Chellis,

The "Scuttlebutt" has been coming through pretty good, but it is delayed a bit by an incorrect address so here is the correct one: Lt. James M. Anderson [...]

It has been some time since I wrote to you, so here is a short history of where I have been: I operated out of Pisa, Italy from Oct. '44 until Feb. '45; then to France—near Nancy, France—until early April; then to our present location which is 15 miles south of Frankfurt. We have good "civilian" quarters and the "chow" is pretty fair. We are one of the few P-47 (Thunderbolt) outfits that are to stay here as part of the Army of occupation. I don't mind that so much because between the two of us "I've never had it so good." Expect to move to our permanent occupation field near Schweinfurt within a month. During combat I managed to get in 65 dive-bombing missions and five escort missions.

I see by the latest Scuttlebutt that Don Strom is down at Heidelberg, so guess I'll have to take a trip down there to pay him a visit.

Enclosed is a check to be used for plaque fund, also a recent picture

As ever
Jimmy [J.M. Anderson][214]

  ✉   ✉   ✉   ✉   ✉   ✉

*In addition to serving in the Occupation, troops in Germany also had to train for possible duty against Japan.*

Neiderseeon, Germany
August—10—45

Dear Chellis;

Greetings from an old Luther undergrad and soldier.

I have enjoyed Scuttlebutt immensely. It is nice to hear about all the family at good old Luther College. I am especially interested in the whereabouts of the members of our great basketball team of '42—'43. I see Davy is Lt. and is ready for Pacific Duty. Of course the married man on our great team—Warren Selbo is Lt. and somewhere in States.

229

How about Paul Eggen, Don McDowell, Don Barth, Skip Herwig and Bill Bierdorf??? Incidentally Chellis—if it's not too much bother have you any L.C. men around Munich, Ger or haven't you a record?? Do not by all means go through any extra work as I know you are very busy. By the way, Chellis, I do request the Scuttlebutt and L.C. Bulletin. My many thanks for your fine help and consideration

I suppose you are wondering what I have been doing now since V-E Day. I have served as an M.P. until just a few weeks ago at which time we moved from Landsberg to Niederseeon exactly 30 kilometers from famous beer-garden of Hitler's at Munich. Now we have half hour of calisthentics and half an hour of foot drill combined with classes on Jap warfare each day. So you can see what kind of life I lead awaiting my future return to the unbeatable institution of L.C. God speed the day.

Enough for now, Chellis

Greetings to all at L.C.

A former student who shall return—P.F.C. Don Estenson[215]

⊠　　　⊠　　　⊠　　　⊠　　　⊠　　　⊠

*Not surprisingly, a common theme in most letters written after V-J Day was reassignment to the U.S. Nonetheless, the men recognized there was still work to be done in Europe.*

Prachatice, Sudetenland
Czechoslovakia
Aug 21 [1945]

Dear Chellis—

Thanks for the Shuttles—they've been arriving regularly. Ashamed to be so late in getting the "plaque" idea thru my head, but enclosed is a little something for that project. I'm back in the division CP again after a period of detached service with the counter-Intelligence in Düsseldorf, Germany. Mighty interesting work that was—catching big-name targets and small fry wehrwolves as well. Along with routine nabbing we laid the hand on the inventor of the tiger tank and the brother (S.A. General) of Joseph Goebbels, and I wound up with passably better "Deutsche Sprache" personally.

Now I'm all mixed up in the all-out I-E program, working out of the Division Information-Education office and getting set to teach in a "unit school"; but my biggest project now is my 81 points and how to shuffle 'em around to get me home! Daughter Margo Linn is growing up, per latest Kodacolors supplied by her mommy, Candy (Margaret Seegmiller Ruid), and I'm not there to watch. Hoping to be released from Czech exile soon—then back to school at Luther for my last year.

> Greetings from Sudetenland, troublespot of
> central Europe (it still is.)
> [Sgt. L. W.] Ruid[216]

# CHAPTER 15

# "Plenty of smorgasbord"—
# Reports from Scandinavia

*Most of the men serving in the "European Theater" were in the British Isles or on the continent itself. However, a few were in more outlying areas.*

[V-MAIL]

Jan.14, 1944 Iceland

From: Pvt Warren Baukol

Dear Chellis,

Received you very interesting letter a couple of days ago and also one from Pete.

As far as I know I am the only Luther man in this rather remote part of the world. My knowledge of Norwegion really came in handy here as the Icelandic language is nothing but real old Norwegion. I have made several friends here and have a rather nice life. I am sure that some of the most beautiful women in the world live here!!! The old Norwegion black dresses are worn by the older women. This is the only mail that travels by air.

Just, "Baukol"[217]

---

Iceland—Feb 21, 1944

Dear Chellis,

I got your second letter to us boys the last one was dated Feb 1 and I believe I got it about the 12th. I really enjoy your letters and hope I will continue to get them. I imagine that many of the other boys have told you this too but it is really hard to write because of sencorship. I will try and get some sort of a letter together and even if you lose interest here and there just keep on reading and you may find something interesting.

I forgot to mention in my last letter that I run into two classmates here in Iceland. Larson (42) from Glenwood (I never could remember his first name but his father is a cop in Glenwood and I believe he put in about two years at Luther) came to Iceland on the same ship but haven't seen him since as he went to a different part of the island. He is in an A.W. outfit. Then one day as I was in Reykjavik I run into "Hyppo" Nelson "42" of Benson who is in the field artillery about all he could say when I saw him (he had been here ten months then) was that he had been here too long

The houses here are mostly made of concrete and need to be because the extreme winds and the terrific amount of rain each year. The Icelandic women are good housekeepers and keep their homes very nice and clean. The majority of streets however are in terrible shape partly because of the new hot water system. By the end of the winter all the homes in this city of some 40,000 will be heated by hot water springs. The water is piped from the springs to the city and then to each house the cooled water running into the sea.

We have had a few planes over here since I have been here but I have not seen any. A couple of these planes were shot down.

I am going to enclose some clippings from our paper the "White Falcon" which I hope you will find interesting.

"The best of the Norwegion people moved to Iceland" is the reply I get from my girl friend when I try to point out that the Norwegions are still superior.

Thats all for now,
Warren Baukol[218]

✉    ✉    ✉    ✉    ✉    ✉

*A graduate of a Norwegian-American college could hardly ask for a better assignment than to be aboard a Norwegian ship.*

[Christmas Card:]
H. Nor. M.S. "King Haakon VII"
*Gledelig Jul og et Godt Nyttaar*

Merry Christmas and a Happy New Year
Nineteen Forty-four
=====

Dear Chellis:

I enjoy "Scuttlebutt" very much. It's very chatty and interesting. I get the impression that L.C. men are definite contributors in this war.

This duty is <u>choice</u>. I'm the liaison officer aboard this ship and with my six men in charge of communications we are the only Americans. That's plenty of smorgasbord, fish balls, fish cakes, as well as "gaffilter," anchovies, etc. And are these Norwegians salty!

Best wishes, Arden [Hesla '31][219]

⊠  ⊠  ⊠  ⊠  ⊠  ⊠

*Rolfe A. Haatvedt was assigned to the American Legation in Stockholm. Even after the war had ended in Europe, his duties there involved matters that were still censored.*

2 June 1945

Dear Chellis,

At long last comes a report from the station which you have no doubt been terming a pocket of resistance. Accept my humble apologies and count this letter as another result of V-E day.

First of all a word of appreciation for the monthly scuttlebutt which is always enjoyed. It is one swell job and has brought many Luther men together. The service will always be gratefully remembered by all of us. It's a fine supplement to Chips, Posten, and the Journal which arrive regularly. Our mail service has always been good, but last weeks effort surpassed all pouches in speed. I read a letter from Helen written only 7 days previously and one from an old pal in the Pacific islands reached me in 16 days.

Well, the censorship lid is still on tight in this business so I can't tell you much more than you have already learned from the Des Moines Register. The whole story will have to wait for V-J day. Our yellow enemies are still with us here in Sweden too and every once in a while we eat in the same restaurant. No courtesies are exchanged.

Both Chris Ravndal and Grant Olson have had their wives over here for some time—one of the blessings of the State Department which the Army and

Navy have not yet accorded officers. I've got my fingers crossed and am keeping the flame of hope burning. What the future has in store remains a matter of conjecture. The powers that be are mysteriously silent, but you know how fast they can expect you to move.

Spring in Stockholm is all sweetness and light—particularly the latter since we are rapidly approaching the days when there is no night. On Sundays and holidays the Swedes take to the woods with a vengeance, cycling or walking into the wilds to commune with the trolls. I'm due for leave the last two weeks of this month so I'm going to do a little vagabonding of my own after the first few days when I have promised to be on the staff of a summer institute in American culture sponsored by the Swedish-American Foundation and Stockholm University. I've inflicted myself as a lecturer on these people on several occasions the past winter—once up at Uppsala. I haven't met a Swede yet who doesn't want to go to the States.

The enclosure is for your rogues gallery. I've had the old blues on more since VE day than in all my time here previously. I'm hoping soon to go on a cruise with the Swedish Fleet so I'll have a chance to wear it without the curtain rope.

Best and warmest greetings to all, and I look forward to the day when I can once again walk up the hill with you. Fair winds and safe anchorage!

Sincerely,

Haat

Lt. R.A. Haatvedt, USNR[220]

# THE PACIFIC THEATER
## AND ASIA

# CHAPTER 16

# "Seeing a lot of history made right now"— Service in the Pacific—1943–1944

*For many students, their musical experience at Luther remained a vivid memory. But in addition to personal details and their usual comments about Luther, the letters sometimes contained grizzly reminders of the horrors of war.*

[V-MAIL]
From: Lt. Helge H. Nasby, USMCR 6 Nov 43
Dear Drs. Evanson and Qualley, (and all the rest that I know)
Received your circular letter of July yesterday. It took some time to get here because of the change in my address and it is quite a change too I can assure you. Nevertheless, the letter was very welcome and I'd like to get some more as you find time to put them out. My job out here is a staff job on the staff of the First Marine Amphibious Corps Quartermaster. It is a tremendous job that will take lots of work before we are through. How does the war in the Pacific look to you folks at home? Our hope and spirits are high and we have every reason to keep them so.

My wife, Isabelle, is teaching at Glenwood under Karl Nordgaard's brother. She likes it fine and says that he is nice to work for. By the way, give my regards to Karl N. and tell him that I never expected that my wife would be working for his brother.I hope that they get along all right. Belle is easy to get along with and never steps on anyones toes.

It must seem very strange to walk around Luther without a crowded campus. I can't imagine what only two hundred students on that spot would look like. How is Dr. Sperati? I wrote him a letter last night. I should write him often but the time does not seem to be available at times.

You should see our tent ornaments, you'd never guess so I'll tell you—Jap skulls! They bother you for a while but you get used to them and soon you start calling them names.

How is the band coming along? Does Dr. Sperati still direct it or does he have an assistant now? It wouldn't surprise me if he is inactive this year. He talked about retiring last Spring when I was there but then you can never tell what he will do from one day to the next. I hope he did retire. If so whom did you get to replace him? I thought that it would be a bit of a relief to get away from music for a few months but you can't take away food and still live. I miss the stuff so much that at times I'd give my right arm to be able to hear some symphony and to have my own band again to watch the kids gradually absorb some line of musical thought. My hands itch to get ahold of my horn again too and I know that even though the flesh is week the spirit might be strong enough to carry me through a few phrases of something or other.

Well, keep the home fires burning and send me some more news. How about the Luther Alumnus? Guess that I will be out here at least two years unless this war ends before then. My foxhole will be deep and the shelter strong. Greet the wives. Say hello to Elmer Anderson and the rest down at Bears, Germann's etc.

Sincerely,     Helge, LC '39<br>
Helge H. Nasby, Lt. USMCR[221]

✉     ✉     ✉     ✉     ✉     ✉

*With a new duty assignment, the men's responsibilities were often subject to change, and they had a period of readjustment.*

Dec-4-'43

Aboard the USS Lyria
Dear Chelis:

Received your latest report the other day and let me thank you right now for it.keep 'em coming.

Sometime after Happy Jenson received his transfer I received mine to the AK. As my ship was not available at that time, I got a 15 day leave & so back to Minot I went. As you can well understand it was a great week. Jack came home from Midshipman School decked out in his gold braid, Thanksgiving, and my twenty-second birthday all within seven days.

Right now I'm sitting in the ward room of my ship, and let me tell you now that it's a lot better than the Crane Hotel-re: your Report.

As to my duties aboard I'm not squared off yet, but it will either be Div. officer, Junior Gunnery or Navigation or a combination of both.

Greet Mrs. Evanson for me and Sara Marie Kohn etc-

Merry Christmas to all—

Bill Aaker[222]

---

*Aaker followed his initial report with a slightly more detailed letter the next month.*

25 Jan, 1944

At Sea—So. Pac. USS Lyra (A.K.101)

Dear Proff. Evanson;

After thirty days at sea and still some more to go I finally get a letter off to you.

Decorah must be plenty cold now, tho it is hard to believe when the temperatures here are well over 100°. This noon while having some general drills such as G.Q., Abandon ship etc. I placed some water on the bridge deck and it evaporated in less than one minuit. Slightly hot, but bearable.

There is no harm in saying that the good Lyra is in a small convoy on its way to a Navy advanced Base in the South Pacific. As our little yellow "friends" have been bothering us of late we have received a number of additional escorts. One escort is a bare 2,000 yards ahead of us. As you can imagine it gives a good feeling, especially when, because of CENCORED items, we are not making our top speed.

So far life has been uneventful—standing four on and eight off, minding my division as a Division officer, and studying Gunnery and fire control on the side. Assist. Gunnery Off., too (oh hum) The latter is my own idea, for my G.Q. station is a battery officer on one of the larger caliber A.A. Guns. This was quite an event for the task assigned was to train this bunch of seamen 2/c and a few 1st into a gun crew. This certainly gave me some sleepless nights for a while.

I haven't heard from Carol Jenson for a long time, but I suspect he is on his way back to the states—tho it wouldn't be a surprise if we should run into each other down here some place. As far as the rest of the L.C. men are concerned I've lost track of them completely—By the way, do you happen to know the where abouts of Joe Magallson (sp?), 1942? Also Gordon Petal, and Ray Franck? I've been looking forward to receiving your newspaper when I get back to the U.S.A.

During those long mid-watches (000-0400) and the 0400-0800 I've been studying the location of the stars—so far I've located Venus or a "mast head light on the horizon" twice—I sure get a kidding from the Exec when that happens—he stands O.O.D. & a Jr. off. as the J.O.O.D.—We use all three sets of signals C Maritime Commission, International, and Navy, so it keeps me jumping remembering all of them.

Well, time to knock off for chow so I close thanking you for your part in encouraging us to join the Navy—the best yet by far.

Sincerely,

W.C. Aaker (1943) Ens. (D-V6) USNR.

P.S. Buy a quart of cherry ice cream and eat it for me—sure could go for a "Luther Special"!![223]

✉    ✉    ✉    ✉    ✉    ✉

*Despite the adjustments they had to make aboard ship, men in the Navy could usually did not complain about their food, especially at holiday time.*

Dear Chellis,

After the last barrage of mail from the old school I'm manning my station to return fire as best I can. This form letter I enclosed helps send greetings and hope for the best of everything to you faculty members and students; they did better in the kitchen than they did in the mimeograph. Our chaplain, we have one Protestant & one Catholic, also wrote up a letter for our Thanksgiving celebration which had more action in the news than we were able to dig up for this event, but you'll get the idea that they feed us not only to keep us fat. Am I subtle!

We certainly enjoy seeing those familiar names and addresses, unfamiliar, you put forth as well for our reference. Perhaps we won't start many new correspondences but this outfit moves, and all the time I know I'll be looking for old friends in places which until now I only knew produced this mineral or that kind of people. It's a real tour aid, no less.

Personally, I'm getting along fine, and think this musician racket will be mine for the duration. We have a good band and enough regulars in the outfit to keep us in line. I naturally look for a day when I can relax on shore duty, but also know I can last as long as the next fellow out here.

I have been getting all the Chips, Alumnus news, Pete's letter, a real kick; and your letters, Chellis, there's no need to say I appreciate them for you know, or they wouldn't be coming. The best of all is to hear of your diligent efforts for the new Main and dorm; if we can assimilate some of your spirit, we should have both very soon. Good luck.

Sincerely Harold S
Harold Carlyle Skilbred, mus. 2/c
"FR" Div.[224]

---

[*Skilbred's letter contained three pages of enclosure: "Season's Greetings" from "the Captain, Officers, and Crew of Battleship 'X,'" a detailed menu of the USS South Dakota's Christmas dinner (featuring roasted tom turkey and roast loin of pork, and traditional accompaniments), and the following form letter, with "Chellis" written in by hand:*]

Dear *Chellis*—Did you like our Christmas menu? We enjoyed it too. This letter will be brief because of space but after our Thanksgiving letter several men brought items to our attention that they thought deserved mention. So here is some more news about ourselves.

Perhaps you no longer have your appendix. If you had it taken out you can sympathize with one of our men. We were at sea a few weeks ago and all seemed to be going well. Suddenly up jumped an acute appendix which demanded immediate surgery. The patient was prepared with a spinal anesthetic and the operation was just in its initial stages when the ship gave a slight lurch and a dull boom sounded through the operating room. "Was that a depth charge?" asked the boy. The doctor kept on working. Then came another and still several more booms. A destroyer had picked up a submarine contact not far from the ship and was giving the Japs a very hot time. "It makes you feel awful funny" said the patient a day or so later, "to be on the operating table with that sort of thing going on along side you". We can understand how he felt. With his stomach open and a doctor probing for an appendix he was in no condition for swimming. Anyway, he can tell his grandchildren that he had musical accompaniment to his appendectomy—the music of depth charges.

243

Early in the cruise we had an airplane alert and everyone made ready as the fighter planes zoomed over us to the attack. On the forward part of the ship manning the machine guns was a group of Marines. One of them gave a "rebel yell" and threw his wallet on the deck. "Everything in that says I get the first one." When finally our guns did tally at least one we could not tell who got it but it sounded like a rooting section at a Army—Navy game. All our boys and the men on nearby ships gave a cheer that must have been heard in Tokyo. How those boys strapped to the machine guns could jump up and down and cheer is still a mystery—but they did.

Well, here it is Christmas. Church services today had the regular carol singing and we are having a community carol sing before the movies on deck tonight. No "White Christmas" but we enjoyed it and thought of you. Remember us in your prayers. We will need them during the new year. Bye now. Will write again soon. Hal S.[225]

*The men serving in the Pacific were not only geographically a long way from home; they also had long periods of uninterrupted duty.*

[V-MAIL]
From: Lt. (jg) M. H. Hanson, Boat Pool, Navy 808 17 March 1944
Dear Chellis:

Thanks for the Luther news sent via your letter to the various servicemen wherever they may be. Its grand to know where the Old Gang is, these troubled days. I'm now completing my fifteenth month of Pacific duty and also my twenty-sixth month of active duty with no leaves so this guy is just a little anxious to see the Badger state once more, and naturally visit you people in Decorah. I was in on the "real thing" a few months past, still keep busy but seldom any interruptions from visitors. I am on one of "those islands" and don't anyone ever mention camping to me again—or I'll _____? Very amusing and educational incidents occur from day to day but I have the wanderlust and want to keep moving. If I remember correctly you were a "bluejacket" back in 19—or 18—??? Duty on the Pinney—I had a cousin on the "wagon" last I heard. Remember LeRoy Larson? "39" Navy pilot. Ran across him at chow a month ago—last time I saw him. I don't know how long I'll be here—Greet Mrs. E. Write again. I wrote to Chellis Jr.

Sincerely Yours

Dusty[226]

✉     ✉     ✉     ✉     ✉     ✉

*Sea duty in the Pacific often involved long periods of isolation and boredom. And when the men did see action, censorship regulations limited what they could describe.*

March 27, 1944

Dear Chellis,

For over a month we didn't get any mail at all on board, but the other day we got all our back mail, including our Christmas presents. Among the letters for me were two of your very interesting letters, and it occurred to me that I should have written you long ago. You know, of course, how hard it is to write letters when one goes a long time without any mail at all, but now that we have mail, I have gone on a writing spree. This makes the fifth letter I have written this evening, and I still intend to write to Chellis jr. this evening. He wrote me a nice letter and it shall be answered pronto.

You might like to know that I am the Ass't. First Lieutenant on board this ship. The job is interesting and at times it is a very busy job. Right now I am in the midst of a damage control bill, which is taking up my time very nicely. We have our toughest job when we are underway, but we have been underway very little. We stayed in one place for almost three months, and that got to be very boring. However, there isn't a thing any of us can do about the situation, so we make the best of it. Reading occupies most of my spare time, and I have had plenty of that up until just lately. I am also the recreation officer and it gets to be quite difficult to scare up movies for the crew every night. Not all the ships have them, which makes it all the harder for us. We also try to get the crew on the beach once in a while on supervised recreation parties. None of us have been in a remotely civilized place for about four months, but we enjoy going over and getting sunburned and swimming in the surf. I'd still like to be back. There are too many things that interest me more than barren islands.

Bill Aaker and myself keep a correspondence going. He is on another ship like the one I am on. We haven't run into each other yet, but it is very possible that we

245

will. We have been at the same places, I am sure, but at different times. Someday we probably will meet. Hope so. It sure would be swell to see a familiar face again. We had a good time together in San Francisco. He got his ship a week or so after I got mine, so we were together almost all the time we were there. We had a few talks with Ole Davidson too. I had intended to write him, but that evidentially was a good intention gone wrong. It's easy to say that you are going to write, but writing is another thing.

My brother Maurice is now at Columbia. As you probably know, he was in the outfit that started the first part of this month. Sherman is in the Maritime Service, and he too has put out to sea. He seems to have landed a nice berth on a new merchant ship. Frankly, I don't have much time for the Merchant Service, but that is only one man's opinion. We had a little trouble with one in one of the places we were, which no doubt accounts for my animosity. There is a lot of bickering going on which seems to be out of place during a war. Looking at it fairly, they are doing a swell job and it is not for me to criticize them. They take the chances we do, and the get a whole lot of cargo transported. But I'll still take the Navy. That is the best branch of the service as far as I'm concerned, and I know you think it is.

I wish I could tell you where we are right now, but I'll have to content myself with telling you that we are seeing a lot of History made right now. Everyone who is out here is seeing the same thing. I shall never regret going to sea, but I surely would like to be back. I had to get engaged by proxy, but I refuse to get married by proxy. The mail helps a lot, but it still gets pretty lonesome at times. However, there are many in the same position that I find myself in, so I will wait just as they are doing. I am looking forward to the first Homecoming I will be able to go to as soon as the war is over. It will be great to see the boys again.

Well, I must knock off now, and I'll try to write more often. I feel sort of ashamed for not writing sooner, but it is sort of useless to apologize for something that is already done.

As ever, "Hap"
C.E. Jenson USS Grumium[227]

⊠   ⊠   ⊠   ⊠   ⊠   ⊠

*For the Navy men serving long assignments at sea, mail gave a welcome morale boost.*

[V-Mail]

From: Lt. j.g. K.I. Olson USNR 7 April 1944

Dear Chellis,

Your last two lengthy and extremely welcome letters certainly deserve more than a v-mail for an answer but for the time being this will have to suffice—Was glad to hear such good news about all of the Luther fellows. How about Jim Crain and Reuben Lund—have you had any word from them? Arie and I have kept pretty good track of one another—had a good letter from Chel, Jr. a few days ago—that work sounds like a good deal for him. I hear frequently from Ted & Freda—they are a lucky pair—that leaves only Chel and I from that gang—we better be getting busy—I really don't have much chance for that sort of thing—one 16 hour period is the longest I have been off this ship in 9 months—though I'm a long way from home my world is pretty small. Am in the best of health—morale good, but am ready to go back to the States any time. Thanks again for the letters.

Sincerely, Kenny Olson[228]

*Although the men could not give details about their location or their specific activities, they often sent information about their training locales. Sightings of other Luther men were also worthy of note.*

April 8, 1944

Dear Dr. Evanson,

Writing time is more or less at a premium for me but with "holiday routine" on the plan of the day, I have managed to gather a few spare moments. I wish to thank you for the very interesting newsletter which I am now receiving. I have often wondered where everyone is stationed, what they are doing, and etc—your letter has brought me up to date on that scene. I learned of your letter from Cal De Buhr, but pushed off to sea a few days after and never had a chance to request a copy. So thanks again and thanks to Cal for being "on the ball."

In May it will be two years I have been away from Luther's campus and with the passing of each day I become more eager to return. It's difficult to imagine two years could flit by so past but, as you know, the Navy keeps a man busy and watching the clock is strictly prohibited. Well, now that I've said I have been so busy you probably are wondering what I have been doing.

247

After struggling through midshipmen's school I received orders to report to San Francisco in twelve days. This allowed me a short time at home and that's about all. I was in "Frisco" just long enough to buy two suits of "whites" and immediately shoved off to my present base. Can't mention the base but "Dyb" wrote the Chips giving my probable location—he hit right on the head. I arrived here Dec 19, 1942, was assigned a ship on the 20th and have been at sea ever since. My first as you probably know was the USS Beaumont (PG60), PG meaning a converted gun boat. I made several long trips on her and was transferred in April of '43 to the Beryl. Have been here ever since. Can't say much about the kind of duty we have except that I'm well satisfied with it. I have one gripe, however,—wished I could get back to the mainland for a little duty.

March 1st I added a half gold stripe to my uniform so am now a Lt. (j.g.).I missed the promotion preceding this one by one day so was plenty disgusted for a spell.

Haven't bumped into many Luther men out here however they seem to be filtering out this way now. Saw Dusty Hanson and Cal DeBuhr, Dusty was in some kind of amphib duty and Cal has taken to subs. I don't envy Cal a bit, that's rugged duty.Ran into Eddie Elickson at an officers club and understand he is navigator in the ferry Command. Have met several doctors who were well acquainted with Dr. Fritchen but understand he is now in San Francisco.Paul Gandrud is also out here. I plan to meet him this afternoon.

Guess I've given you about all the dope censor regulations permit but will keep you informed from time to time on news from out this way.

Keep those letters coming. I know it means many hours of extra duty but it's greatly appreciated

Radtke [Lt. (jg) Loyal C. Radtke USNR.][229]

✉ ✉ ✉ ✉ ✉ ✉

*Navy duty took the men to a number of well-known locations. If they did not get too specific in their descriptions, they were able to pass along some information to Evanson.*

New Guinea
May 10, 1944

Dear Chellis,

I received the Newsletter you sent out a few days ago and it was most interesting to learn where the boys are stationed through out the world. Some of them went to Luther when I was there and was glad to know where they are located. I also receive Chips and look forward to the time when they come. Karl keeps me informed concerning the news.

Our ocean voyage lasted 38 days and were mighty happy to set foot on dry land after that journey. We came by the way of the Panama Canal and that was an interesting experience in itself to pass through the canal. Conditions here are better then we had anticipated and no reason to complain.

We have talked to some of the natives and they seem quite friendly.

We have movies and other entertainment three or four times a week and we appreciate that.

It is quite warm here but cools off in the evenings which makes fine sleeping weather. This is the rainy season and it really comes down.

It's getting dark so must close.

I trust that all are fine in your family. Am looking forward to the time when can return to the Luther Campus.

Sincerely,
Paul G. Nordgaard[230]

✉   ✉   ✉   ✉   ✉   ✉

*Unless they were in active combat conditions, the men found much of their Navy routine uneventful.*

3 August 1944
Central Pacific

Dear Dr. Evanson:

Please don't be too shocked when you receive this letter, but believe it or not, I have been intending to write for quite some time now. Trouble is, there isn't much to write about that will pass censorship.

Have been on this broncho of the seas for about 2 months now and cant really say that I do like it. The skipper, other officers, and crew are a pretty fine bunch of guys. We are doing convoy work behind the lines, and very little happens that is of any excitement. Maybe a G.Q. once in a while or something like that, but that, so far, is the extent of it. Before I came aboard, this little baby did chalk up a Jap sub, though I sincerely hope they (or we) will come across a few more of the yellow devils before I leave. The latter probably won't occur for some 12–16 months yet, so lets hope it's the duration.

Saw Bestuel while I was in Pearl Harbor. He is on a Navy oiler. Compared with our quarters, he is living in a palace .I missed DeBuhr while there, but may get to see him sometime.(I hope.)

What's news around Luther and Decorah. Haven't had any mail in 2 months except a couple of V-mails, so really don't know the news.

Will close for now—and am hoping to hear from you—

> Sincerely,
> Cyc
> [Ens. Paul Schroeder]

P.S. Give my regards to all.[231]

⊠ ⊠ ⊠ ⊠ ⊠ ⊠

*Duty at sea meant long periods without mail, and in the Pacific, the men were very conscious of the great distances between them and home.*

9 Aug '44

Dear Chellis,

I've managed to get hopelessly behind in my correspondence lately. All our mail comes in bunches—then comes the task of getting a months letters written in two or three days.I've been getting your letters every month.

I've been aboard this ship for over a year now. I still wouldn't care for any other duty but sure could go for a little <u>stateside</u> liberty. No one can gripe like a sailor.

Everything is going 4.0 in this area. This war is getting a bit one sided now and getting more so every day.

I had a chance to see Bob Thayer a while back. It was just for a few minutes but I have hopes of seeing him again in the near future.

I get an occasional letter from my kid brother at Luther. He is quite impressed with the school and seems to have no doubt as to where he someday will get his degree. By the way there's still two or three at home who will be ready in a few years.

I haven't much hope of getting back until after the war but am planning on a trip back there as soon as its over. And it had better not be 'Golden Gate by '48.' Looks more like '45 to me.

If you think of it how's about saying 'hello' to Dr Keiler for me. I may get around to writing him a short note one of these days. I don't think I'll ever forget his 'debit! and credit!' drawers in Accounting class.

Most of the interesting news is censored so will give up at this time
[Ens] Harold [Bravick][232]

&#9993; &#9993; &#9993; &#9993; &#9993; &#9993;

*Despite the dangers, men in the submarine corps took great pride in their branch of the Navy.*

[Aug 23—'44]

### U.S.S. Skate (SS305)

Dear Chellis,

Must take off a few minutes to drop you a line—let you know that the U.S.S. Skate hasn't failed to reach the surface every time we've hit for depths.

We're all squared away down on the boat again after two weeks rest, so it won't be long before we depart again for another crack at the slant-eyed sailors. Have been pretty successful thus far.

Thanks again for putting out the dope sheets; I'm sure all the other fellows appreciate it as much as I do. Seems good to come in after several months cooped up in this sealed over-grown gas-pipe and get caught up on all the news of the Norsemen.

It might be espirit de corps, but I'm still sold on the submarine Navy. Probably one of its biggest points as far as I'm concerned is the chow situation—never a hungry moment! 'Course we do run out of spuds toward the end of each run, but rice or noodles are a fair substitute, as long as the steak is there.

Sounds to me as though Larson Hall will be a new place next time we see it! I've been gone only a short time and already so many changes have taken place back there I can scarce keep up with them.

251

Cyc's address: Ens. P.C. Schroeder, [...]

As the war progresses it seems the big Homecoming is not so far in the offing, and we're all more and more impatiently awaiting that day. Guess we've all found the old adage "Absence makes the heart grow fonder" quite true—those Luther associations are something that can't be equaled.

Saw your old ship again several months ago; did you know she's the flag ship of one of the fleets out here? She's really doing a good job, truly in keeping with her history.

You'll have to forgive the garbled condition of the letter—I have the duty tonight and am continually being interrupted. Every time we get back to the boat after a rest period chaos reigns supreme the first day, so many things to get squared away.

Have made some connections and acquaintances out here which are quite valuable to any young swains who might find themselves out here.So in case you hear of anyone coming out this way tell them to find out whether the Skate is in and I'll try to fix them up.

Time has come for me to hit my sack—reveille at 0600, which is early after two weeks of no keeping of hours! So I'll knock off.A chance exists that I'll be back there in several months.

Respectfully, [Ens] Cal DeBuhr[233]

*The men quickly found out that their idealized visions of a paradise in the Pacific were often far different from what they experienced there.*

10 September 1944

Dear Chellis,

Thanks a lot for your "poop" sheet, believe me mail is a very much looked for item in these parts.

My brother is now overseas, where he is I haven't the slightest idea, I don't have his proper address yet but hope to soon. A rather strange thing happened when we left the states, I believe that we were at the same P of E and at the same day also. Of course neither of us knew that. Apparently he left a little later than I did for my folks are getting my mail but not his.

I am on an island in the SW Pacific, not a bad one either. We have lots of Japs here too, lots of live ones and lots of dead ones too. Also an active volcano complete with earthquakes and tropical storms. About the first thing that happens to all visitors to this part of the world is the exploding of the myth of the glamorous South Sea Island Gals. Out here they are black, half (exactly) naked semi-pygmies. One look is enough to last for the duration plus 6.

The jungle is thick and complete with millions of types of insects and a plentiful sample of each, centipedes being the worst problem. They have a nasty bite and are brown slimy looking things about 8 inches long.

Enough for now, I'm awaiting more news from Luther. How did the drives for building funds make out? Have you been able to do any work on a new Main yet?

Sincerely
[Lt Robert H. ] Babe Hanson[234]

✉    ✉    ✉    ✉    ✉    ✉

*In the Pacific, even men not serving in the Navy spent a considerable aboard ships.*

New Guinea
21 Sept/44

Dear Chellis:

Have been receiving your scuttlebutt pretty regularly so I thought I would drop you a line and let you know how I appreciate your efforts to keep the boys informed of the progress of Luther and the boys in the service.

I have been overseas now for a year, spent three months in the Hawaiian Islands and until now in New Guinea Have been in two amphibious operations so far, one operation I landed on D. Day half an hour after the first waves. It is quite a thrill splashing thru the water to the beach without knowing what is behind the jungle to greet you .As yet I have had only one narrow escape, a bunch of bombs lit a few yards away, but I was in my air raid shelter. We had received air raids pretty regularly until the invasion of Palau & Halmaheras. I guess the japs have their hands full up there.

Have spent so much time on board ship traveling half way around the world and making amphibious operations I almost feel as much like a sailor as a soldier.

As yet I have not run into any Luther College men but hope to someday. Would appreciate some of the addresses of the L.C. men in the Pacific.

We have shows three nights a week, also have a daily news sheet so we are not entirely isolated. Will send a copy along. My wife is working in Kansas City while I am gone. I guess her brother (Kenneth Fagerhaugh) is working on some important war materials. Well must close,

Capt. A.L. Enger[235]

⊠        ⊠        ⊠        ⊠        ⊠        ⊠

*The men who had taken Evanson's history classes had studied war as an academic subject. Now they were experiencing it firsthand.*

8 October 1944

Dear Chellis,

Have been going to write to you for quite some time now, but have never seemed to get around to it. But I'm in hopes that the adage, "Better late than never" still goes with you.

First of all I want to say that I think your "Scuttlebutt" is a swell idea; I've enjoyed every one I've received, I assure you. Keep up the good work. I think of college days and friendships made there very often of late, and it is certainly good to hear what the L.C. grads are doing around the globe.

Our Division has been pretty busy lately on Peleliu island of the Palau group "West of Tokyo". Those first few days were neither fun or thrilling. Wars in history books used to sound so very thrilling when we discussed them in the class room, but the real thing is quite different.

Ran into two L.C. men enroute here. Leo "Gabby" Sebastian, 1st Lt., USMC (sorry I don't have his address) and George Scale (Dick's kid brother) Cpl. USMC, H & S, 1st Mo. Trans. Bw. 1st Marine Div. % FPO Frisco. George wasn't a L.C. man but was around for homecomings and holidays so much that we nearly considered him one of the gang. We three had quite a number of Bull sessions during the time we were aboard the same transport and you can imagine what we talked about most.

I see where my ex roommate <u>Capt.</u> Holmlund has been around quite a good deal of Europe and seemingly is the same old boy.

College reports sound good. I hardly know however, just how you can operate. Am certainly proud of the place. The male to female ratio is about reversed from what it was when I started. How's the band coming along?

My greetings to Nargaard, Larson and all the old friends there. I think of all of you often and will be up to see you all in a year or so when I get my second leave. On my first one I had such a short time up there that I didn't get to see half of the people I wanted to see.

Take care of the home front there, Chellis. I know you can. We'll take care of these—Nips as fast as we can and be back for a real Homecoming when it's all over.

Very Sincerely
Perry Dungey

P.S. Just now got a letter from Dick Skale, flying B—17's in England. He's really doing a job.[…][236]

*There were relatively few Marines who corresponded with Evanson, but they displayed their characteristic pride in the Corps.*

Somewhere in Central Pacific
Oct. 15, 1944

Dear Chellis;

Just received my copy of the August 'Scuttlebutt' this morning and decided that I had Prolonged the letter that I have owed you for so long, long enough. I don't know of any mail that I look forward to receiving quite as much as I do our Scuttlebutt. (If you will permit me to say our.I still like to call myself a Luther man even though I am a long ways from there now.)

I still haven't been fortunate enough to run across any of the Luther fellows since I came into the service but there isn't so many of the Luther men in the Marines and those of us who are in the Marines are probably pretty well seperated. Ever since leaving the states I have been on the lookout for the U.S.S. Cabot which Harold is on but as yet I haven't had any luck and as far as that goes I probably won't, although I really would like to run across him.

I really got a big kick out of Coach Pete's article in the August Scuttlebutt about his football team. I suppose its quite a change for him after having fellows like Curt, Bud, Gabby, Settji and etc. But then I suppose all the schools are having to face the same problem this year. I am in hopes that after we finish off the slant-eyed rats that I will be able to get back to Luther and maybe this time I won't have to spend quite so much of my time working and will be able to come out for at least one or two sports. My younger brother Don writes that he is even out for football, I can just picture him as small as he is for a football player in a uniform. But I still wish him all the luck in the world, I'm sure that the team Coach Pete has this year will be fighting just as hard for good old Luther as any previous team has.

You mentioned in the August Scuttlebutt something about filing these letters until after the war when we have the big argument as to who was in the best outfit you can be sure that I'll be right there arguing for the 5th Mar. Div. The big five as we call it is tops with me. Although I am still a boot I can say that I have learned a lot, not only about fighting but about things in general. As my dad always told me after being in World War I that ones experiences in the service are worth a million but you won't care to go through them again for another million after you once get back home.

As you probably already know I am in the infantry, and as much as I detested the thought of becoming a boot soldier as a civilian I finally wound up as one myself, and now I can say that I am proud of the fact. The nucleus of this division is composed of the *[following line cut out of page, presumably by censor]* and I can think of no men that I would rather have over me than these fellows. But enough of this bragging about the outfit that I am in.

I'm sure by this time you have come to the conclusion from this scrambled up bunch of words that I need some more English especially some work on letter writing.But I will try to at least make my address plain enough so I will be sure and keep getting all my Luther mail.

Greetings to Chellis Jr., the rest of the family, the faculty, as well as all the students. There has been many a day that I have wished that I was sticking my feet under the table at the boarding club, especially since we came overseas and the chow isn't always the best. I'm sure that I will also never forget the swell pheasant dinner at your home one Sunday while I was a Luther.

Best of Luck
Wayne [Bravick][237]

⊠　　　⊠　　　⊠　　　⊠　　　⊠　　　⊠

*While they had serious duties to perform, medical officers also benefited from some conditions envied by their fellow officers.*

[Oct. 18—'44]
Somewhere in the Pacific

Dear Chellis—

Received your note too late to look up those two men you mentioned in the San Francisco area—However, was glad to hear from you & enjoyed getting the "Scuttlebutt." As an old Navy man yourself you realize that such means of news transmission is quite fast and amazingly accurate—

You will perhaps recall that on our European trip, I was one of the few who did not get seasick. I don't know if it was the Cashton moonshine, the Iowa beer or just descending from a long line of Norske sailors—However, duty on a "tin can" is a real test & so far I am doing fine—The scenery is beautiful even if it has a monotonous sameness but it will probably liven up a bit soon—

You perhaps have such vital statistics as the fact that I finished Marquette med. school & interned at Columbia Hospital in Milwaukee, Wis. before entering the service on an active duty status, That is, in case anyone is interested—Right now I am the medical officer on the best destroyer in the Pacific Fleet—the stalwart <u>Stanly</u>.

My address is and will be for some time to come

Lt (j.g.) Joseph E Homstad M.C. U.S.N.R. [...]

Like the rest I certainly do appreciate your interest in us boys & always did enjoy stopping to see & listen to you—you can bet that I could go for a cup of that good old Norske Coffee again instead of the Navy idea of that good old beverage—

By the way, I surely would like to know more about Ted Normann, Dr. Kaasa, H.<u>T. Mo</u>en & some of the boys of my vintage—1938 was a good year, eh Chellis?

As medical officer, I don't have to work too hard and have no regular watches to stand & consequently am the envy of my fellow officers (the other 19) when I sleep all night without interruption. They are a fine bunch of young fellows and so life is quite congenial aboard this ship. No Luther boys present except me but one from Drake and one from Notre Dame (former track Capt.) have heard of Luther. Incidentally, there are no other <u>former</u> Trombone players either.

I have three pharmacist mates to do most of my work so if anyone does write, I'll answer eventually—Hope you had a good time at homecoming entertaining among others, my father-in-law & his two beautiful daughters. Give your family my regards & anyone else that might remember me—Will look forward to more news—

Sincerely,
Joe Homstad[238]

⊠        ⊠        ⊠        ⊠        ⊠        ⊠

*Many of the men in the Pacific saw heated action, but others enjoyed less dangerous conditions.*

New Guinea
22 October 1944

Dear Chellis,

Today your August "Scuttlebutt" arrived with alot of news of the boys I hadn't hears about for along time.I hadn't been able to get Rod McConnells address since he got in the navy so it was really welcome.

Things north of here have really been breaking, but we haven't come close to it, nor do we expect to for quite some time yet, although I wouldn't mind eating Christmas dinner in Manila. It's so quiet down here that we cuss the birds for waking us up in the mornings.

Ever since I got out here I've been stationed at a very nice base, in fact those who have been farther north say this is the best base they've seen, and I must admit we live the life of Riley.

The base is in a large bay, surrounded by mountains with the remains of a former cocoa nut plantation all around it. We live in huts, twelve men to a hut, have a very nice officers club, excellent chow, plenty of recreation in the line of volley ball and soft ball, and nothing else to do.In fact I've had such an easy life that the old bread basket is growing; top the scales at 195 now.A good basketball game would kill me. However, that will all change in a couple of days when I go aboard ship.

A few days ago the army engineers took my ship down to a small native missionary village for a picnic. It was really a very interesting day. The missionary had been there for over sixty years, so the natives were quite civilized and all spoke English, but their homes, clothes, and food were much the same as before, that is everything except the head hunting.

I've written Kenny a couple of times since I've been here, but no answer. He's probably having a little more interesting time now though, and is too busy to write. Maybe I'll catch up to him someday.

I haven't seen a Luther man yet. I did run into a St. Olaf man last week, so we had a big time talking in a Scandinavian accent, but he didn't come up to a Luther man.

Received a letter from Chell the other day too. He said he hoped to get home for Christmas again this year too. That would really be swell. I only wish I could be there to have some of the good old times. Maybe next year.

I haven't seen or heard from Archie since I left the states, but I imagine he's somewhere up in the Central Pacific. When it comes to writing he usually has a pretty bad case of writers cramp.

Say hello to the family and give Lucky a scratch behind the ears for me.

As ever,

Jake [Ens. T.L. Jacobsen]

The new idea on the "Scuttlebutt" is good, however, see to it that the greatest share comes from Pete and yourself.[239]

✉   ✉   ✉   ✉   ✉   ✉

*Once news of a battle had been officially released to the press, the men were free to report it in their own mail. But even then, they usually limited their details.*

25 Oct 1944

Dear Chellis:

Just received your July copy of "Scuttlebutt" and was sure glad to get it. It reminded me to write to you as I have planned many times but never got around to it.

According to your sheet the Luther boys are well represented all over the world. I haven't seen any Luther boys for a long time now but saw John Boe, a Lt (jg), at the time, at the first stop west of the states. Also saw Otto Sheel at the same place and Erling Jordahl there also. The next Luther man I saw was Bob Lee at a little island quite a way. farther out. He was on his way back stateside & I the other way

Since I've been out here we have been in on a couple of the big shows and plenty of excitement. Our squadron was the one that sighted the Jap Fleet which resulted in a big battle and destruction of a large part of Jap sea and air power. I can tell you this as it is old news & has appeared in the newspapers some time ago. We have a good outfit and a good reputation out here.

I'm enclosing a money order for $25. which I pledged about a year ago for the rebuilding of Old Main. Sorry I'm so slow but I never thought of it near pay day and later it was too late.

Hope to receive more of your "Scuttlebutt" in the future.

Sincerely,

[Lt ] K.O. Hotvedt

P.S.—My wife and I are expecting the stork sometime in December.[240]

⊠     ⊠     ⊠     ⊠     ⊠     ⊠

*In the Pacific Theater, conditions might remain very dangerous long after troops had initially secured a new area.*

[V-MAIL]

From: Lt. T. E. Overby Nov. 2, 44—Philippines

Dear Friend

Just a short note to let you know what happened to one of your students. I hope you will pass it on to the old gang.

Landed shortly after D-day & have really seen the sights. Saw all of it from the ship & then came in when things were still hot.I still spend time in a fox hole as the Jap planes wouldn't have missed it for anything.

My job is registrar in a Station Hosp & keeping records out here is rugged. However, battle or no the paper work must go on.

I hear from Enger once in a while. He is a Capt. & now on New Guinea. He has really been in the thick of it but is O.K. the last I heard.

I read one copy of that paper you put out & I think it is grand. How about a copy once in a while.

Hope to hear from you some time.

A friend,

Ted Overby[241]

⊠     ⊠     ⊠     ⊠     ⊠     ⊠

*While the correspondents tried to give Evanson as much information as possible, they had to be sensitive to censorship regulation, which seemed particularly tight in the Pacific Theater.*

The Mariannas<br>5 November 1944

Dear Mr. Evanson,

I have intended to write and thank you for the "Scuttlebutt" which I have been receiving, many times but have been a little careless in that respect I guess.

I received one copy while in Port Hueneme, Calif. And found that "Brooklyn" Christianson was there but my outfit left the states before I could look him up. This issue (August) informs me that a former classmate and friend has been commissioned. Ens. Clifford Ellingson at Ft. Pierce, Fla.

I enlisted in the Navy in October, 1943 and in January 1944 was transferred to the Seabees.I am now in the 31st Special Naval Construction Battalion which by way of explanation is a combination Construction and Stevedore outfit. We left Port Hueneme, Calif. on Sept. 11, 1944 and after a trip of 26 days at sea landed in the Mariannas. I cannot specify the exact island due to censorship regulations. Our trip out here was marked by stops at Pearl Harbor and the Marshall Islands. We were not permitted to get off the ship which was an Army transport. The U.S.A.T.

I have been hearing a lot about Luther since September as one of your freshman is a very close friend of mine. She's Miss Verna Amdahl and then of course I hear all the happenings from Jackie Sand too.

From what President Preus writes of the changes in Larsen Hall I guess the dormitory must be quite a place now. Was sorry to hear that Wartburg and Central had the strength to be Luther. Seems rather different that when I was there. I'll say good-bye for now and will look forward to the next issue of "Scuttlebutt".

Sincerely,<br>Bob Sand [S 1/c][242]

*Because of the vast distances involved, sailors and soldiers stationed in the Pacific Theater sought to keep their addresses up-to-date so that they would continue receiving news from home.*

[V-Mail]
From: Pvt Dean M. Penney 37680164
[No Date—probably early November 1944, preceding the next letter by a brief interval]
Dear Chellis,

Just a few lines to let you know my change of address, as it seems pretty good to get the news about the Luther boys. Seems like it shouldn't be too long before the boys can come home and back to the things they care for.

How are things getting along at school? Suppose there is quite an enrollment there for summer school.

I'm located in Hawaiian Islands on the island of Oahu. Seemed good to get back on land after being in the water for a while. Guess I wouldn't make a very good sailor.

Everything going along about so so but glad I'm not any further. I will close hoping this finds you and the rest of Luther folks all okay.

Pvt Dean M. Penney             As ever
                                          Dean[243]

---

*Soon after arriving in Hawaii, Pvt. Penney had to report yet another address change, with additional news as well.*

Nov 11, 1944
Oahu T.H.

Dear Chellis,

Received the August & September editions of Scuttlebutt and have changed addresses, so thought it would be best to drop you a line. Enjoying reading about the Luther boys but as yet haven't run into any of them. Guess some of them come into Pearl Harbor regular.

Assignment allright but still in question as to what the outfit is bound for. Taking training everyday so suppose one can hope for the worst and never be disappointed.

I hear from Lorrie Ugland quite regular. He was home on furlough and getting married from the way his last letter read.

Did the election turn out as you had planned it? Seemed like quite a landslide. Maybe after politics are straightened out they can wind things up in Europe.

Going seems to be pretty rough over there from the way the papers read. Hope it doesn't take too much longer over there. Philippine invasion proved to be pretty tough too. Well I guess I'm no prophet and would hate to try to predict when it would be over.

How was homecoming last year? My Sister, Ruth, was there and had a nice time. Maybe next year all the boys can be back.

Hoping this finds all well at your house and at school I remain.

Respectfully yours
Dean[244]

✉   ✉   ✉   ✉   ✉   ✉

*Some of the men found themselves performing duties that seemed unexpected in terms of their previous academic records.*

U. S. S. Lyra (AK-101)

13 November, 1944—Sunday

Dear Chelis—

Haven't heard a thing from the Alma Mater for some months, so will send this along to stir the place up a bit.

At the moment I'm sitting on the boat deck—gazing over the most vacant So. Pac. Island I've seen yet. Altho it's cool enough, what with rain pouring down every few hours, this being anchored for a month in one spot is boring. Have had a little excitement of a sort, but everything is quit now.

Bye the way, if Tutor Ellingsen or one of the math proffers should show up you might tell them that I, one of the worst mathematics students ever, is now taking an active hand in navigating this ship around. At that it's very interesting & one thing for certain, you're on your own!

My brother, Jack, whose on a "tin-can" has been in a bit of action—some time ago. Saipan, Teanean, and some shore bombardments. He's a Fire Control Officer on his ship.

Haven't seen a thing of former Luther men here, although I've looked carefully—ah yes Carol (Happy) Jenson ship is now a IX 112, instead of AK112—a spare parts ship.

Here's wishing you a happy holidays, New Year, & greet "All hands" for me—

Regards,
Ensign W.C. Aaker USNR[245]

✉    ✉    ✉    ✉    ✉    ✉

*Although Evanson received some details of combat action, the men usually downplayed its severity, as with this description of battles experienced by the U.S.S. Killen.*

[Letterhead: U.S.S. Killen (DD593)]

18 November 1944

Dear Chellis,

It has been my desire to write to you for a long time just to say "hello", & in remembrance of one happy year spent at Luther. Now that you have so kindly included me on your mailing list of "Scuttlebutt," writing to thank you for it seems a must.I appreciate the Navy influence on your newssheet.

Most of the names you mention, naturally, are strange to me, but often I get news there of one of the old buddies like Dusty Hanson, Kip Weyke, Paul Preus, et al. Most of them alas I haven't seen since I left Decorah. But I have kept close touch with Kermit D. Hanson, who is now out here somewhere as supply officer on an escort carrier. I also had a good visit with Paul Preus & Solveig in San Diego last summer. He was attending West Coast Sound School while my ship was in there for a few weeks. Unfortunately, our schedules did not permit an evening of Luther gossip.

My own Navy career has been varied. Three years of it in March, & it seems a lifetime. I spent one year in Alaska on patrol duty, & most of last year going to school in the states putting this new destroyer in commission and getting her organized. We left the states in midsummer. I'm primarily the anti-submarine officer aboard, but also act as 1st division officer, deck watch officer, & navigator .Lots of things to learn, but we keep very busy & I like it very much.

We haven't been out here very long, but our combat record already shows a part in the 1st landings in the Philippines & in the battle of Surigao Strait. We have official credit to date for torpedo hits on a Jap battleship, a cruiser, & a few Jap planes definitely shot down. Lots of excitement going on lately.

Hope you are all well. What is young Chellis doing now? I still remember vividly the waffle dinner that the news bureau staff enjoyed at your home, & Pug

Nelson had to stop with only six waffles down. Give my regards to Prexy Preus, Pip Qually, Pete, Dave Nelson, & and others I know around Luther. I'm looking forward to my next visit there, & dedication of the new main hall. Enclosing a small donation to the fund.

As ever,

[Lt] Bob Jarnagin[246]

*[Ed note: It is interesting to compare Jarnagin's description with this one from the Navy Historical Center:*
*<http://www.history.navy.mil/photos/sh-usn/usnsh-k/dd593.htm>:*
*Department Of The Navy—Naval Historical Center*
*805 Kidder Breese SE—Washington Navy Yard*
*Washington DC 20374-5060*

*Online Library of Selected Images:*
*—U.S. NAVY SHIPS—*
*USS Killen (DD-593), 1944–1975*

*USS Killen, a 2050-ton Fletcher class destroyer built at the Puget Sound Navy Yard, Bremerton, Washington, was commissioned in May 1944. She arrived at Manus, Admiralty Islands, in September 1944 to begin combat operations against Japan. A month later Killen was part of the huge armada that assaulted Leyte, in the Central Philippines. After several days of providing gunfire support for the landings there, on the night of 24–25 October she took part in the Battle of Surigao Strait, in which one of her torpedoes damaged the Japanese battleship Yamashiro. On 1 November 1944, while still off Leyte, the destroyer was attacked by several enemy planes and shot down four, but was hit by a bomb that killed fifteen of her crew.*

*Repairs at Manus and at San Francisco, California, kept Killen out of action for the rest of 1944 and the first four months of 1945. She rejoined the Seventh Fleet in early May. In June and July 1945 Killen supported the invasion of Borneo, then went to the North Pacific for the final month of the war. After Japan's surrender she covered the occupation effort until departing the Far East in mid-November to return to the United States. Decommissioned in July 1946, Killen spent the next dozen years as part of the Pacific Reserve fleet.]*

⊠        ⊠        ⊠        ⊠        ⊠        ⊠

*Even the letters that gave relatively detailed information about the men's battle experience also included insights to their thoughts about their alma mater. While the earlier change to a co-educational institution may not have been universally popular, many recognized that if the change had not been made, the College probably would not have survived the war.*

Nov.21, 1944

Dear Chellis,

Have received two "Scuttlebutts" and really appreciate them. Keep them coming will you please. This first one arrived when I was aboard ship just shortly prior to our landing on Angaur Island.I meant to write and thank you but I just didn't have time to get around to it.

You probably read about the 81st Division taking Angaur. I came ashore on D-Day about 3 hours after H-hour. Rode around in a landing craft for about 5 hours before landing watching the Navy bombard the beach. Is a pretty sight to see them laying off shore firing broadside from battlewagons, destroyers, cruisers—knocking out everything on the beach except those Japs that were dug way down and there always seem to be some that are. Then planes would come over and peel off to bombard strafe the beach.By this time I was really glad I was on the right side.

When we finally got orders to land I got a hollow feeling in my stomach which stayed until we'd been on shore a while. Had to get out of the LCVP about 30 yards out, in water to the waist and wade in. There were potholes underwater and quite a few of the fellows in our outfit fell down. Luckily, I kept my feet so didn't get bathed all over. We were all carrying heavy communications gear on our back which was cumbersome.

On shore the beach was crowded with shore party, "cats" building roads, supplies beginning to come in, etc. We went in about 100 yards and stopped to set up our communications. My section set up in a deep shellhole which felt good. About 50 yards away combat engines were blowing Japs out of installations and there were a lot of guys standing around waiting for them to come out.

The first night was plenty tough to go through. One's imagination plays so many tricks on you and every little noise is a Jap. Didn't sleep much—just lay in my fox hole and dozed. Was called in the middle of the night to help decode a message and that helped the night pass more quickly. Don't believe I ever hated to see night come on so much in my life. After the first couple nights I was so tired

I slept soundly all night. That is as soundly as the rocks (this coral is tough to dig and sleep) would permit.

After 4 days the island was declared "secure" but plenty of fighting took place after that in cleaning up a pocket. I really understood what one of those "pockets of resistance" are now. Used to read about them before but didn't realize what the were. They holed up in a natural bowl which had caves galore and crevices, pinnacles, trees, and rocks. The whole area had to be gone over with a fine comb, blasted every cave to blow them up. They won't give up and fight to the end no matter what the odds are. They're just like rats to get out of holes.

They're small but as long as they have a weapon, ammunition or grenades they are satisfied as long as they can get plenty of men before they get killed or commit suicide.

Must seem awfully funny to have more girls than boys for students now at Luther. For you people who knew it before it was co-educational it must be even more so. Would be a small school population if it weren't for them now, though.

Mother wrote and said Capt. Bob Wilson was home again and was leaving for the Pacific again soon. Hope he gets more planes.

The news is good to hear now with the Philippine campaign going well, the Navy running the Japs home (those that were left), and the European Campaign still moving if slowly. Can't be too good to suit me.

Met Bob Olson (from Hatton and went to Luther for his Frosh & Soph year) on board ship on the way to the landing. He's in the Artillery unit attached to us. He's the only Luther man I've run into so we had a lot of fun reminiscing.

Sorry to hear that the football team wasn't too successful at Homecoming but the Big Team is certainly doing it's bit and winning all over the world.

It's time for lights out so must close. Would certainly like to be sitting in one of your history classes right now though. Say "Hello" to the Pete's, Pip, Prexy, and all the faculty from me.

Sincerely,
T/4 John P. Halvorson[247]

*Some letters contained less about the writer's current activities than they did about their reminiscences of time spent at Luther, even though that may have only been a semester or two.*

November 22, 1944

Dear Scuttlebutt

Well here I go finally writing you a letter. I realize I should have written sooner but have just put it off and off. But now you are stuck with a letter. To start it off I had better straighten out my address. You still have the old one for when I was in school. But since then lots of things have happened and now I'm overseas. So here is my address:

~~Elmer Robert~~ Bob Tone FC (R) 3/c

(The old gang wouldn't know me        USS Lamons D.E. 743
with a John Henry like that.)

Boy you don't know how really swell your "Scuttlebutt" paper is. It keeps a fellow in contact with the states and the old college. And another swell feature is that I have located some of the old gang. By the way do you by any chance have Paul Johnson's address? I have lost all contact with him since we were roommates in good old room 89, Larsen Hall U.S.—well the impossible always seems to happen.

Ah—yes I am full of good old Luther College memories. The things we did & didn't do.I have one regret and that's that I couldn't complete my first year to say nothing of the others that most certainly would have followed. But I'll be back you can count on that.And once more "Jake" can ride me in that class of his.

Boy was I ever amazed to read of your changing Larsen hall into a girls dorm. The place will never be the same without the boys in there. But say where are the fellows housed now?

Do you think that in one of your future "Scuttlebutts" you could list the gang now attending Luther. We out here would love to know.

Say hello to all the gang both at college and in the armed forses.And thanks a million for the paper.

Yours

Bob Tone[248]

   ✉       ✉       ✉       ✉       ✉       ✉

*While the Marines were often involved in heavy fighting, the Navy provided their transportation, which frequently brought the Navy men in and out of combat areas as well.*

Nov 23, 1944

Dr. Evanson,

Just received the Sept. issue of the "Scuttlebutt," so thought I would drop you a line to let you know I'm receiving it. Thanks a lot. I can't think of anything else you could send that would be more appreciated. It's a sure way to keep in touch with former classmates and friends.

Glad to hear Luther put out another football team. Where did they get the material? This is the second homecoming I've missed, and I sure miss them. I hope to be there for the next one, I've got my fingers crossed.

I'm still on operations. We are working with the 1st Marines and they are resting up after the last "blitz", so I've got it pretty soft. We'll be moving up front soon, seems like you can't keep those Marines quiet, they want to be on the move all the time.

I haven't seen Ted Jake since we left Mare Island. I guess he's around New Guinea somewhere.

I think "Gabby" Sebastian (sp) is around her somewhere.

I have to move off the beach so guess I'll close for now.

Thanks for the "Scuttlebutt." I really appreciated.

Greet everyone

Arch [Ward]

Excuse the writing but these LCT's just won't sit still.[249]

⊠     ⊠     ⊠     ⊠     ⊠     ⊠

*In addition to the letters, postcards, and V-Mail, Evanson also received information from other sources: word of mouth on campus, telephone calls, and letters from other family members. As the following series of correspondence with Karsten Ulvilden suggests, sometimes that information did not correspond exactly to what the men were experiencing, particularly when their own reports were subject to censorship regulations.*

[Letterhead: United States Navy]

Nov. 26, 1944

Dear Dr. Evenson

I don't know how long it will take this to reach you but its apt to be some time.

I have finally reached my destination & should stay put a few weeks. I should have written while I was yet in the States because I can't say anything about why I'm here. You can ask Irene Struxness or Mona what kind of a school I'm going to. I haven't started yet & it may be about a week before I get in.

This is a swell place out here. It's the nicest camp I've been in. The climate is swell and I should be able to get a good tan. We can get anything we want including the best brands of chewing gum by the carton. I could help you out on the cigarette problem if I could send them. They don't hardly sell cigarettes by any thing but the carton out here.

So far I haven't done anything, not even while I was on the way over. I think the navy must have slipped up someplace, at any rate it hasn't happened to me before.

There is a theatre across the street that runs 3 shows every afternoon & of course they are free. It's not a bad life at all yet but nothing beats home. I'll still take Luther for my school.

I'd better knock off for now. You can send chips & scuttlebutt this way anytime now.I haven't had any mail for a month.

Sincerely

Karsten Ulvilden S 2/0[250]

---

*Evanson obviously followed Ulvilden's suggestion and got the information from another source, because in the December 1944 issue of "Scuttlebutt," Evanson reported, "Another sailor, Karsten Ulvilden, S2/c, Box 5, Pacific Fleet Schools, Navy 91, %FPO.Frisco. now in radio school at Pearl Harbor. Good going, boy." That prompted this reply:*

[V-MAIL]

From: Karsten H. Ulvilden S 2/0 Jan, 18, 1945

Dear Dr. Evenson

Well I have received the "Scuttlebutt" now and was really glad to get it.I want to inform you of a mistake. <u>I am not a radio man</u>. I can't tell you yet what I am but will be able to after tommorrow.

I got my orders today and tommorrow I go aboard a D.E.I go with a buddy of Bob Tover. His name is Ramlo and they hail from the same town I guess.

My school didn't last long but it seemed plenty long. They throw things at a guy pretty fast. I liked my school fine and think I have interesting work.

Hows the Iowa snow and cold weather? I haven't been bothered with any of that this year & now from what I hear I am going to get all the sunshine I want. The climate might appeal to me. It isn't to hot and is cool at night. Of course I wouldn't take it before good old South Dakota or Iowa.

I'd like to trade with Don Thompson-saw by "Scuttlebutt" where he is in Sioux Falls. I'm sorta running out of space so I better sign off.

Sincerely<br>Karst    Karsten H. Ulvilden S 2/0[251]

---

*After a few weeks, Ulvilden could finally pass along his real activity directly. In the earlier, indirect communication to Evanson via the other source, "radar" had apparently become confused with "radio," which was probably not surprising given the relatively new technology of radar.*

Feb. 9, 1945

Dear Dr. Evenson

Guess I'm finally in the navy. Been getting in a little sea duty lately & it hasn't been bad at all. I was seasick the first 3 days but take it like an old salt now. I figure I did pretty good tho, only lost one chow and made it to the rail for that.

I received a envelope with all the back Chips and Scuttlebutt's I hadn't received. It was swell to get them and they have kept me busy in my spare time.

Well I can finally break down & tell you what kind of work I'm doing! I am a radar operator. I like the work fine and it seems like a pretty good deal aboard ship. I've still got plenty to learn tho.

Right now we are down in the part of the world where it is plenty hot. We got past the International Date Line but are on the way back to where we started from.

I am with a pal of Bob Tover. His name is Don Ramlo, guess Bob's around here someplace but haven't run into his ship as yet.

I'm hoping to see Jim when we pull into port. He should be getting out here about now. If I can get a liberty it might be possible to hunt him up.

271

I better close for now. Have to get in a little sack duty before I go back on watch.

> Sincerely
> Karst    [Karsten Haraldsson Ulvilden][252]

---

*Evanson corrected the error in the February 1945 issue of "Scuttlebutt," noting,* "V Mail from Karsten H. Ulvilden, S2/c,Box 5, Pacific Fleet Schools) Navy 91, %FPO, Frisco. Says 'QUOTE' I am not a radio man 'UNQUOTE'.O.K. boy, but that's the way I 'Heered' it, Campus Scuttlebutt, you know. Going aboard a D.E." *That, in turn, prompted the following reply:*

March 9, 1945

Dear Chellis:

I just received "Scuttlebutt" today & noticed I'm no longer a radio man. I can now tell you what I am. I'm a radar operator on a D.E.

This is as good a deal as a fellow can get aboard ship, it seems to me. There is a good deal of sack duty connected with it.

I've gotten in quite a bit of sea duty now. It had me a little sick at first but that's all a thing of the past now. Don't figure I did so bad tho, only hit the rail once

The duty we have now is the real stuff but I'm getting tired of it already. I'd just as soon start moving on. We are at sea practically every day but get [censored—part of sentence cut out of page] a good deal of the time. We took one trip that kept us out about 17 days, that is the longest I have been out at one time.

Jim is out here now but I haven't seen him yet. Hope to run into him before one of us pulls out tho. Guess he saw us come into port one day but I missed him.

I'm studying for S1/c now but haven't taken any tests yet. That is another good thing about radar it is an open rate yet, so maybe someday I'll be able to make a rate.

I'll knock off for now.

> Sincerely
> Karst [Karsten H. Ulviden][253]

---

March 12, 1945
Dear Chellis

Boy I'm really on the ball with this letter writing now.

I'm writing to ask for information this time. Could you give me the address of a fellow by the name of Schroeder? I think he was at one time captain of the football team. One of my officers would like to know. I guess Schroeder was his Exec. at one time.

It's not so long since I wrote so there isn't much news. I am at sea again, have been for a few days & will be for a few more. I'm hoping that when I get into port I'll be able to locate Jim.

We are getting some rough riding out here these days. A fello has to spend practically all his time below. Going topside is just asking for a salt water shower.

I still haven't a bunk so am sleeping topside. I sleep on the boat deck & generally manage to keep out of the way of the spray. We ran into a rain scwall the other night and I really got a soaking. It's all in the life of a sailor, I guess.

I'm kinda run down to I'll sign off for now.
Sincerely
Karst [Karsten H. Ulviden][254]

---

*In the April 1945 issue of "Scuttlebutt," Evanson noted:* "Karsten Ulvilden, again from his D.E., I had Cyc Schroeder's address sent to you. An officer aboard the DE knew Cyc, Sleeping on the boat deck made a real 'salt' out of Karsten, with benefit of a bit of rough weather."

⊠    ⊠    ⊠    ⊠    ⊠    ⊠

*Men who actually witnessed battles sometimes became a bit cynical regarding official reports. In addition to meetings facilitated by "Scuttlebutt" reports, some men recognized each other by their distinctive Luther College class rings.*

28 November 1944
Dear Chellis,

I have been enjoying your scuttlebut (very much a Navy term, incidentally) for several months and find no end of pleasure in each copy. I have the names of a number of LC men, whom I hope to run across out here, thanks to the publication. Only last week an officer stepped into my cabin to listen in on the Grieg Piano Concerto, to which some of us were listening, and after a rather casual conversation we accidentally observed each other's rings. The officer-Lloyd Larson of Caledonia-'42's small class mid year graduate. We have since had a good many evenings together. I hadn't seen my brother Sylvan for twenty-two months, when we dropped our hook at Kwajelien within five hundred yards of his ship. We had a pleasant three days together. It develops he has made Lt.(jg) and is Captain of his Subchaser. He arrived at Eniwetok about three days after we had left there; however, I expect to see him show up here any day.

We aren't a spectacular ship-don't have a long list of stars on my uniform (honestly, our uniform out here couldn't house stars) which is a pair of shorts. We are doing some of the errand running that has to be with a fleet such as ours is. My big eyes have observed most of our major warships in the last three months, that is of those that are out here. I have been very cynical upon reading of the great victories out here. I didn't know that victories were of the sort that are so d——— shallow. We get an overseas edition of Time, published at Pearl Harbor, that is quite fresh-five days.

The daughter of the King of these islands was killed when we took over these islands, where we now are. They are quite friendly, however, as they were badly misused by the slant-eyes. They took all their girls of ages 16–20 with them on their ships. They say that one can tell the virgins from the others by the fact that the virgins wear grass skirts. Don't look at me like that, I haven't been on terra firma for three months. You might be interested to know that once a man is married in the tribe, he shares his bride with his brothers; A ruling of the king. No doubt he has no brothers. They are a christianized tribe, catholic. They live on coconuts and fish. They have an ingenious sail boat. Made from coconut leaves, that is the sail, and the boat itself is hewn from the tree. They have dozens of them and are seen on the area always.

I should like to send greetings of the seasons to all the friends at Luther and especially to Dr. Sperati and his wife.

Thanks again to all your good work on the Scuttlebut

Sincerely,

Alvin Mikelson

How did Talle come out? I had a good visit him the last time I was in Washington.[255]

⊠     ⊠     ⊠     ⊠     ⊠     ⊠

*As the holidays approached, Christmas cards offered the men an opportunity to give Evanson a brief update of their activities.*

[Christmas card—No Date, probably 12-44]

Still under pressure here and it looks as if the tempo is increasing on the Pacific:

Had lunch on one of the new Battle Wagons last week. No wonder the Japs haven't been too anxious to tangle with us.

Haven't found any Lutefisk yet but haven't given up yet.

Dave [Preus][256]

⊠     ⊠     ⊠     ⊠     ⊠     ⊠

*While most of the men stationed in the Pacific enjoyed tropical weather, a few served in the Aleutians, where they found the weather much less enjoyable.*

Tuesday night, 26 Dec. 44

Dear Scuttlebutt

Here's a few words to let you know that I've been receiving your four page volume for some time and enjoy it very much. It's swell to read about all the other fellows, what they're doing and where they're at. Although I was at Luther only for a short time and barely long enough to get acquainted I'm sure I did acquire some of that everlasting Luther Spirit and I'm proud of it, as everyone else is.

Right now my job is flying P-38's in a fighter squadron up in these cold, cold Aleutian islands. This isn't a good place to be I can tell you that but there are many that are worse too.

I've run into only one Luther man since leaving the states., That was Bill Luther and his wife. Ran into them up at Anchorage, Alaska in October. Bill is with the Army Engineers up there.

Had a leave last April but was home only a few days so didn't quite make it up to Luther. I'm hoping to get back there sometime in the future though.

I'll sign off and want to thank you again for sending the Scuttlebutt.

Heres my new address […].                    Sincerely

Lt. Arvel D. Perry                              Arvel D. Perry[257]

# CHAPTER 17

# "A pretty doggone big place"— Service in the Pacific—1945

*Although letters from soldiers' wives did not go through the same censorship as their husbands' letters, the only additional information they could provide was often primarily theoretical.*

4908 James Ave. S.
Minneapolis 9, Minn.
1/9/45

Dear Chellis:—

Not much information is available other than Stan's address. We would appreciate your getting this new one on the mailing list:

Capt. John S. Henderson, USMCR [...]

He is flying R4Ds—his choice of duties if he could have chosen. It's just the job for an old man Stan says—meaning himself. He is in the vicinity Perry lately vacated, which he knows to be the Palau islands. Evidently transporting men and supplies into the combat area. My suppositions are always plentiful, not necessarily accurate

Sincerely,
Helen Henderson[258]

✉        ✉        ✉        ✉        ✉        ✉

*Some men got their sea legs more quickly than others, but that sometimes had unfortunate consequences, as they had to make up for the incapacity of their colleagues.*

Somewhere in the Pacific
12 January 1945

Dear Chellis:

First I wish to thank you for sending the "Scuttlebutt." It sort of brings back memories of a little place back in Iowa that many of us will never forget.

I tried to tell the navy they were making a mistake by not accepting a perfectly good (but smooth mouth) sea faring Viking back in 1942. But they seemed only interested in young blood with a few less miles on the speedometer and 28 yrs or less of seasoning. So they stuffed me in the MPs—with a stick in one hand & a gatt on the hip, spoiling a GI's definition of fun.

Instinctively upon my maiden voyage I developed sea legs & an appitite that wouldn't lend an ear even when a very rough sea said give. The elements must have been working for the fishes—we hit rough weather the second day out and I must say it made the galley look like a haunted house. Never have I witnessed such a waste of groceries. The sad part of it was that some of us less fortunate who didn't get sick volunteered to clean up those 2nd hand vitamins that our brothers had spewed on every available place but the latrine.

Yes, I enjoyed every day of my trip over—hope I can say the same for those yet to come. There is very little I can say of news until we settle to a permanent location. I'll try to keep in tough with Luther until I can be there in person.

Always Floyd
[Omundson][259]

✉   ✉   ✉   ✉   ✉   ✉

*The Pacific theater was immense; nonetheless, there were several key points where Luther men and women crossed paths, so duty in the Pacific offered hopes for future meetings with fellow students.*

Jan. 29, 1945—2000

Dear Chellis,

Today I received the Jan. "Scuttlebutt" and was sure glad to get it. I'm back at Heuneme and intended to look up Heltne but evidently he's quite a ways from here now.

The latter part of Nov., I was home on leave and had quite a pleasant surprise when I met Erling Naeseth. He sure looked good and even though we didn't see each other long, we managed to have a quick telephone gab about "times" at Luther and the boys.

I didn't know if Gerhard is any relation to Erling but will try to look him up when I get the chance.

Very soon now, we'll be shipping out and maybe I'll meet a few of the other boys in the Pacific.

Enclosed is a donation for the plaque.

The address: John D. Christiansen [...]

Very best regards to all
"Brooklyn"[260]

⊠          ⊠          ⊠          ⊠          ⊠          ⊠

*Naval service in the Pacific was often rather isolated. By early 1945, the men there were hoping for a quick end to the war in Europe, knowing that would mean more resources for the struggle against Japan.*

[Letterhead: U.S.S. LCI ₺ M 431

30 January 1945

Dear Chellis,

I suppose by now you are about ready to cross me off your mailing list—I surely hope not though I probably deserve it.—I have fully intended to write for months—always those good intentions but they still fail to materialize—Other people seem to keep up their correspondence but I find it increasingly difficult as the months go by—I'm either very busy or else doing nothing. The former leaves no time and the latter leaves nothing to write about—however it has been so long since you have heard from me that I can surely find a few items of interest other than the fact that I'm in the best of health and anxious to get back to the States and of course pay Luther a visit—Right now we are underway and in our case that means that something is up. We now have some very interesting duty.—Don't suppose that I can write much about it but the change in the letter head may give you a hint—the M stands for mortar.—So we are now a fighting ship instead of a troop carrier.—I'll be home in another 4 or 5 months and will tell you about it then.

Ted and I finally got together out here—I suppose you have heard that by word through Freda. Surely was good to see him again—He was the first I have seen since leaving the States that I knew as a civilian—naturally Ted and I had a lot of things to talk over.—We got together for about 4 days in New Guinea—I doubt very much if I shall run into him again out here.—He has put on a bit of weight since I last saw him—might also add that he's doing a darn good job as skipper of his L.C.T.

Harlan Moen is still out here—I have seen him only once and that was last June.—To you that no doubt seems a long time ago but to us out here it doesn't.—Although the over all time spent out here seems very long, four, five, or six months back seems like nothing at all.

The figures you quoted on Luther men with commissions was very interesting—I rather imagine that is a percentage pretty hard to beat.

What happened to that other war we are fighting Chellis—I had thought it would have been over with long before this.—It looks right now as though the Russians are going to reach Berlin first.—Maybe that's a good thing.—The past month out here still has me buffaloed. On the last big one I was all set for anything, that is I hoped I was, and it turned out to be a lot of fun for us.—We've a long way to go out here though even if we have come a long way in the past year.—I certainly wouldn't make any predictions about this theater.

My one big concern right now is getting back to the States—I now have 17 months in and ordinarily the Navy is pretty good about its rotation policy.—If I get orders within the next four months I'll consider myself very fortunate.—One gets just a bit tired of not seeing any civilization after a while—the last we saw was Australia and that was 14 months ago now.—Actually I'm not complaining—our life as compared to a lot of them out here has been one of luxury.—I might add that it's easy for me to make such a statement right now for the sea is like glass and the ship is functioning perfectly.—There are times when that statement seems out of line.

Thanks for the greeting from Pres Preus and also the Student Body President—Those letters are just what we appreciate most Chellis.—Do you have any word of Reuben Lerud or Jim Cain? I have heard nothing of either of them for about a year now.

Well Chel, this lets you know that I'm still around and still complaining—also that your letters are coming thru nicely and are very welcomed.—Give my regards to Dr. Preus, Karl Hansen, Dr. Keiler, Pip Qually, Dr. Jacobsen and any of the rest of the faculty that might happen to remember me.

Sincerely

Kenny O. [Lt. K. I. Olson USNR][261]

☒     ☒     ☒     ☒     ☒     ☒

*The long periods of training were especially frustrating when the men heard about the contributions of their friends and colleagues. The opportunity to actually become involved in the "real" war effort was something they looked forward to.*

[Letterhead: Officers' Club, Kearny Army Air Field, Kearny, Nebr.]

2 February 1945

Dear Chellis,

Just a hurried note to inform you that I will have left the states by the time you receive this. My duties will be those of bombardier-navigator on one of the "big birds" and I hope to run into at least a few of the many Norsemen who have been seeing so much action against the Japs. Can't ignore the somewhat sentimental feeling that the real he-men like Gabby have opened a big hole over there, and I certainly intend to deliver some good punches on into the Jap backfield. I've hesitated in writing to you because I've been parked on the sidelines all this time. Have derived some satisfaction from learning of the accomplishments of some of my students who have completed their tours. I have been constantly impressed with the close parallel between an effective bombing team and a good football team. Enough of my rambling.

My wife and daughter are located in West Salem, Wisconsin and will have my new address as soon as it is available. Please keep me on you mailing list, and extend my best wishes to all the fighting Norsemen.

I nearly forgot to mention that I'll be coming back to Luther to "clean up" my shameful scholastic record and try to <u>earn</u> a degree. The army has taught me some lessons in application and effort. The two and one-half years experience teaching and supervising teaching should be of some value later, too.

My airplane-commander is a lanky Texan named Anderson.

Please convey my respects to "Pete" and "Pip."

Sincerely,

Woody [Capt. L. W. Woodiwiss][262]

&#9993;    &#9993;    &#9993;    &#9993;    &#9993;    &#9993;

*The experience of sailing aboard a Navy ship was in marked contrast to the experience enjoyed by the men who had traveled to Europe with the Luther Concert Band.*

4 February 1945

Dear Chellis,

After reading a couple issues of your "Scuttlebutt", I decided that an informal letter would be the only appropriate thing for me to write. Yes sir, Chellis, the sheet has some good old "bull" in it and do we like it! Once more I am finding out the whereabouts of the classmates and college chums of years back.

I doubt if you remember me, Chellis, because I wasn't particularly interested in history so kind of took a side track around those courses while at Luther. However, I was one of those from the class of '35 who enjoyed the band tour across the Atlantic in '36. Must say that I enjoyed that a little more than the cruises currently being taken.

I am in the Seabees, the 112th Naval Construction Battalion to be exact, and we are in the Marianas Islands. My work is in the disbursing office of the battalion.

The "Luther Alumnus" and "College Chips" also reach me, for which I am pleased.

Inclosing two dollars for the "Jones Plaque Fund". I think the idea good and know that it will be backed in true Luther spirit.

Will be awaiting the next "Scuttlebutt" Sheet, Chellis, and keep 'em coming.

Sincerely,

Alvin O. Mosbo[263]

&#9993;    &#9993;    &#9993;    &#9993;    &#9993;    &#9993;

*The men's orders sometime changed as quickly as the climate in which they were serving. Many of their assignments also seemed far removed from actual combat.*

[Letterhead: Construction Battalion Replacement Depot
Camp Parks, Shoemaker, California]

16 February 1945

Greetings—

Well I think that this is my first epistle to you, and at that it has to be a brief one. Letter writing is one thing that I haven't had much time for, and if it hadn't been for my change of address (and my want of the scuttlebutt) then I probably never would have gotten around to this sort of thing.

Here goes with the highlights ... been in the Aleutians for the past year and a half and have just returned from spending thirty wonderful days at home in the Windy City. Was there for Xmas and New Years for the first time in three years and boy what a treat. While home I had a visit with Gladys Budd, and dinner with Gertrude Sovik. However while in the still windy Aleutians I was attached to Armed Forces Radio (although in name I'm a Seabee). We were a small detachment if thirty men, and by the time our tour of duty was up we were scattered from one end of the chain to the other. Worked with sports most of the time, and was the island Sportscaster over the local station. It made me think of Luther each time I made a station break as our call numbers were WXLC, and they come mighty close to the old campus station. Believe you already know that Rev. Tolo and I were on the same island for a while, and spent a year ago Xmas Eve & New Years Eve together.

Our small draft of thirty Seabees sailed under the Golden Gate on November 30th, and after my leave I reported to Providence, Rhode Island, but was sent back to California four days later. Then something happened that I never thought was possible ... yep I'm assigned to station force here at Camp Parks outside of Oakland, and should be here for some time to come. They have a radio program here that is presented by the fighting Seabees each week, and is supposed to go on a nation wide hook-up soon. When this happens I'm to join the staff, but at the present time I am doing the dirty work of making up overseas drafts in the transfer section of the Personnel office. Toughest thing about the assignment is working with the Waves ... am I kidding?

Well it goes without saying that I actually miss those history classes, and hearing you tell about Adams climbing on that white horse, cracking his whip, and riding to victory. I'll be back there on the campus with the other fellows when this thing is over, and love every hour of it. My greetings to Coach Pete and the others. Thanks loads for sending the scuttlebutt, and it's nice to get the Chips. Please note this change of address.

Best regards,

Don Flikeid[264]

✉    ✉    ✉    ✉    ✉    ✉

*While the men frequently commented on everyday matters, their casual references to combat experiences indicated that the realities of war were never far away.*

[Letterhead: United States Navy

USS LST 745

17 Feb 1945

Dear Prof. Evanson

Cannot express my appreciation for these issues of scuttlebutt that have been coming out this way. Just what we need, something chatty and informal and yet something that gives us a contact with our Luther buddies all over this globe. That is certainly no understatement. As far as I have been able to ascertain, no other colleges have taken such a personal interest in the boys as you have. It means a lot for us and also for Luther.

This "ole" Pacific is a pretty doggone big place. Have so far run into only one class mate thus far and that was quite a coincidence. On one invasion Irwin Knutson's outfit had passage on our ship. We had some fine bull sessions during our trip together. We were both pretty eager to exchange our Luther news. He'd been in Hawaii before coming out here. Was a B.A.R. man in the Infantry. A little since that operation I've heard that he was a pretty rough customer as far as the Japs were concerned. That Leyte operation was a pretty muddy deal for the army. "Ole Mother Hubbard" has been flitting around quite a bit out here and is in fine shape, the crew included. No more visible damage than some gnawed finger nails. Have witnessed a little air action, a Jap plane shot down in flames at night was very spectacular to say the least. This blue jacket gunnery is pretty deadly.

Am Navigator and Ship Service Officer, those duties filling my time very well and I find them, especially the navigation quite interesting. Our gunnery officer R.J. Norgaard (Ens) is also from N. Dak., and we don't let each other forget our Norsk ancestry. His father, J.R. Norgaard, is an old Luther "Grad", one of

Dr. Sperati's crack clarinet players, way back in the European touring days. He certainly had a high regard for Sperati and "Dick" says that he's made inquiries about him.

It's been pretty rainy out here, which is natural at this time of the year. Imagine that the wind is whipping its icy fingers across the Oneota as usual—that's for me!!

Enclosed is my contribution to the plaque fund.

Hoping the big homecoming day comes soon. Please greet Prof. Qual and all from me

A "Semi-Alumnus"

Rolf O Norstog[265]

$$\boxtimes \qquad \boxtimes \qquad \boxtimes \qquad \boxtimes \qquad \boxtimes \qquad \boxtimes$$

*Evanson's correspondents were often frustrated because they either had nothing exciting to write about, or they could not describe their activities because of censorship regulations.*

U.S.S. Cahoba

Feb. 19, 1945

Dear Dr. Evanson,

Received another copy of the "Scuttlebutt" this afternoon, and I think it is time to write and thank you and all of the others who make it possible for we out here to get it. I look forward to getting each copy as it is so full of interesting news of good friends.

As you already know I am on a tanker. Paul Eggen was the first person I saw when I came aboard—it shouldn't be necessary for me to say I was surprised. He is in my division so we have a daily chat.

Received a letter from Ness a few days ago. I guess he has seen quite alot. He said he likes his new assignment, although he was disappointed at first.

I like duty aboard this ship, even though it gets monotonous at times. We expect to get to go back to the states soon. We have been at this atoll for about a month now. We are leaving here soon on another operation. Wish I could write about the more interesting things, but you know censor regulations won't allow that.

I am enclosing a contribution for the plaque. I think it is a very good idea. Its something Luther College will always be proud of. I know I owe alot more to Luther College than that.

Will close now knowing that this is not very interesting.

Best Wishes,

Lyle [Ens. Lyle W. Bestul][266]

    ✉      ✉      ✉      ✉      ✉      ✉

*Service in the Navy took men to some of the less commonly visited areas in the Pacific, such as the Netherlands East Indies (N.E.I.) and Dutch New Guinea (D.N.G.).*

[Letterhead: American Red Cross]

N.E.I.

February 27, 1945

Dear Chell and all,

I'm sorry I have neglected writing for some time but I decided to wait until I got permanently settled for at least some time. That we never know.

We flew in from Guinea day before yesterday. This place is quite a bit like the last one but at least, we're out of that red, gooey clay. It is supposed to be somewhat hotter here but it has been raining much of the time since we got here. I woke up last night in a little puddle. Guess I'll have to fix the tent one of these days.

I'm very glad to finally get down to my regular job. When we were in D.N.G., we got into a construction battalion for about 6 ½ weeks building an AACS station. Practically Seebees. I still believe that the natives could have done a better job. They built the orderly room and it really looked neat. Thatched roof, etc.

The natives are quite the "boys." They are small but considerably smart. Some can write better than I with apologies to the natives. There names run something like this: Adrionous Sokoi, Abraham, Socrotus, Ike, and Mike. They are exceptional business men. They nearly ran me out of house and home one day. I bought a pack of Jap coins and a pack of Japanese cigarettes but they argued me out of an extra amount of cash in the big deal. Some talk fluent English, and Adrionous could speak Dutch, English, Malayan, as well as his native tounge. Well, so much for the "boys." Incidentally, the Jap cigarettes are really strong.

I'll try to get ahold of some more and send them to you but I'm warning you. I smoked two of them one day and I could feel them without a doubt.

This place is going to be all right as all indications point that way. I believe I'll like my work as most of the fellows do. I can't state it for security reasons or at least that is my belief. I don't believe that it is anything extraordinary though.

I went to a quaint little chapel when I was in Guinea. It was made entirely of local materials. Native logs bound with vines and a thatched roof as well as thatching behind the altar. The chaplain was exceptionally good and as all are, a regular fellow. The name of the chapel was Mt. Olive and I enjoyed it immensely.

I got my hands on a baseball when I was there and it really felt good. It's been quite awhile since the last time. I got "conked" between the eyes on one occasion. The ball went through the webbing or at least that is my excuse, and I admit it is a poor one.

I saw a U.S.O. camp show last night and take it from me, they are good and I mean good. Some of the songs kind of get the sentimental side of us but they do a world of good to our morale. They are exceptional.

I also have seen many shows since I've been overseas. "The Conspiritors" was the last one, night before last. I didn't go to sleep this time as the first time I saw it but maybe it was caused by overwork, or do you know me better than that?

Well, I've "batted the breeze" long enough so better close. I've got a considerable amount of letters to write, in fact, about 31. Write if at all possible but I imagine you are busy to say the least. I used to gripe when I didn't get mail down at Luther or in the states but you should hear me on some occasions when I don't get a letter for 2 or 3 weeks which often happens. I'm waiting for the Scuttlebutt and the Chips to catch me. Another thing, I surely would like to walk down to the Parrott and fill myself with ice cream until I dropped. Tell all hello.

Sincerely,
Tommy [Pvt. P. L. Thompson][267]

✉    ✉    ✉    ✉    ✉    ✉

*Because of censorship restrictions, the men were not able to describe much of their activities, but they nonetheless attempted to give Evanson a feel for what their duty was like.*

U.S.S. Jason (ARH—1)
Feb. 28, 1945

Dear Chellis,

It's about time I'm writing, I know, I'm very sorry that I've neglected you this long, after having received Scuttlebutt nearly every month since it was begun, I should be very ashamed of myself, and I am indeed. I am a little behind now since I had a change in address and that always causes a couple months delay in mail.

At the moment I am reading your Jan. issue, I have Chaplain Tolo's copy. It is needless to say how happy I was to find a Luther man out here. And he is <u>not</u> the only one. I have met 5 Luther men in this place during the four months that I've been here. These men are Alvin Mikels (he's a Lt. (j.g.) now, by the way), Lt. (j.g.) Bob Lee, Lt. (j.g.) Happy Jensen, Ensign Vernon Bly, and Lieut. Tolo. I see you were wondering about the Chaplain's rank; he's a full Lt. Now all of these meetings have been accidental, they were experiences that I'll never forget!

The day before yesterday Bob, Al, Chaplain Tolo, and I had a little reunion on the beach. In the morning Al, Bob, and I had a steak fry; the Chaplain joined us later in the afternoon. We had quite a "bull reunion"—everyone talking at the same time. Truly the Luther spirit which blends perfectly with the Navy ways.

As you know, I had duty in Pearl Harbor for quite some time—15 months to be exact. From there I was transferred to the U.S.S. Hector (AR7), where I spent 3½ months and then to this ship. I just reported aboard this ship the 19th of Feb.

I have 19 months consecutive overseas duty now, so I expect to be going back pretty soon. And you know that I have not so little to come home to; my son is over 14 months old now. Dorothy is living in Minneapolis; her address is 3300 First Ave. So. Our son's name is David Lee (Dorothy—Lloyd); he looks just like me—at least that's what Dorothy says. Since <u>I</u> have never seen him except through pictures, I cannot rightly judge.

I met a number of Luther men in Pearl Harbor, Although I missed many more. Some of them I met were Lt. (j.g.) Cal De Beehr, Lt. (j.g.) Gerry Quam, Lt. (j.g.) Bill Aaker, Lt. (j.g.) Loyal Radtke, Lt. (j.g.) Dusty Hanson, Bob Bonnerup, Ph M 1/c, and Bill Ehrman, Hospital Corpsman. More of them visited me at my station there—the Pacific Fleet Camera Party. We would spend as much time together as possible—i.e., as long as their ships would be in.

Scuttlebutt really means a lot to us out here. You're doing a remarkable job on it, Chellis, and we can't thank you enough. I've shown it to many of my friends at Pearl and here; they are always very much impressed with your paper.

Very glad to read that Luther is winning in basketball; more power to you. I hope the Norseman spirit prevails even among the women. I'd like to come back to good old L.C. some day—as a student, I am. Maybe I'd study a little more then too. You remember that my time was pretty well taken up with a certain brunette. I surely don't regret that now either; those are mighty nice days to look back upon. Since my address has been changed four times in the past four months, my mail service has been bad. I haven't had a Scuttlebutt of my own since the Nov. issue, but Al Michelson has given me his copy since that. Now the Chaplain here is looking out for me. That Feb. issue really came fast air mail; I can't tell you how much I enjoyed it.

I read that young Chellis was home for Christmas; I hope to be home next one. I've been out there the last two now. It hasn't been bad, though; I've had all the comforts of life in the Navy. I've had excellent duty; I'm asst. officer in charge of the Central Pacific Fleet Camera Party Branch here. Our unit is stationed aboard the Jason; we are not attached to the ships' company. So you see that I am quite independent, since I am no. 2 man in our unit. I'd like to tell you all about our work, but I'll have to save that until I get that 30-day leave. When I do Dorothy and I will be down to visit you. I'll also bring some samples of our pictures taken out here. Most of them cannot be sent by mail, so I'll have to wait until I can carry them with me.

Since I began this letter I've seen Bob Lee again. I stayed with him on his plane, a PB2Y just last night. Bob, Al and I are planning a hop together in the very near future.

I see Tutor has been called back into the service. The Navy couldn't get along without him, eh? That's not difficult to understand.

As I sit here daydreaming, I just remembered one very pleasant afternoon that I spent with you, Mrs. Evanson, and your family in a Rochester park. Remember when Chellis and I were roommates while we worked at the canning factory? That was a most delicious picnic dinner that we had. That's something that I really miss—the good old Norwegian cooking.

I am indeed privileged to have the opportunity to hear a Lutheran sermon every Sunday now. Of course, Navy chapel services are pretty much alike. I've attended many nice services; it was all very inspiring except the sermon. That is where I felt something lacking; I am more at home now on the Jason with Chaplain Tolo.

I would like to ask a favor of you, Chellis. Could you make arrangements to send Scuttlebutt to Dorothy? I repeat the address: Mrs. Lloyd A. Iverson, 3300 First Ave. So., Minneapolis (8), Minnesota I really would appreciate if you would do that for me.

Enclosed you will find $2.00 for the plaque fund. Also a couple of pictures— not examples of our work, however. My striker did the one; besides he had bad film. So much for alibis! So long for the time, Chellis; greet all good Luther men from me and keep us up to date out here. Very Sincerely,

Iver [Lt. (j.g.)L.A. Iverson USNR][268]

✉    ✉    ✉    ✉    ✉    ✉

*Because of its central location, Hawaii continued to be a focal point of activity throughout the war. "Oahu" is known as "the Gathering Place;" for men serving in the Pacific, it was aptly named.*

[Letterhead: Design of wings with propeller insignia above:
Bud Potter]

Thursday
March 1st [1945]

Dear Chellis, Scuttlebutt, and all

First of all I want to thank all of you who are responsible for my getting the "Scuttlebutt" every month. The address is not very recent but I'm all to blame for that. Everytime I'd get a copy I'd say to myself I'd better get busy and drop you a line but something always came up. Today I got a copy and I said that it was about time I let some of my friends know where I am etc. First off I'm on the island of Oahu of the Hawaiian group. I'm a teletype operator in one of the busiest message centers in the world. I like it very much, no kidding, I really do, never a dull moment so I guess that's the reason.

We have been getting lectures on our rights from the G.I. Bill and it convinces me more and more that I'll be coming back to school.

I hope you haven't gotten the idea from my stationary that I'm a general or something—had a birthday while back and result—stationery from kid sister. By the way Luther had better take Hamline or I'm in for a bad time. She's a foreigner and attends Hamline—guess my brotherly love doesn't have much influence!

Its just about that time for me to close and go to work. Just in case you can't make out my outside address; you see I want to be sure and get my copy—

P.F.C. Vernon H. Potter [...]

Best wishes to all

"Bud"[269]

 

&#9993; &#9993; &#9993; &#9993; &#9993; &#9993;

 

*With training completed, in addition to the pressures of the war the men had to endure transportation to their new assignments, as well as new environments.*

Ensign M. C. Bachman

5 March 1945

Dear Chell,

'Just dropping a line to say hello from a little island "'way out there" somewhere. I haven't quite become accustomed to the heat, rain, meals, routine, etc. out here, but am gradually learning.

I flew all the way out from Calif., having a swell trip. A guy surely keeps an eye on those engines, however, with all that water underneath. We stopped at quite a few of the old battle spots coming over.

I laughed at the beards some of the boys had, when we stopped over at various ports. But, by the time I arrived here, I had more hair on my face than on the top of my head.

I'm hoping to move up a bit—before long, but don't know where. However, it's pretty interesting right here.

I'm sorry I didn't get to talk with you again before I left, but the time pretty well ran out on me. It's too bad I can't throw you a few packs of cigarettes. The matches are more scarce than cigarettes here. Hi!!

'Guess I 'd better close for now. Say hello to Mrs. Evanson and Chellis Jr. for me!!

As ever,

Marv [Ens. M.C. Bachman] [270]

⊠      ⊠      ⊠      ⊠      ⊠      ⊠

*Even before V-E Day, some ships were being redeployed in the Pacific Theater in anticipation of the push toward Japan.*

Mar. 3, 1945

Dear Chellis,

Since I changed F.P.O. Address I've not received your greatly appreciated "Scuttlebutt." No doubt the missing copies will eventually reach me but thought it advisable to notify you of my new address nevertheless. I desire very much to have my name retained on the mailing list.

We finally got out of the "Bush league" about the first of the year and since then have been on the "go." I've been assigned to the ship for almost a year, being with the group that formed the Ship's Company at Newport, R.I. After two months as a pre-Commissioning detail at the station, we put her into Commission at the Construction yard. Soon thereafter we took her on a shakedown Cruise for several weeks. Our first assignment was that of a Training Ship which gave officers and men a chance to become thoroughly familiar with her as well as teaching green crews. It was after this tour of duty that we finally passed through Panama the first part of January.

I've been in Service 18 Mo. Previous to that time I instructed Radar for 8 mo. in the Army Air Force Tech Training Command. I held a War Appointment in the Civil Service. Have been out of Public School work for almost three years, but I am looking forward to reentering after the war.

I'm happy to make the belated announcement of the arrival of the third son into our family. John Thomas was born Sept. 26, 1944. He now tips the scales at 20 pounds and is going strong. Steven Rolfe is 5 years, Craig David is 3. Was fortunate enough to have a short leave before taking out on our last cruise so had an opportunity to see my family including of course John for the first time. It will be a great day when I can be with them again.

It has been my pleasure to meet up with several former Luther men during these past three years. Paul Preus, Alvin Mikelsin, Red Norman were at Cornell U. at the time of my indoctrination Course in late '43. Also one of the Strom brothers—he was an instructor at the time. In Newport I met an Olson who after graduating, taught in Maxwell. I can't recall his first name. There have been others too that I was not well acquainted with.

Since coming out here I've had no opportunity to meet anyone since I've had but one short liberty.

My duties aboard include those of a Junior Division Officer besides being Range-finder and Optical officer. It keeps one busy all the time. Days and weeks go by swiftly.

In two hours I have the mid-watch which behooves me to "hit the sack" but quick.

Remember me to Pete, Pip, Karl and others. Good luck to you all and to good Ol' Luther.

Respectfully yours,<br>
[Lt. (j.g.)] H.L. Ritland [USNR][271]

&#9993;    &#9993;    &#9993;    &#9993;    &#9993;    &#9993;

*In some cases, the men's wives forwarded information to Evanson.*

[Letterhead: Mrs. L.W. Woodiwiss]

March 3, 1945

Dear Mr. Evanson,

Woody wrote and asked me to send you his address for the Scuttlebutt, which is Capt. L.W. Woodiwiss [...]

We both enjoyed reading the Scuttlebutt while living in Texas. Woody isn't much of a correspondent and, then too, he is one of those fellows who didn't think he was doing much toward winning the war while "on this side," but now that he's across I feel free to develop a little information.

He's stationed in the Marianas, flew across in a B-29 on which he's the Bombardier and in general likes his set-up. Major Ted Steel of The Army Hour made the trip with them for the purpose of making a recording of it. Woody wrote the record was made and I've been listening to the program the past few Sundays but have failed to hear a voice resembling his. Maybe tomorrow will be my lucky day.

Woody has been trying to get in touch with Gabby but, so far, hasn't heard anything pro or con.

Never having been a pupil of yours you probably don't remember me but nevertheless, I'm proud to say I was a Lutherite (active) in '39 & '40 and went by the name of Phyllis Nelson—or I should say Normy Nelson's sister.

Thanking you, I am

Very sincerely,

Mrs. L.W. Woodiwiss [West Salem, Wis][272]

✉      ✉      ✉      ✉      ✉      ✉

*Many of the men who attended V-12 courses together kept in contact with one another across the Pacific*

[V-MAIL]

From: Ens. Clifford Ellingson U.S.S. Towner [Undated]

Dear Sir;

A few lines to let you know that Luther is well represented out here in the Pacific. I've been out here for quite some time now and have met up with a lot of the fellows. Just the other day I had quite a good old chat with Douglas Simondet. I've also met quite a few of the boys from my class at Midshipmen School.

The "Scuttlebutt" has been reaching me all the time, however, they have not been coming by the right address. I left Fort Pierce about three months ago and failed to write and tell you.

I am on an AKA which is a 14,000 ton ship. It was commissioned on the 1st of December so we are beginning to feel right at home.

At the present time we are at a port out here at a well known place but expect to be underway in a few days for—well, I'll leave the rest out for a number of reasons.

How's everything back at Luther this year? Do you have a basketball team? I noticed that you were keeping up the football spirit last fall.

I'm fine and going strong. Hope to clean up on this mess pretty soon.

Sincerely,

C.T. Ellingson

Ensign USNR[273]

✉      ✉      ✉      ✉      ✉      ✉

*While it was often difficult for the men to be out of the U.S. for long periods, it was particularly hard on married men, especially for those who had children born in their absence. For those who had brothers serving in the war, news of their exploits could also add to the tension they felt.*

4 April 1945

Dear Chellis,

First I must tell you of the 'big event' which has happened. Frances and I are the very proud parents of a baby girl, Carole Jane. She arrived the 25th of March a little over a month after I waved farewell to the Golden Gate Bridge in San Francisco. Had I known what becoming a father was really like by correspondence, the Navy probably would have found me A.W.O.L. for a month. Now that it is over and have received a letter from my wife I am much relieved, as I can assure walking around in a daze <u>does</u> cause incidents, such as delivering a "hot" dispatch in a Captain's dining room with my <u>hat</u> on. As you know that just doesn't work.

I want to thank you for "Scuttlebutt," I and I know all the other fellows appreciate it a lot. News of Luther & Luther fellows is most welcome.

I received a letter from Arie Gaalswyk the other day. He says his wife is now at Luther. I wish you would give her my best regards should you run into her on the campus.

My brother, Rod, has left the states now too. I am hoping to see him, the chances should be pretty good. My marine brother, Willard, as far as I know, is still on Iwo Jima. He said it was far worse than Bouganville last year. From the reports I can understand that.

I have lost track of Kenny Olson, could you tell me where he is now? Also I haven't heard anything about "Rube" Lerud or Jim Crain in a long time.

I can tell you I was in Honolulu the other day, so if any of the fellows happen this way I shall be on the lookout for them.

Greet Chellis Jr. from me and tell him I promise to answer if he should be inclined to write.

I hear "Tutor" is back at Luther. I wish you would qreet him and Bob Jacobson from me.

I hope this finds you & Mrs. Evanson in the best of health

Sincerely
Bob McConnell[274]

✉       ✉       ✉       ✉       ✉       ✉

*Some of the men had significant periods of service in the Pacific Theater, and saw a great deal of combat action.*

[Letterhead: U. S. S. Montpelier]

6 April, 1945

Dear Chellis,

I too have been receiving "Scuttlebutt" regularly, and I hope you will forgive me for being such a procrastinator in making acknowledgment, and telling you how much I thoroughly enjoy such issue.

Permit me to relate just a little of my experiences since I left Luther in 1940.

Following graduation in June of 1940, I entered Naval flight training. I received my commission in June of 1941, then instructed flying at Pensacola for three months, and at Corpus Christi, Texas for twenty four months. I married a little Texas girl in March of 1942, and our marriage was blessed with a little girl (Dolores Ann) in June of 1943. In October of 1943 I began my tour of sea duty and to date I have eighteen months. I hope that I shall be permitted to return to the States for leave and reassignment soon. Last April I became Commander Scouting Squadron Twelve with additional duties on Cruiser Division Twelve's staff. By no means do we fly the fast and new type aircraft in this branch of Naval Aviation, however our planes and pilots have a specific mission, and I personally believe we have done quite well. We have done a great deal of spotting for Naval gunfire in the Solomons, the Central Pacific, and the Philippines.

I am enclosing a money order for twenty five dollars as an initial donation for the "Luther Building Fund", and two dollars for the "Jones Plaque Fund".

If I be granted the customary thirty day over-seas leave, and if travel conditions permit, I hope that Mrs. Lunde and I may come to Luther for a visit in the near future.

Perhaps you would like a little souvenir of the Corregidor operation. I had a ringside seat for this one, and believe me it was an unforgettable sight to see the transports coming in one after the other and dropping their load of chutists. It will always be remembered, because it meant the recapture of the little island where our troops held on so tenaciously about three years ago.

Sincerely,

Don Lunde[275]

✉   ✉   ✉   ✉   ✉   ✉

*By the spring of 1945, with the end of the war appearing to be a realistic possibility in the near future, many men began thinking of what they would do after the war. For those whose studies had been interrupted, a return to Luther was high on their priority list, especially with the possibility of benefits provided by the "G.I. Bill of Rights."*

11 April 1945

Dear Mr. Evanson, and all:

Been quite a while since I last wrote. Sorry to be so tardy, but things have been happening fast and furious.

Before I forget, my address has been changed. It now reads: [...]

Got a whole pile of chips and scuttlebutts when we got into this port. Seems as though they had been held up because of wrong FPO. Hope you get this straightened out 'cause I really enjoy them.

Saw Eugene Clark while we were in Pearl. We had a big confab on the good old days.

Received a letter from Mary Kvasse yesterday. She tells me she isn't attending good old L.C. anymore. Sorry to hear it, 'cause she made a very welcome addition to the "Norsemen" student-body.

By the way, how is the pulchritude around there now?

From the looks of the b-ball scores, you had quite a team this year. Sure wish you could have beaten Dubuque as I went there to V-12, and they are much too cocky.

How is old Dr. Sperati? Is he still beatin' the drums on "Stars and Stripes Forever?" Whenever I hear that song I can see him up there beatin' for all he's worth.

Excuse me, I just noticed that I turned the paper Navy style. I try not to do it with letters, but it has grown to be quite a habit.

From the picture in the G.I. Bill of Rights booklet, the campus is in great condition. You can bet I'm going to take advantage of the gov'n'ts offer, and go back to Luther.

Well, its time for me to take the deck so I'll have to secure. Say hello to everyone for me.

Yours,

"Meatball" (Warren G. Berg)

P.S. I'll have to try to get a money order, and then will send something for the placque fund.[276]

⊠     ⊠     ⊠     ⊠     ⊠     ⊠

*As the war continued in the Pacific, the men there hoped for relief following the anticipated end of hostilities in Europe.*

Phillipine Islands
12 April/45

Dear Chellis:

Thought I would drop you a line to let you know I appreciate your monthly letters.

I have seen all of the combat I want. The D-Day here show was a thrilling and exciting time with all the Navy letting go with everything in the book. Have been in continuous combat since then, had a few close ones but not too bad. I am sending our daily news sheet and a Jap invasion bill, we found several thousand pesos in a cave. You better show Pete the paper, I believe he was in the Sixth Division last war.

Had a letter from Capt Overby, he is on one of the islands close by. Also rec'd a letter from Walter Johnson, he is at Ft Leavenworth with his wife.

As yet have not met any Luther boys over here.

Am glad to hear the basketball team is doing so well on the small enrollment, it will be nice when we can all get back for Homecoming again.

I don't imagine the boys in Europe will enjoy coming over here but we sure can make good use of them.

At present we are set up in a former college that we chased the Japs out of.

Saw Irving Berlin's "This Is The Army" last night, it was very good

Well must close,

Le Roy

P.S. We fought in two campaigns in New Guinea at Maffin Bay & Sansapor. I also got some invasion money the Japs planned on using in U.S. territory, will try and send some to you next time. Will send a victory peso, used by American Troops in the Phillipines.

Le Roy [Capt. A.L. Enger][277]

⊠     ⊠     ⊠     ⊠     ⊠     ⊠

*Most of their attention was directed toward their duties and conditions aboard ship, but the men were also conscious of significant events transpiring elsewhere, such as Franklin Delano Roosevelt's death on April 12, 1945.*

USS LST 1023

Sunday Night, April 15 [45]

Dear Dr. Evanson,

Finally the slow Navy gave us the word and we pulled out. We sure waited long enough after we were loaded. We have quite a cargo—850 tons of beer! Reckon the boys will be glad to see us pull in to some island "out there."

Had a letter from Al Jacobson last week. He is a paratrooper. Got in on the Philippine Isl. Says "Editor" Olson plans to go to Harvard after the war. Guess we'll have to do some fast talking with Ole. Doc Strand is going to Supply School in Boston—a darn good liberty town.

We are heading for Tutor's former hang-out now. Just for onward routing I believe. These darn LST's roll like the dickens even fully loaded. It's almost impossible to write.

Our World and our Navy lost a wonderful man this week. He gave his life for his country, the same as any of those in active service.

Greetings to the faculty,

Sincerely,

[Ens] E.O. Naeseth[278]

⊠    ⊠    ⊠    ⊠    ⊠    ⊠

*Even though assignment stateside may have been safer than duty overseas, the men were often eager to get to actual duty stations as soon as training was finished.*

[Letterhead: The Plaza, Overlooking Union Square,
San Francisco, California]

Tuesday, 17 April 1945

Dear Sir:

Guess it's about time for me to sit down and get things squared away.

These copies of Scuttlebutt's have been chasing me around enuf. As you know you've been sending them to me on the PC 1077. I left her about 2 years ago and every time I get one they chase me about. So here's the dope. After I left I went aboard an AKA then to an AP (the best in the fleet). I left my AP and got myself some gold braid which makes me an Ensign, now. After the commission I was sent to the Univ. of Arizona for indoctrination. There I ran into Ens. Paul Preus (Luther '38). After Univ of Ariz I was sent to take Communications at Harvard University. I left there last December and did some duty in Seattle, Wn. Then I went to Bremerton, Wn. To the CVE School there.[279] I left there a few days ago and my future address will be—[…]

While at Harvard I ran into "Andy" Anderson (Luther '38). Andy and Paul are the only two Luther men that I have run into since coming in the navy in '40. Have looked for more but just don't seem to be able to find them.

Would appreciate your sending me John Wenberg's address. He left Luther in '39. Also Verner W. Bitter (Luther '39).

That seems to be about all, might say I'm just waiting transportation to my ship out in the Pacific some where. It will seem kind of good to get back out there. I spent a little better than three years out there already and figure I've had enuf duty here on the beach for one time. There is too much work to do out there to be sitting around here any longer.

Will let you know as soon as I get squared away.

May God Bless you all,

Ens. R. Gerald, Mitchell, U.S.N.R.

P.S. Forgot to say that I'm now a Communications Officer.[280]

⊠ ⊠ ⊠ ⊠ ⊠ ⊠

*By the spring of 1945, the U.S. Air Forces were actively bombing the Japanese home islands. Despite censorship restrictions, the men were able to provide Evanson with some details of their missions.*

[Letterhead: Army Air Forces]

The Marianas Islands
22 April 1945

Dear Dr. Evanson,

Here it is a beautiful, hot, sunshiney Sunday morning out here on the islands and it's about time I was writing you all a letter letting you know approximately where I am.

I want to thank you again for the swell time that I had visiting with you folks the last time that I was home. It was certainly great to talk over old times. After my leave was over I went back to Walker A.A.F. for a few weeks more training, then down to Cuba for the second time on detached service. We spent a couple of weeks flying training missions down there then went back to Walker until about the middle of March. We spent a couple of weeks staging at Kearney A.A.F., Neb. and about three days at our P.O.E. in Sacramento. We had a rather interesting trip out here from the States. Came by-way-of Hawaii and had two passes into Honolulu, Pearl Harbor, Forde Island, etc. We all had a swell time seeing everything. From there on I can't mention anything about our trip. Since we've been here on the island my crew and I have already had four actual combat missions over the Japanese Empire. Just a word about each of them: Our first mission was over the Koriyanea Chemical Work on Honshu. You probably heard that mission described over the radio as being "the longest bombing mission of the war". I might add that nineteen hours in the air at one time isn't exactly fun. We naturally received our "baptism of fire" on our first raid and even managed to bring back some flack holes in our plane. Our second mission was over Tokyo proper and was termed the longest raid of the war so far. The third mission was over the Kawasaki Power Plants in the Tokyo Area, and our last mission was over Konoya Air Field on Kyushu, Japan. We've had very good results on all of our missions thus far.

Say Dr., will you do me a favor if you have time when the next "Scuttlebutt" comes out? I would like very much to know if there are any "Lutherites" with the same A.P.O. and Unit as mine whom I might be able to look up while I'm here. I received the "Scuttlebutt" dated March 22; it was forwarded to me here from Walker, and I certainly want to keep right on receiving it. It's really great to be able to keep track of all the old gang this way.

I haven't mentioned anything about our living conditions here. Actually they aren't so bad when you consider that there are still quite a few Japs on the island and that we're living in just a small clearing in the jungle. On top of all that we are quite a distance from our source of supply. We live in Quonset huts, however, and our food is good.

Guess that is all of the news so I'll say so-long for now.

I'm enclosing a picture and a small contribution to the Plaque Fund in a separate envelope.

Most Sincerely,
Les Fels
P.S. Thanks again for all of your trouble

Three of my crew are good old Iowa men. Airplane Commander, 1st Lt. D.B. Baker, Cedar Rapids. Pilot, 2nd Lt. R.C. Beason, Montezuma. And myself from West Union. As for the rest of my crew: Bombardier, 2nd Lt. R.G. Reasoner, Roswell, New Mexico. Radar Operator, F/O F.J. Rose, Lansing, Mich. S/Sgt. C.A. Skrutvold, International Falls, Minn. S/Sgt. E.E. Folwell, Horseshoe Bend, Idaho. Sgt. J.W. Malley, Providence, Rhode Island. Cpl. A.A. Mecker, St. Louis, Mo. Cpl. R.A. Billings and Cpl. L.G. Rondeau, Norwich, Connecticut.
Leslie R. Fels[281]

✉     ✉     ✉     ✉     ✉     ✉

*The men in the Pacific followed progress in the European theater with great interest, hoping that redeployed troops would help bring a quick end to fighting there as well.*

[Letterhead: American Red Cross]

May 7, 1945

Dear Chellis,

It has been sometime since I have written to anyone at Luther. Have been getting the Scuttlebutt and Chips quite regular, but have changed addresses a couple of times just lately, so it will speed them up with the new address.

Have yet to run into a Luther man out here in the Pacific. Hear from Eddie Larson & Lorrie Ugland quite frequently but otherwise not much correspondence with Lutherites. Would you try to find out Carsten Lukvold's address and put it in the next Scuttlebutt?

Sorry I can't tell what island I'm located on but censorship pretty strict right at the present. Have a pretty decent go here. Japan ought to be beginning to wonder where U.S. will strike next when the war is over with Germany. War news sounds as if it could end anytime on that side.

Luther must be really rebuilding and remodeling. Hope the war ends real soon so they can begin their work at school!

301

Very little to write of at present so will try to write again soon.

P.F.C. Dean M. Penney

> As ever
> Dean[282]

   ✉      ✉      ✉      ✉      ✉      ✉

*Although the war in Europe was over, and progress was being made in the Pacific, men were still beginning new training programs in the spring of 1945.*

> Radar Maintenance Sch.
> San Francisco, Calif.
> 5/27/45

Dear Mr. Evanson

It's really high time I am getting a letter off that way. I should have did it long ago but I guess I'm not much at writing letters

The first thing I want to do is thank you & I hope in turn you will thank everyone else who has a hand in getting "Scuttlebutt" to all the fellows in the service. I have received it regularly & I certainly wait for it & read it through thoroughly, sometimes a couple of times. I also really enjoy getting "College Chips" & it has did alot to let me know where alot of the Luther fellows are at.

I haven't been very lucky as I have never ran into any of them yet but now that I'm in Hawaii I hope to get to see a few of them.

By this time I'm quite an old Salt myself, if I may use that term. I have been on the same ship for fifteen months & we have covered practically the whole Pacific. We have been from the states, went beyond New Guinea & from Australia as far north as Alaska so that is covering quite alot of water. We spent about ten months around New Guinea & were in on two invasions & also have one Jap sub to our credit. The way I'm writing here its turning out to be an autobiography but I hadn't started out with that intent & hope you don't mind to much.

Right now I am temporarily detached from the ship as I am going to Radar Maintenance school here & will be here for about five months. I read in scuttlebutt that Karsten Leigvold was going here also but I have looked through the files & failed to find his name so he must be at another school out here.

Right now I'm really enjoying the nice sunshiny weather after flying in from the Aleutians only a couple weeks ago, that's where I left my ship.

I'm going to ask a favor of you also, I wish you would have College Chips and Scuttlebutt sent to this new address now as I'll be here for five months as I said before & I'll notify you again when I go back to the ship.

I was wondering if you have any kind of a list from which you could pick out the fellows who are stationed here in Hawaii, I'd really appreciate getting a list like that so I could see a few of the fellows again.

I am going to enclose a money order for the Plaque fund & soon I'll have to get my check to the building of Old Main also.

I have been following the sports & from the number of men you have there they have really been doing alright. You must have had some real basketball games there throughout the winter season. I also noticed that you have some very regular writers & I hope or rather resolve to do better from here on.

I'm hoping after I finish school here that I'll hit the mainland for a thirty day leave & then maybe I could get down there for a football game also.

No, for this time I guess this had better be all Chellis. Here is hoping you & everyone else at Luther are enjoying these summer months along with all the others and for now its "so long for a while."

Sincerely yours
Jennings S. Aske[283]

✉     ✉     ✉     ✉     ✉     ✉

*Not all men in the Pacific were in dangerous combat positions. Some had responsibility for the morale and general well being of the troops.*

31 May 1945

Dear Chellis & Ruth:

Many thanks for including me on your lists for your news letter and "Chips." I imagine you got the address from Chuck Weiser.

However the address has been changed again. It is Naval Air Bases, Navy 128, F.P.O. San Francisco Calif. I am on Admiral Mason's staff now and have jurisdictional supervision over the physical training and recreation personnel and program at the Naval air stations in the districts. This included Midway, French Frigate, Johnston, Polynesia, Canton as well as those in the main Hawiians. So I do a lot of island hopping myself but none of the beach heads are tough.

There are a lot of familiar last names in your communications but the first names do not designate any of the fellows that I remember. I guess they are all raising families etc and were smarter than I was and knew enough to keep out of this mixup. It is not quite as bad as that sounds but I sure am ready to don a snap brim hat, a striped tie and some flashy socks any time the final gong sounds.

I gather that Chellis Jr. is in Denver but there was no clue as to what he is doing. Also your daughter mentioned but not which one.

I imagine Chuck gave the dope on our family, Babe and Mary in Princeton and Frank has been in Navy 18 mo. now. Right now I think he is with them in Princeton on leave. I am in my 30th month as a Lt. now and it does not look as though they are going to get to my name or date for promotion during this war.

Would appreciate a note giving details of the where, what and well being of your family and any other news of the old timers that I know. Even the store ads seem to show that not too many old timers are still going. Kindest regards to all of yours

Cordially<br>Cap [Lt. F.C. Cappon]284

&#9990;  &#9990;  &#9990;  &#9990;  &#9990;  &#9990;

*While many of the Navy men sailed aboard large ships, such as aircraft carriers, destroyers, and battleships, others were on smaller craft, such as Arch Ward on an LCT (Landing Craft Tank).*

June 6, 1945, p.m.

Dear Evanson—"Scuttlebutt"

I received your March issue today and it really boosted my morale. Thanks a lot. Too bad you had to quit sending addresses. They really kept us in contact with the fellows.

Just finished a 3400 mile jaunt aboard this barge. Believe me I don't want to do that again. I have faith in the "1324", but not 3400 miles worth. After it's through and think back it really was interesting. Thrill in every "knot." I think it's the longest trip an LCT has ever made on its own power.

Glad to hear Luther is having a baseball team. Got a kick out about having to show the boys how to hold the "trademark" up. Bob Jake must be having a time.

Sending a couple of pictures of my "battleship." Notice our washing machine on one of them. That's our pride and joy.

Only Luther fellow I've met out here was Chuck Fairchild who was at Luther for one semester, he's also from my hometown. He's going back to Luther along with me after the war.

Hope this finds you well and hearty. Greet everyone for me.

Arch

Sending $5.00 for the Plaque Fund[285]

---

*Evanson referred to Ward's letter in the June 1945 issue of "Scuttlebutt," noting, "Also two pictures (including washing machine in plain sight) "Archie's Joy" from the Pac from Ens. Archie Ward, just after his ship had completed a 340 mile cruise, a record for that type, he says. And a Plaque contrib. too. He's on an LCT." He began the July issue with a note of correction: "First off, an apology, and that to Ens. Archie Ward and "Archie's Joy" when I said in the last issue that his ship had just completed a record cruise of 340 miles. That should have been 3400, and it was my mistake too. Of course any Navy man would have known it didn't add up, but some of you G.I.'s who don't like the water any too well anyway might have figured that that cruise was far enough for anyone and too far for most people." That, in turn, prompted the following response from Ward.*

Sept. 21, 1945

Dear "Scuttlebutt,"

Received the July issue of the Scuttlebutt today, and am a very relieved sailor. Thank you for the correction from 340 miles to 3,400 on the little cruise we recently completed.

A 340 mile trip in one of these barges is a feat in itself, let alone a 3400 mile jaunt. I'm not to eager to do it again. Getting to old.

Am now operating out of Guam loading all these lucky high point fellows. Tiresome work, especially with the war over, and me with all of 29-1/2 points, long way from 49.

Just reserve me a billet at Larsen Hall, I'll get there by some hook or crook method.

What kind of material has Coach Pete got for a football team this fall? Sure would like to be there, if only to be a spectator.

Thanks for the Scuttlebutt. It really keeps us going out here, a good morale builder.

Ens. Arch Ward

Will put in my request for "Chips" and the "Alumnus" Thank you[286]

    ✉      ✉      ✉      ✉      ✉      ✉

*In addition to facing the dangers of combat duty, many of the men in the Pacific also contracted malaria.*

Mobile Explosives Investigation Unit No.1
C/O Fleet Post Office
San Francisco, California

[undated]

Dear Chellis,

It's Sunday morning and I'm over at the house doing a little work. I've been out on an operation for the past month and am back now with the unit.

There's little new from here that you haven't already seen in the papers, I guess. Things have been pretty hot, figuratively and literally speaking.

I had some sixty letters and papers when I came back to the unit the day before yesterday. Amongst them was a very welcomed issue of scuttlebutt, which I enjoyed very much. You're doing the guys out here a real service, one which we won't forget. A guy always likes to hear from the bunch back at Luther.

Please pardon the typing. These typewriters out here are pretty well beaten up. Also my typing leaves much to be desired.

It's hotter than blazes this morning and I'm sweating like a butcher. The heat plus a little malaria make a guy suffer once in a while.

I'll have to cut this short and get to work, I believe. 'Hoping this finds you all well, I remain

As ever,

Marv [Bachman]

PS Say hello to Mrs. Evanson for me.[287]

    ✉      ✉      ✉      ✉      ✉      ✉

*Although many men were redeployed from Europe to the Pacific after V-E day, some factors made that transition earlier. In this case, although the area of duty had changed, the ship remained the same.*

7 June 1945

Dear Dr. Evanson,

It has been my intention to write for some time but good intentions don't count for much unless they are carried out.

I have enjoyed your Scuttlebutt pages a great deal and also the Chips.

To start with the most recent news, I entered holy matrimony with Dalora H. Nichols of South Bend, Indiana on March 20th of this year. That happy event took place shortly after I took command of this ship.

It seems that some more overseas duty, this time in the Pacific, will be my lot, sooner or later. At present, we are on the west coast undergoing a program of training. I was over in the Mediterranean for 16 months. We left Africa a few days after Christmas last year. It was surely wonderful to see the good old U.S.A. again. I have been on the same ship since I reported aboard in '43.

It will be a grand day when we all can come back to visit and to celebrate that first homecoming after victory.

Sincerely,

[Lt(J.G)] Evans L. Knutson[288]

⊠          ⊠          ⊠          ⊠          ⊠          ⊠

*After V-E Day, the military concentrated fully on defeating Japan. While some men were able to return home from the European theater, others were redeployed directly to the Pacific.*

[Letterhead: U.S.S. Blackford (APB—45)]

13 July 1945

Dear Mr. Evanson,

I know that I have been neglecting all my friends at Luther for some time now, but really I have been so busy that I haven't had much time for anything including letter writing. I'll try to do better in the future.

As you probably noticed, I'm at sea again. Where at sea, is immaterial because it all looks the same, and the heck of it is, your only looking at the top of it.

We are shaking the Blackford down at the present time but we shall be off for parts unknown in a very short time. I dont think it is a military secret to say that I'm going to the Pacific. At least it wont be as rough there as it was on the North Atlantic on the Destroyer I came off of.

Mr. Evanson, I know that many of the Luther boys are on Small Craft in the Pacific. Here's the story behind that statement. This ship is to act as a mother ship for small craft and if I knew which of the ships had Luther men aboard I'd surely look them up. I'd like to get a list of the fellows if I can. I know that they would like to have some one greet them that faraway from home. If you could put me in the way of obtaining such a list I'd be very grateful to you. (I hope you dont mind, but this typewriter doesn't spell right.)

I'd like to have you greet my friends on the faculty and all of my other friends there at school for me. I'll be writing to many of them as soon as we get caught up with the ship's work.

I received your June issue of "Scuttlebutt" today. It had to follow me around a bit but it finally caught up to me. Thank your very much for it and I hope it keeps coming. I'd also like to have you change my address for Chips, if you will

If I can obtain that list that I mentioned I'm sure that there will be a goodly number of Luther reunions in the Pacific. Thanking you in advance for your help for this, I remain

Respectfully yours,
"Mack" Ens. C.F. McDonald. USNR.

P.S.

I forgot to tell you what I do on this bucket of bolts, so I'll add that now. I'm Damage Control Officer, Athletic Officer, Ward Room Mess Treasurer, On the Survey Board, Censor Mail, On the Hull Board, On the Summary Court Martial Board, Ass't to the first Lt. and when I'm not busy they find a few odd jobs for me to do. Oh Yes, I'm also the First Division Officer. Let me tell you, as you probably can recall, that it is quite a job to handle a Deck Force. Oh Well, things are tough all over.

If you ever have the opportunity, I'd like to have you greet especially the Peterson and Nordgaard families for me. You can also tell Mr. Reque that with my new glasses I'd probably be able to hit the ball for him if I were given the opportunity again.

C.M.[289]

⊠        ⊠        ⊠        ⊠        ⊠        ⊠

*Men serving in submarines had their own perspective on the war. Because Evanson had served in the Navy in World War II, Navy men kept him up-to-date on sightings of his former ship, the U.S.S. Pennsylvania.*

[Undated]

Dear Dr. Evanson,

Arrival of the last "Scuttlebutt" reminded me that it's been a long time since you've heard from the underwater Navy. My correspondence has been shameful since we arrived in the states—didn't write letters while we were on leave, upon returning to San Francisco we were so busy getting the boat back together and making good liberties that Luther-writing was neglected, and when we got out here we were underway almost every day training to get everyone back into shape so we could give the Nips a bad time when we got back out there.

I see mother gave you all the dope on the small Luther reunion although she had it a bit fouled up—we never did get to see Rob McConnell; at least, I didn't. But seeing the rest of the boys was swell.

Guess all the training we had here before we left on this last patrol did some good because we caused the J-boys a good deal of woe. The skipper is getting the Navy Cross for the last run and the boat has been recommended for the Navy Unit Commendation, possibly even the Presidential Citation. Time will tell which one. Our trouble was that we didn't have sufficient torpedoes to fire. Got rid of our usual load and still saw ships which almost made us weep! So stand by for a good sea story when I get back.

Am enclosing a picture of your old home—Still recognize her? Thought maybe it might interest you to see what she looks like.

We had a photographer aboard this last run—they're sending one out with every boat to take colored movies of any action and also life as it is lived out on patrol. They're planning a picture of submarines similar to "Fighting Lady." Don't know how it'll turn out though—the real action aboard is hard to film, especially if they want pictures of the enemy. During an approach the scope is used as little as possible and then <u>only</u>, to get a set up for the fire control party. And after the fish are fired the target is usually below the water surface before we can get the camera attached to the scope, focused, etc. We're all wondering therefore, what the outcome will be.

Have been taking life quite easily since we got in—swimming, sunbathing, lounging in general. Plan to take a hop over to one of the other islands tomorrow to take a look around. The more I see of this place the better I like it.

Glad to hear Davy Preus finally got his bars—which reminds me, I owe him a letter. That's the trouble, we accumulate so many letters while we're out on patrol that it's a rough time we have trying to get them all answered during our stay in port. 'Course if we didn't get lots of mail when we came in we'd gripe like blazes.

Remind Chellis, Jr. that he owes me a letter. He's probably mad at me because I didn't look him up when I was in the states—however once on a plane we stayed on because it was no trouble to get bumped off. Getting another would turn out to be a tough job.

Time to hit the sack so I'll knock off. Greetings to Mrs. Evanson, the family, Pete & wife, everyone in Decorah.

Sincerely,

Cal

Took a picture while out on patrol which I'm sending Andy. You might ask her for a look at it if you see her.

Cal [Lt. (J.G.) DeBuhr][290]

    ✉    ✉    ✉    ✉    ✉    ✉

*As the end of hostilities approached, many of the men had an opportunity to see firsthand the war's impact on local populations.*

July 20, 1945

Dear Chellis,

Thank you for the May issue of "Scuttlebutt" which arrived today. I really enjoy hearing about the home front.

My ship, the U.S.S. Towner was commissioned on the 1st of December. Since that time I've visited quite a few places, a few of the more interesting ones being Panama, Pearl Harbor, Honolulu, New Caledonia, the Admiralty Islands, Leyte, Somar, New Guinea, and last but not least, the great city of Manila

It was our first opportunity to see the ravages of war. Many people are starving as there is very little food.

The inflation has gone sky high which makes it practically impossible for the poor people to buy food or clothing. A very poor grade of shoes sells for

$32.50 a pair. I doubt a co-ed back at Luther would appreciate paying such high prices.

While on Leyte I visited a native Priest. He had received his education on Leyte and Somar.

I've visited many native villages and learnt quite a few of their customs. In fact, I think I'll be an expert on native culture after the war.

I've been close to the Japs a number of times. Picked up one sub. contact but we lost it.(poor hunters)

We have traveled over 25,000 miles since we left the states so we figure we are getting salty.

Hello to everyone at Luther.

> An Alumnae.,
> Clifford [Ens. Clifford Ellingson][291]

⊠        ⊠        ⊠        ⊠        ⊠        ⊠

*With the Navy's "points system," many felt that the only way they would be returning home soon would be if the war ended. Even then, the process might be a long one.*

Aug. 1, 1945

Dear Folks,

Just finished noon chow so I have a few minutes, so will drop a few lines to you people back there in "God's Country."

Well, believe it or not I finally got away from the states. Got an awful long ways away from the good old U.S. too. We are over in the Ruyukus group of islands. It's really a pretty nice place. The weather is hot in the day time, but the nites are very cool. In fact I have used a blanket every nite I have been here.

We left the states on 17 May. (The day we always had those good old rope pulls at Luther) We stopped at Pearl Harbor for a few days. I run into "Cyc" Schroeder there & we had quite a gab for a few hours. Stopped at the Marshalls, & the Caroline islands for a few days too. After 51 days on a ship we finally arrived on our island here. The land scape here is much like the country around Decorah. The natives here are really something. You can't imagine how filthy they really are. I would much rather live in a hog house back in Iowa than in one of their houses.

Say we have a Dr. in our outfit by the name of John Donlon. He is a cousin of the Donlons that have that drug store in Decorah. You might mention it to them there in the drug store if you should drop in there some time.

I suppose that summer school is going strong. In fact your second section should be starting now.

Betty and David are now back in Lake Mills for a while. Surely wish I could be there with them for a few days. Would love to get back to Luther for a few days too. Maybe it won't be too long. Of course, with the point system the Navy has now, I only have 4½ years of overseas duty in order to get out. I'll take my chances that the war ends.

About time to go to work, so will close for now. Greetings to you all, I'm waiting for the day I can drop in and have a "cup of Joe" with you.

So long
Just [Lt(J.G.)] Harold [Heltne][292]

⊠     ⊠     ⊠     ⊠     ⊠     ⊠

*The end of the war also meant the end of most censorship restrictions, so that the men could finally report some of what they had seen and where they had been.*

29 August 1945

Dear Chel,

Here is a letter from one of those pacific sailors who rates the common two overseas ribbons with no stars but who has been a few miles from the states anyway and wished once more to express his sincere appreciation for "Scuttlebutt". I can't even report that i have been in the forward area like most of your correspondence, but i will attempt to put forth something in the next few paragraphs which might be of interest to you. Enough of this dry humor—i might also insert a request for the Chips and Alumnus now also. Thanks!! I really look forward to getting all three every month.

Since we are allowed to tell where we are now and where we have been, I, for once will have something to write about. You will probably realize that being on a small craft we don't move around too much which makes it impossible for us to tell where we are because we don't move out of the immediate area long enough.

At present I am or rather the ship and crew is working out of Midway with some excellent duty since the conclusion of the war. We are in port for about a day

312

and a half and the night of the second day we are out on patrol but we return to port bright early the morning of the third day. I imagine that you can relate from that what good duty we are really having. We naturally waiting for further orders every day. We hope that they will be to return to the states to decommission this ship. Of course this is only wishful thinking but it should happen within the next six months because these ships are much too useless and expensive to run during peacetime.

Before the war was over we were working with submarines and stayed out most of the time. Prior to that we worked out of Pearl Harbor. While there we got to see most of the islands of the Hawaiian group. Most of the crew liked the island of Hawaii the best.

During our duty at Pearl we escorted a large passenger and cargo ship to four different islands. That was the longest trip we ever made. We went to Palmyra, Fanning, Christmas,—stopping so we got ashore on Palmyra only. We tied to a buoy at Fanning and dropped anchor at Christmas. Our last stop and destination was Canton, the northernmost island in the Phoenix group. It proved to be interesting but in my estimation, after you have seen one small Pacific island you have just about seen them all. They seem to be either a bunch of sand or coral with a small amount of vegetation on most of them.

This just about exhausts my book of travels on a pc[293] for tonight so will sign off. The only battle that I can report is the one we take whenever we get in a rough sea and bounce and bounce and bounce which goes on for hours, and isn't exactly enjoyable.

Forgot to tell you that I am one of King Neptune's members, being fully initiated when we went to Canton. Our captain and two members of the crew were the only old salts aboard, so had their fun initiating the crew and officers.

Just another of Luther's sailors waiting to return—

(anxiously)

Very sincerely yours,

Chester Porter [Sm 3/c][294]

✉ ✉ ✉ ✉ ✉ ✉

*After long periods of training or stateside duty, some men were transferred to the Pacific just as the war was ending.*

Sept 4, 1945

Dear Dr. Evanson—

Just thought I'd drop a few lines to give you my new address & would appreciate it very much if you'd send Chips & Scuttlebutt again this year. In case you are wondering what kind of a ship this is it's a hospital ship. It's just a new ship so this is her first trip out. We are going to cross the date line tonight so I'll wake up in the morning and it'll be Thurs the 6th. Since censorship has been lifted I guess I can tell where were headed. First stop is Okinawa & from there I'm not sure, probably Japan to pick up allied P.W.'s. Sailed under the Golden Gate on the 14th of last month. We were almost directly under the bridge when the good news came. Came as far as Pearl on LST & then picked this up there. Had a little liberty in Honolulu but the liberty there isn't much to talk about.

Well I guess this will be about all for now. Am planning for summer school at Luther next summer. Hope we're all out by then. Best wishes to all.

Milford "Bucket" Lunde[295]

# CHAPTER 18

# "We intend to get up to the homeland before long"— The Philippines

*For some men, their love of music overrode their fears of what was happening around them.*

Philippines, 4 Feb 1945

Dear Dr. Evanson,

I surely enjoy receiving the Scuttlebutt and the College Chips. Thanks much.

I received a fine break in the Army being assigned to General MacArthur's Headquarters as a statistician in the G-3 section of the General Headquarters of the South West Pacific Area. I keep my direction arm in shape by having the GHQ Chapel Choir.

Did you hear my choir make its broadcast from the Philippines? My GHQ choir broadcasted to the States on Christmas Eve over networks from coast to coast. Just after the broadcast the Japs gave us a Christmas Party. My choir had planned on going caroling so we couldn't let the Japs stop us. We caroled for General MacArthur at his home, and just as I finished directing my group in Silent Night our guns brought down a Jap plane in flames. The bombs and guns didn't bother me as I conducted cause I played bass drum and cymbals in the Luther Concert band!!!!! We caroled at many of our Generals homes and at various places throughout the city even though the Jap raid was on all the time. We have received much praise for continued caroling under such conditions.

On Christmas morning I was asked to lead 250 Filipino children in the singing of Christmas carols at a party we gave them. That was some experience.

315

About half of them couldn't speak 'Americano' so I had a couple Nuns relay what I wanted them to sing in Filipino. They all knew the melodies so everything was jake. In the afternoon my choir visited the hospitals to sing for the sick and wounded soldiers.

I am well acquainted with the Supt of a large Filipino school. He has had me at his home many times for traditional Filipino meals and all. The History books they use are 1917 models!! The Japs made them paste paper over passages not good for the Filipinos to know, so the Supt. foxed them by pasting transparent material over the restricted material, and he got by with it!! Supt Kapili gave me some Jap text books that they had to use. Will show you the books sometime when I visit Luther, and I hope that will be very soon!

Sincerely,

[PFC.] A. Maya Savold

Greetings to all.[296]

✉    ✉    ✉    ✉    ✉    ✉

*Most men found their duties in the military very different from what they hoped to do in civilian life.*

Cpl. Kenneth Kastner (37568867)

"Somewhere in the Philippines" [Feb 11, 1945]

Dear Editor,

I received your first and grand issue of the "Scuttlebutt" and certainly enjoyed it. It's the real thing and I just can't explain what it does to a G.I. I noticed most of the fellows were officer's and that is certainly good. I was just lucky to get a corporals rating. I'm in Communications and am supposed to be a Radio Operator. I went to Radio School and learned Code, so am a key and voice operator. It's a good racket and I like it, but I doubt very much if I will keep up with it after the war. I still want to get a Music Major if the College still thinks I'm eligible.

I've only been overseas for 14 months but I've been all over this South Pacific Islands. Beautiful South Sea Isles with their women, phooey.

Give Prof. Hoslett my congratulations in his new addition, and greet any of the other Professors I had while I was there.

316

Will close now and am looking forward to returning to Luther College and try to do a better job than I did the first year. Keep sending the Scuttlebutt."

I know Mayo Savold is in the near vicinity, but have not seen him. I haven't seen any L. C. men yet. Will see you in the next issue. I hope you get this alright as I am addressing this the best I know how.

Sincerely,
An L.C. Student
Kenneth Kastner[297]

✉  ✉  ✉  ✉  ✉  ✉

*Although Evanson's field was history, at a small liberal arts college, it was not unusual to find students from very different majors in his classes. In some cases, their undergraduate majors were good preparation for their military assignments.*

Philippine Islands
4 March 1945

Dear Dr. Evanson,

A professor is supposed to be able to recall names, faces, and facts about hundreds of former students but I imagine that you have forgotten quite a few by this time. Of course students remember their teachers and that gives them some advantage in recollection. Maybe 1940 isn't so very long ago insofar as memory goes. Somehow I did manage to acquire a degree in that year. I had the peculiarity of desiring a major in history on top of one in chemistry. Chemistry for bread and butter; history for the love of it. Never expected to use history and probably never will but I never regret having taken it from a cultural viewpoint. The stuff fascinated me and I couldn't help reading it when I was supposed to be studying something else. That was one hell of a student for you to have.

Is there some way of getting Dr. Waldeland's address? The last I heard from him was about the time he left Luther. Never did find out what his address was after that.

I left the States on December 31 so am just a newcomer. My tentmates are praying for a Jap air raid so they can initiate me properly. Can't say that I would welcome one.

317

Spent fourteen months in the infantry with the 6<sup>th</sup> Division, which is now in Luzon. Then came thirteen weeks in Chemical Warfare O.C.S. Spent two years in the Central Flying Training Command as Base Chemical Officer at two different places and now am on duty with the Fifth Air Force Service Command. We're mainly concerned with supply. When the call comes for incendiary bombs, I get some work. Otherwise it's mostly routine work. Have to inspect units for their defense against chemical attack. Should poison gas be used, I'll have a terrific job.

Bumped into Kenneth Quam in a camp at Dutch New Guinea. Played a few games of chess and lost, as usual. We used to play quite a bit at Luther—which accounts for some of my unexplained absences from class. I was surprised when censoring mail back there to get one of his letters. I knew he was in camp before that though.

Have bumped into a few Luther men while in the army. First one I saw was Chet Horen in Edgewood Arsenal, Md. while at Chemical Warfare O.C.S. I was cadet corporal of the guard one night and when inspecting the guards saw that one was Chet. He was sent to California, I believe, after getting his commission. See that he's in the European theater now. When I was base Chemical Officer in Liberal, Kansas, Lloyd Ritland was one of the Ground School Instructors. In Dutch New Guinea I met a cousin of Sig Reque's. He was working in Headquarters and noticed my personnel form showed that I graduated from Luther.

Got married in Texas in 1943. My wife swears she'll make a Texan out of me after the war. Since she's half an inch taller, I can't argue.

Have received some literature from Luther including a couple of Scuttlebutts. Move around so much that I'll probably receive most of the publications in an old soldier's home.

If I could get Dr. Waldeland's address, I would appreciate it.

Sincerely,

[Capt. Roger V. Krumm]              Capt. Krumm[298]

✉     ✉     ✉     ✉     ✉     ✉

*With combined air, naval, and land forces, the American advance in the Philippines went rather quickly once it had begun.*

19 Mar 45
Somewhere in Philippines

Dear Chellis:

I'm sorry I haven't written you, at least, a little note of thanks for getting the Scuttlebutt out. I enjoy it a lot even though a lot of the boys names are unfamiliar to me but every once in a while I see one that used to be with me.

I got a direct commission in the field on the 26th of December and since that time we have really been on the move. I have seen quite a bit of the Philippines already and have just finished on this campaign that we came in with. We didn't have much opposition here because the bombers had really done their work before we got here. I'm surely glad that I don't have to be on the receiving end of the bombardment our ships give the old shore before the infantry heads for shore.

The Philipinos seem quite friendly to us here but are very undernourished because most of them have been up in the hills for nearly three years.

I have only met one Luther boy since I have been in the army these three years. And that was Chaplain Howard Lybeck who I met at Fort Leonard Wood right before I left the states a year ago. Paul Nordgaard and I keep in touch with one another out here but I have moved so much it's hard for anybody to catch up with me. I'm still waiting for my xmas presents.

I have a little girl now too that is waiting for me to come home, she was born in October, I'll bet she will be quite a girl when I get home. I was hoping I could have had a boy, so he could of gone to Luther and tried to make a better record than his dad had.

I'll bet things are nice and green at home now and the boys are most likely out on the diamond, getting ready for another season. I haven't played any ball since I've been over because the temperature has been too high.

Who would have thought that those little Japs, Gil and I pitched against from Hosei University over ten years ago would be getting me to come over to see them. I don't think that I will be so friendly towards them if I ever get to Toyko.

I've tried to give you the latest and I hope the news keeps coming. I've only had mail once in the last two months.

Sincerely
Al. [2nd Lt. Albert H. Bell,][299]

✉     ✉     ✉     ✉     ✉     ✉

*In addition to censorship regulations, stereotypical Norwegian humility meant that most of the men would not "blow their own horns" too strongly. For example, Al Jacobson's unit, the 503rd Parachute Infantry, was an important part of the airborne invasion of Corregidor.*

25 March 1945
Philippines

Dear Professor Evanson,

I don't know if you remember me as I was only in your history class for one semester. Anyway, I've certainly enjoyed receiving your "Scuttlebutt" and reading about all the boys.

Lately, I've been moving and finally today, about three months supply of "Scuttlebutt" came in the mail. And now I'd like to give my latest address so I'll get them regularly.

I've always liked things a little out of the ordinary and I really hit it when I joined the parachute Infantry. There's nothing like it.

We just came back from a mission; getting a little rest at last. Maybe you read about our outfit in the papers not long ago. Then yesterday, we received notice that the regiment had been given a Presidential Citation for our last action.

Have you heard from Gene Olson? I correspond with him quite regular and he's been rolling around France with his Tank outfit.

About the only thing I have to look forward to is coming back to Luther after the war. I've been writing to Naeseth and he's all for coming back again. That will be a happy day when we're all back there again.

Is College Chips still operating as usual? It must be rather tough with a small student body.

Well, I guess I've gone on enough. Hope to continue receiving the dope on all the boys.

Sincerely,
[Pvt.] Al Jacobson[300]

✉        ✉        ✉        ✉        ✉        ✉

*Because mail often came infrequently, it was always important. But the men obviously put a high premium on getting the most recent issues of "Scuttlebutt."*

[V-MAIL]
From: Pvt. Orland L. Hansen May 23rd 1945—Somewhere in the Philippines
Dear Chellis:

Just received the Mch issue of Scuttlebutt along with 58 other letters. Required several hours time to read them all. Don't know when I'll be able to answer them. "Tuff" about U.S. censorship forbidding listing of addresses—but Security is security! Have read the aforementioned news letter three times & many of the names recall certain incidents & memories associated with them—while studying at L.C. Incidentally, Chellis, hope to send a contribution for plaque & Old Main—when I can get hold of a money order. S'pose the class of '45 are on their way by now—starting out in life. Remember, vividly—three years ago, May 18—'43—a great day. Also think back on that fateful day—May 25th wasn't it—when Old Main spit her last words from a fiery tongue—"Ressurgam"! Have been taking things easy of late—doing plenty of reading & studying, too! Have a young Filipino, a former guerilla, teaching me "Tagalog" dialect, and find it quite easy & truly interesting! These peoples were hard hit, their clothing consists of odds & ends—including "gunny sacks." All for now—best wishes to L.C. family & students. My heart is with you. Good luck & God Speed—Orland "Ole"
P.S. would like Krumman's address if possible![301]

⊠       ⊠       ⊠       ⊠       ⊠       ⊠

*Duty in the Pacific Theater often covered a wide geographical area, with the ultimate goal being Japan.*

June 14,1945

Dear Chellis,

Received the April Scuttlebutt today. Hadn't received one for some time because I've moved again. I've seen quite a bit of the Pacific—mostly water. I've been to Hawaii, Angaur in the Palaus, Guadalcanal in the Solomons, Mannus in the Admiralties, New Caledonia and am now on one of the islands in the Visayas Group, [Censored] Philippines, I'm enclosing today's issue of our Division newspaper—"The Wildcat." Also a snapshot of a buddy and myself "going native."

An exhibit of this war sounds interesting. One of the items could be "war money". I'm enclosing a "Victory Peso" which is all that is used in the Philippines.

It is worth 50¢ in American money and quite confusing. When we go back to American dollars again we'll probably think that it's worth only half its value.

We're living fairly comfortably here in pyramidal tents. We're located in a grove of coconut palms about 100 yards from a nice ocean beach. We also have fresh water showers. We have our own theatre for the Bn with movies three or four nights a week—I run the projector part of the time. Our chapel is located about 500 yards away with services on Sunday mornings and Thursday nights. Hope the Japs are finished soon so we can all get back to Luther to finish college.

Sincerely,
Bob Olson (ex '44)[302]

✉    ✉    ✉    ✉    ✉    ✉

*Although Navy personnel expected sea duty when they began their duty, Army men also had to endure conditions on troop transport ships in order to reach their combat assignments.*

[V-MAIL]

Luzon, 21 June 1945

From: Cpl. M. E. Lore
Dear Chellis:

Every night I get down upon my knees and thank God that I'm not in the Navy.

This is great—the hardest part to becoming an overseas veteran is coming-over-seas.

I do have great respect for Uncle Sam's troopships—manned by competent crews, they get the job done. Good chow, spacious accommodations (sometimes you can even turn over in your bunk) but the monotony was horrible.

Best regards to you,
Marv Lore[303]

✉    ✉    ✉    ✉    ✉    ✉

*For many serving in the Navy in the Pacific, direct contact with the enemy was often limited, though intense.*

The Philippines
Sunday, 24 June 1945

Dear Chellis,

The faithful arrival of your scuttlebutt manuscript each month offers a rather shameful contrast to my complete neglect to acknowledge receipt of them. I really look forward to each arrival and enjoy very much reading of the varied activities of my many Luther acquaintances. It's a shame the censors had to clamp the lid down on the printing of exact addresses of the fellows; I'm sure they must have been instrumental in many a pleasant overseas reunion. I haven't run across very many Luther fellows in my travels so far tho I'm sure there must be a large number hiding in the hills somewhere. I did have Rolf Norstag aboard for dinner and a bull-session a few weeks back. I also did some operating with the ship Jim Ylvilden is on during the early part of the Year.

Florence tells me Chell was home for a vacation recently, says she had a nice long chat with him on a variety of subjects. Still claims to be unattached with all the surplus of women about I see; I guess he figures he may as well look the field over carefully as long as the odds are all in his favor. My correspondence with him has been no better—guess I'll have to get on the ball or people will begin giving me up for lost.

I'd like to enclose a contribution for the plaque fund, a worthy project which should command support from all Lutherites in the service. American money is quite scarce out here; even the Army gets paid off in pesos and the Japs counterfeited so much of that a guy seldom knows whether he's flush or broke.

My contact with the Nips has not been too extensive so far. My ship supported one landing in which the Nips beat a hasty retreat to the hills in the face of a stiff barrage. These little boats pack more punch per ton than any ship in the Navy. It really has been quite an experience to command on all the way from commissioning to action against the enemy. I haven't seen anything of your old ship; it really is a pretty meek little lamb along side these new monsters. Equipment grows obsolete awfully fast at the clip events move out here.

I suppose the golf season is on full swing now after a fairly slow start. Dad claims his only lack is golf balls sufficiently round to putt with. Undoubtedly the West Side tournament will come off with all of its usual rivalry. It generally resolves itself into whoever is the fastest talking anyway and doesn't necessarily indicate who is the better of the best.

323

Well, keep 'em out of the rough and wheatfields and give my regards to your scuttlebutt audience everywhere.

Sincerely,

Tom Lynch [Lieut T C Lynch, U.S.N.][304]

⊠      ⊠      ⊠      ⊠      ⊠      ⊠

*For some, V-E Day meant reassignment from Europe back to the U.S., and a quick discharge. Others, however, were reassigned to the Pacific Theater. Because of the vast distances they had to travel, some of them barely made it across the Pacific before V-J Day.*

2 August 1945

Near Manila, P.I.

Hello All:

Guess a change of address must surely call for a letter, and that's for sure what I've done. My outfit, the 1636th Engineer Construction Battalion is now located at an airfield near Manila in the Philippines, and being kept plenty busy.

We were the first re-deployed troops to arrive in the Southwest Pacific directly from Germany and France, so received a great deal of publicity. A photographer from Life magazine made the trip with us, and took several pictures. Even though I haven't been out of the states so long, I've surely travelled. We first went to Europe, through France and up into Germany. On V-E day we were building a big PW camp to accommodate some of the many of Adolf's boys who were "Kaput" about this time. As a result there was very little celebrating done by our outfit on the big day. It was surely a wonderful feeling though to realize that everything was over in Europe. A few weeks after V-E day we were back on the transport and headed for new worlds to conquer. We had a really long trip from France to Manila, but it also proved to be quite interesting. We passed through the Straights of Gibraltar, so theoretically, we saw Africa in our portside and Europe on the starboard as well as the famous rock. It looks exactly like the pictures that that Life Insurance Company, Prudential isn't it, uses. Then we passed through the Panama Canal, which is quite a thing—must be experienced to really appreciate. And now it's Luzon of the Philippines. The natives of all the countries we have seen, all seem to have their peculiarities. This Army is an experience and an education nearly like living a history book.

Well good people and fellow Norsemen, guess I'd better knock off. It's raining outside, which isn't exactly a rarity among these parts. My regards to everyone at Luther, and I still intend to be free and at Homecoming in 1946.

Sincerely,

Ted. ('41) [Cpl Ted V. Jensen][305]

---

*Jensen followed his report with an update a few weeks later.*

3 September 1945
Luzon, P.I.

Hello All:

Talk about your changing world, we've really seen it. It just seems that I never get settled in one place long enough for the Scuttlebutt, Chips of any other publication from Luther to reach me directly. I've been quite fortunate in their having been forwarded to me, so your newsy letters have been keeping me well posted even though a bit old. You have been doing one swell job with the news though, it's a treat to receive each and every copy.

At the moment I am stationed in northern Luzon in the Philippines and rather expecting to go to Japan itself soon. Now that I have come this far, I rather hope that we do go to the land of the Rising Sun before returning home, as it's a leadpipe cinch that I'll never go as a civilian. I've had just about enough of this travel, and especially by way of the high seas. No doubt I have mentioned in previous letters just how well this 1636th Engineer Construction Battalion is travelled. But anyway, here's a quick sketch. We originally went to La Havre, France and on up to Germany and across the Rhine river doing considerable work as we went. Soon after V-E day we were sent back to Marseille, France and were on the first ship of troops redeployed directly from Germany to the Southwest Pacific, arriving in Manila. Had two projects at an airfield near Manila, where the Jap representatives came to negotiate the surrender terms, and then up here no doubt preparatory to Japan itself. As a result of everything, I am perhaps a bit over optimistic about everything, but I still have high hopes of being back home shortly after the turn of the year. Be this as it may, I have certainly seen my share of the world. This man's Army is an education in itself, though at times I believe a fellow has the right to call it a warped program.

I have still to see my first Luther man outside the continental limits of the United States too. Seems a bit funny that I have been able to miss them all so consistently as I know we are represented all over the globe. I guess I'll make up for that though when I come to Homecoming in 1946. How about arranging for an extra glittering occasion that year, as surely the most of our boys will be back by that time. Think of the extra special bull sessions that we could have when we all come home again. I spend lots of time thinking of things like that.

How are we going to do in football this fall? Any of the old boys back from the wars to bolster the team, and any outstanding prospects lined up to enter Luther? The boys have done a wonderful job to keep the old tradition alive in spite of all obstacles, so I'm sure that we'll come through okey. Give the other fellows the old Pri Sec and Luther will never be beaten in fight. Now that all wars are over, Luther will regain its winning habits, and again become the scourge of the small colleges in Iowa and vicinity. The best little school in the nation, that's our Luther, whether it be scholastically, in sports, socially, or what have you.

For now, I am forced to call this a letter. As my APO's change in number, I'll do my best to keep you posted, as I certainly look forward to receiving any news of Luther which might come through. Greet all the good people on campus, and everyone connected with Luther College itself.

Regards, Cpl. Ted. V. Jensen '41[306]

⊠　　⊠　　⊠　　⊠　　⊠　　⊠

*Even after hostilities ended in an area, the U.S. forces were involved in reconstruction of damages left by Japanese occupation.*

4 August 1945

Dear Chellis,

Received the May issue of the Scuttlebutt this morning and decided to drop you a line and also send a money order for the rebuilding of Main Building. Have also been receiving the College Chips recently.

At the present time I am waiting orders to return to the US and should have them before long. I have been here in Manila since the 22nd of March and the place sure looks different now than when I arrived. A lot of it has been cleaned up but it will take a good many years before the place will be rebuilt. There were only a few buildings left standing after we pushed the Japs out. Personally I don't care very much for the place and will feel much better when I get my feet back in the U.S. again.

Should be seeing you all before to long and hope to be able to see a few football games this fall.

Enjoy reading the Scuttlebutt and finding out where the boys are located. Haven't seen very many L.C. men around here. I'll see you soon.

Sincerely,

George A. Pfister[307]

⊠     ⊠     ⊠     ⊠     ⊠     ⊠

*The men listened eagerly to reports of the impending victory over Japan, but until the treaty was finally signed, they anticipated continued fighting.*

9 Aug '45
Luzon

Dear Chell,

Good intentions never did get letters written so I've thrown them to the wind and "gotten" down to brass tacks. If I remember, they (the tacks) always did bring good results, at least, the boy in the seat in front of me in sixth grade hit the ceiling from one.

I'm still nestled (?) snugly in the wooded hills of Luzon, suffocating from heat during the day and shivering from the cold at night, with frequent downpours which aren't afraid of running up a water bill!

We've a good setup, Chellis, resting up, etc.—for any task that may be ahead! From the news, maybe we won't have to conduct another campaign. At any rate my fingers are crossed. Am in a "right pert" locality; located halfway up the mountains overlooking a spacious valley which is filled with rice paddies, irrigation ditches, coconut trees, and a multitude of Filipino settlements with their "stilted" bamboo huts & thatched roofs.

-Aug 11-

I must confess—that my letter writing was interrupted by the chow call—and this epistle has lain unfinished the past day and a half.

Last evening, Fri—about 10 p.m., I heard the first news of Japan's acceptance of the pact drawn up at the Potsdam conference. I quickly relayed the text of Japan's message to the members of the company who were enjoying a bit of coffee & cake in the mess hall—following a movie. This news aroused quickly their enthusiasm, which, however, lasted but a few minutes, when they came to the realization—that officially the hostility with Japan had not been terminated; no, the men of the 98th Chem. Mortar Bn, a unite whose services and assistance are considered an absolute necessity by the various Infantry Div in their sector, went to bed, with no more optimism than had been evident during the past few weeks. A much different attitude than that manifested by many of our brothers in the service—revealed by news reports from Manila, Okinawa & other points of allied occupation.

It is my opinion that even should a peace settlement come to be, most of the invasion landing plans will be carried out as scheduled. Japan must be unarmed completely!

I'm in radio communication and thoroughly enjoy my work and am much more satisfied than if I were in any other combat union or in any other type of work. I have the opportunity of listening to the many Jap. propaganda programs broadcast to the U.S. forces in the Pacific and Far East. Little do they know that their broadcasts are truly morale boosters in that their amusing, warped side lights on the war situation provide many a hearty laugh to the G.I.

Incidentally, the mosquitos here give us more trouble than the Japs have in the past. Yeah, they have a million and one air-strips and conduct bombing missions every night, undaunted by inclement weather conditions. Ship bombing has been thrown aside for the newer dive bombing technique. Have you ever cowered 'neath a flimsy mosquito net very much alive to the fact that those hundreds of squadrons of that dreaded insect are gathering for a final plunge which will leave you in the morning with the integumentary characteristics of the horned toad? Even the Minn. & Wis. Lakes have nothing in comparison! Am enclosing two money orders for the plaque fund and century club. You'll have to do my share of golfing for this season! Hello to the faculty & students. Just received the May Scuttlebutt.

Sincerely, [T/5] Orland L. Haugen '42

P.s.: incidentally, sent you yesterday a pictorial map of N. central Luzon—it might prove interesting.[308]

*Public Relations specialists had a wide range of experiences, even when not in active combat areas.*

Southern Philippines
Friday, August 31ˢᵗ [1945].

My dear Chell:

I've been meaning to keep in contact with you, Doctor, because inasmuch as you're Public Relations Director of the school, and I'm a public relations "specialist" out here, we have something in common (I think).

I imagine that just about now, it's back to the grindstone for you. Certainly wish I was back there for this term, enjoying one of your History courses. I haven't recorded a whole lot of it out here (I was a "combat" correspondent for about a month). During that time I covered the longest raid ever made by B-24 Liberators to Soerabaja, Java, from base on Morotai. I rode supercargo as always, of course, trying not to get in everybody's way at once.

In my stupid eager manner, I also volunteered to ride piggyback in a P-38 over Singapore straits. That's the closest I've come to "the war" in World War II.

Shot full of luck as always (even when I don't recognize it) I just received word that my 18-year-old bro. Jim, Seaman Second in your United States Navy, has arrived at Samar. That's not too far from where I am, so am making arrangements to see him.

The crux of this letter is to greet you, hoping this finds you in luxuriant health & good humor.

The same guy,
[Cpl] Marv. Lore[309]

✉     ✉     ✉     ✉     ✉     ✉

*After long months at war, many joined eagerly in the V-J celebration. Some were more cautious, however.*

[Letterhead: Ensign M. C. Bachman]
[Hand-lined box around "Ensign" with line to:
I'm still sweating out the j.g. ALNA]

8 Sept. 1945

Dear Chell,

Well, the war is over and here I sit in Manilla (the censorship's off) wondering when I'll get home. 'Guess I'm not alone on that score.

How're things back at Luther? I s'pect a big schedule of events is being planned for the post-war period. I'm anxious to see old Maine rebuilt, bringing things back to normal. Also I'd like to see the Norsemen out running through Loras on Nustad field. I had some of he best times of my life out there, and that's the truth.

I haven't been in the field since coming back from my last operation about June first. Since then I've been instructing a bunch of Army & Filipino classes in Jap ordnance. Frankly, I've talked until I get sick of hearing myself repeating the same stuff week after week.

I've managed to get in a couple of operations since coming out, but have had life easy the remainder of the time.

V-J nite was pretty wild in Manilla. People were drunk and firing all sorts of guns around. I wouldn't have gotten out of my sack for the world. I didn't get shot when the war was on, and don't intend to collect the "Heart" from some drunken V-J celebrant. Several were killed on Okinawa that night. Everyone went wild.

I have no news on what's in store for me. We intend to get up to the homeland before long and then <u>may</u> get home. I'd like to de-booby trap the emperor's palace. Some fun.

Well, Chell, I'd better sign off. I've enjoyed the Scuttlebutt very much, and know I'm not alone. It's a real pleasure to have someone publish a letter of that sort.

'Hoping to see you before long, and thanking you for all, I remain
> as ever,
> Marv [Ens. M.C. Bachman U.S.N.R.][310]

   ✉      ✉      ✉      ✉      ✉      ✉

*The men who had earned enough points were sent back to the U.S., while others were shifted from one unit to another. For some, their assignments remained the same, but others had some new responsibilities.*

6 November 1945

Dear Mr. Chellis;

Have been receiving the Luther College Scuttlebutt for quite some time now, and I thank you very much for sending it to me. Been going to write you for quite some time to thank you.

I started this out as a business letter, but I guess you would appreciate it more, by me writing just a friendly letter. So here goes.

Have been keeping up on most of the news through a girl I write to at Luther. She works off time at KWLC.

Came overseas the 15th of May 1945 and joined up with the 37th Division. Was in Hq Co 1st Bn of the 148th Infantry. Acting as company clerk. Being that the Division is going home, that is the men who have over 60 points, I was transfered into 175th Finance Disbursing Section. Where I am now. Working in the accounting section, doing a lot of typing and figuring. Like my new job much better than the one I had with the 148th Infantry.

I see by the Scuttlebutt that you have to request for the College Chips. So I wonder if you could put me on that list of requests along with the other fellows. Thanks.

Haven't seen any of the boys from Luther that I know over here in the Philippines as yet. But I am still hoping. Saw some of the fellows while I was in the states, but that is all.

One nice thing about living around here, is that we have electric lights and running water. And the food is very good too. That is the main things of course. Suppose you are getting better things at the boarding club by now too. Now that the war is over and everything. Maybe, you want have for long, if these strikes don't quite in the near future.

About all for now. Have to go back to work, so will bring this letter to a close. Be seeing you by next fall, I hope.

A Luther Student,
Pfc Keith K. King [311]

# CHAPTER 19

# "Out here on Tojo's stoop"—
# Okinawa and Japan

*After the taking of Okinawa, some of the men hoped to return to the U.S. soon, anticipating that other troops would soon arrive to continue the assault on Japan.*

May 6, 1945
Okinawa

Dear Chellis:

Inasmuch we've been having it a bit easy of late and my weapon is cleaned and oily, my clothes all washed, the whiskers shaved off, my belly full of how chow and am feeling on top of the world, I shall write some letters and you're no. 1 on the list, I've been putting off writing to you to long.

This has been a rather easy campaign for the outfit. By far the easiest I've ever been in. The army seems to be doing all the work and catching all the hell—but I guess you can read all about that in the paper.

The hot scuttlebutt around here is that the old salts (that's me) are going stateside after this rock is secured. So I may be home sometime this summer. Hope the Navy can spare a ship or two, any old creaky tub will do.

Thanks a lot for continuing to send me "Scuttlebutt" with nary a peep out of me that I was getting them, a thank you note or anything. Keep 'em coming, I enjoy them immensely.

Excuse the scribbling. Mom Leikvold is very adept at transcribing my letters, so maybe she can help.

Sincerely,
Carsten [PFC Carsten D. Leikvold][312]

⊠    ⊠    ⊠    ⊠    ⊠    ⊠

*As bombings of the Japanese home islands increased, the men anticipated a more rapid conclusion to the war.*

July 2, 1945
Okinawa, Shima, <u>Japan</u>

Dear "Chips' Staff":—

Just dropping you a short line, hoping you'll see fit to keeping me posted on Luther—news. Would like to see issues of Chips sometime—have only been receiving Alumni News & the "Chellis Specials."

Everything is proceeding along with the pressure ever-increasing on Tokyo—we're just methodically battering 'em down. I'm waiting to see the results of our soon-to-be 1,000—2,000 B-290 Air Raids on Japan! They won't be able to last long once they commence. It'll greatly hasten their defeat—lead to a quicker "unconditional surrender"!

Greetings to all Luther—folks and especially the President Preus family.

Notice my change in address:
Ens. John Ingvoldstad[313]

✉  ✉  ✉  ✉  ✉  ✉

*Because of the vastness of the Pacific Theater, it was sometimes difficult for men to reach their duty assignments quickly; their ship often left a port before they arrived to board it.*

24 July, '45
U.S.S. Salt Lake City

Dear Dr. Evanson,

I am finally able to carry out a desire which I have had for such a long, time, but haven't been able to do it until I arrived overseas to find nothing on which to spend my money. That desire has been to contribute something toward the erection of New Main back there on the campus. Therefore, I am an enclosing a $20 money order which I would like to have serve two purposes. First, would you take out a suitable amount for the Plaque Fund and turn the remaining portion over to the building fund. I realize I am making some extra work for you personally, but I am not sure as to what constitutes the usual contribution to the plaque fund, so I'm sending it in one lump sum. Thanks a lot for whatever extra work it involves for you.

333

Received the May issue of Scuttlebutt a few days ago, and as usual it was swell to receive. It's too bad the Censorship Bureau jumped on you and forced you to stop including addresses, but it still remains intensely interesting. How you are able to take time to write it up every month along with your other work is more than I can figure out, but I certainly hope it can be continued. You really deserve a lot of thanks.

Like many other Luther fellows I, too, became involved in the campaign at Okinawa. In fact, that is where I finally caught up with the Salt Lake City. We left on May 28, and believe me everyone aboard was only too glad to clear out. The ship had been there for 63 days, I believe, (from the latter part of March), and had spent most of the time shelling fortifications on the island. Air attacks were virtually a nightly occurrence, so everyone was pretty well "fagged out" when we left. This old ship has been in on virtually every major engagement out here & still she fights on. Most of the crew feels she is charmed because of her continual luck in escaping damage. Who knows?

I have very little time left before going on watch, so I shall be forced to close. Thanks again for your efforts & let's hope this coming year turns out for the best for dear old Luther.

Only the best to you all<br>
[Ens] Paul [Narum][314]

&#9746;    &#9746;    &#9746;    &#9746;    &#9746;    &#9746;

*Even when the men had an opportunity to describe their previous exploits, they were reminded of the constant danger as the war continued around them.*

Somewhere on Okinawa<br>
5 May 45

Dear Chellis:

After numerous attempts I'll try at least to get of a few lines to thank you for the "Scuttle Butt." It has come regularly and even though a bit late by the calender, it's hot of the press to us out here on Tojo's stoop. It works both for good and bad—it's nice to read of all the old Luther boys and where they are, but the bad part is I've probably been on the same islands with many of them but never knew they were there until I found there where abouts through the "Scuttle Butt" and College Chips.

334

If all goes well and we get back in good health—this will have been a wonderful experience & education. One can read of the natives, customs, climate etc of the south sea islands but it seems more like a myth then a reality, until you become a part of it.

Some of these groups are beautiful islands and some of the people could be made into human beings if they could be unharnessed from the Japanese yoke—others again appear almost hopeless and seem to be satisfied with their lot as a matter of circumstance. My only explanation would be ignorance, lack of a liberal education & centuries of slavery under the Nip empire. Chellis, sometime I'm going to see if the historians of tomorrows' history books gathered their data from hearsay or they drew it from fox holes where many of us are watching it being made. ha

Japanese war fare is interesting & demands some respect but I wonder if it doesn't cloud some of the rays of their rising sun when we are blasting their play house it took them a century to build.

We have quite a contrast out here as compared with old Luther—on Sunday we used to shed our sweat shirt & corduroy pants when we went to church. Here we go in a Fatigue suit, steel helmet & your gun—perhaps a granade or two in your pocket. Oh, yes we trust the Lord but not a Jap.

Okinawa Shima or Jima is about 270 mi on this end of the Japanese archipelago. It is one of the main islands of the Luchu group. You may have some difficulty finding it on the map as it's only 27 miles long and from 3 to 10 miles wide. Nevertheless it is one of our key positions in cutting Japan from the China Sea and her outlying former possessions. With a good base here we could slowly starve out these lesser islands—even starvation is a hard proposition among people that live & fight on a handful of rice a day. One peculiarity of this island is that the inhabitants of the principle city Naha. It is the only island city under Japanese control where the women enjoy equal rights with men. Nevertheless where the horse is the beast of burden in our country—the female seems to be in the South Pacific. And don't ever let me hear of a Luther coed who can't carry her own books home. ha These underfed, appearingly spindly native lassies can cary a load on their head that takes 2 men & a boy to lift up there. And I know it's heavy, after helping one with her basket I stood and wondered how a little woman could travel miles of hilly country with a basket as heavy as that balanced on her head & a baby strapped on her back. They also work all day in the fields with their full field pack (baby) Beats me that the kids don't get sun stroke or dry up like a potato chip.

I started out by a thank you letter but it appears as though I'm stretching it a—

Later

Excuse please but I just heard "Whistling Pete", that's a big artilery piece that has caused us a lot of sleep the past 2 weeks. When we hear the whistle or whine of the 1st shell you dive for the fox hole & wait for the feet to come. They really make believers out of you.

Well Chellis greet everyone at Luther & give my regards to all responsible for the overseas edition of College Chip & Scuttle Butt". We'll soon be back & when we do one of my 1st places to visit will be the Luther Campus.

Always<br>Floyd. [Omundson][315]

&#9993; &#9993; &#9993; &#9993; &#9993; &#9993;

*After the war ended, some of the men had an opportunity to observe conditions in Japan first-hand.*

Oct. 24, 1945<br>Soma, P.I.

Dear Dr. Evanson,

I was very happy to receive a copy of Scuttlebutt before sailing for China. Won't get any mail now until I get back to the Philippines.

It's wonderful to hear that few of the boys will be back there for school this fall. I'm afraid the Navy is going to keep us in for a while.

As I'm the Photo officer aboard ship, I've had an opportunity to take a lot of pictures. In the very near future, I'm going to send about eight 8X10 enlargements of various scenes in Manila, Japan, and China. I might even send one of myself. I've been spending a lot of my spare hours in the photo lab.

My other duties are Civil Readjustment officer, Junior officer of the Deck, and Assistant First Division officer, our main job under the Civil Readjustment Program has been to explain the various phases of the G.I. Bill of Rights to the members of the crew.

After making this trip to China, we'll have traveled 43,000 miles since we left the states. We saw Tokyo for the first time on the 15th of Sept. Our convoy brought troops to Tokyo and Yokohoma from the Philippines. The big event of the day was when a Jap tug, manned by a Jap crew, pushed us in along side the dock in Yokohoma.

The Japanese people do not enjoy the high standard of living that we have back in the good old U.S.A. About 85% of them wear wooden shoes, and their clothing is old and torn.

A Japanese home is very clean and empty of all furniture. They sleep, eat, and sit on the floor, usually around a fire place in the center of the room. A Japanese will always remove his shoes, upon entering his home.

Will stop for now. Hello to everyone back at Luther.

Sincerely,

[Ens.] Clifford [Ellingson]316

# CHAPTER 20

# "So crowded one could hardly walk"— China-Burma-India Theater

*In addition to the men who were serving in the direct attack against Japan, there were also a number who were stationed in the "China-Burma-India Theater" (CBI). Some of their duties involved weather or air reconnaissance, which provided opportunities for them to travel through different areas.*

Somewhere in India
December 20, 1943

Dear Evanson's,

I sure was glad to receive your letter of Christmas Greetings today with all the news in it of my old classmates. Nothing could be more welcome than a letter like that telling us where they're all hanging out. We're sure scattered around the world. Surprising what can happen in a few years.

There is one reason I was especially glad to get your letter and that is you gave me Prof (or rather Lt) Hastvedt's address so I can contact him and may be able to arrange to see him sometime later if he stays here a while yet. That sure would be a pleasure. I haven't seen a Lutherite since I stopped in Decorah at your place last summer during my leave.

Since I came over here, I've received two letters from your son Chell, and have written him at least that many. He seems to like it quite well in Colorado. I sure hope it improves his asthma. Glad he gets to be home for Christmas.

I am now settled down and back to work in my own line. I've had enough traveling for a while. This going at least half-ways around the world is a long ways. I only want one more trip that far and that is when I go back. After that I intend to stay with my darling wife for a while.

However, I must say I have a pretty nice set up over here. It's very similar to what I had back in the states. I like it very much. Of course we have a few hardships here, but I'm not complaining because I know there are many who have it worse. Anyway our aim is to get things thing over so we can all go back home.

Along with this letter I'm sending about 81 rupees worth of American dollars as a donation to the Luther College Building Fund for the "New Main". I, as many other, want to be sure Luther "grows up" again after the war like it used to be only better. I know there is about 8 or more of us made a sworn statement we'd be back the first Homecoming to celebrate. You probably know approximately who I mean: I still remember definitely how we were having a big "bull session" before the 1st one left. I believe it was James Crain who was the first one of that crowd.

Another reason I want Old Main back up is that I have a sister graduating from high school in about 2½ years and I have high hopes of her going to Luther too. I know I'll do all I can. And after her there is also a possibility of my kid brother. I won't look into the future any farther than that at present but you'll very likely think of another statement I could have possibly added.

My most common past-time is writing letters over here. I'm glad you included some of the boys' addresses because now I can write some of em. I had a nice long letter from Kenny not to long ago. Sure glad to have heard from him. No letter from Ted for some time, but I'm expecting one soon, at least that's what "young" Chellis wrote me.

Well, I guess I better stop for now. Thanks again for that "newsy" letter of yours. I hope you'll be able to come out with the second edition soon.

Please observe my change in address. This should be quite permanent for a while.

With Best Wishes or The New Year,
[Lt.] Arie [Gaalswyk][317]

---

20 March 1944

Dear Mr. Evanson,

I received another one of your most interesting letters. Very glad to receive them. I also received one a week or so ago from Mr. Hanson, or should I say "Tobak". Anyway I enjoyed it also very much. Luther news is dear news to all of us. Like someone said the other day it seems like the friends one makes at college are usually the ones, one keeps in touch with. I know I find that very true.

Mr. Hanson asked if any of us were receiving the Chips. Well I don't believe I've received hardly a copy since I left there. However if they aren't mailed first class overseas there isn't too much future in it. I know over here it would take about 3 mos. First class mail gets here in 10–20 days. I'd sure appreciate receiving the Chips if it possible. I'd be glad to pay the subscription note if I could get it.

Had a letter a few days ago from Young Chellis. Told me about his new job. Seemed to like it better, especially to be out in the open air. Colorado has a nice climate. I remember Denver had more clear days a year ago this winter, than any station within 500 mile radius from where I was at in Nebraska.

From your letters it sounds like a lot of the Luther boys are making good. I'm sure glad Ted got to go to Officer's Training School. He had to work his way in the hard way all right. Anyway the experience he had will do him in good stead there. Frankly I believe a little experience in ranks will later help one as an officer.

Everything is going along fine here. By now I have everything pretty well set up. I believe I have the best station around. I especially like the swell bunch of men I have in my outfit. It sure means a lot, I think.

At present I'm sort of sweating out a Captaincy. Really I'm not counting on it too soon, but should get in the next few months.

Since I've come to India, I've had a chance to see a good share of the country. Strictly speaking, I'm not in love with the place. The Indians are sure plentiful, that is for sure. The other day I happened to be driving back from a near-by place, and it happened to be market day in a certain village. One saw them come from all directions. Really it didn't seem to be a too densely populated district. I guess it's surprising how many live in one bamboo hut. The same goes for China. I believe it, when they say ¼ of the world's population live in these two countries. One thing that interested me about certain areas in China, they're missing a certain age in civilization. They're still in the wheel-barrow stage and then go to the airplane age. Really it must astound them.

I believe I better get to a few other letters. I'll be anxiously awaiting your next letter. Now take it easy on those history students. Until next time best wishes to all.

Sincerely,
Arie Gaalswyk[318]

---

[India] 6-3-44

Hello Chellis:

Well here goes. I thought I would acknowledge your letter this evening. That is if the candle holds out and the mosquitos calm down a little. It was very interesting to hear where the fellows are now. When I left quite a few of them were still there. Maybe if I had used a little sense and stayed longer I wouldn't be sitting here arguing with mosquitos now. Say you shouldn't plug the navy quite so much. They haven't got anything on us. They may get thier navy beans once a week but they don't get corned beef (dehydrated steak) as often as we do. We live on the stuff. That is what CBI stands for. Corned beef indefinitely. This country on a whole is inhabited by a race of oppressed people. They don't know how to smile. That is they didn't until we came. They call us a happy people. The country is hot and up until now it was dry and dusty. The monsoons are almost here and it rains almost every day now. The people live in houses made out of bamboo and mud for the walls and the roofs are rice straw. Every house is built up on a mud platform to keep snakes and water out. You should see the roads over here. If you find a place where you can go 20 miles per hours you have an exceptionaly good stretch of roads. That isn't true around the biggest cities. There they have fair roads. On the whole this country isn't worth having. All kinds of tropical fruits grow here and some of them are very pleasing to the taste. Mostly we stick to eating mangoes, coconuts, bananas, and dates. They all grow wild and all we have to do is get someone to climb the trees for us. The coolies recieve 1 rupee or about 30 to 32 cents a day so you can imagine how high thier standard of living is. Thier chief food is rice. Over here the cow is scared and it is much better to kill a man than a cow. If a cow is killed it will cost you from 2 to 3 hundred rupees and if you kill a native you will be charged from 10 to 50 rupees. That doesn't mean a person should go around killing natives but at times I believe it would be a very good idea. They can be very disgusting at times but it is best not to strike them because you might hit the wrong person and you will have a whole village out to get your hide. That is about all there is to tell about this country. They have a lot of queer customs in thier different religions. Over here if you enter one of thier temples you leave your hat on and remove your shoes. Some of the temples have some beautiful work of decorating. The Jain temples are the most luxurious because the Jains are a more wealthy class of people. Well Chellis don't know if it will make sense or not. I guess I don't have the longest address anymore. It has been shortened a good deal. Well

So long

Harlan [Twenge][319]

---

[Letterhead: 10th Weather]

July 6, 1944

Dear Chellis,

I hope you don't mind me addressing you that way. It makes it more of an informal way of putting things.

I've been very happy to receive your monthly letters. Always anxious to hear what the rest of the gang is doing. We're sure all spread far and wide. I guess I can safely say I'm the most distant of all?

As you probably notice on the envelope, I'm a Captain now. Sure glad to get it. I must say I've worked hard over here, and I have a weather station I'm proud of. Next to the Aleutians we have the worst place in the world to forecast for. I guess you have heard of "The Hump". Anyway, one doesn't just stick a wet finger in the air and decide whether it's going to rain or not. Really it's not an easy task.

I received another letter from Chellis, Jr. today. I must say he's a very faithful writer. He and I correspond quite regularly.

I hear Prof. Haatvedt is back there. Had sort of planned to see him sometime, if he'd still be here. He's probably given you all the dope on India. I've been over nearly the whole country by train so far. It's quite a country, but I'll take the U.S.A. anytime.

Glad to hear Ted and Freda were married. They're one grand couple. I feel somewhat the blame (or should I say have the honor) for it all. You see I sort of instigated their first date together. I had one with Freda's room-mate and sort of fixed Ted up at the time. Yes, surprising what things will turn into sometime.

Carolyn, my wife, is working in Pontiac, Michigan. She and her sister recently went on their vacation to New York City. They enjoyed it very much. Carolyn, much interested in music, had to get in on some of the concerts there. On their way back they spent a day in Washington, D.C. She likes her work quite well. Naturally we're very anxious to get back together. It's been a year now since we last saw each other.

Glad to hear Bud Eiden is getting back. I admire those boys that fly those planes. I make a few trips myself so know pretty much what what they do.

Better sign off for now. It's time to get some sleep. Greetings to all of you there at Luther. Sure would enjoy being able to visit the Campus again.

Sincerely,

Arie Gaalswyk[320]

---

22 October 1944

Dear Chellis,

I guess I haven't been too regular with my letters to you lately. Not that I have any legitimate excuses. However, I have been very busy the last few months. I was a little short of help. The situation is a little better now.

I enjoyed a 20 day leave here recently. Was up to Musoorie, a place up in the Himalaya Mountains north of Delhi. The climate sure was nice. Really quite a change from what it's been here in Assam all summer. (We can now say we're in Assam.).

I received a nice long letter from Ted J. in New Guinea, yesterday. It was the first one he had had time for since the big event of he and Freda getting married. So far he hadn't gotten in on any doings. I've got a hunch he might've on this landing in the Phillipines a few days ago.

You undoubtedly have had a talk with my wife there on the campus by now. She's really happy to be back there. I'm glad she has this opportunity to go. I only wish I could be there also. She says the 3rd floor in Larsen Hall really looks marvelous. One really wouldn't believe it unless he had seen it, she said.

I was glad to receive your last copy of the Scuttlebutt a few days ago. There are very few things I enjoy more over here. It also was good to hear a few words from Dr. Preus and Coach Pete. Sure wish I could be out there playing football with the boys. I'd sooner do my fighting on the football field, then out here.

Well it's nearly time for chapel services so I better get shaved. Just keep the Scuttlebutt coming. Greetings to all.

Sincerely,

[Capt] Arie [Gaalswyk][321]

---

343

5 February 1945

Dear Chellis,

It's about time for me to write you a few lines again. All your letters (Scuttlebutts) are coming in very regularly. They surely are interesting.

I'm not sure but I believe I've written you since I was moved last November. Anyhow, my new APO is 493. Still the same outfit only on DS at a different place. That's the kind of outfit this Weather Squadron is. We're attached to nearly every Air Force outfit over here. At present I'm with the Bomber Command which has these big B-29's. What a marvelous ship that is. Before I was with the Air Transport Command. Anyhow as a result I get varied experience. My opinion is they're all a part of the best branch of the service. I guess I shouldn't say that to an old navy man.

Looks like the Navy got most of my buddies at Luther. The navy went over pretty big there. I'll admit they's a great outfit. I got quite a kick out of that remark you made in one of your letters in reply to Lt. Commander Jones' comment about the guy who chose to be a weather prophet in preference to joining the navy. However, I'm still not sorry.

My present work keeps me pretty busy. I'm Area Weather Officer and have control over a number of stations. It means for a good share of traveling. Really I like it very much. One of the reasons is that it's more Administrative and less of this routine technical work. Most of the problems which come up concern personnel. All in all it makes it a very interesting task.

My hopes are to get back there next fall. There is some possibility of going to a refresher course at Channte Field, Ill. That's what I'm hoping for. However, being there are only a few openings for each course, I don't believe I should figure on it too strongly.

Carolyn is really enjoying it at school there. I'm glad she's there. According to her last letters she was working pretty hard with her studies as the exams were coming.

Sounds like Luther has a pretty good basketball team this year. Sure glad to hear that. Keeping up good old Luther traditions.

Well, I better sign off now. It's getting near my bed-time.

By the way tell that son of yours he owes me a letter.

As ever,
Arie [Capt. Arie Gaalswyk][322]

⊠    ⊠    ⊠    ⊠    ⊠    ⊠

*The men serving in the CBI were not only distantly removed from home geographically; they were also in a very different cultural environment.*

[Letterhead: American Red Cross]

March 17, 1945

Dear Scuttlebutt Personnel,

I received your Feb. issue of the Scuttlebutt today. I really enjoy hearing from good old Luther College, and especially after not having received any other mail for about two weeks.

I guess maybe I've moved around so much lately you couldn't keep track of my address. In fact, I was moving so much that I didn't send you my new address as I didn't know from one day to the next where I was going to be.

After I left Ft. Monmouth, I went down near Washington, D.C. I got to see Dave Preus a couple of times while I was down there. Then I went to New York City and stayed there awhile.

After spending a short time in New York the Army decided it was about time for me to go overseas after spending about two years in the Army in the States. I was lucky as I didn't have to come by the boat. I climbed into a shiny plane and flew over. I made quite a few stops on the way over so I got to see a lot of interesting sights. I got to see the Sphinx and Pyramids when I was in Egypt.

I finally reached my destination here in New Delhi, India. New Delhi is a new and modern city so we have it very nice here. We live and work right in town. Our barracks are big cement structures that look almost like a hotel from the outside. They are the nicest barracks I've been in since I left Ft. Monmouth, N.J.

We have it very nice here. We have Indians, whom we call bearers, that sweep the floors, make our beds, shine our shoes, and keep the barracks in general in good condition.

I really lead a rough life here. I get up at 7:30 in the morning and eat breakfast. Then I go to work at 8:30, take a twenty minute break in the morning for lunch, and quit for noon chow at 12:30. I go back to work at 1:30 and quit in the afternoon at 5:15. I also get one day a week off.

A person sees many strange sights here in India. Besides the historical points you see camel caravans, often pulling carts, and almost everyone riding a bicycle. We also see a lot of crippled beggars sitting on the streets and trying to take advantage of the soft hearted Americans. The soldiers have all caught on to these people by now—and just pass them up. Besides these people there are a lot of people trying to sell you little trinkets which are of no value. If you'd buy them you can be well assured you just got hooked.

I must close as I have to write a letter to the little girl back home yet tonight too.

This is my present address:

An Ex-student,
Vernon Sorem[323]

&#9993;    &#9993;    &#9993;    &#9993;    &#9993;    &#9993;

*In addition to "Scuttlebutt," Evanson sent personal letters to some of the men. (Such correspondence does not survive.) In some cases, he apparently asked them to purchase items for him which were difficult to obtain in the U.S.*

7 May 1945

Dear Chellis,

I received you letter of the 17th a few days ago. Always glad to hear from you. Very much interested in hearing how things are going, including all about good old "Luther" and also anything you hear form the rest of the gang.

Yes I am now in China. Really I'm most happy here, principally because of the much favorable weather during this season. Frankly the last two weeks I spent in India were almost unbearable. This is more like good old Minnesota or Iowa.

Sorry, but now that I am in China I can't get an evening bag as you requested. Those are only available in India. Instead, however, I got something which I'm pretty sure you'll like. The silverwork one can obtain here are probably among the best in the world. I bought you something of a bracelet type, along with a pin and ear rings to match. Something like that one can wear possibly with an evening dress. Now if you don't particularly care for this then you can give it to Carolyn as I intend very likely to get her something like it someday. Then later, if and when I go through India, again, I'd be able to get you one of those hand bags. Also if you wish to keep this now and later want me to get the handbag in addition if and when the opportunity arises I'll do that too. Probably could bring that back with me if I get to come home this coming fall (I hope). This silver set I bought comes to about exactly eight dollars counting the postage for mailing. I sent it 1st class so it probably will reach you almost the same time as this letter. You can give Carolyn the money if you wish.

Concluding from the news VE day will have been before you get this letter. From now on the focus will be on Japan. I hope it won't last too long. Personally I'm an optimist about the situation. I bet she's really going to get a licking.

I guess Carolyn has told you of my new job. I handle all the administration and correspondence for the Weather Central here. We live in a hostel by ourselves here so are solely responsible for the upkeep of it. My work includes supply, mess, utilities, PX supplies, adjutant, transportation, Chaplain, and what have you. Really I like it. Have a swell bunch of men to work with.

Word just received that this is "it" in Europe. Probably will have a confirmation before morning.

Better write Carolyn a few lines now. Best Wishes to all.

As ever,

Arie [Cap't. Arie Gaalswyk][324]

---

16 July 1945

Dear Chellis,

About time I answer your letter of 26 June and also some of those most interesting Scuttlebutts. Been playing so much bridge here lately that it has interfered with my letter writing. That's a pretty poor excuse, I guess. Anyway we are now in the midst of a bridge tournament and it really is a lot of fun and an excellent past-time.

Had a nice letter from young Chell the other day. Sure was glad to hear from him again. I guess I had delayed answering his previous letter so the long time in between letters from him was my fault. Chell seems to like it quite well in Denver. It must be a pretty nice city, from what I hear. I would expect you folks would take a vacation down there this summer.

Back on the gold standards again; I made major this month. Pretty happy to get it. It is practically the top one can go in weather unless one is head of a whole region such as ours here covers India-Burma and China Theatres. They're usually WestPoint men and most of the time have a pilot rating. Only other possibility is staff weather officer for a Air Force. So I am qutie honored to get it. It also helps

347

from the pay angle. Of course that is not what I am in here for. I sure hope it is over soon so we can all go back home and carry on with our careers.

Reference to your request on something for your two daughters I will be glad to get something for them. You mentioned a ring. They have some pretty nice Jade rings here. They come fairly high. I believe $15 to $20 if you want a pretty good one. Really I am not sure about those prices. I myself have not bought any as yet so I can't tell for sure. If you want something for around a few dollars they have some very nice silver bracelets here. There is one kind which wraps around one's wrist like a snake, sort of the springy type. Also they have some silver rings which you can have made. You can get your name imprinted on it in either American or Chinese. Well you let me know. Maybe a Jade ring is not exactly something for a young girl. Perhaps it would be okay for Marilyn as she is a little older than Beth.

The big thing on my mind these days is whether I am going to get home when my two years are up in September. There is quite a bunch in our unit ahead of me so until they go our chances are very slim. So the next thirty days should sort of tell the story. At least is will be a good indication.

So Mary Jane Talle's husband was stationed at this base. Yes it is perhaps the best in China and we live in the best hostel on the base, so I have no complaints in that respect. I have been pretty fortunate all along that way.

I will try to get a snapshot sometime for your picture collection. I don't have a camera with me but some of my friends do. So some sunny day I'll see what I can do. I'll be anxious to see your collection someday. Maybe I can make it sometime near the end of the year, I hope.

Young Chellis tells me that the three McConnells met in the Pacific That was pretty nice. I can imagine they had quite a time. Also was glad to hear Ted and Kenny got together ther a while back. You have probably seen Kenny there lately. At least I understand he was home for a short stay. Maybe he spent all his time in Texas, for I hear he got himself engaged to a nurse from there. Surprising what happens.

Won't be so long again before the school doors will open. There probably will be a fair number of students who have gotten out of the service on points. I am not doing so good on the point system. Have 73 and I doubt if they will ever get that low before Vj Day. Where I missed out was twelve points for a child. However I sort of want to see this thing through. Sort of gets in one's blood.

Better call this short now as it is time to "hit the sack". For some reason I was sort of tired all day so I better get a fair nite of sleep.

I will await your answer on getting something for the two girls. Reference to the evening bag if I ever get an opportunity I will get one. In fact I want to get about three of them since a good friend of the folks also asked for one. The one Carolyn got seems to have made quite a hit.

Will be waiting for your next Scuttle-butt. Be sure you keep that thing a going if possible. It has been a great thing to keep in touch with all the Lutherites. So I hope you keep up the good work.

Sincerely
Arie [Major Arie Gaalswyk][325]

&#9747;    &#9747;    &#9747;    &#9747;    &#9747;    &#9747;

*Word of the atomic bomb attack on Hiroshima, and the Soviet Union's subsequent entry into the war, greatly improved hopes for a rapid end to the war.*

10 August 1945

Dear Chellis,

Have a little time to spare so will drop you a line or two.

I'm presently in the hospital. Hadn't been feeling too well the past month so decided to get a check up. Possibility I may have a slight case of dysentery and if so I want to take care of it now. It's not very serious as in most respects I feel quite well. They should know in a few days what's wrong with me. In the meantime I'm taking life pretty easy.

The news the past few days has been so startling that everyone around here is becoming very optimistic concerning the possibility of a sudden ending of the war. First the news on the use of the "Atomic" bomb and yesterday word of Russia's entering the war against Japan. Who knows what may happen in the coming days, maybe before this letter may ever reach you. I know we all feel the end cannot come too soon.

With the possibility of the war soon being over and getting out of the army relatively soon thereafter, I'm thinking quite a lot about what to do in civilian life. I'm pretty well decided on taking advantage of the G.I. Bill of Rights and at least take a year of post graduate work. The question is what to take up. As you know I'm pretty much interested in mathematics, however there's very little practical use for it except in its application in scientific work or else towards business. Personally I don't feel I'm interested in doing any work dealing with the physical

349

sciences. Rather I'd like to get into some Administrative or personnel work or else go into the teaching field. Someday before to long I'd like this whole thing over with you. Also with respect to what school I should go for my post-graduate work if possible I'd prefer staying in the mid-west somewhere. Having been so far away from the folks and other old friends for these past couple of years makes one want to stay in that neighborhood at least for a while, once one gets back.

I'm here in the hospital at Kunming. Understand we can say that much. It's a relatively cool place with a lot of rain these days. The reason for its coolness is because of its height above sea level. In a normal atmosphere the temperature averages about 3 degrees Fahrenheit cooler for every 1000 feet. Since this is a little over 6000 feet above sea level, it makes for about 20 degrees cooler than a similar place at sea level. So really it is quite comfortable around here. One crawls pretty well under the blankets at nite, even though it's mid-summer.

I haven't had any mail now for nearly 2 weeks. It's been about a week since I came down here and the week previous to that the mail had been held up for some unknown reason. So as a result I'm pretty anxious to get some. Our weather plane was to have brought my mail back yesterday but for some reason forgot. I didn't know I'd be here this long or I'd left word to have it forwarded. All I hope is I get some soon. There should be another Scuttlebutt arriving soon too and perhaps is amongst it all.

Hoping to see all of you before too long. In the meantime I suspect you are all getting ready for the fall opening of school. There should be a fair number of veterans amongst them. Should help out making for a good football team. Say hello to Pete and tell him I wish him and the team a good season this fall. Even would like to get in and watch one of the later games.

As ever, [0-856986]

[Major] Arie [Gaalswyk][326]

---

*By October, Gaalswyk was anxiously awaiting orders for reassignment to the U.S.*

5 October 1945

Dear Chellis,

In your Scuttlebutt you had asked a number of times for a snapshot of some kind so now that I have one I'll send it to you. I got one of the boys to take a picture and develop a few I guess it resembles me somewhat.

Well I'm not on the ship as yet but believe it can't be but a matter of a few days before I get my orders. At least that is what I hope. Heard one of the other officers who was on my shipment has left and don't see why I need either stay here much longer. Sure not doing anything requiring my presence. That's what I told headquarters in a message a few days ago and should get a reply by tomorrow. One thing is sure I'm anxious enough to go back. Doubt if I can make it for homecoming. However I would like to get back to see Luther play at least one football game.

Haven't received your August Scuttlebutt as yet. Perhaps you have discontinued it because of the war coming to an end and figure the boys starting to come back soon. I suppose there will be quite a number coming back soon. Should be a fair number of veterans enrolling in Luther this fall.

I know I am already considering strongly of starting school, perhaps, by the first of the year if I can get out soon enough. If nothing else take some refresher courses at Luther. If advanced calculus is offered next semester I might consider enrolling as a special student and take it. Also try getting in some education courses just in case I want to go into teaching. Frankly I'm very undecided as to what I do want to go into. Anxious to get back and consult people and get a little advice on the matter. First thing though is to get back and get that release from active duty.

Don't know if you seen Carolyn lately. Anyhow she is directing the Spring Grove High School Band until I get back. Mr. Blugstad is on leave to the Army so they decided to give her the job until I get back. She likes it fine and seems to be doing okay. Sure was swell of them to ask her. Nothing could be more ideal, because they told her she could leave whenever she gets word I'm back.

Well, better write the little girl a few lines now. After that it'll be bed time. Here's hoping to see you soon. In the meantime cheer that Luther team to victory for me too, will you?

Sincerely,
Arie [Gaalswyk][327]

⋈    ⋈    ⋈    ⋈    ⋈    ⋈

*While many of the bombing raids over Japan were launched from the Pacific, some originated in the CBI.*

351

1 October 1945

Dear Sir,

I have been getting the "Scuttlebutt" now for some time and am sorry for not writing sooner and expressing my utmost appreciation toward you for sending me a copy. I don't think many remember me as a Luther student because I only attended there a very short time due to lack of funds. I regretted having to drop out but it was only a short time after that the Army got me anyway.

I was there in 1940 with John Thompson of Elroy, Wisc., and I knew others—Knutson, Amundsen and others. John was my room-mate and we graduated from the same High School. I think John went about 3 years there.

At the present time I'm stationed at Rupsi, India which is not too far from Calcutta. We are in the Assam Jungles and find it very humid and hot. However, the best is yet to some for us as we are getting ready now to go to the States. We are to move in a couple of weeks. Everyone of us are very enthused and also very impatient at the present time. Our aim is to be home for Thanksgiving dinner with our families. Our group which have the B-24's are known as the "Libs of China". They made many raids on Jap installations.

Thanking you and saying that I enjoyed very much the time I spent at Luther.

Sincerely,
[S/Sgt] Donald C. Ormson[328]

⊠     ⊠     ⊠     ⊠     ⊠     ⊠

*Serving in photo reconnaissance also gave men an opportunity to cover a great deal of territory. While many men spoke highly of their encounters with Navy enlisted personnel, some were less impressed by the officers they encountered.*

Calcutta, India
13 Oct. 45

Dear Dr. Evanson:

Just received the August edition of Scuttlebutt and was glad to get it.—I left Greensboro, N.C. the 20th of August for the New York POC. Was at Ft. Hamilton out of Brooklyn. Had a fairly good time there. Left there the 1st of Sept. for India via Gibalter, Suez Canal and Ceylon. The trip took 27 days. We are quartered at Camp Angus which is about 25 miles out of Calcutta. It is just a distribution Center for the Air force and all our orders have been out to fly us on into China. Am going to a place called "Schwamglia." Don't know where it is. Is a photo recon outfit. The ship we came over on was a Navy Transport called the "USS. Gen. Hase."—Was just a converted supply ship and you could easily tell it. Had about 400 officers on board. I don't know whether you were an officer or not when you were in service and any way you were in the Navy but it is sure awful easy to loose all respect for those "gentlemen" on board a transport. This isn't a gripe sheet so I'll cut that out.

These natives here do all the work for us so there isn't to much doing. They are paid 35 Rupees a month, equivilent to about 12 dollars. They don't earn anymore however.—Downtown in Calcutta is the dirtiest place I have ever seen. After 10 pm all the kids seem to just lay down where sleep overcomes them. Grown ups are the same. Had lots of fun buying some stuff however bargaining.—

Not much more to say—

As ever

Pfc. David Tate[329]

☒       ☒       ☒       ☒       ☒       ☒

*Observations in postwar China gave an accurate appraisal of the conditions that ultimately developed into Mao's Communist Revolution.*

18 October 1945

Dear Chellis,

When I think of all the fun you have given me by your magnificent production "Scuttlebutt", and of all the hours I have spent reading them, I feel downright ashamed because I haven't helped you out on them. So, here goes a belated effort.

I have been very unfortunate in not running into any ex-Lutherites. And does that make things lonely. I still hope that someday I can change things.

Life has been rather monotonus on the whole. With few exceptions this "git up and go" philosophy doesn't intrigue me any more.

The star in our life out here the past year burst forth a week or so ago when we pulled into Shanghai for liberty. That made up for a good many things.

Enclosed you will find a couple of banknotes. Yi, is it ever fun to carry around hundreds of thousands of dollars!!!! One type of currency was issued by the Japs during the occupation. Its value when we left China was $140,000 to one American "gold" (the Chinese say "gold" instead of Americas or US money, or dollar). This currency is called CRB ; the bill says what it stands for, I cannot remember at the moment.

Another bill is the CNC or Chinese National Currency which the Chinese used before the war. Its rate of exchange was $700.00 to one gold.

Silver money for change is practically extinct.

In the stores a person may pay in any type of money. Quite confusing when one starts bargaining in three different types, especially when the merchant brings out that dog gone adding machine of his with the beads on.

In the few weeks that the Americans had been in the town before we arrived the Chinese had caught on to the "rich American is a sucker" idea. So, prices went sky high. An OPA China version is attempting to hold it down, but not to satisfactory are the results.

I really did enjoy some real Cantonize food. An old time British tar we ran into taught us the way to order and eat such a dinner. Ah me, my palate tingles now as I think of such delights as "sweet and sour pork", "beef with onions" "port (fried) with bamboo shoots". They sound simple enough, but the way the stuff is cooked, oh man, oh man.

Russian food also hits the spot. Those Russians must be rugged to eat such heavy food. it is flavored like nothing I have had before. As for vodka, I like it, but not too much. A bit on the potent side.

The Chinese people, from the several people I talked to are quite a grafting, corrupted type. In fact the whole town seems to be filled with sharpies. However, when one does get a bad deal in a store the salesman does it very nicely.

Particularly noticeable on the streets were the many white Russians; Money changers.

I was surprised to learn from a couple of people that nothing was being done about the Quislings in the town. They were roving the streets just as they used to. I hope, but I may be wrong, that something will be done, if such a status is present.

The shops will ordinarily raise their prices 100 to 200 percent over the expected price received. The buyer is supposed to state a price then the bargaining begins. However, enough Americans aren't too good at such practices so the merchant will wait until a real sucker comes along and pays double the price an experienced Shanghai-ite pays.

The political situation is rather tense over here. So much so, that on the nite of the Chinese celebration of the double-tenth (something like our July 4 combined with victory celebration) all servicemen were sent back to their stations. No-one seemed to know what the Communists might try to do, or what the thousands of Japs in camps about the city (not really camps, more like a staging point, very little to hold them back if they wanted to start trouble) might do. Some people cannot see how a civil war will be averted.

The filth of the streets was amazing. The odors terrific. Thousands of coolies throng the streets with hundreds of rickshaws. Street vendors by the scores, prostitutes, beggars all form the crowds.

The beggars fascinated me. Never have I seen as beggery beggars as they. They reminded me of the beggars in "Les Miserables" or of the beggars of early France and England. I actually had to stop and look at a couple of them.

At the moment we are at Kiirun, Formosa. Just sitting after bring some Chinese troops to occupy the place. Unfortunately, we do not get any liberty here.

The war may be over but those mines still go off with just a big a bang as ever.

Enclosed is a bit for the Plaque Fund. Swell idea.

Hope to see you before next spring.

Best regards

[Lt (jg)] Jack Aaker[330]

---

[Letterhead: U.S. Marine Corps]

2 Nov. 1945

Dear Chellis,

Received a Scuttlebutt yesterday that had been beaten to a frazzle all the way from North Carolina out here but it sure was welcome. I'm in Tientsen, China and what a place this is. I've heard how the Chinese live but I didn't ever dream they were as desolate as the reports said they were but now I realize they are more desolate than anyone can realize. I'm working in the Engineer Company and so far our main duties have been getting supplies unloaded and I have about 50 coolies working for me everyday. They average about 15 years of age and do a really man's size job 12 hours a day for $500 Chinese money or about sixteen

355

cents our money and they're making more now than they ever did. I saw a 14 year old boy put a box weighing 405 pounds on his back last night and walk away. And I thought the Norsemen were strong! These Chinks have absolutely no strength in their arms but their backs seem to be made of cast iron.

I'm enclosing $500 in Chinese money since you said you were receiving money from all over the world. Today it's worth about $.16, but the exchange varies here every hour so it's no telling what it will be worth tomorrow morning.

I spent a few weeks in Transient Center at Guam and bumped into Red Henderson in the mess hall one noon so you can imagine how we both felt. He's the only Luther man I've seen for quite some time. He was headed for the states when I saw him and left about three days before I did.

I sure was happily surprised aboard ship one day just off Okinawa when a sports broadcast announced, Luther 25, La Crosse Teachers, 0. That was one game I really couldn't lose, but I guess you know where my support was. Anytime Luther can beat that miserable outfit they call La Crosse State will be a happy day in my life. Hope Luther can keep on winning but it's a little but too much to expect with so few men. But I'll bet they never get beat for lack of trying! But by next fall things should be back to normal and with old students returning and the building program starting, we'll win our share of games again.

Well, so much for now. Keep up the good work on Scuttlebutt—you'll never know how much it's appreciated in every part of the world.

[Lt.] Warren Selbo[331]

⊠　　⊠　　⊠　　⊠　　⊠　　⊠

*Although the postwar assignments gave the men the opportunity to visit a number of cities in Asia, they were clearly ready to return home as quickly as possible.*

Nov. 17, 1945

Dear Friends,

Received the August issue of Scuttlebutt a few days ago. It is the first mail I have received from the College in some time—due to a foul up in the routing of our mail. We have moved about so much lately that routing our mail isn't easy. One sort of looses interest in writing better when one doesn't receive any, but I guess that cannot be helped. I always enjoy reading Scuttlebutt, even if some issues are late getting here.

Right now we are in Hong Kong. Before coming here we were at Okinawa, Shanghai, and Formosa. Of these places I thought Shanghai the most interesting. At Okinawa there are too many typhoons for one to care to stay long. We went there to reload when we left Shanghai. We were there twice before that, and once after that. We were in one typhoon there and that is the last one I care to see. The Navy wanted to keep Okinawa as one of its major bases, but I believe they have changed their minds.

We were at Formosa for a little over a week. We were at the harbor of Kiirun on the northern tip of the island. The harbor is surrounded by high mountains, with the city built along shore, and on the slooping mountain sides. The city is small, with small factories, naval yards, and a business district. The harbor was filled with sunken ships. Nearly every building in the city had been bombed. It rained every day we were there, so we were glad to leave after we had completed fueling L.C.I.'s that brought Chinese troops in to occupy the island.

Shanghai and Hong Kong aren't much alike. Hong Kong is more fashionable and somewhat cleaner, but both cities are filthy. The streets in Shanghai were so crowded one could hardly walk—someone was always begging or trying to sell me something. The prices are very high in both places. The more Americans that arrive the higher the prices go. They know the Americans have money, so they raise the prices to twice what they were before the Americans arrived. I had better change the subject as I have rambled on long enough on where I have been.

Paul Eggen is still aboard this ship too. We have long chats about the days we spent back at Luther.

The ship is scheduled to return to the states in December, so we are all looking forward to being back soon. There doesn't seem to be very much for us to do here. We fueled some transports carrying Chinese troops to Northern China a few days ago.

I was very glad to see that some of the fellows are already discharged and back in school—I hope to do the same. By next fall things should somewhat be back to normal again.

Will close now by wishing you all the best. I will enclose some Chinese money, and a snapshot of myself. Hope to see you all soon.

Lt (jg) Lyle W. Bestul[332]

# RETURNING FROM OVERSEAS DUTY

# CHAPTER 21

# "Counting my discharge points in anxious anticipation"—The End of the War and Discharge—European Theater

*With the end of hostilities in Europe, the men hoped to return to the U.S. But many realized that they might also be reassigned to the Pacific to help defeat Japan. A "Points" system was supposed to equitably distribute reassignments home, but like many other elements of the military experience, to many men it must have seemed like the scenes later portrayed in the novel,* Catch-22.

---

*When the war ended in Europe, Evanson received numerous reports of reassignment back to the U.S. The men were often turning their attention toward life after the military.*

7 June 1945

Dear Chellis,

Just a note of thanks for the many editions of "Scuttlebutt" received. My address is no longer Navy 416, but Navy #948, c/o F.P.O., N.Y., N.Y. I would appreciate it very much if you'd make the change on your distribution list and pass along a note re same to "College Chips" & "Alumnus".

At present I'm in London for duty with ComNav for Germany. Undoubtedly you have seen pictures of my skipper, Vice-Admiral Ghormley, or read of his assignment. Today his picture was in the London papers as attending the 4 powers conf ab at Berlin regarding control of Germany. As personnel officer for his command, which includes subordinate commands, my work is interesting and

361

enables me to obtain a good overall picture of the set up. For your information Dick Ellingson is handling the religious needs of one of our subordinate commands on the continent. Hope to see him shortly. I have 5 chief yeomen in the office now besides other ratings. Really an efficient outfit. (was once a yeoman myself) Morris Ness paid me a visit last weekend. I believe your editions for him are still going to the LST #54. He is now on the USS Southland, c/o FPO, N.Y., N.Y., an accommodation ship, at present tied up at Weymouth. Together we visited the Tower Bridge, London Bridge & the Tower of London last Sunday after attending services at Westminster. We enjoyed the afternoon at Royal Albert Hall.

Don Gjerdrum came up to my last base at Navy 416—(Dartmouth) for a good dinner before he left for the U.S. It was certainly enjoyable conversing with him.

Thanks again for your fine efforts put forth.
                    Sincerely
                    EN Larson
P.S. Might add that I'll be needing one of those rooms at Larsen Hall one of these years and still have a year to complete at Luther. I am counting my discharge points in anxious anticipation of rejoining the fold shortly. (have 3½ years of active duty now).

                    ENL [Lt. (j.g.) E.N. Larson][333]

&#9993;    &#9993;    &#9993;    &#9993;    &#9993;    &#9993;

*While all of the men looked forward to seeing family and loved ones, some of the men anticipated seeing their young children for the first time.*

                    France
                    12 June 1945

Dear Scuttlebutt—

I have a couple of things to tell you but will first ask that until I know what my future address will be, will you kindly send "Scuttlebutt" & any other mail <u>to</u> Canby, Minnesota. We are waiting to be shipped back to the U.S., which will be very soon. There I expect to see my family & then to another theatre.

Another member has recently been added to my family. Mary Irene was born on April 27, 1942. Just in case you don't know it I also have a little boy, Mark Lawrence, who is now almost 21 months old. I haven't seen Mary Irene yet & am anxiously waiting to get home.

I might also add that I have been promoted to Captain, as of June 1, 1945.
I am getting Scuttlebutt regularly & appreciate it very much.
Respectfully
Lawrence B. Nesset, Capt. M.C.[334]

✉     ✉     ✉     ✉     ✉     ✉

*With Japan's surrender, the men still serving in Europe could expect reassignment to the U.S. It was simply a question of "when."*

Berlin, August 29, 1945

Dear Chellis,

I don't believe I've written you since the end of the war. That certainly was sudden, but very welcome, news. I was on leave in Edinburgh, Scotland at the time the news first broke and then was in London for the official V-J Day celebrations. It was pretty fortunate for me to be on leave when it all happened. The people joined in the celebrations a little bit more in England than here in Berlin.

I think I wrote you once before about not being lucky enough to meet any Luther men over here. Well, Bob Inman was assigned to our squadron about 3 weeks ago. I guess I was the first Luther man he had seen over here also. It's good to run into someone from back there. I didn't know Bob really well, because I think he went to school just the first semester of my last year, but just the same I was really glad to see him. I'll try and send you a picture soon.

I haven't had much news of a possible trip home—my 84 points should help me out a little though. According to the Stars & Stripes, everyone over 74 points should be home by Christmas. I'm keeping that paper, so if I'm still here, I'll have somebody eat it. It's all a question of getting replacements. Our outfit is going to stay here, so someone has to take the place of the ones that go back to the states.

I'm going to put in my request for Chips and the Alumnus. However, if something should happen, and I accidentally was sent home there may be a sudden change of address. There is a slight change in my address: [...]

I really do appreciate reading your letters and Chips.

We are pretty well settled down now here in Berlin. It's pretty much routine, more or less like an airlines. Our planes take leave personnel to England and the Riviera besides carrying mail and freight and things like that.

Once in a while they keep in touch with what they did in the war by having airborne exhibitions. They had one the other day with the 82nd Airborne Division and got a good commendation on it. It was quite a show, with gliders & paratroopers. It all came off like clockwork. The 82nd went into Holland in our ships, among others, so it was sort of a reunion.

This stay in Berlin has been very interesting, but I hope it's not too long.

I'll write again soon—

Sincerely,

Lt. Vern Larson

P.S. I found a snapshot, so I'll send it along. I'll try and get one of Bob Inman and myself and send that.[335]

⊠          ⊠          ⊠          ⊠          ⊠          ⊠

*There was a competition to see who might have been the first Luther man to enter Berlin. Weston Noble's correspondence (included in the "Individual Writers" section) indicates that he initially thought he might have been the first, but Vern Larson seems to have won that honor.*

Berlin, 5 September [1945]

Dear Chellis,

You'll no doubt be surprised to get another letter from me so soon—but it's a good occasion for once. I wrote last when I met a fellow from Decorah—Bob Inman. Now I met two fellows from Riceville—one was Weston Noble. He dropped in on me last night and really surprised me. I guess I must have changed a little, because he asked me if Lt. Larson was in. When he looked closer, it dawned on him. It has been quite a long time since I saw him, and I guess I must have changed a little. Weston got here July 5th—one day after I did, so I guess I at least have him beat for the honor of being the first Luther man in Berlin. There may be someone else from Luther here—if you hear from any, mention it in your letter and we could have a big reunion. Bob Inman said he heard that there were a few fellows from Decorah here in Berlin, but so far, I don't know if he has seen them.

It was a long time over here before I met anyone from Luther; but I've had a pretty good average here in the past week or so. This other fellow from home works practically next door—you might say. It's funny we haven't run into each other before.

364

I'm way up there with the points now—92, with the recount, but my classification has been declared essential—for how long, I don't know. So I don't have the slightest idea when I may be going home. I'll just hope for the best.

I'll write again—

> Sincerely
> [Lt.] Vern Larson[336]

⊠ ⊠ ⊠ ⊠ ⊠ ⊠

*Some of the men remained in the Army to serve in the occupation of Germany, while others returned in civilian positions.*

[Letterhead: American Red Cross]

Sept 7 [1945]

Dear Chellis:

It is now about 30 days since I saw the last issue of Scuttlebutt and longer than that since last I found time to do any correspondence. My itinerary for the past weeks will cover it well I believe.

Left Keesler Fld. Miss July 21st, discharged at Ft. Sheridan, Iola, Wisc for 1 day, Wash D.C. and University of Maryland a couple of weeks, New York, London, and various other cities in England, Dieppr, Paris then to Granville and tonite I'm billeted/sleeping in a large school building in Jullouville where Eisenhower was headquartered for a time. Tomorrow I leave for Karlsruhe Germany via Avranches, Mortain, Domfront, Alincon, Monaucourt, Dreux, Versailles, Paris again, Choisy le Roi, Nograt-Sur-Marne, Meaux, Chateau Nuerry, Crezancy, Chalone, Verdun, Metz, St. Avola, Saarbrucken, Hamburg, Kaiserlautern, Mannheim, etc, which is pretty close to the route.

It is quite likely that I will be rather permanently located in the U.S. occupied southern part of Germany and of course would welcome addresses and names of Lutherites etc in this theatre.

I am a civilian working as an administrative officer with the United Nations Relief and Rehabilitation Administration so can be located thru UNRRA in Karlsruhe or any of the many stations we operate.

I saw Rep. H.O. Talle very briefly in Wash. D.C. prior to leaving for London and really enjoyed talking with him again.

The important part of this letter is selfish of course but is to change my address so when mail finally catches up with me it will finally bring me Lutherite news.

With best regards to all I remain,

Very truly Yours
Melvin G. Aasen,
UNRRA[337]

   ✉    ✉    ✉    ✉    ✉    ✉

*Although there were always rumors circulating about reassignment to the U.S., the men had little certainty about what would happen to them next.*

England
1 November, 1945

Dear Chellis,

As you can see, I've left Berlin. I'm on the way home, but don't have any idea just when it will be. England is a lot closer home than Berlin was. We had a sailing date of approximately Nov. 20, but now that's been cancelled and something else is cooking. It may get us out sooner, I really don't know.

Most of us were sent here to England to join outfits slated to return to the states. They are the remaining 8th Air Force outfits—fighter and bomber groups, although their personnel is made up now of nearly every kind of Air Force outfit. There isn't anything to do but sweat it out. We spend most of our time in London which is about 2 hours' train ride from the field, which is located near Ipswich.

I've seen a few Luther scores in the paper—not doing too good, but I'll bet they are trying plenty hard if I know anything about Luther football teams. I may get back home in time to catch a basketball game or two. I'm going to try hard to get to Decorah even if it's only for a short time.

I guess you'd better stop sending the monthly newsletter and Chips. They'll never get to me now—

Here's hoping I'll be seeing you again soon.

Sincerely,
Vern Larson[338]

# CHAPTER 22

# "At least there are hints of peace"— Reassignment After V-E Day

*Some men were being reassigned from Europe to the Pacific Theater, but many who had already spent a considerable amount of time in combat zones were rotated back to the U.S.*

[Letterhead: USS J. Fred Talbott—AG81]

June 1, 1945

Dear Dr. Evanson,

I wish to inform you that each issue of scuttlebutt has been reaching me on schedule, and, as always, enjoy it immensely. I realize a news sheet like "scuttlebutt" takes a great amount of time and work but I, like other Luther people in the service, are very appreciative to you and your staff. As a Navy man I say, "well done."

My change of address all came about last March when I received orders for a change of duty. I spent twenty-eight months in the Pacific and was overjoyed when I discovered that my new station would take me to the East Coast. With my change of duty I received a thirty day leave plus twelve days travel time which wasn't hard to take. On my way home I had a delay of a week in San Francisco and while here saw Lt. Davidson out at Treasure Island. I spent the month of April at home and had a wonderful time while it lasted. The middle west is still the greatest spot in the universe according to my calculations. I wanted to spend a few days on the campus but the time and gasoline shortage restricted my desire.

I reported to my new station May 10th and am completely satisfied with my new duty. In fact, the fellow in Washington who gave me this assignment must have been aware of my likes and dislikes. At present my duties consist of ass't

Executive officer and Senior Watch officer. Up to a few months ago this ship was classified as a (DD), one of the old fourpipers, but since conversion she has lost a few of her original characteristics. Still a good ship however.

Your Plaque idea is an excellent one and I'm enclosing a five dollar money order as my contribution to that fund.

Guess that winds me up for now

Very respectfully,

Loyal [Lt. (jg) Loyal C. Radtke USNR.][339]

⊠          ⊠          ⊠          ⊠          ⊠          ⊠

*While it was still possible that more men would be needed in the fight against Japan, for many, the summer of 1945 gave a welcome sense of relief.*

July 11 1945

Dear Chellis:

Just to let you know of a slight change in my address (the post office insists!): [...]

The change means that I have been put in charge of the Base Library of the Advanced Base Receiving Barracks, the only big library at Port Hueneme, As you might guess, this is right down my alley, and life is very pleasant at the moment. I get down to Long Beach occasionally to see sister Elaine and the Twetens.

Scuttlebutt coming through fine!

Gerhard B. Naeseth[340]

⊠          ⊠          ⊠          ⊠          ⊠          ⊠

*Stateside duty offered a much safer environment than assignment overseas, but many men still looked forward to the possibility of serving outside the U.S.*

[Letterhead: Construction Battalion Replacement Depot, Camp Parks, Shoemaker, California]

28 July 1945—Saturday morning

*[Ed note: Except for the handwritten greeting and ps, this is a typed "form letter," which the writer obviously felt warranted the apologies at the beginning and end.]*

Hello Prof.—

This happens to be the one thing that I've always said I would never do. I'm quite sure if I were to receive a letter written like this it wouldn't get an answer, but believe me when I say that working as I am at the present time just doesn't give me a chance to write as much as I should. When I worked nights there was time for it, but working days presents a different problem. For one thing there is always 'gold braid' looking over your shoulder, and then too my telephone never seems to know when to stop ringing.

As far as my work is concerned—things are going along rather smoothly, but am beginning to feel as tho I've had my share of Stateside duty. A friend that I had the pleasure of working with on Armed Forces Radio Station WXLC in the Aleutians is one of the five Naval Correspondents assigned to the 7th. Fleet stationed in Manila. He tells me that there is an opening (or will be in two months) for a man in Public Relations. Seems to think they could request me if I wanted to go out there. I'm seriously thinking about the possibilities it has to offer. It would be interesting work, and being stationed at Manila would be better than another small uncivilized island like the/?_@*)(_&&%$# Aleutians. Waiting to hear from him now.

Mom is still here and I went down to Los Angeles again last week-end to be with her. Flew down on United Airlines (two hours from Frisco), and drove back Sunday night with a friend in camp. We went up into the mountains early Sunday morning for a steak fry—what a breakfast that was. After that I played a couple sets of tennis, and spent the rest of the day taking it easy. Sounds nice eh? It was.

Well the Japs just don't seem to know when they are licked do they? At least there are hints of peace, and that's something—but I'm all for having it last just a little longer and whip them to their knees instead of handing them an easy peace on a silver platter. If we fail to land an army of occupation it means a moral victory for them, and they will only use it to spur the people on to another attempt at this thing we have fighting for three long years. By the way I just realized my enlistment date was three years old on the 8th of July—it really feels like much less, and is hard to make myself believe it has actually been that long.

Our work here has really let up—I'm transfer yeoman you know, and we haven't had a commissioned unit on the base for almost two months. We're sending the men out in Casual Drafts now, and the majority of the barracks here in Camp Parks are empty. A lot of the fellows have just been back from their rehabilitation leave (30 days plus travel) for little as a week, and we've had to ship them right back out. Makes it rough, and I can't say it's a popular job (in one sense of the word) although I'm treated like a king, and don't have too much trouble getting what I want done such as laundry in two days, tailoring free, watch fixed pronto, no details etc. Now I wonder why??

Wonder if I have ever mentioned living quarters here? We live in barracks of course, but I've a room (only two rooms located in each barracks) with three other fellows. I'm what they call a section head (Transfer Section) with a few fellows and gals (Waves—bless them) under me, and so we get a private room with table, chairs, drawers to put our small items in, and lockers to hang our uniforms in. I assure you the Aleutians were never like this—although the weather here in Livermore Valley is the next thing to it. They can have this 'Bay Area' section of California, and I'll take the good old Windy City.

Believe me when I say that I'll try not to send out any more epistles of this sort, but I was stuck for time and wanted you to know I hadn't forgotten. Please answer, and consider this as personal as you know I want it to be.

As always,
Don Flikeid, y2

P.S. You can see how far behind I was in my letter writing. Have had several Luther "sessions" as of late. "Dated" Ruth Barth several times while she was here awaiting embarkation to Pearl. We paid a visit to sick-bay and saw Phyl. Knutson (Mrs. Skilbred) with the new addition (6 lbs.). Had a date in Frisco to see Cliff Bruland (Chaplain for Coast guard), but fouled up. Will see him soon[341]

# CHAPTER 23

# "Quite a hankering for civilian life"— Reassignment from the Pacific Theater

*Many men remained in combat zones until the end of the war. But by late 1944 and early 1945, some men who had served in the European or Pacific Theaters were being reassigned "stateside."*

[Letterhead: United States Navy]

1-4-45

Dear Chellis:

Better I write you tonight as I just finished one to "Pete" and I seldom get in the mood for any extensive letter writing. I was home finally for thirty days after twenty three months in the Pacific and I certainly contend that is the grandest place to be of all. It was my first visit home in three years so my folks had to look twice when I walked in but we managed to get along very nicely. The weather was perfect while I was there (November) but that cold atmosphere did cause me some discomfort. I know you have had snow and cold the past month as these Calif. papers have on the front page daily. It isn't so crazy out here evenings in fact one has to wear a top coat up until ten A.M. when it does warm up. The weather has been grand <u>even sunshine</u> consistently but the rains are soon to fall.

I saw and talked to Doc. Moore on a visit to Sp. Valley while home. He was up there from Durand doing a little hunting. Told me Don had shipped to England and also that his wife was expecting his summer—suppose you have that scoop already? I know Harriet is married and that Beth's husband is in the service. Here I am still "Free, White and 2?!" Thought it best I remain the bachelor temporarily—this is not to released in Scuttlebut? O.K.!

371

I did receive your Dec. copy and have since received the ones sent previously to the Pacific. Frankly, I look forward to its arrival because it contains the kind of dope a person wants to read and how you obtain it is beyond me but it is remarkable how fellows will write you and try to keep the ball rolling so that it will be enjoyed by all. I get a bang out of "Pie Crust" Strom and his meandering around Italy and now France. Always the "weaker sex" mentioned—I'll bet he is the life of his company.

Enjoyed a nice visit with Ove Berven and Lars Bjerking at Thanksgiving outside of that all the old friends are gone. I have lost contact with Chellis Jr. so please forward his address. I saw Kermit Hanson a short while before I left Pearl H. He's on one of the baby carriers—we enjoyed a "short one" at the club together. I was with the Amphibious Forces all the while in the Pacific—saw it start with so little but now its one big thing out there and will continue to do so from all indications.

Presuming your daughter is quite the young lady now. Greet Mrs. Evanson and write if you ever have time between classes and Scuttlebut?

Sincerely
"Dusty" [Lt. (jg)] M. H. Hanson [USNR][342]

*Returning to the U.S. not only meant a change of duty assignments. For some, it meant adapting to the demands of family life as well.*

Hayward, Calif.
June 30, 1945

Dear Chellis,

The time has finally arrived when I again can relax, enjoy a cigar & write a few letters. The baby is getting along fine, & so am I with the diapers.

I want to enclose a picture which was taken on Majuro Atoll, in the Marshalls, in March, '44. You can see a part of our swing outfit; the fellow who is singing the vocals with me is now sharing this house in Hayward with me. We were playing ashore for a hospital this day, under the most glaring & hot sun I've yet seen.

Also, if you're yet taking on new donations for the placque fund, I'm enclosing a couple dollars as my entry.

Our best wishes to you, your family, & the school.

Respectfully,

Harold C. Skilbred[343]

⊠　　　⊠　　　⊠　　　⊠　　　⊠　　　⊠

*The end of the war was long awaited by the men in the Pacific, who could now turn their attention toward the next chapters in their lives, including academic matters. Some were also attempting to recruit new students for their alma mater.*

[undated]

Dear Chellis,

Have a bit of information for you or maybe I should say, a prospect. Consequently, don't allow amazement at another letter from me get you down; you probably realize by now that I'm not much as far as a correspondent is concerned.

We took a young seaman aboard this time in port whose name is Anderson, Wm. R. Anderson, hailing from Waupaca, Wisconsin. He's a Dane, but I guess Danes get by at Luther as well as an Irishman or Dutchman would. The boy has completed high school.

At present that is the extent of my info concerning him, but I have hinted to him about attending Luther and I plan to really give him the business, now that we're all done giving the J-boys the business. But maybe a little literature, etc., probably a letter from Karl, would further the cause to some extent. Don't know what his extra-curricular activities or interests are and I have no idea of his financial status, but I'll see what kind of an intelligence agent I am and give you the answer later.

He's a good-looking dude, clean-cut, and in the short time we've had him aboard here he's impressed all the officers as a good boy. So you might give him the works from that end and I'll do my best here. His address is the same as mine, his rate is S. 1c. Home address is 326 West Fulton Street, Waupaca, Wis. and his mother's name is Mrs. Wm. Anderson.

Funny thing—we took one boy aboard last fall name of Glaab. I immediately took him into a corner, thinking he was a dyed-in-the-wool Scandinavian, and tried to talk him into going to Luther—he was a man-mountain—good at f.b. or b.b. Come to find out he's a Czech and his ambition is to go to Notre Dame and I'm sure he'll make it.

Certainly good news the other day, wasn't it? We fired all our pyrotechnics and the deck gun, came to all stop and held swimming call right out in the middle of the ocean. It's a great feeling—having this fiasco at an end. Now comes the big task of converting this Navy back to a peace-time canoe club. And it seems as though they want us to stick around to help them—judging from the point system they've set up for a release.

I had planned to stay in for about a year and then go back to school—but from the looks of things I'll be in for quite some time yet. Not that I don't like it, but I've developed quite a hankering for civilian life again, and I'll have more of a chance to get back for a homecoming occasionally if I get out. Will have to wait and see.

How long do you plan to continue sending out "Scuttlebutt"? I imagine the mailing list will be decreasing quite a bit in the near future. By the way, could you please give me Tutor's address? I'd like to drop him a line.

'Spose you're all busy getting things back in the groove for the coming year—how soon do you think the student body will become rational again? Not fifteen girls to every boy!

You've been asking for pictures in your "Scuttlebutt" the only one I have available just now is enclosed—mind you, it's not much of a picture. It was taken on the bridge of our boat last July—at sea.

Must get off another dozen letters before we reach port tomorrow, so I'll close. A further bulletin on this guy Anderson will be forthcoming.

Respectfully,

[Lt.(J.G.)] Cal [DeBuhr] [U.S.S. Skate (SS305)][344]

⊠　　　⊠　　　⊠　　　⊠　　　⊠　　　⊠

*The most anticipated day of the war was "V-J Day," when Japan surrendered and the war was finally over. But once the war in the Pacific was finally over, no one knew how long it would take for everyone to return to civilian life. For example, it was not clear what type of occupation would be imposed on Japan, and how large an occupation force would be required. As a result, many of the men in the Pacific felt like they were "in Limbo."*

USS La Mar (APA47)

16 Aug. 1945

Dear friends:

With the arrival of the welcome Scuttlebutt today (which had been forwarded of course) my memory was given the needed jolt to get busy and give you my new address. I had every good intention of doing so before I left N.A.S.—Seattle, Wn. but in the rush of being ordered to sea I didn't get around to it.

After being detached back in July from N.A.S., and while in Frisco I had the good fortune to run into Lt. Davidson out at Rev. Brown's church one Sunday morning when Chaplain Norstad was preaching then. Needless to say we had many things to talk about as we had been at Luther together way back when.

The duty here is needless to say a bit different from that of a shore station, but I enjoy it as much as it is possible apart from my family.

Now that the war is over, what the future holds for us in length of service, is a question, and I suppose it will be for some time. We have much to be thankful for that victory is ours at last. That many were thankful was evident at a service we held on board the evening that word came through. A greater portion of the men have seen a lot of action and joining in the prayers and hymns brought tears to a good many.

It will be a great day when we are all home again to take our place in carrying on in home, church and community. God speed the day.

Sincerely in Christ

Chaplain B.T. Anderson

P.S.: By the way the spelling of my first name is: Bjarna <u>Not</u> Bjorne[345]

✉    ✉    ✉    ✉    ✉    ✉

*When the war finally ended, the "points system" often created hard feelings among those who were not lucky enough to be reassigned to the U.S. quickly.*

[Letterhead: American Red Cross]

August 28, 1945.
Okinawa Shiwa, Japan.

Dear Chellis:—

Everything continues O.K. out this way! As yet, the Navy hasn't seen fit to give any Pacific combat-veterans "a break"—so, guess "those of us", who got stuck out this far, prior to Tojo's surrender, are just "out of luck", when it comes to trying to get back to a Civilian Status (or, at least, duty in the States!) Let thousands of those "Duration of War" Stateside Sailors get out here and relieve us—it's safe out here now!

That "Point System" is sure the most unfair one that could be concocted by any human mind! Maybe it took several, though, to figure that one out—that is, several of those who didn't wish to come out this way for their turn, so's some others could get back home! That's pretty good—when a man whose been in combat several months gets no more consideration than a Stateside flag—waving "Red, White, & Blue"—cutie!!! You figure that one out—I can't!

Certainly hope that some red-blooded American, who knows what the term, "fair play", implies—likewise, a job "well-done"—I hope such an individual might have "guts" enough to bring proper pressure to bear on those responsible parties who saw fit to make such a dastardly mistake—let's "right that wrong!" That's the very least that can be done for those veterans who were willing to lay down their lives, so others might "live in Peace." Now, their job completed—fortunately, many of them had their lives spared—now, and soon, they wish to share in peaceful living, at home with their respective families (in a civilian capacity)—they want their rightful, well-earned, hard-fought for place in the New World—and, Now!

Respectfully yours,
Ens. J. Ingvoldstad.[346]

✉      ✉      ✉      ✉      ✉      ✉

*The end of hostilities did not mean that everyone would immediately be discharged. Some, especially in medical fields, expected to remain in the service for some time.*

[Letterhead: National Naval Medical Center Bethesda, Maryland]

4 Sept. 1945

Dear Dr. Evanson,

No doubt you maybe knew I was transferred from Great Lakes to Bethesda. It was something I was hopefully anticipating all the while at Great Lakes.

My aunt (Pa's sister-in-law) met you not so long ago at an American Legion "shindig" at Charles City, I believe. She relayed to me that you were very sorry that I didn't come to see you one of those times I got home for the week-end. Well the truth of the matter is that one time I did stop to see you but you nor anyone else was home. You seem to be quite hard to track down as I remember that I didn't see you the first time that I sought you when home in February.

This is really one swell place at which to be stationed. As it's only twelve miles from down-town Washington, it takes only a little while to reach there. Quite as you'd expect of me, I spend practically all my time chasing around from one public bldg. to another, and have seen practically all of them in the 4 weeks I've been here. I've seen the Capitol, Lib. of Congress, Lincoln & Jefferson Memorials, Washington Mon. (Still haven't gotten to the top of it), Arlington Cem., the Pentagon, Mt. Vernon, and a great many more things of lesser interest.

You ought to have been here the night that peace came—t'was some place. As usual I was gazing at something and this time it was Jefferson Memorial. I heard the good news in a very strange sort of way—no one told me, I didn't hear it over the radio, read about it or anything else. While staring about I noticed an unusual am't of racket—all the cars were honking, like-wise the trains & the Potomac river boats. When I realized why I proceeded to the White House where I knew all the excitement would center. It was just mobbed—the street cars literally had to plow thru the people. That was one time when it was advantageous to be tall as I could see over the heads of everybody and therefore had the good fortune to see Pres. & Mrs. Truman from a great distance. They came out twice while I was there but for all of me it could have been any middle-aged couple since I couldn't distinguish their features. After plowing thru the wildest village I've ever seen for a while, I came back to Bethesda. They drank enough alcohol to flood the Potomac.

The reason I'm here is to take a 6 week course in malariology but that is somewhat of a misnomer as only about 1/3 of is was actually malariology. It includes Helminthology, entomology and a little more. I really thoroughly enjoy it.

When I finish it in a couple of weeks I'll most certainly leave Bethesda, but as to where I don't know for sure—likely Calif. Under normal wartime conditions I'd go overseas, and still likely will.

In a matter of days school will be starting so it goes without saying that I'd like to be there. I'll consider myself lucky, however, if I can start it next year at this time. The Drs. & corpsmen in the Navy are quite pessimistic about their chances of getting out very soon.

Jimmy Peck is the only person I've met here whom I previously knew, except for a relative. Neil Jordahl came to Washington (from Camp Lejeune) the first week I was here, but didn't know I was here; I'm still hoping to see him but the chances are getting slimmer it seems.

Me thinks I've gobbled long enough so I'll call it quits.

Best to you all,

Donn [Gordon Luce H.A. 2/c][347]

*Those who avoided injury during the war were often conscious of how close they had come to danger, in some cases simply because they had chosen one form of transportation over another. But with the end of hostilities, they could now focus their attention on postwar life.*

10 September 1945

Dear Chellis,

Greetings from yours truly out here on the island of Maui, one of the Hawaiians. I feel that I am indeed fortunate to be able to send these greetings because, as you know by now, I just barely escaped the holocaust which befell the Franklin. Yes, I was lucky. It all hinged on the fact that I insisted on getting surface transportation instead of air the first time out from Frisco (I had quite a lot of baggage). And so I missed the Franklin by a few days in Pearl Harbor. Although I spent six weeks chasing her all over the Pacific I never quite caught up with her. Thank God for that! Most of the radio—radar personnel were killed.

After that episode I had a change of orders and was assigned to a Carrier Aircraft Surface Unit (CASU). I have been here about four months now. Many Air Groups have been stationed here, training & practicing before going farther out or aboard a carrier. It is our job to service the planes, repair them, make installations, etc.—in general, to keep them in A-1 condition. Some groups come in with planes & take them along when they leave, others use our planes. My job is Radio—Radar officer. I am in charge of the shop and the line crew. I have about 70 men. Have one assistant officer. We have day and night crews and work seven days a week. It's a grind all night, but work is slacking off now. In fact, this unit may fold up by 1st Oct.

This is a rather pretty island—a big valley with high mountains on both sides. Crops are sugar cane & pineapple. Surely have had my share of pineapple and pineapple juice since coming out here. 10¢ a can and no points! The climate here is very uniform and pleasant. Haven't seen any rain in the time I've been here, but it doesn't get very hot. Nights are always cool.

During the time I was in Pearl Harbor I saw quite a few Luther boys: Marv Nelson, H. Welch, R. Franck, Orlo Walstad, the McConnells, Jennings Aske, "Cyc" Schroeder and several others. We got together several times and had a good old gab-fest

Well, the war is over and everyone is thinking of home and "sweating out" the points. The latest is ¼ point credit for each month overseas. I'm a little short yet (I have 46 at the present time) but at any rate I don't think I'll have to go any further out when this place folds up. I hope to be out of the Navy within a few months at the most—maybe sooner if they lower the points. I imagine Tutor is eligible for release—Haat for sure, now. It will be wonderful to get back to a decent living again. Almost 3½ years of this is enough for me.

I have no definite plans as yet. I hope to get back to graduate school for at least a year and I think the time is now while things are still unsettled. I can get at least a year—perhaps more on the G.I. Bill. I would be foolish if I didn't take.

I have been receiving the Scuttlebutt, which I appreciate very much. Since I will probably be here at this address only a few more weeks I wonder if you would be kind enough to send future issues to my wife at Preston, Minn., c/o A.H. Langum. Also I would appreciate it if I could get a copy of Chips and Alumnus sent to her. She can send them to me, wherever I may be, by airmail. Thanks a lot.

Elinor has been staying with her folks the past seven months while I've been away. Lately she's been visiting friends in Kokomo, Ind. and Chicago. She'll probably be down at Luther again soon. She really likes the place and especially the people. I guess we all do.

Enclosed find a couple of bucks as my contribution toward the Plaque Fund.

You might slip a word to Mr. Hansen or Pip that there will be a lot of surplus electronic equipment for sale <u>cheap</u> in the near future and I think Luther ought to get in on the bargains. We could use all kinds of parts especially. Tutor, Bob. J., or Dr. Docken should be able to advise on what we could use.

Regards to Dr. Preus and the faculty members. Hope to see you all again before many months. Best wishes to you and Mrs. Evanson.

As ever,<br>[Lt.] Emil Miller [U.S.N.][348]

&#9993;     &#9993;     &#9993;     &#9993;     &#9993;     &#9993;

*When the war was finally over, ships were sent to a number of ports for decommissioning. That required some men to remain in active duty to process them.*

[Letterhead: USS Varian (DE 798)]

18 Sept. 1945

Dear Chellis,

I suppose by now Luther's in full swing—more new faces and I do hope a great number of old faces. We who don't have enough points will undoubtedly be drifting back sometime this school year. I know yours truly would much rather be back in school instead of bouncing around on a D.E.

My ship happens to be one of the D.E.'s they are going to keep in service. In a way it's O.K. with me because this is the only ship for me while I'm in the Navy. I've been 1st Lt. since last May so you know I have plenty to do.

At the present time we are on duty here at the New London Sub Base, New London, Conn. We go out almost every day and work with different subs—It's very interesting, but tiresome. I'm in hopes of seeing Cal DeBuhr here in the near future—My only reason for thinking he will be around is that the scuttlebut has it that a large number of Pacific subs are due in here very soon. So I was wondering if you could give me Cal's address—you can't tell maybe I'll see him much sooner than I expect. The Navy moves in mysterious ways, you know.

Oh, yes. when is homecoming this year? I would like to get a leave about that time—I know if everyone feels like I do there should be quite a gathering especially for the boys and girls who have been off to war—

380

By the way how's Luther's football team this year? Honestly I can hardly wait to see (Lut) the white & blue out there giving their all. I certainly would like to be putting on that uniform, but duty calls—maybe next year—with Archie & the rest of the ol' gang.

Hoping to see you during homecoming, I remain

As Ever,

[ENS.] Curt [Larson] [U.S.S. Varian (DE 798)][349]

✉    ✉    ✉    ✉    ✉    ✉

*The points system continued to be a matter of frustration for the men. For most of them, it seemed as if someone else was always eligible, but not themselves. As they awaited their return home, they eagerly received any news from their alma mater. A sad report came when Carlo Sperati, for whom many had played in the Luther Concert Band, died on September 12, 1945.*

30 September 1945

Dear Chellis,

Hope that you don't mind the informality but after having received your Scuttlebutt news for so long, I feel that I can write to other than as a former professor of mine.

I realize that your work on the "Scuttlebutt" has taken much of your time but I assure you that it has been appreciated by the fellows all around the world. Others can not but feel the same as I do and your work has definitely been a tie which kept us in contact with old friends and former acquaintances. Yes. Chellis, I've really appreciated what you've done for us. Thanks a million.

A few days ago I received a clipping of Dr. Sperati's death. He was a grand man, and I am happy to have known him, certainly the "unforgettable character" of all of those of us who were fortunate enough to have been associated with him. Perhaps our Norway Tour made me realize more than ever just what a man he was. That trip was one which has memories for all of us.

My brother, Alton, wrote me that another Mosbo enrolled at Luther this fall. I wasn't surprised to know that my cousin was there, guess that my brother and I had always drilled the idea of Luther into him. My brother also wrote that Luther certainly has a building program under way. If and when everything is completed, the college will have a very nice plant.

Out here we're all anxiously awaiting the word which will take us from Okinawa back to the states. Transportation seems to be the big hold-up. Although I have the required forty-four points for discharge, I am in disbursing and we are not eligible for discharge at this time. Where that leaves us, I really don't know. Rotation has been at a standstill on this island but believe that it'll go into effect again, hoping that it does so that some of us can at least hit the states and get some stateside duty instead of being out here indefinitely.

Thanks again for all the pleasure that came my way for your efforts on "Scuttlebutt" somewhere there should be a campaign ribbon for you.

Al Mosbo[350]

---

[Letterhead: Fleet Airborne Electronics Training Unit Pacific]
[N.d., but after Sperati's death in 1945]
San Diego, California

Dear Chellis,

The enclosed contribution is for the plaque fund.

The August issue of the "Scuttlebutt" was late because I neglected to send you my new address. Since my present address is on the envelope I will not repeat it here. I would appreciate it if you would notify the "Alumni Bulletin" and "Chips".

I learned of the death of the "Old Maestro" through an accidental meeting with Don Hastings, '38. (He is working in an aircraft factory here.) Do you have an extra copy of "Chips" containing Dr. Sperati's obituary? I missed that copy and I would like to know the details of his life and his passing. His death surely marks an end of an era at Luther, but his memory should be an inspiration to keep Luther on the top in the field of music.

I visited Decorah and the Luther campus while on leave during August. That was my first visit since 1939. I wandered around the campus noting many changes, the absence of Old Main especially. I spent a couple of days in Decorah, visiting Frank and Esther Miller and Tom Roberts, Jr. By coincidence, I bumped into Lt. Sheel USNR in Shell Haven. We were next door neighbors in Hawaii for a whole year.

Thanks for "Scuttlebutt." It is appreciated.

Sincerely
Erling Jordahl[351]

⊠　　　⊠　　　⊠　　　⊠　　　⊠　　　⊠

*While the men who arrived in the Pacific late did not avoid all danger, they recognized that men who had served there longer received higher priority for reassignment back to the U.S. However, that did not deter them from thinking about their own futures once they were finally reassigned.*

Guam, October First 1945

Dear Dr. Evans o—o

As far as writing the college in the last two and a half years I'm afraid I've been guilty of that ancient evil of procrastination. Each time I've received a copy of your "Scuttlebutt", I've promised myself to write to you. Yesterday I received one, and I want to thank you for sending them.

I'd like to continue at Luther what I so sadly started before I entered the service. I don't know how much credit I will be able to get from my army training, but I've heard that the college itself must decide. If you could give me an idea I'd appreciate it greatly.

I'm a navigator on a B-29. I've been overseas for four months—just long enough to get in on the last few bombings of Japan. We had a few close calls, but outside of a couple of scares I'm none the worse for my small part in the war. Since V.J. day we flew a few supply missions to prisoner of war camps in Japan, China and elsewhere, and a few miscellaneous missions to other islands of the pacific. Until two weeks ago I was in the 73rd Wing on Saipan. They disbanded, and the high point men went home. Now, those that were left are in the 315th Wing here on Guam, and have no idea when we'll be getting home, but I believe I can at least be sure of starting Luther next fall at the very latest.

If you would like a list of the schools I've attended in the army Signal Corps, pilot training, and navigation training—to help compute any credits I may derive from them, I'd be glad to send them on request.

I intend to take a business course, and have been preparing myself for it thru the U.S.A.F.I. I am taking a correspondence course in business law, and right in our wing they started an educational program taught by competent personel, and sponsored by the U.S.A.F.I. program. I am taking bookkeeping, Spanish, and advertising: All courses which I have not taken before, and will get no college credit for. I am taking them primarily for preparation for Luther.

I believe the army has done me a great deal of good. Of the benefits derived the main thing is that I've learned the value of an education. Before I entered service, school was more or less a monotonous duty to be performed, and it seems I put little into it and got little out of it. I intend to take full advantage of my educational opportunities thru the "G.I. Bill of Rights".

I am enclosing $15.00 for the New Main building or any other edifices that you are planning. It would barely cover the cost of the postage you've spent on me.

Well here's hoping it won't be too long before I start school again.

Yours truly,

[F/] Les Gorder

P.S. I'm working on another Luther prospect—I think I've got him convinced.[352]

&#9993;     &#9993;     &#9993;     &#9993;     &#9993;     &#9993;

*The soldiers and sailors were eager to return home, but in many cases there was significant reconstruction work to be completed before all of the troops could be demobilized.*

Oct. 2, 1945

Dear Mr. Evanson,

I just received my July issue of "Scuttlebutt" so shall write you a letter. We didn't receive any mail for four weeks so that is the reason I got it so late. We were taking over Marcus Island at the time so didn't get any mail. We are now back at Saipan but are planning on going back to Marcus. They are making an Air Field there as it is the shortest route between Frisco and Tokyo. The Seabees are doing the job and they really know their business. There was only about five thousand Japs there and they were really glad to see us come and take over. All the Japs will be taken back to Japan the 3rd of this month. We have a rumor going around the ship that we are supposed to leave for the states the 1st of November so are hoping to hear the official order soon. We had pay day today so anytime will be alright. In fact I have my dress blues clean and pressed.

Well I guess I miss the start of another school term at Luther but hope I shall be on hand for the next one. Have any of the service men enrolled for this semester?? In the "Scuttlebutt" I received it said if we want College Chips or Alumnus we should request them. I surely would like to have them sent to me as I enjoy them very much. How is the football team coming this year, I hope they are able to carry on.

384

I think it has rained every day we have been in Saipan the last few months and it seems like a continuous rain and not the five minute showers we are use to. We are also try to paint our ship a battleship gray instead of the jungle colors we now have.

Well I have to go on watch so will have to close and I'll be waiting to hear from Luther.

Sincerely,
Truman [Stelloh 2M 2/c][353]

✉     ✉     ✉     ✉     ✉     ✉

*Many positions became obsolete when the war ended, but that did not necessarily mean that the men who performed such duties were discharged immediately.*

4 October 1945

Dear Doctor Evanson,

I hope you will, as a result of this letter, straighten out my address with Scuttlebutt and Chips. I believe the last address you have for me is West Coast Sound School. I've been here in San Francisco now for some time being shifted from one command to another and with no permanent address but as of 1400 tomorrow I will get an address which will be permanent for quite some time (Longer than I'd like with the war over). Anyway, now it is: [...]

That's the important part of the letter and "mange tak." I want to be sure I hear from you and all the people at Luther. If you want to stop reading now it's okay with me because the rest isn't important (it's about an Ensign).

At Diego in Sound School I learned all about Sonar and Anti-Submarine Warfare and that is supposedly my capacity as far as they are concerned. However, now there is no need for Sonar Officers and on a PCC there are only about 5 officers I believe so I'll probably be a division officer, stand deck watches and be head of the gunnery Dep't in addition to Commissary officer, Ships Service Officer, and probably Capt of the Head or something.

You might be interested to learn that I saw Lloyd Iverson in Diego. He's got permanent duty there with the camera party. I also saw Evans Knutson who was there for an emergency ship-handling course. He's skipper of his LCI now. I also saw Chaplain Cameron Hoff and heard him conduct services in one of the local churches. It felt good to hear a Luther man again.

385

Here in Frisco I spent 3 weeks on Treasure Is. and had one week of instruction in Lt. Davidson's School, Pre-Commissioning Training Center. I had several nice visits with him. I also had the good fortune to spend about 8 or 9 days with newly commissioned Ens. Clayton Ammondson who is now on his way to an Oiler, the Kennebago AD 61. I roomed with him at Luther and was in boots with him so you can guess how glad I was to see him.

I get a little news from "Lefty" Dahl once in a while. She misses Luther as we all do. Said in her latest letter that she saw Luther play Hamline in football but forgot to tell me the score or any particulars. She also plans to attend Homecoming. Needless to say I would enjoy that immensely myself. She seems to find Kiester all right.

Give my best to everyone, especially Mr. Jacobsen & Dr. Docken and thanks again for the help.

Sincerely,
[Ens.] Bob Larsen[354]

✉    ✉    ✉    ✉    ✉    ✉

*Even after the war had ended, the men still had some restrictions on what they could describe in their letters. But their focus was increasingly on their personal postwar plans.*

[Letterhead: U.S.S. Effingham (APA-165)]

7 October 1945

Dear Mr. Evanson,

I've meant to write you before and thank you for the "Scuttlebutts" that have been coming my way, but am just now getting around to it. I have not been as fortunate as others in meeting up with old classmates from Luther, although I have seen several fellows from my V-12 and midshipman days. Certainly glad that the war is over and am looking forward to getting back to civilian life. Will have 39½ points at the end of the year, at which time we are hoping to be back to the States. We left the States in January and were back for three weeks (no leave) in June. My wife had just finished her last examination when I called, so she left for San Francisco the next day. Speaking of exams and college, I plan on getting out of the Navy the first part of next year so if everything goes all right I'll be back in September. I would appreciate your estimate on the possibilities of renting an apartment for the school year. We're expecting an addition to the family next March, so we'll need more room than if just the two of us were to come.

Before I forget, I would like to take advantage of your offer to make a request for Chips through this channel. It may seem strange, but the ship has been out of envelopes for quite some time, and my supply is nearly exhausted. I even put several letters in one envelope. We're on our way to the Philippines now, and will be able to get supplies there-I hope! I expect that we will tip the 50,000 mile mark by the time we get home next time. Our stops include New Caledonia, Guadalcanal (we were there at the time of the Serpen's disaster), Russell Islands, Purvis Bay, Ulithi (saw the Franklin on her way home-also several other ships of the fleet), Okinawa, where we landed just in front of Yonjan airfield and from there back to Pearl. Stayed in and around there for a month, during which time I saw Don Melaas, just commissioned and on his way out. The next stop was the most welcome of all! Our second cruise took us to Pearl, Eniwetok, Ulithi and then Okinawa, where we finished out the war. Your old ship was hit just a few days before it ended. We've made two trips with occupation forces—Korea and China. Have my camera with me and am getting what should be interesting shots, even tho the field is still restricted (armament, etc.).

Would like to give you facts and figures about the ship, but that's still on the confidential side. I can tell you that we did get a Zero during the first mass air attack on the invasion fleet off Okinawa, however. It was making a suicide dive on a battleship when one of our forty MM's knocked the tail off. The battlewagon thanked us as it pulled out of the transport area. Strange, but true.

Have just a few minutes before I go on watch. Thanks for taking the time to compile "Scuttlebutt"—it's certainly interesting. Best regards to everyone.
Sincerely,<br>Bob Hulsebus[355]

---

Oct. 7, 1945

Dear Chellis,

For quite a few months every time we hit port after a time at sea, there would be a copy of your "Scuttlebutt" for me at the first mail call. Lately there haven't been any. I know that is my fault and I'm trying to rectify it now. Perhaps with the war ended, "Scuttlebutt" is no more, but then I want to tell you I enjoyed each copy and appreciate the work and time you spent for all of us L.C. alumni. Would you please put me on your mailing list, if the dope-sheet is still alive, and in any case ask them to send me the "Luther Alumnus"? That would also be appreciated.

For all that the Allendale has been pounding around the Pacific for about a year and nearly 50,000 miles, I have yet to meet my first L.C. man. You have often mentioned numerous who have passed through Pearl, and I'm sure there have been some there when I have, but somehow our paths haven't crossed. I have been particularly watching for my cousin Paul and Chaplain Jimmy Amundson whom you have mentioned.

We did have 2 Decorah boys on here, John Hovden and an Ericson. Hovden has already left for home, lucky fellow.

Of those 50,000 miles, only a few have been in hot spots. We spent the first 10 days of the Okinawa action dodging kamikazes, but except for the occasional submarine scares, that is about all the war we saw, but an awful lot of ocean at 15 knots. This is being written from the Philippine Islands, so we have still more to look forward to—and they aren't talking about sending us home yet either.

I am one of the world's worst correspondents, so you would be doing me a favor if you would greet my relatives there and my food friend Dr. Tingelstad.

You will find a small gift for one of those funds—your choice. Wish it could be more, but my bankroll is making a slow recovery from 2 enjoyable weeks in San Diego. You, being an old Navy man, know what happened when you get a little stateside liberty.

Thank you again for enjoyable hours and pleasant memories brought back by your letters. I think that you did more good for L.C. then you can realize now.

Sending best regards to you and Mrs. E.

Yours,

Paul K. Preus '37, USS Allendale (APA 127)[356]

 

 

*Military personnel who had served significant periods in active combat zones, had received citations for valor, or had been wounded, received priority for discharge under the points system. Others simply had to wait until the military forces were demobilized and the majority of the men were discharged.*

[Letterhead: U.S. Naval Small Craft Training Center
Roosevelt Base, Terminal Island, San Pedro, California]

1-1-45

Dear Chellis:

There has been quite a lapse of time since I wrote you last but since my coming here I have skipped considerably in keeping up my correspondence. Your dope sheet "Scuttlebut" is read regularly and it is always looked for, believe me. I have been with Nick "The Mad Russian" Shiftar several times and I passed my copies on to him. Nick, by the way, together with his wife will be headed La Crosse way soon as he was discharged today. He has no definite plans. Met a boy from Mabel, Minn (Gabrielson) last week—he graduated from Hamline Univ. and is an Ensign here for assignment by the bureau. He played against my teams at Preston and naturally he was pleased to meet someone.

Is Chell Jr. still in Denver?—I saw the Luther La Crosse FB score and hope the Norsemen can pluck a few Peacock feathers this Sat. I presume homecoming this year will be a little more like the days of old. I hear from home and many of the boys are home to stay. Don Moore should be out soon. I saw S.Calif beat St. Mary's Pre Flight last Sat & will see UCLA and Calif this Sat. I'll still take the big ten brand of ball. Minn. may be the top team this year.

I'm lacking points for discharge but they should be lowered within two months which should make me eligible—I have nothing planned at present—don't know as if I'll go to school for a year or back to work. Sorry to read of Dr. Sperati passing. What a grand man he has been and his memory will live forever.

Are you still teaching the same classes or are you executive these days? Best regards to Mrs. Evanson and to the Peterson's and Qualley's.

Sincerely,
Dusty [Lt. M.H. Hanson U.S.N.R.][357]

✉     ✉     ✉     ✉     ✉     ✉

*When the war had ended, many of the wartime units became part of the Occupation Forces.*

389

13 November 1945
Nagoya, Honshu, Japan

Greetings from the Land of the Rising Sun:

ETO[358] to Tokyo would seem to be a fairly good motto for this outfit to which I belong, in fact some people thought enough of it to have the same printed on all the vehicles of the 1636th Engineer Construction Battalion. And now it has materialized as we have been both places, and are more or less patiently awaiting that one more boat ride. I suppose that it goes without saying that the one more boat ride is the States bound one. The same ride that most all of the boys over here are looking forward to. We first set foot on the soil of this country the 4th of November, and nearly by the 5th had seen enough of it. This duty here is entirely too much like garrison duty back in the States, and serves primarily to impress the Japanese people.

I ran into the first Luther man I have seen since leaving the States a very few days before we left the Philippines. He is a Chaplain with the 37th Station Hospital near San Fabian by the name of Butch Ranum and originally came from Northwood, Iowa. While I never knew him before, we still had a nice session and seemed to have all sorts of things in common which isn't unusual. He has spent some twenty-six months over here in the Pacific area, and is certainly awaiting that well earned return to the states. I seemed to have missed seeing Orlando "Ole" Haugen class of 1942, and of Decorah by a matter of days. We had the same APO for a short time, which we both discovered by way of Scuttlebutt, but I left Luzon before we could make contact. I have since heard from him that he is still in the Islands, but perhaps someday he will also come up here, and we can have our reunion on Japanese soil.

I have one request to make at this time. If possible, could you please see that all Luther publications receive this up to date address of mine so that it is possible for me to receive Chips, Bulletins, Scuttlebutt and such so welcome issues. It's really great to receive them, so keep up the good work for those of us who aren't fortunate enough to get home too quickly. Thanking you again for past favors and for your efforts to keep track of some of we roving service men which I know is a big job.

Regards,
Ted '41 [Cpl Ted. V. Jensen][359]

# CHAPTER 24

# "Wondering what will come next"— Planning for Postwar Life

*By late 1944, the men started to hear reports about the "G.I. Bill of Rights." With the financial assistance that might provide, many of them could realistically consider returning to college after the war. Many also hoped that courses they took while in the military might be applied toward completion of their college degrees.*

Somewhere in the Pacific
Dec 30, 1944

Dear Luther,

The other day I received a copy of the Nov. Scuttlebutt and was very pleased to receive it. I do not know to whom I'm indebted for giving you my address but I deeply appreciate it and hope I'll continue to receive it. I ran into John Victor Halvorson on a troopship when we were on our way to attack Angaur Island of the Palau Group as a part of the 81st "Wildcat" Division and have seen him a number of times since—he looks none the worse for being in combat. It might interest you to know, if you haven't been informed, that my cousin, Roland O. Hegg (Hatton, N.D.) is now an Ensign USNR but as yet I don't have his new address.

I found the address of a good friend I met when I was at Luther ('40—'41) of whom I had lost track. I plan to write him as he is somewhere out here too.

Do you plan to accept for credit any subjects taken by service men through the U.S.A.F.I.? I am attempting to extend my college training through this means and would like to gain a degree after the war by taking advantage of the "G.I. Bill of Rights". Have you established a policy on this as yet? I have also heard rumors to the effect that college credit may be given, at the discretion of the college, for things learned in the army and army schools. In my case this would consist mainly of Radio work. At present I am a radio operator and have attended army schools on both repair and operation of radios used by the Field artillery. I would appreciate any information you could give me in regards to this.

Here's hoping the war will be over soon so we can come home. I'm looking forward to the next issue of Scuttlebutt.

Sincerely
Bob Olson [Tec 4 Robert E. Olson][360]

&#9993;   &#9993;   &#9993;   &#9993;   &#9993;   &#9993;

*Postwar readjustments took many forms. Individuals had to plan the next phases of their lives. But on an international level, the victorious Allies began planning for a postwar organization to help maintain peace. In place of the failed League of Nations, they began work to create a "United Nations." The groundwork for that organization was established at the San Francisco Conference, which lasted from April to June 1945.*

12 May 1945

Dear Chellis:

It must be about graduation time. I had hoped to be back this time but Treasure Island gets busier all the time. We thought there was a lot of activity here last year when we were pushing ships and supplies out in such large amounts, but action is really going on now.

The Conference is interesting in many ways. It brings a great deal of color to an already colorful city. It is hoped that its objectives are reached in such a manner that a better world organization will function. I have been out with the Norwegian delegates, and they are quite an outstanding group. I've been with them at the Consulate General's home, the Consul's home and at a Dinner Party. They are well thought of and are being given important positions in the conference.

Quite a few of the boys have stopped in, the last few months. Off hand I can think of Chaplains Sorlein and Amundson, Loyal Radtke and several others. I'm expecting Paul Strom any day.

What is this Plaque business? I must have missed a letter explaining it. Anyway, here's five dollars. It must be all right if you and T.F. are pushing it. Since I promised a picture back in 1942, I'm sending one now. That will be one less thing I have to answer for when I get a little leave and can come to Decorah. I haven't had any since Oct. 1943.

Enough of this for now. I hope it isn't too long until I can return to Luther for good.

> Sincerely,
> Dave [Lt. A.O. Davidson][361]

   ✉      ✉      ✉      ✉      ✉      ✉

*In order to resume civilian careers, it might be necessary to locate official documentation that had been misplaced in the chaos of going to war.*

> Germany
> May 18, 1945

Dear Dr. Evanson,

I didn't know exactly who I should write to but I trust you will put it in the proper hands for me. It concerns the whereabouts of my Teacher's Certificate. I made the necessary arrangements to get one when I graduated in the spring of 1942. That fall I took a teaching job at Kensett, Iowa. While there, I was asked to send my teacher's Certificate to the County Supr. of Education. I informed them that I hadn't received my Certificate as yet but would send it to them as soon as I got it. Then in November I was drafted and I haven't seen my certificate yet. Now I'm wondering where it is, to whom I could write, or if you have any way of tracing it there at the College. About two months ago I wrote the school board at Kensett asking them if they had any record of it. As yet I've received no answer. So if you can help me in locating it I would really appreciate it.

Now for a bit of other news. I've been receiving "Chips" and "Scuttlebutt" regularly and enjoy both very much. The issue of Chips containing the picture of the gym and a part of the campus really made me homesick. There should be more pictures like that. I'm working on a buddy of mine as a prospect for post-war Luther.

Some time ago I met Gerry Johnson and we had a lot to talk over during the one hour we were together. Joe Magelssen and I are still corresponding regularly and also Ole Haugen & Babe Nordby.

V-E Day is now a part of history and most of us over here are counting our points over and over again. Sorry to say I lack quite a few for a discharge and am wondering what will come next.

I hope the baseball team comes along as well as of old this year. I get time now and then to play some catch and get in a few softball games. From now on I think we'll have more time for sports for a while.

Well, I must close for this time. Tell Pete and Sig Reque "Hello" from me.

Sincerely

[S/Sgt] Arleigh Kraupa[362]

⊠        ⊠        ⊠        ⊠        ⊠        ⊠

*For some, the transition to peacetime "normality" began with new assignments even before they were discharged. But perceptive men recognized that the end the war would not be without problems of readjustment.*

Brooklyn, N.Y.
28 May 1945

Dear Dr. Evanson,

This matter has been on my mind for quite some time but for one reason or another I haven't had the opportunity to attend to it.

I would appreciate very much if you would send me the "Scuttlebutt." Up until this time I've been on the go so much I haven't had a chance to settle down for any length of time. It appears now that I shall be here for sometime so I hope to become established and contact all the Luther men I possibly can.

My status and stations have been varied. I spent last year on convoy duty in the Atlantic. The beginning of this year was spent at Great Lakes, from the Lakes to San Diego and now in New York. While in San Diego I was fortunate in contacting my brother, Maurice and Jim Ulvilden. I also had frequent visits with Cameron Hoff who is stationed at Camp Pendleton.

My duty in New York has been at two stations. I was originally attached to the educational services staff at St. Albans Naval Hospital. A short time ago I was transferred to the Naval Medical Supply Depot here in Brooklyn. My work here consists of drug analysis. I'm very pleased with the set-up. I'm doing work I've had some experience in as well as having studied for it. I consider myself very fortunate in that there are only sixteen of us doing this type of work in the navy. I'm actually doing the same type of work as I was doing as a civilian. I'm tickled that I'm able to keep my hand in my line. Aside from the pay I could as well be a civilian. I live on subsistence. My hours are from eight to four-thirty with every nite and every weekend off. I'm very lucky and realize the fact. What amazes me is the fact that I don't know a single soul in this vast political organization called the navy that helped me out. I was merely drafted into the job.

I hear from my brothers who are spread thru out the South Pacific. From what they say all are faring just fine.

I find that being practically a civilian again rather awkward after the short period of time I've been in the service. I wonder how it will be for the boys who have been in for three or more years. I have a feeling we're going to have a terrific readjustment problem on our hands.

> Sincerely yours,
> Greet Chellis when you have the chance
> Sherman M. Jenson '41[363]

✉ ✉ ✉ ✉ ✉ ✉

*As the end of war became increasingly imminent, Evanson's correspondents began thinking of what they would do after the war. For those who left Luther before they had received their degrees, completing their education was often a high priority. Many of those who had graduated were also considering graduate or professional school.*

30 May 1945

Dear Mr. Evanson,

Well, it looks like what I've been waiting for the past year has arrived.

While at Newport, R.I. I was assigned to the U.S.S. Consolation—a hospital ship—which was commissioned 22 May, and the way it looks we'll be to sea soon.

Could you tell me if Luther accepts the correspondence courses that the Navy is offering to the men, as credits toward a degree? There are several of us that want to take a couple courses but I would like to know in order to choose the right courses.

Just one more favor—would you send me Chet Porter's and Ray Fuller's addresses. Thank you.

I wish to thank you for the college papers.

> As ever
> "Bud" Baer [Ronald D. Baer, S 1/c (SC), USS Consolation][364]

✉ ✉ ✉ ✉ ✉ ✉

*Even as they described their current activities, men were outlining their future plans.*

Somewhere in the Pacific

30 May 1945

Dear Mr. Evanson,

I should have written you long ago but seems like the time passes by so quickly I don't have much time for writing. I have been almost around the world now and have received College Chips, Scuttlebutt, or Luther Alumnus everywhere. I enjoy them a great deal and always wait anxiously for them to come.

When I first came into the Navy I took my boots at Great Lakes and from there went right to sea and have been there every since. I had a few months rest from the sea while taking Amphibous training at Little Creek, Va. I'm on an Amphibous ship now and like it a great deal but still in favor of going back to the fleet even if I do have to wear the uniform of the day after 1630. Ha! At Little Creek I ran into my old roommate "Red" Mathre which was an enjoyable sight to see. I have been in Africa several times and now are in the Pacific. I picked this ship up in Philadelphia were we put it in commission and came west. We have only been out here a few months but no trouble as yet. One thing we have had is plenty of rain & also heat. Of course we hit Philly in January. Ha!! Most of our liberty time we go swimming or play softball just so it is something to get a little exercise. I'll be waiting to get back to Luther and play baseball instead. I remember the first six weeks I spent at Luther and how I hated it. Than I began to like it more everyday until the day I left. Now I can't wait until I'll be able to go back. You always said Luther would grow on you and I sure believe it now and every paper I receive brings back pleasant memories. I think I'm eligible for the G.I. Bill of Rights as I have had ninteen months of sea duty. Even if there was no bill I'd sure try and find someway to get back. I hear they have changed the college some and the girls are mostly running it but the main thing it is still going.

I like the Navy real well and haven't a thing to complain about. In fact I have even gained a few pounds. I'm in the quartermaster racket and like it alot as there is always something to do or new to learn. I also never realized how big this Navy really was until you see some of these ports with all there ships. I have met several fellows from the mid-west and they all seem to have heard of Luther.

I haven't heard from my cousin Marv lately but it sounds like he is having a real time out in the field he likes. My mother said he even preached a few Sundays at our church in Salem.

Well I have to go on watch in a few minutes and I better get my cup of "Joe" in so I don't fall asleep. Thanks for sending all the papers and I'll be waiting to get back to Luther.

Sincerely,
Truman Stelloh[365]

✉  ✉  ✉  ✉  ✉  ✉

*Those who were fortunate enough to be discharged soon after V-E day had to find jobs in the civilian world. In some cases, their course work at Luther was directly applicable to their new positions.*

July 23, 1945

Dear Chellis:

I had meant to drop you a line much sooner than this, but I was never very prompt in writing.

I wrote to Pip as soon as I got out of the service and got my transcript so I could go to work. I landed a pretty good job with the Lincoln here in Fort Wayne and like it fine. There's a bunch of nice fellows to work with and advancement opportunities look good.

Chellis, I would like to have the address of Paul Narum if you have it there. We were roommates at Newberry and I have never written to him or heard from him.

In my spare time I am studying for actuarial examination I. It is tough and I am glad that I had a lot of math at Luther.

When you see Bob Jacobsen, say "hello" to him from me and if he is teaching Hall and Knight this summer tell him I'm now on page 50, and have done every problem with lots of difficulty!

I hope to hear from you soon and best of regards.

Sincerely,
Bill [Winter][366]

✉  ✉  ✉  ✉  ✉  ✉

*Some men encountered medical problems not related to combat. Even though hospitalized, however, they eagerly followed the news coming from Japan, which ultimately culminated in the Japanese surrender.*

Aug 10<sup>th</sup> [45]

Dear Chellis,

Received the Scuttlebutt the other day and was glad to get it. Received some December Chips too. Kind of old but still glad to see them.

I promised to write and let you know what happened to me. Well, I'm in the Naval Hospital here at Mare Island. Don't know the whole story yet but I think I will be operated on tomorrow for hernia. What else will happen, I don't know

Jeepers! I surely hope the Japs are really through now. If they are maybe we vets can get back to Luther by the fall of '46. That would really be swell.

Got to see Dr. Olson the other day for just a few minutes. Hope to see more of him in the near future.

I didn't get to stop off at Denver like I had planned. I didn't get away from home in time. Ha!

There is a band giving a concert out here on the lawn. We have the windows open so we can hear it. Only one thing wrong, it's not the Luther College Concert Band. I don't think that there is another band in the world that can compare with the Norsemen outfit.

This is quite the place. A cute red cross girl just came through the ward and showered us with Gardenia's. This place smells like a flower garden now instead of a surgical ward.

You'll have to greet everyone at Luther for me. Tell Coach "Pete" I surely was sorry to miss him while I was there.

This is short but will have to do for this time. Will try to keep you posted as to what is in the wind for me.

Hope to see you soon,

A Norsemen
Willy [Wilbur M Johnson][367]

⊠     ⊠     ⊠     ⊠     ⊠     ⊠

*For men who had married during the war, returning to Luther to continue their studies was slightly more complicated than if they were single and could return to regular student housing. Before the war, married students were an oddity at Luther College.368*

21 August 1945

Dear Chellis,

It is a wonderful feeling being able to write a letter knowing the war is over. We all hope it won't be too long before the country can get back to normal and everyone can live a regular life again. This fall begins the post-war era for Luther, and if all the plans are carried out, Luther ought to progress greatly. May God guide her and help her.

Some of the fellows, when they return to finish Luther, will be married, and will want their wives to be with them. What can Luther and Decorah do to help them find a place to live? 3 or 4 of us have written to each other and that is one of the things we are wondering about.

Sally is enjoying her work up in Alaska. Looks like we will be out here quite a while yet. I hope to be back for the fall of '46. The way Strus wrote, the enrollment at Luther sounds good. That is what we like to hear. Had a good letter from Chell Jr. the other day.

Best regards to all. Sincerely, Erling [Lt. (jg) EO Naeseth]

⊠　　　⊠　　　⊠　　　⊠　　　⊠　　　⊠

*Postwar assignments often relocated the men to different areas of the globe, but with the fighting ended, their thoughts increasingly turned to their own plans for the future.*

5 Oct. 45.

Dear Prof. Evanson:

Just a line to give you my new address. Have been transferred into the [...]

This outfit is a long range mapping sqd. using B-24's for their flights. The base is located at Gushkara, Bengal which is about 70 miles from Calcutta. We are supposed to be transferred to the So. Pacific for a job there pretty quick. So far all we've been doing is getting our equipment ready and doing routine flights for training.

Have been wondering if Luther is going to try to make any living quarters available to married students after they get back. I know myself and suppose a lot of other fellows will be influenced by the same thing, that if there are places to live there with your wife and family—if you have a family, you will go back to Luther, but if not, will have to go someplace which does make arrangements for the married students.—I'm just curious because I intend to return to Luther if this is possible.

Had a letter from Dick Ulvilden day before yesterday.—Have seen no one around here who has gone to Luther. Hardly any fellows from Iowa at all.—
Best wishes to you—
Very Sincerely,
Pfc.Dave L. Tate[369]

✉        ✉        ✉        ✉        ✉        ✉

*While the men may have had lofty ambitions for their postwar lives, their discharge also gave them an opportunity for much needed rest, and a chance to adjust to civilian life again.*

Rio, Wis
Oct 10, 1945

Dear Chellis:—
A quick note to tell you that M/Sgt Harlan Kittleson of HQ Btry 79th Div Arty became <u>Mr</u> Kittleson again at high noon of Oct 12th. The Separation Center at Fort Sheridan, Ill. performed the honors. The process of obtaining the honorable diploma was pleasingly swift.

Leaving Schweinfurt Ger. on 2 Sept by the 40 & 8 for Marseille sailing on 16 Sept, stepping off the boat at Hampton Roads POE on 27 Sept and receiving my discharge 5 days later left me in a daze. I returned as a high pointer with the 99th Div.

Plans for the present are rest, rest, & rest.

Thank you so much for sending me your lively "Scuttlebutt" no one else in my unit received such newsy, monthly letters.

In haste with best wishes,
(Mr.) Harlan Kittleson
Rio, Wis.

P.S. Just read the Lutheran Herald account of Sperati's funeral. Very sorry. He was a man's man that I will always remember.[370]

✉        ✉        ✉        ✉        ✉        ✉

*With the rapid reduction of troop levels, the men who were not among the first receiving their discharges often had to assume a wider range of responsibilities. But even while they completed their work, they were also planning for their own futures after they left the military.*

[Letterhead: U.S.S. Eugene A. Greene
With handwritten note next to drawing of ship:
"Trim Ship, isn't she?]

At Sea, 10/13/45

Dear Chellis:

Am enclosing some literature on Colonial Wmsburg which you may enjoy.

The medical officer was transferred last Monday—The CPhM's enlistment expires in 10 days—and orders came in for the 2/c to be transferred—so that will leave me as the medical department! And all I want is to get out—go to L.C. one semester and then back to medical school.

We are on our way from Norfolk, where we have been a training ship—to Casco Bay, Maine, where we will operate with the Atlantic fleet on maneuver.

The ship will be at New Haven Conn for Navy Day from 10/25 to 10/30/45.

My brother Rolf is a RT 3/c in the Navy and it is our hope that we can be together at Luther College. He hasn't decided what he wants to do yet, but his latest fancy is to follow in my dad's footsteps as a lawyer.

In case you would be interested to send him any literature his address is: [...]

Thanks a lot for "Scuttlebutt" and greetings to Luther College, students & faculty.

Fred Giere [PhM 3/c][371]

✉   ✉   ✉   ✉   ✉   ✉

*Because most of the men expected to be discharged during the school year, they often needed to find temporary positions until the next year began.*

[Letterhead: U.S. Naval Training Station, Newport, R.I.]

Oct. 17, 1945

Dear Chellis:

Greetings to you, other faculty members, & friends at Luther College.

I have planned to write to you so many times & thank you for the work you have been doing & are continuing to do for the Luther men in the service. Now that the war is over and I'm almost ready to be discharged, I'm getting around to write a few lines to express my thanks & appreciation.

Your work in keeping the men of Luther in contact with each other & keeping us informed how Luther has been carrying on is a glowing and true example of the friendliness and spirit of democracy which exists at Luther. I know your work in keeping up the "scuttlebut" & other projects has been greatly appreciated by all the Luther men & women in the service. Again I express my thanks to you, Chellis.

Pete, no doubt, has informed you of the fact that I am the proud father of a son. I have a big husky boy who will be eight mo. old the 21st of this month. If he continues to grow as he has & remains as active and swift of movement as he is now, he should be a football prospect for Luther some day, at least I hope so! He weighs 22 lbs. now which, I think, is very good for a boy of eight months. I hope I haven't given the impression of a braggart in this paragraph.

I hope to be discharged from the Navy in December as I will have sufficient points by then. I wonder if you could give me any information on the possibility of getting a teaching & coaching position for the remainder of the school year beginning in January. I would appreciate any information you could give me, & I would be happy to send the money necessary to be given to the Placement Bureau.

I have been considering returning to college for another semester if I'm unable to get a coaching position before next fall.

Perhaps you have already noticed by the address on the envelope that I have finally been promoted to chief. There finally was an opening here on the station just before V-J Day so I took the test & was promoted to chief. It really was a grand feeling to finally get into a good suit of clothes & wear a shirt & tie again.

Since I have remained here at Newport & have continued working in the Ath & Rec department, I haven't much of any news of interest to write of.

I'm enclosing $3.00 as a contribution to the plaque fund; the souvenirs you will have to get from my brother, Wilmer, who is in Tokio Bay.

I hope to soon see my many friends at Luther. I hope this finds you & your family in the best of health.

Sincerely,
Percing Fure[372]

# PHOTOGRAPHS

James Anderson

Roger W. Anderson

Lyle W. Bestul

A. O. Davidson

Wayne, Harold, and Don Bravick

Cal DeBuhr Receiving Bronze Star

Clifford Ellingson (r.) with
Ens. Lockman, Guam

Les De Noyelles and Dick Reed

Don Estenson

Lyle O. Estenson

Ray Franck

Leslie Fels, Navigator, with Crew

Don Gjerdrum

Alvin Gisvold

Fred Giere

Arie Gaalswyk in Himalayan Mountains

Fred Giere, Bob Rasmus, and Red Mathre

Rolfe A. Haatvedt

Leland Harris (l.) and Flight Officer Stanley J. Kvam

Ens. Ted Jacobsen

Ted Jacobsen

Bob and Beverly Hulsebus

Lloyd Iverson in Pearl Harbor

Vernon Larson

Carroll E. ("Hap") Jensen

Milford ("Bucket") Lunde

John Meyer

R.G. Mitchell

Paul D.Linnevold and Kenny Nesset

Carsten D. Leikvold and Buddies

Robert Olson "gone native" in the South Pacific

Sailors crossing the Atlantic for the first time ("Pollywogs," like Chester Porter) were initiated to become "sons of King Neptune."

411

Kenneth Olson

Rolf Norstog

Marvin Rohm

Paul ("Cyc") Schroeder

George Strum

Sigwart Steen

Leo ("Gabby") Sebastian

Lloyd ("Woody") Woodiwiss

Clarence Winden

Merald Wrolstad and Willard Conradson

# ENDNOTES

1   "Scuttlebutt," April 24, 1944. As noted later in this introduction, I have not corrected spellings or grammatical errors, nor have in indicated such errors with "[sic]."

2   Andrew Carroll, ed., *War Letters: Extraordinary Correspondence from American Wars* (New York: Scribner, 2001), 34–35.

3   For a description of V-mail, see <http://www.smithsonianmag.com/issues/2004/may/around_the_mall.php>, accessed November 20, 2006

4   For a detailed history of Luther College, see David T. Nelson, *Luther College 1861–1961* (Decorah: Luther College Press, 1961).

5   The V-12 program was designed to meet the growing need for commissioned officers in the Navy. For a brief history of the program, see <http://homepages.rootsweb.com/~uscnrotc/V-12/v12-his.htm> (accessed November 20, 2006).

6   Nelson, 360, 370, 371.

7   Ibid, 271.

8   130:4:68–71. For an explanation of the notations used in these citations, see "Introduction."

9   130:19:1.

10  130:6:1.

11  130:18:3–4.

12  130:9:71–72.

13  A number of correspondents mention sending him cigarettes. In the February 1945 issue of "Scuttlebutt," Evanson acknowledged this by noting, "My personal thanks to Marv. [Bachman], John Sorlien and Erling Naeseth for helping me to keep the 'tan' on my fingers."

14  130:26:35.

15  130:11:24–25.

16  130:17:19–20.

17  130:9:20.

18  130:20:25–27.

19  130:9:33–35. Harris was a 1941 LC graduate.

20  130:26:25–26.

21  130:5:1–2.

22  130:4:3.

23  130:26:42.

24  130:22:17.

25  130:6:18.

26  130:11:40.

27  130:25:57.

28  130:7:17–18.

29  130:11:26.

30  130:25:58.

31  130:25:59.

32  130:25:60–62.

33  130:6:2.

34  130:4:82.

35  130:3:23–34.

36  130:22:6–7.

37  130:4:65.

38  130:4:40.

39  130:22:41.

40  130:4:54.

41  130:9:12–13.

42  130:14:1–3

43  130:10:16. Hof's letter is not dated, and Evanson made no reference to him in "Scuttlebutt."

44   130:4:55.

45   130:14:72–74. The letter is undated, but it is mentioned in the March 25, 1944 issue of "Scuttlebutt."

46   1130:17:61.

47   130:9:31.

48   130:19:3.

49   130:17:10.

50   130:19:33. David Preus' father, O.J.H. Preus, was President of Luther College

51   130:22:42–44.

52   130:24:1.

53   130:24:12.

54   130:24:14.

55   130:19:34.

56   130:4:2.

57   130:8:2.

58   130:2:40–41. The location is not identified in Bachman's letter, but in the August 1944 issue of "Scuttlebutt" Evanson notes that Rod McConnell was at the Hollywood Beach Hotel,Hollywood,Fla, as well as "Bob and Bob McC." Rodney McConnell's letter of August 21 (130:15:55–56) indicates that he, "Bob" and "Marv" are all there.

59   130:2:27–30.

60   130:24:2.

61   130:19:35.

62   130:9:76–77.

63   130:24:3.

64   130:4:33–37.

65   130:4:78.

66   130:15:15.

67   130:24:15–16.

68   130:2:42–43.

69  130:15:3.

70  130:9:78.

71  130:24:4.

72  130:18:37–38.

73  130:8:1.

74  130:15:57–58.

75  130:17:23.

76  130:11:51.

77  130:15:8–9.

78  130:15:50

79  130:11:45.

80  130:11:1.

81  130:22:46.

82  130:15:4.

83  130:6:10.

84  130:20:39–41.

85  130:3:22.

86  130:11:2.

87  Warren Berg recalls that in V-12 training, a "tree" was a disciplinary warning, indicating that if you made a similar mistake again, you would receive disciplinary action. (Conversation with Warren Berg, February 19, 2007.)

88  130:9:73–74.

89  130:22:4–5.

90  130:25:6–9.

91  130:2:73. The Catholic college is not identified, but in the September issue of "Scuttlebutt," Evanson noted, "Lt. (j.g.) Luther Berven in a Navy V-12 unit at Carroll College, Helena, Mont. With no sea duty as yet, but still hoping. Carroll is about like Loras, a Catholic school."

92  130:7:22.

93  130:19:23.

94  130:2:66.

95    130:5:33.
96    130:14:22.
97    130:18:13.
98    130:7:31–32.
99    130:22:45.
100   130:6:3–4.
101   130:17:54–55.
102   130:17:56.
103   130:8:11–12.
104   130:20:45.
105   130:25:1–2.
106   130:25:3–4.
107   130:19:26.
108   130:19:27.
109   130:19:28–29.
110   130:6:8–9. The Bond sheet is not included with the letter.
111   130:10:19.
112   In the December 1944 issue of "Scuttlebutt," Evanson heeded her sugges-
      tion, and simply noted that he had received "a good letter from Vivian Hamre
      Bergan, that's Kenny Bergan's wife. He is an Ensign, now at 36 Oxford St.,
      Arlington 74, Mass. He's a Project Engineer at Mass. Institute of Technology,
      on "hot stuff".
113   130:2:68.
114   130:4:62.
115   130:4:63.
116   130:15:16.
117   130:21:21
118   130:20:10.
119   130:9:39–41.
120   130:10:24–25.

[121] 130:14:62.

[122] 130:2:39.

[123] 130:11:37.

[124] 130:11:41.

[125] 130:17:62.

[126] 130:21:22.

[127] 130:21:3–4.

[128] 130:6:31.

[129] 130:7:12.

[130] 130:21:18.

[131] 130:22:8

[132] 130:17:60.

[133] 130:10:3

[134] 130:10:4.

[135] 130:4:56.

[136] 130:21:72–73.

[137] 130:21:74.

[138] 130:22:24–25.

[139] 130:9:75.

[140] 130:4:57. The letter does not contain the return address mentioned, and Evanson did not include it in "Scuttlebutt."

[141] 130:17:2.

[142] 130:21:58–59.

[143] 130:17:11.

[144] 130:22:13–15.

[145] 130:18:6.

[146] 130:14:11.

[147] 130:14:12.

[148] 130:20:22–23.

[149] 130:26:2–3.

150 130:26:29.

151 130:4:72–75.

152 130:14:64–65.

153 130:14:66.

154 130:14:67–71.

155 130:15:63–64.

156 130:4:5.

157 130:9:38. Although the V-Mail is not dated, in the February 1945 issue of "Scuttlebutt," Evanson noted, "Now for mail which I couldn't squeeze into the last issue. Sgt. James A. Haugen 37678685, 773rd.Bomb Sqdn.,463rd. Bomb Grp.,APO 520,%P.M.,N.Y., a V-mail from Italy, a tail-gunner on a B-17. No flying as yet, getting acquainted with Italy, mud etc."

158 130:10:26–27.

159 130:10:28. The misspelling of Holmlund's name is in his original letter.

160 130:10:29.

161 130:22:11.

162 130:26:45.

163 130:16:2–4. Meyer's mother sent a photo on August 21 (130:16:1).

164 130:14:32.

165 As a result of the change of ribbons mentioned in the next sentence, the print becomes much darker at this point.

166 130:4:66–67.

167 130:8:15–16.

168 130:8:14.

169 130:17:58.

170 130:14:33.

171 130:20:50. Ruid's comments notwithstanding, Evanson did not mention his whereabouts in the next few issues. Ironically, in the March 1945 issue, he refers to correspondence from Ruid which is not included in the archival collection.

172 130:21:80–81.

<sup>173</sup> 130:14:20.

<sup>174</sup> 130:17:59.

<sup>175</sup> 130:14:31. Although the V-Mail is not dated, Evanson refers to this letter and gives Larson's address in the January 1945 issue of "Scuttlebutt."

<sup>176</sup> 139:16:14–15. The news release is not dated, but in the February 1945 issue of "Scuttlebutt," Evanson reported, "Here's one for the books, especially for the older Luther men, who remember Mills from Fort Dodge, who used to cavort at end for Pete, and how. He's a chief pilot on a B-17, flying out of England, 30 daylight missions over Germany. Brought his plane home on three engines once, following low altitude bombing (forced), and practically repeated the same again. He's with the 305th Bomb Group. Has Distinguished Flying Cross, Air Medal and three Oak Leaf Cluster. Is married and entered AAF Dec. 9, '40."

<sup>177</sup> 130:26:1.

<sup>178</sup> 130:17:24.

<sup>179</sup> 130:14:17–18.

<sup>180</sup> 130:13:64–65.

<sup>181</sup> 130:13:61.

<sup>182</sup> 130:20:11.

<sup>183</sup> 130:22:10. In the September 1944 issue of "Scuttlebutt," Evanson commented, "From one of the "Old Salts", John Sorlien, a picture card of the port of Marseille, which I am sure several Luther men have seen by this time. By the way, John, I still await the evidence of that Kraut plane. No hurry, but don't forget it. Guess we know you were in or close to the D-Day in southern France."

<sup>184</sup> 130:14:50.

<sup>185</sup> 130:21:7.

<sup>186</sup> 120:2:29.

<sup>187</sup> 130:6:24–26. The date 1-11-44 is typed; the Nov. 5 '44 entry is added in Evanson's handwriting. Since no American troops were in France prior to June 6, Estenson may have typed the date to indicate "1 November," i.e., in military or "continental" style.

<sup>188</sup> 130:14:37.

189   130:14:28.

190   130:18:5. Olson's comments about the Navy prompted this reply from Evanson in the January 1945 issue of "Scuttlebutt": "Cpl.Eugene B.Olson,… writes from Eastern France, still trying to catch up with Noble, which will be in Berlin, <u>for</u> <u>sure</u>. Praises the G.I., and I join you, boy, 100%, but you just can't blame a guy who has been aboard ship for shouting (and I certainly don't mean to do it too loudly) the praises of the Navy. That's why we will have to take a week for the first Homecoming."

191   130:6:23.

192   130:25:44.

193   130:13:28.

194   130:18:20.

195   130:14:23–27.

196   130:16:51.

197   130:11:57.

198   130:14:60.

199   130:23:72. Although the letter does not indicate the year it was written, in the April 1945 issue of "Scuttlebutt," Evenson noted, "Danny [Lien] met both Paul Borge and 'Jumbo' Strom on the way across." It was thus undoubtedly written in March 1945. Although Strom does not indicate his location, on March 6, Danny Lien wrote a letter from "Somewhere in France" (130:14:60).

200   130:14:63.

201   China-Burma-India Theater

202   130:17:28.

203   130:6:27–28.

204   130:3:6–7.

205   130:14:51.

206   130:9:47–48.

207   130:3:31.

208   130:25:44.

209   130:14:29–30. No specific date is given.

210 130:14:52–54.

211 130:6:32.

212 130:13:25.

213 130:15:23.

214 130:2:24–25.

215 130:6:19–21.

216 130:20:52.

217 130:2:58.

218 130:2:59–60.

219 130:10:11.

220 130:9:2–3.

221 130:17:21.

222 130:2:4.

223 130:2:5–6.

224 130:21:68.

225 130:21:67.In the February 1944 issue of "Scuttlebutt," Evanson noted, "Skil-bred, that Xmas menu sure reminded me of a similar one from the "Pennsy" Xmas, 1919, they know how to put out the chow on Battleship X too."

226 130:9:15.(The underlined blank space is in the original V-Mail.)

227 130:11:28–29.

228 130:18:7.

229 130:20:1–2.In the April 1944 issue of Scuttlebutt, Evanson reported, "Wel-come Air Mail from Lt. (j.g.) L.C.Radtke, USS Beryl, PY23, %Fleet P.M., Frisco., yesterday, the first, but not the last letter from the boy who used to burn 'em in at the insistance of the fans in the bleachers, myself included. Congrats on the j.g., Radtke.His experiences have been varied and interest-ing too.Has met up with Dusty Hanson, Cal De Buhr, Dr. Fritchen (Com-mander), and expected to see Paul Gandrud the afternoon he wrote, 4/8.Has been at sea ever since his assignment to a boat Dec. 20, 1942; so he's a real salt, that's for sure."

230 130:17:52–53.

231 130:21:10–11.

[232]  130:3;25–26.

[233]  130:4:43–44.

[234]  130:9:32.

[235]  130:6:11–12.

[236]  130:4:79–80.

[237]  130:3:27–28.

[238]  130:10:20–21.

[239]  130:11:13–15.Jacobsen's closing comment refers to the September 1944 issue of "Scuttlebutt," in which Evanson had noted some changes in format.
First, it would be typed by two women who worked in President Preus' office,
which would improve the quality of typing and production of the newslet-
ter.Second, Evanson announced, "I will place in the hands of each member
of the faculty a copy of the last issue and ask that each one submit a line or
two from the letters he receives from men in the service so that we widen the
scope of the idea.I also plan to have various members of the faculty write a
greeting to all of you from time to time.This should certainly improve the
project.In other words, we will try to make it "all faculty" in character.Hope
you like it."

[240]  130:10:33–34.

[241]  130:18:35.

[242]  130:21:2.

[243]  130:19:8.

[244]  130:19:4–5.

[245]  130:2:8.

[246]  130:11:22–23.

[247]  130:9:7–10.

[248]  130:24:37–38.

[249]  130:26:4.

[250]  130:25:11–12.

[251]  130:25:13.

[252]  130:25:14–15.

[253]  130:25:16–17.

254  130:25:18–19.

255  130:16:6–7.

256  130:19:38.

257  130:19:11–12.

258  130:10:5.

259  130:18:23–24.

260  130:4:1.

261  130:18:8–9. In the letterhead, the letter "L" is crossed out, and "M" inserted.

262  130:26:37–39

263  130:16:52.

264  130:7:9.

265  130:17:63–65.

266  130:2:69.

267  130:24:18–21.

268  130:11:8–11.

269  130:19:31–32. The date on Potter's letter does not include the year, but in the March 1945 issue of "Scuttlebutt," Evanson noted, "Bud Potter, a teletype operator in Hawaii."

270  130:2:44–45.

271  130:20:19–21.

272  130:26:40.

273  130:5:41. The V-Mail is undated, but in the March 1945 issue of Scuttlebutt, Evanson reported, "Ens. Clifford Ellingson writes from the Pac. to say he has seen Douglas Simondet as well as several from his midshipmans class."

274  130:15:51–52.

275  130:15:14.

276  130:2:65.

277  130:6:13–16.

278  130;17:7.

279  CVE: Escort Carrier—Precommissioning School in Bremerton

280  130:16:16–17.

281  130:7:3–6.

282  130:19:6–7.

283  130:2:32–35.

284  130:3:34.

285  130:26:5–6.

286  130:26:7–8.

287  130:2:47. The letter is undated. Evanson referred to it in the June 1945 issue of "Scuttlebutt," when he noted, "Ens.Marv Bachman, in a MEIU outfit, in the Pac. had 60 pieces of mail waiting for him following an operation, inc Scuttlebutt O.K. Marv, we'll keep it coming at you. It's warm in Decorah, finally, but not that hot."

288  130:13:32.

289  130:15:62

290  130:4:51–53. The letter is undated, but in the July 1945 issue of "Scuttle-butt," Evanson reported, 7/28. A good letter from the "underwater Navy" Cal De Buhr, good hunting on the last mission, will mean something worth-while for the crew. The Skipper really rated a top flight decoration. Sent me an airplane photo of the "Pennsy", still pouring it on. About all that looked natural were the four turrets, one of which had just fired a salvo when the picture was taken. That picture goes up on the bulletin board for sure, Cal, and THANKS."

291  130:5:34–36.

292  130:9:80–81.

293  Patrol Craft

294  130:19:30. Sailors were inducted into "King Neptune's Court" when crossing the Equator.

295  130:15:19.

296  130:21:5.

297  130:13:22.

298  130:13:66–67. Conrad R. Waldeland had served as chair of the Chemistry Department from 1932 to 1942.

299  130:2:62–64.
300  130:11:17–19. For more information about Jacobson's unit, see <http://corregidor.org/heritage_battalion/index.htm>
301  130:9:42.
302  130:18:18–19.
303  130:15:6.
304  130:15:24–25.
305  130:11:33–34.
306  130:11:35.
307  130:19:25.
308  130:9:43–45.
309  130:15:7.
310  130:2:46.
311  130;13:23–24.
312  130;14:59.
313  130;11:3.
314  130:17:15–16.
315  130:18:25–29.
316  130:5:37–40.
317  130:7:33–36.
318  130:7:37–39.
319  130:24:48–52
320  130:7:40–42.
321  130:7:43–44.
322  130:7:45–47.
323  130:22:1–2.
324  130:7:48–51.
325  130:7:52–53.
326  130:7:54–55.
327  130:7:56–59.

328 130:18:34.

329 130:24:9–11.

330 130:2:1–3.

331 130:21:23.

332 130:2:70–71.

333 140:14:21.

334 130:17:26.

335 130:14:39–43.

336 130:14:45–47.

337 130:2:12–14.

338 140:14:44.

339 130:20:3–4.

340 130:17:9.

341 130:7:10–11.

342 130:9:16.

343 130:21:70.

344 130:4:49–50. Although the letter was not dated, from the context, it was undoubtedly written in July 1945.

345 130:2:20–21.

346 130:11:4–7.

347 130;15:10–12.

348 130:16:9–12. The aircraft carrier USS Franklin was damaged by a kamikaze attack on October 30, 1944, refitted, and then received extensive damage from Japanese bombing attack on March 19, 1945, suffering casualties totalling 724 killed and 265 wounded. For a brief history of the Franklin, see http://www.hazegray.org/danfs/carriers/cv13.htm

349 130:14:13–16.

350 130:16:53.

351 130:11:55.

352 130:8:20–22.

353 130:22:37

354 130:14:9–10.

355 130:10:35.

356 130:19:43.

357 130:9:18–19.

358 European Theater of Operations

359 130:11:36.

360 130:18:15.

361 130:4:38.

362 130:13:62–63.

363 130:11:38.

364 130:2:51.

365 130:22:34–35.

366 130;26:33–34.

367 130:11:53.

368 David T. Nelson notes, "Many veterans were married and had children. They had to be housed and cared for. The old policy (not unique at Luther College) by which a student marriage was treated almost as moral delinquency, was relegated to oblivion overnight. The ex-servicemen, after life in foxholes and subsistence on the delights of army rations—especially canned ones—were determined to have homes of their own and enjoy normal peacetime life. Although barracks and other makeshift quarters could hardly be called normal, the young married folk, happy to be together, took them in stride." (Nelson, p. 295.)

369 130:24:7–8.

370 130:13:26–27.

371 130:8:5–6.

372 130:7:24–30.

# Index of Correspondents

www.ingramcontent.com/pod-product-compliance
Lightning Source LLC
Chambersburg PA
CBHW030412100426
42812CB00028B/2925/J